PEASANT RUSSIA

1. Woman carrying buckets of water in a village in Nizhnii Novgorod province. Photograph from the California Museum of Photography, Keystone-Mast Collection, University of California, Riverside.

PEASANT RUSSIA

FAMILY AND COMMUNITY IN THE POST-EMANCIPATION PERIOD

Christine D. Worobec

PRINCETON UNIVERSITY PRESS   PRINCETON, NEW JERSEY

Library of Congress Cataloging-in-Publication Data

Worobec, Christine.
Peasant Russia : family and community in the post-emancipation
period / Christine D. Worobec.
p.   cm.
Includes bibliographical references and index.
ISBN 0-691-03151-7 (acid-free)
1. Russian S.F.S.R.—Rural conditions. 2. Rural families—Russian
S.F.S.R.—History. 3. Peasantry—Russian S.F.S.R.—History.
I. Title.
HN530.R87W67   1991
305.5′633′0947—dc20   90-41811   CIP

This book has been composed in Linotron Galliard

Princeton University Press books are printed on acid-free paper,
and meet the guidelines for permanence and durability of the
Committee on Production Guidelines for Book Longevity of the
Council on Library Resources

Printed in the United States of America by Princeton University Press,
Princeton, New Jersey

10   9   8   7   6   5   4   3   2   1

To My Loving Parents, Nicholas and Olga

Thus the peasant court to all appearances is absurd. . . . But as long as our peasant wears that gray homespun coat which he has been wearing since the time of Askol'd and Dir; as long as he has those same bast shoes in which once upon a time he fought the Radimichi and the commander Wolf-Tail; as long as he has the same shaggy beard as Perun and his hat remains that of the tiller that the tribal Scythians had in the colony Traian; as long as he has a chimneyless hut which he had when he was still a Dregovich rather than a Russian; as long as he has the grain with the bran and crackle that he had as far back as the time of Vladimir Monomakh when the Polovtsy drove his horses away and trampled his fields; as long as he has the mounting arrears which he had after Tokhtamysh invaded Moscow and as long as he has eaten his 1874 harvest already in 1870; as long as he has corns on his hands that are tougher than the humps on camels, and a gray-and-black face like his ancestral compatriot, who was ruddy-cheeked and white only in his mother's womb, [that is] if his mother did not strain herself pulling a heavy bucket from the well; as long as salt is for him the same price as treasure, and iron is also expensive for him and is as rare in his economic pursuits as it was for the man of the Stone Age; as long as literacy is [as] harmful to him as is a lord's overindulgence that stops the small child [i.e., his peasant] from taking geese out to pasture [or] harrowing, and the care of babes in arms who are often fed by pigs because their laboring mothers are too busy; in short as long as the Russian peasant remains a Russian peasant, why does he need another higher court that does not understand his people just as the people do not understand their court?

Besides this, if the peasant court is bad, then let the gentry's court itself be the first to cast a stone . . . when it considers itself to be without sin; but I will not cast [that stone].

—Anonymous, "Krest'ianskii sud"

Contents

Illustrations _____

Tables

Acknowledgments

THIS BOOK has been enriched by the generous support of institutions, scholars, and friends. It began as a doctoral dissertation at the University of Toronto under the guidance of Harvey Dyck and Robert Eugene Johnson, and John Keep. The Social Sciences and Humanities Research Council of Canada sponsored numerous research trips abroad. The staffs of Robarts Library at the University of Toronto, the Library of Congress, the New York Public Library, Columbia University's Butler Library, the library of the University of Illinois at Urbana-Champaign, the British Library, and Bibliothèque Nationale were all invaluable in helping me to locate rare materials. I would like to give special mention to the librarians at the Helsinki University Library who never tired of lugging huge volumes of bound records to my carrel or fulfilling my innumerable photocopying requests.

Since that time I have benefited immensely from other research opportunities and the generosity of numerous scholars. Grants from Kent State University and the Kennan Institute for Advanced Russian Studies allowed me to immerse myself in the larger world of Russian and Ukrainian peasants. Special thanks must go to Daniel Field, who not only encouraged me in my work but enthusiastically read the manuscript more than once, each time providing me with invaluable criticisms. Brenda Meehan-Waters, Barbara Alpern Engel, Ben Eklof, Teodor Shanin, and Alan Wildman all took time to read the manuscript and offer excellent suggestions. Gerald Newman demonstrated how to make historical materials come alive; I hope I learned my lesson. I owe an incalculable amount to Barbara Evans Clements, whose wisdom and inexhaustible willingness to guide a novice in women's studies opened up a new world of ideas to me. Barbara also helped hunt down several photographs, for which I am most grateful. Timothy Mixter was extremely generous in sharing his large photographic archive with me. Stimulating discussions with Stephen Frank, Timothy Mixter, Esther Kingston-Mann, and others at the 1986 National Endowment for the Humanities Boston Conference on the Peasantry of European Russia, 1800–1917 helped me to formulate my ideas and gave me the confidence that I was on the right track. Thanks also need to be extended to my graduate student, Maureen Tighe-Brown, for proofreading the manuscript in the final states of preparation. Gail Ullman and Lauren Lepow of Princeton University Press were a pleasure to work with. Their support and advice were invaluable. This book also owes a great deal to my husband,

David Kyvig. His constant encouragement and delight in discussing my work with me made the task of rewriting more pleasurable, while his red, blue, and sometimes green editorial marks often saved me from myself. Lastly, I owe a great deal to my parents, who lived through this book with me. Their love and concern sustained me throughout.

Sections of chapters have already appeared in print. Chapter 2 is a revised and expanded version of "Customary Law and Property Devolution among Russian Peasants in the Post-Emancipation Period," *Canadian Slavonic Papers* 26, nos. 2 and 3 (June–September 1984): 220–34. "Victims or Actors? Patriarchy and Russian Peasant Women," in *Peasant Economy, Culture, and Politics of European Russia, 1800–1921*, ed. Esther Kingston-Mann and Timothy Mixter (Princeton: Princeton University Press, 1991) incorporates sections of chapters 4, 5, and 6. I appreciate the cooperation of the respective editors in reproducing these materials.

I have followed the Library of Congress system of transliteration from Russian, though the plurals of weights and measures have been anglicized. Place names ending with a soft sign have had this diacritical mark deleted in the anglicized version, except in those cases where the sign significantly affects pronunciation, as in Iaroslavl'. I have used the anglicized versions for well-known names and places. Dates are given according to the Julian calendar, which in the nineteenth century was twelve days behind the Gregorian.

PEASANT RUSSIA

2. Bathing infants along the Volga River, 1897. (The children's clothes are made from factory-produced cotton.) Photograph from the California Museum of Photography, Keystone-Mast Collection, University of California, Riverside.

Introduction ————————————————————————

IN A REMOTE northern province of tsarist Russia in 1872, an angry peasant widow, Aksin'ia Tifanova, decided to battle the male leaders of her village. The village assembly of Nizhneborets, Kurgominsk canton, Archangel province, had taken away her land. Eleven years earlier, the same assembly had recognized Tifanova as household head and permitted her to retain her deceased husband's and son's land allotments. Now, however, the commune undertook a land repartition and, in accordance with tradition, reapportioned the arable to married males only. It thus transferred Tifanova's allotments to another household without compensating her. Tifanova appealed the commune's decision to a justice of the peace, then to the district arbitration board, and finally to the provincial administration for peasant affairs on the grounds that the emancipation statutes of 1861 had given communes authority to seize lands only from those members who had arrears or from households whose families had died out from a lack of male heirs. Tifanova vehemently argued that she had a right to her land allotments because she had successfully farmed them for over a decade and had met all of her household's tax obligations and redemption payments. She also pointed out that she had already sown the winter crop on the property. That grain, she stressed, constituted the only sustenance for her and her two daughters. But the widow Tifanova's hopes for justice were dashed. After four long years of litigation, all her appeals were denied. At the same time the authorities reaffirmed both the commune's traditional right to reallocate lands in the manner agreed upon by a two-thirds majority of household representatives and the exclusive title of married males to communal land allotments. Nonetheless, they granted Tifanova permission to harvest the sown grain, which, in the eyes of customary law, represented her inalienable property.[1]

Just a year earlier, in the central industrial province of Iaroslavl', another local dispute had broken out, this time between two co-villagers. The peasant Shishov accused the eighteen-year-old Katalov before a cantonal court of ruining his marriageable daughter's reputation by loudly cursing her within earshot of community members. The incident had taken place during the August grain harvest. The defendant Katalov testified that Shi-

---

[1] Cited in Nikolai Petrovich Druzhinin, *Iuridicheskoe polozhenie krest'ian: Izsledovanie, -s prilozheniem statei: I. Polnopravnyia sel'skiia obshchestva i bezpravnyia seleniia. II. Krest'ianskaia zhenshchina. III. "Vy" i "ty." IV. Nakazanie bez suda. V. Preobrazovannyi volostnoi sud. VI. Iuridicheskaia bezpomoshchnost' krest'ian* (St. Petersburg, 1897), pp. 245–48.

shov's fifteen-year-old daughter had made a blatantly suggestive offer, telling him "to make a bed in the rye," to which he replied with a succession of curses. He freely corroborated testimonies of eyewitnesses who asserted that his words were so unsavory that they could not be repeated in front of the court. The judges, following customary practice, suggested that the plaintiff and defendant end their quarrel amicably. The plaintiff Shishov, however, refused to accept Katalov's apology. After all, the honor of his daughter, family, and household was at stake. Shishov feared that unless Katalov was punished for his actions and made to retract his false accusations, villagers would shun his daughter as a girl with loose morals. The risk of her becoming a spinster and not fulfilling her social, economic, and reproductive duties as wife and mother was too great. Consequently Shishov was appeased only when the court found Katalov guilty of falsely shaming his daughter and punished him accordingly. In addition to receiving twenty lashes, Katalov was required to deliver a public apology before the village assembly, declaring that he had shamed the girl Shishova without cause and that all his words were blatant lies.[2]

In the same year in nearby Klin district, Moscow province, another dispute arose between feuding peasants who, in this case, were all members of the same household. Here was an instance of ongoing quarrels between a patriarch, on the one hand, and his son and daughter-in-law, on the other. The household head, one P. E., protested before a cantonal court that his son was unwilling to contribute all of his annual wages to the household coffers. He further charged the son and his wife with disrespect and disobedience. The son denied the charges, contending that his mother was to blame for the family's trouble. He accused her of making life miserable for him and especially for his wife, who was never free from her incessant demands. He then proposed two alternative solutions to the family's problems. Either he and his wife would move out of the house and set up an independent household, or else they would remain in the father's home, providing a fixed monetary sum for its maintenance. The judges convinced father and son to settle their differences on the basis of the son's second proposal. This meant that the son would remain in his father's household and turn over fifty-six rubles, or a third of his wages, to cover the communal dues and taxes. The settlement also specified that the house

---

[2] *Trudy Kommisii po preobrazovaniiu volostnykh sudov: Slovesnye oprosy krest'ian, pis'menny otzyvy razlichnykh mest i lits i resheniia: volostnykh sudov, s"ezdov mirovykh posrednikov i gubernskikh po krest'ianskim delam prisutstvii* 7 vols. (St. Petersburg, 1873–1874) 1:280, #25. Hereafter cited as *Trudy Kommisii*. In several sources, including the *Trudy Kommisii*, compilers assigned numbers to court records, folk songs, or bibliographic entries. I have included those numbers, designated by a #, after the page reference for the convenience of the reader. All translations from Russian to English are my own, unless otherwise noted.

and all other farmstead property were henceforth to be held in the common ownership of father and son.[3]

One more case, equally connected with peasant morality, property, and family life, may be cited. At the end of the nineteenth century in the central agricultural province of Orel, Anna Akulicheva, a peasant woman of the hamlet Meshkovo, Bolkhov district, was charged with stealing a piece of linen and was subjected to a public shaming.[4] Community members tore her kerchief from her head, tarred her shirt, and unraveled one of her own linens, which they tied to her body as a sign of the stolen object. Then, tying her to a cart, they led her down the village street, banging oven dampers and shouting insults at her. The ritualized shaming ended when the villagers reached the nearby river and went through the motions of washing the tar out of Akulicheva's shirt. But as soon as she was escorted home, the humiliated and vindictive Akulicheva took the law into her own hands. Stealing a whip from a village administrative officer, she attacked everyone who dared cross her path. She escaped the village elder's threat to arrest her and reported the public shaming to the district land captain. He in turn arrested the elder. At a meeting of the village assembly the land captain admonished the household heads for allowing such an illegal shaming. According to the law, he said, criminal offenders were to be handled by the appropriate court and not by traditional extralegal public tribunals.

The matter was not ended, however. Village assembly members remained indignant because Akulicheva had transgressed community norms. Not only had she stolen property from a neighbor, but by soliciting outside intervention in what was to them a local matter, she had brought disgrace upon the entire community. Akulicheva had to be properly chastised and the village sufficiently compensated before she could be welcomed back into the fold. The assembly therefore ordered her husband, who up to this point had been unsuccessful in containing his willful wife, to whip her in the village square. The crafty Akulicheva, however, remained one step ahead of her co-villagers. She hid all her personal belongings, which no doubt included some coins, thwarting the assembly's customary demand for compensation. In the end, family and community drove the unrepentant woman out of the village.

What do these apparently ill-assorted squabbles among Russian peasants reveal? Widow Tifanova's dispute with her commune, Shishov's concern over his daughter's and family's reputation, the quarrels of an extended peasant family in Moscow province, the public shaming of a petty thief—each of these is a microcosm of post-emancipation Russian peasant society. The fabric of that society, in every case, is shown to have been a compli-

---

[3] Ibid., 2:562, #22.

[4] V. V. Tenishev, *Pravosudie v russkom krest'ianskom bytu* (Briansk, 1907), pp. 41–43.

cated network of ritual, law, and custom, upholding the patriarchal village and family, in the face of a multitude of challenges, through the distribution of property and punishments. Family, community, and commune formed a tightly interwoven complex of peasant institutions that perpetually interacted with one another in the constant struggle for survival in a hostile and unpredictable world.

Peasant societies are, by definition, built on relations firmly tied to the land. Land generally provides the means for peasant existence, and around that foundation institutions develop in turn to perpetuate peasant society. It is not enough for peasants to reap the benefits of the land. Of necessity land must be apportioned among households and worked in a productive manner. The economic viability of peasant communities depends, furthermore, upon family and community cooperation on various levels. In a three-field system cooperation is essential in the allocation of communal arable land, the timing of agricultural activities, the grazing of animals, and the organization of collective labor on communal meadows. In this regard the Russian village assembly of male household heads was extremely important in supervising and coordinating the labors of their family members to meet household and community needs.

Family and community cooperation must also exist on welfare and social levels. Not all community members are able to contribute laboring shares in the fields or in the home. Some are too sick, others too young or too old. But the system must nevertheless accommodate them in some way. When hardship strikes individual households, neighbors are called upon to provide temporary aid. In normal times, on the other hand, the family is the focal point of peasant life: besides being an economic unit, it is a consumer, welfare, and social institution providing for all its members and acculturating them in the values of rural society. The community collectively decides what behavioral norms must be respected for community survival. It is up to families to inculcate those norms and values in their children and to punish any deviance. When an individual's actions threaten the community as a whole, however, the family defers to community authority.

Community solidarity is also important in combating governmental interference and mitigating the challenges that economic changes pose to traditional life. Within such a rigidly defined world—"we" of the community vs. "they" of the outside world—individuals have to conform to community interests or risk expulsion. Indeed, individuals cannot exist outside the collective. Only as members of a household can they enjoy rights as community members.[5]

---

[5] Martine Segalen, "Life-Course Patterns and Peasant Culture in France: A Critical Assessment," *Journal of Family History* 12, nos. 1–3 (1987): 220.

Within their inner world emancipated Russian peasants had to deal with many levels of institutions, including commune, village assembly, and household, which had evolved in response to various external pressures. The hierarchy and patriarchalism of the state that the peasant world mirrored cannot be separated from the ecological conditions which gave shape to them both. A short growing season of five and a half to six months, inclement weather, and, in some areas, poor soils rendered the line between poverty and destitution precarious. A rigid system of authority and command wherein individual activities were tightly controlled for the common good evolved to meet the challenges of a hostile environment.

This is not to suggest a romanticized picture of rural Russia in which peasants were constantly concerned with their neighbors' welfare. Villagers provided temporary aid to those households visited by natural disasters, such as fires or illnesses. On the other hand, households whose destitution was the result of an irresponsible and alcoholic patriarch received neither sympathy nor help. The petty squabbles that embroiled Russian peasant society demonstrate further that peasants were not averse to stealing from one another, lying, falsely accusing each other of misdemeanors and deviant behavior, quarreling over property rights, or avoiding their tax payments. Generational tensions were ever present in the extended family household.

To ensure that such conflict did not threaten community interests, the community emerged as arbiter, jealously guarding prerogatives, scrutinizing behavior, and punishing delinquency. Through its own chain of command, from elected village elders to household heads and informal groupings of women and youths, it maintained rigid control devices to ward off potential danger. In this context the Russian peasant was not only the victim of oppression, but very much the actor and oppressor as well in the tightly interwoven universe of family and community.

The widow Tifanova, by virtue of being a woman, found herself discriminated against in a patriarchal system. Yet she had never deviated from the commune's belief that only economically secure and responsible taxpaying households were assets to the community. She would also have heartily supported the premise that a woman should become household head only when the household did not have adult male heirs. She and community shared the belief that a peasant was entitled to the fruits of his or her labor.

The peasant Shishov and his daughter's assailant Katalov both subscribed to the community's moral values, which insisted that a bride be a virgin (even if she had to resort to using chicken's blood on her wedding night). A shameless, promiscuous woman was viewed as an unstable community member, incapable of assuming the responsibilities of wife and mother that were crucial to the perpetuation of family and community. Although intent on protecting his own daughter's reputation, Shishov would have cast the first stone at another peasant's daughter accused of immorality. In the Klin district extended-family household, generational tension, exacerbated by the intrusion of money into a largely subsistence household economy, may have disturbed relations. In the end, however, the son was willing to accept, even if somewhat reservedly, his father's patriarchal authority. There is no indication that he would have acted differently had he been in his father's place.

Lastly, Anna Akulicheva clearly felt victimized by her oppressive male-dominated society. Yet she played by some of that society's rules, choosing those which best served her cause. She met violence with violence and, when that proved unsuccessful, resorted to the one weapon to which the community was vulnerable: the power of officialdom. In defying her husband's authority, stealing, and subsequently refusing to submit willingly to community censure and rehabilitation rites, Akulicheva was a rebel and hence an outcast. Her actions threatened the patriarchal and moral sinews of her community and therefore could not be tolerated. A few of her female co-villagers may have secretly applauded Akulicheva's boldness and independence, but the majority were just as horrified by her conduct as the men. Unlike Akulicheva, they had accommodated themselves to a patriarchy that both oppressed and rewarded them. Women carved out their own spheres of influence within the domestic household and larger community. As laborers, as bearers and nurturers of children, and as guardians of tradition and ritual, they had a vested interest in preserving the system.

By studying informal community structures, interrelationships among all village members, formal male-dominated communes and village assemblies, and family households of post-emancipation Russian peasants, as well as rituals that bound peasants together and aided them in reproducing their society, it is possible to uncover the inner world of peasant Russia that retarded, cushioned, and even impeded the beginnings of Russia's economic modernization. A few historians have already demonstrated how post-emancipation Russian peasants succeeded in subverting external agencies of change and protecting the moral fiber of their daily lives. The late nineteenth- and early twentieth-century army, school, urban culture, and Stolypin agrarian reforms were of themselves unable to transform Russian peasants into modern citizens who controlled their environment and embraced the ideals of a national rather than parochial culture.[6] By concen-

---

[6] See for example, John Bushnell, "Peasants in Uniform: The Tsarist Army as a Peasant Society," *Journal of Social History* 13, no. 4 (Summer 1980): 565–76; Ben Eklof, "The Myth of the Zemstvo School: The Sources of the Expansion of Rural Education in Imperial Russia, 1864–1914," *History of Education Quarterly* 24, no. 4 (Winter 1984): 561–84; idem, *Russian Peasant Schools: Officialdom, Village Culture, and Popular Pedagogy, 1861–1914* (Berkeley, 1986); Anthony Netting, "Images and Ideas in Russian Peasant Art," *Slavic Review* 35, no. 1 (March 1976): 48–68; Julie Brown, "Peasant Survival Strategies in Late Imperial Russia:

trating on external elements, however, these historians have not examined the substance of traditional Russian peasant society, the focus of this study. Only through an understanding of the normal functioning of Russian peasant society prior to the changes of the late nineteenth and early twentieth centuries can the historian of modernization appreciate the resilience of peasant customs and institutions. As Michael Confino has aptly pointed out, if historians are to understand "the effects of the agents of change (such as the market economy, modern communications, schooling) . . . we should first carefully analyze the agents of cohesion, the force of traditions, and the peasants' moral and material strategies for maintaining the precarious equilibrium of rural life."[7]

Until Russian peasants could be convinced of the superiority of a new worldview and modern ways of doing things, they stubbornly clung to tried-and-true methods of survival. These methods may have been powerless in the struggle against poverty, bad harvests, and other environmental disasters, but they assured some measure of security if only because countless generations had used them and survived. The fact that Russian peasants chose to reconfirm and, in some areas, resurrect the repartitional commune in the wake of the Russian Revolution provides striking testimony to the tenacity of traditional rural institutions and mores.

It is the task of this study to penetrate the very fibers of Russian peasant society in the decades immediately following emancipation. It examines the strength and vitality of the traditional patriarchal family and community in the central industrial and central agricultural regions of the Russian Empire. The family, with its productive, reproductive, and cultural functions, and the community, embracing all families in a network of economic and social relations, were at the root of peasant traditionalism. The customary practices and values undergirding this normative world formed within the subsistence-oriented economy a survival strategy that was perforce accepted by most community members. The land tenure and property devolution practices, the dynamic family life cycle, the various household structures, the rigid patriarchalism, and the elaborate set of social

---

The Social Uses of the Mental Hospital," *Social Problems* 34, no. 4 (October 1987): 311–29; George Yaney, *The Urge to Mobilize: Agrarian Reform in Russia, 1861–1930* (Urbana, Ill., 1982); Judith Pallot, "Khutora and Otruba in Stolypin's Program of Farm Individualization," *Slavic Review* 43, no. 2 (1984): 242–56; and Robert Eugene Johnson, *Peasant and Proletarian: The Working Class of Moscow in the Late Nineteenth Century* (New Brunswick, N.J., 1979). Postreform Russian peasants were not at the same stage of development as their French counterparts, who by the First World War had become modern French citizens subscribing to a national French culture. See Eugen Weber's brilliant study, *Peasants into Frenchmen: The Modernization of Rural France, 1870–1914* (Stanford, 1976).

[7] Michael Confino, "Russian Customary Law and the Study of Peasant Mentalités," *The Russian Review* 44, no. 1 (January 1985): 38.

restrictions that Russian peasants had devised all have to be understood as components of such a strategy.

In exploring the multitudinous dimensions of traditional Russian peasant life this study takes the macro- rather than micro-level approach and thus risks being charged with reducing the peasantry of central Russia to a homogeneous group. However, general cultural and economic patterns do emerge, despite tremendous regional variation and differences even between neighboring villages. Teodor Shanin has argued in his most recent work that "the ways peasant households operated, peasant property customs, peasant agriculture and diet, the economic functions of the peasant community, etc." were remarkably similar throughout European Russia.[8] The central industrial and central agricultural provinces shared similarities in historical development, ethnic composition (Russian in the main), and demographic profile. Internal migration also characterized both areas, although industrial wage labor and peasant craft industries were far better developed in the central industrial than in the central agricultural belt, where agricultural wage labor was more pronounced. As the nineteenth century progressed, however, differences increased between the mixed economy of the northern industrial region and the monoculture of the predominantly grain-producing south, causing some variation in household structures. Nonetheless, common cultural patterns between north and south remained.

The structure and culture of the Russian peasant household displayed a marked continuity, as this study demonstrates. Over several centuries plentiful land resources and the gradual development of serfdom had given shape to the multiple family peasant household. In the post-emancipation era the commune's allocation of land to all married males, together with male partible inheritance, continued to promote early marriage and the incorporation of new conjugal units into the patrilocal household. The larger a household's laboring capacity, the larger its landholdings and the greater its economic well-being. This contrasted markedly with Western European societies that allocated the bulk of the patrimony to only one son, forcing other male siblings to develop strategies of resource accumulation in order to marry and establish independent households.

Far fewer Russian than Western European peasants were lured from the countryside to the distant city as a place of permanent occupation and residence. This may be explained to some degree by partible inheritance, which encouraged Russian sons to remain in the village and perpetuate the complex family. The emancipation settlement also discouraged permanent migration elsewhere by constraining peasants from abandoning their com-

---

[8] Teodor Shanin, *The Roots of Otherness: Russia's Turn of Century*, vol. 1: *Russia as a 'Developing Society'* (London, 1985), p. 83.

munity responsibilities. Legal constraints were particularly evident in the central industrial regions, where acute land shortages became an increasingly pressing problem in the late nineteenth century. Most sons forced into migrant trades to supplement their families' meager agricultural incomes returned to the village to marry, work in the fields at peak periods of the growing season, and retire.

The patriarch of the Russian peasant household held absolute power over management of the household economy and the labor input of family members within limitations set by commune and community. If extra income was necessary to supplement meager agricultural revenues and thus to guarantee the household's survival, the patriarch encouraged a son to earn wages at a domestic industry, or perhaps on a neighboring estate, or else at a migrant trade out in the larger world. He expected that son to remit his wages, minus any expenses incurred while he was away on the job, to the household coffers. A married migrant worker normally left his wife and children behind in his father's household to farm the communal land allotments. The extended family, together with laws enforcing communal land tenure that made it difficult for a peasant to abandon his communal land allotments, impeded the sweeping changes inherent in industrialization.

The incorporation of newly married couples into patrilocal households provided the labor strength necessary to meet household agricultural and tax obligations and to support young and old nonlaboring family members. Consequently, the division of a single household into two or more independent ones, as a result of internal family changes, was normally postponed until married sons had children of their own or the patriarch died. Previously dependent sons became the supporters of their elderly parents within the patrimonial household. Bringing their wives into their father's home, they were often content to remain there several years. When a patriarch died, uncles and nephews or, more frequently, brothers divided the household property and obligations, setting up independent households that would more effectively meet their security needs. Impatient sons who wanted to become household heads before their fathers died left the paternal household with or without permission. If the fathers approved the decision, they awarded their sons some household property to help them get started. The sons, in turn, made provision for their aging parents' welfare. Sons who defied their fathers' wishes by demanding a separate household usually did not receive any parental aid. That threatened loss of aid deterred some sons from taking such independent action unless they had alternative resources, perhaps savings from wage labor withheld from household use.

Post-emancipation Russian peasant households were fluctuating and adaptive structures, as this study will demonstrate. Due to natural changes in family composition and household divisions, Russian peasants over the course of their lives lived in a variety of family household structures, ranging from the complex to the simple. A detailed reconstruction of 230 late nineteenth-century Russian peasant family households in agricultural Voronezh province reveals their complexity and diversity, the rhythms of the family life cycle, and the role of division or fission within that cycle. Examination of areas more closely affected by industrial pursuits and migrant trades further attests to the durability of the extended Russian peasant family after emancipation.

While the large household remained the model for family development, the Russian peasant family did experience change in the second half of the nineteenth century. The growth of capitalist relations in central Russia and the pull of urban centers for supplementary income had an effect upon household structure but were insufficient in themselves to destroy the extended family. The penetration of a growing money economy into the countryside, the result of increased out-migration and monetary wages, fostered some individualism. And the normal generational tensions of a multiple family household did at times explode when wage-earning sons demanded greater independence from their domineering fathers. At other times strained relations between women in the multiple family household fostered partitions and the establishment of smaller household units. As a result of an increase in premortem fission, i.e., households dividing before the patriarch's death, and the abolition of serfowner controls of peasant families, the simple nuclear family became more visible in post-emancipation rural Russia. The normative extended family, nonetheless, remained predominant.

Various levels and institutions of Russian peasant society—cantonal court, the community at large, formal commune, village assembly, and household—combined to perpetuate the complex Russian peasant family and the patriarchal system, as this study will demonstrate. They upheld the sanctity of marriage and the mutual responsibility of spouses, which were vital to reproduction and production. Ritual and the oral culture surrounding the major life-cycle event of marriage illustrate well the ways in which family and community strove to inculcate the youth with conservative patriarchal values. Since marriage was such a dramatic change for women, more so than for men, family and community expended a great deal of effort on preparing young girls for their responsibilities as wives, mothers, and daughters-in-law. Girls were expected to safeguard and enhance their reputations by maintaining their virginity until marriage and learning numerous domestic skills. Family and community also provided opportunities for marriageable youth to socialize at both formal and more intimate gatherings, permitting arranged marriages to give way slowly to individual

choice. Despite the increasing frequency of the latter in the post-emancipation period, economic and social concerns ultimately remained the criteria by which a prospective spouse was judged.

The many levels of Russian peasant society also cooperated in upholding
the patriarchal ordering of family and community relationships. Male cantonal judges and village elders supported the patriarch's authority against
recalcitrant family members, believing that patriarchalism was the basis for
a smoothly functioning peasant society. Over time, peasants had strictly
delineated tasks and functions according to gender and age in order to
meet the demands of their predominantly agricultural economy, adapting
similar divisions of responsibility to domestic industries. Increasing land
shortage, the precariousness of subsistence agriculture, and the peasantry's
burdensome obligations to family, community, and state reinforced rigid
and oppressive power relations within the village. Russian peasants developed a set of behavioral norms and a moral code to buttress the status quo.
They feared and punished severely delinquent activity that threatened the
collective interest and community solidarity by challenging the subordination of woman to man, child to parent, young to old, and weak to
strong.[9]

Russian peasant women were second-class citizens, but at the same time
they supported or, at least, accommodated the patriarchy. They did not
have any political rights in the village. At home they owed complete obedience to their fathers, husbands, and fathers-in-law. Beatings and sexual
abuse were sometimes the rewards they received for their double burden
of labor in the home and fields. In addition to these difficulties, women
could not always depend on their spouses to fulfill their economic and family responsibilities. Despite the oppressive conditions of their existence, the
majority of Russian peasant women were reconciled to their lot as subordinates in a male-dominated world. They remained so because the oppressive and misogynist patriarchy also compensated them, allowing them,
within certain limits, to be actors in their society. While fearing the female
body, men honored women as mothers. Women's reproductive abilities
were obviously critical for a society's survival. Just as important, women
taught children society's values, passing on words of wisdom from previous generations, and helped them find suitable marriage partners. The patriarchy also protected women from false slurs on their reputation, rigorously punishing slanderers. Finally, it allowed women to carve out their

---

[9] I have made similar observations in regard to post-emancipation Ukrainian peasants of
the Russian Empire. See my "Temptress or Virgin? The Precarious Sexual Position of
Women in Postemancipation Ukrainian Peasant Society," *Slavic Review* 49, no. 2 (Summer
1990): 227.

own subsystems of oppression and authority within the domestic sphere and larger community of women.

Incipient industrialization could not of itself destroy the extended family household and patriarchal society of Russian peasants. Other peasant institutions had to be torn asunder and replacements created to alter the extended family's economic, social, welfare, and cultural functions. The demise of the large family household, for example, necessitated a disruption of the communal land-tenure system and its provisioning of all males with land resources, however minimal such resources became by the turn of the century. Intensified capitalist relations were necessary to lure the peasant away from traditional subsistence farming on a collective basis to profit-oriented individualistic farming. That dramatic transformation required more than access to credit. A wholesale revolution in thinking was a prerequisite for the adoption of new labor-intensive techniques, complex crop rotations, sophisticated fertilizers, and modern agricultural machinery and the abandonment of collective rights and obligations. Only a significant reduction in infant mortality rates could provide peasants with the security to lower fertility rates. Furthermore, fundamental changes in the legal system, including incorporation of customary law into the civil law code, were required to terminate the peasantry's isolation as a separate *soslovie* (estate). Some of those prerequisites for the destruction of the Russian extended peasant family were realized between the revolutions of 1905 and 1917 and others not until the Soviet, particularly the Stalinist, period. Yet even Joseph Stalin, in his war against the Russian peasantry, was unable to destroy the peasant household. Collectivization rid the countryside of the commune, but not of the household with its precious garden plot and few animals.

Culture is the slowest of all human creations to adapt to change. The rituals that post-emancipation Russian peasants observed and the mores and behavioral norms they set were remarkably resilient, indeed fairly static in terms of development. Peasants continuously improvised their songs and tales, but rarely departed from the patriarchal values of their normative world. They might have selectively incorporated a few urban ways into their culture, once again, however, without abandoning their traditional worldview. Until the city could penetrate the village by improving standards of living and creating a standardized national culture, peasant Russia would thrive. However, even economic and educational improvements are insufficient to challenge patriarchalism, which is as much a cornerstone of urban as it is of rural life.

When you have seen the collective farmers selling their produce in the street markets of Soviet cities or have been rudely upbraided by a passing *baba* (old woman) for not walking upright or wearing proper clothing,

you know peasant Russia is very much alive today.[10] The distinctive character of modern Soviet society stands more fully revealed through comparison with the traditional society of an earlier day. The central value and
purpose of this study is to advance understanding of the complex and
unique culture of post-emancipation peasant Russia.

[10] I am indebted to Alan Wildman for pointing out this connection to me.

3. A village scene. (Notice the thatched roofs.) Photograph from the Library of Congress.

4. Village officials. (Notice the detail of the carvings along the roof line.) Photograph from Fotomas Index, London.

I

Resources and Obligations

ALONG the mud street, amid the wooden and clay structures of a post-emancipation Russian village could be heard a cacophony of laughing, cursing, crying, and shouting voices, animal cries, and the noise of industrious peasants at work. Not audible, but always guiding and shaping peasant life, were the ever-present institutions of the commune (*obshchina* or *mir*) and village assembly (*sel'skii skhod*). Central features of the Russian peasant world, their economic and political tasks were innumerable.

The emancipation legislation of 1861 did not give formal recognition to the traditional peasant commune (obshchina) and its assembly of household heads, but created in their place the village community (*sel'skoe obshchestvo*) and its assembly (*sel'skii skhod*). The village community became responsible for collecting taxes and dues, enforcing law and order, and regulating land use. Catering to the needs of former serfowners, the 1861 laws defined a village community as peasants settled on the land of one landlord. In some cases, neighboring peasants from landed estates of several noblemen or peasants of adjacent settlements who had common use of some lands could make up one of these communities. As a result, the official community did not always coincide with the boundaries of a traditional land commune or village. In these complex village communities a large village administration was superimposed over the disparate communes or portions of communes to coordinate matters of common interest. Each obshchestvo had an assembly of male household heads who elected an elder, a tax collector, a scribe, a fire marshal, a guard for the communal grain storehouse, and other officials necessary for the community's welfare. The assembly also bore responsibility for military recruitment, and for maintaining roads, bridges, and churches, as well as for providing welfare services to widows and orphans.[1]

Two-thirds of all the repartitional communes of central Russia were co-

---

[1] Geroid Tanquary Robinson, *Rural Russia under the Old Regime: A History of the Landlord-Peasant World and a Prologue to the Peasant Revolution of 1917* (Berkeley, 1972), pp. 67–69; James Ian Mandel, "Paternalistic Authority in the Russian Countryside, 1856–1906" (Ph.D. diss., Columbia University, 1978), p. 47; Thomas S. Pearson, "Authority and Self-Government in Russian Peasant Village Administration (1881–1917): Problems and Perceptions" (Paper presented at the Conference on the Peasantry of European Russia, 1800–1917, University of Massachusetts-Boston, 19–22 August 1986), pp. 1–5.

terminous with their sel'skie obshchestva.[2] With well-established mechanisms for dealing with their common interests, the peasants in these communes easily incorporated the new functions of the village community into the traditional land management and juridical roles of the commune and the assembly of household heads. Where the new sel'skie obshchestva were artificial conglomerations of several communes and thousands of peasants, peasants largely circumvented them. They chose instead to preserve their traditional identities as separate communes. They used their own assemblies of household heads to deal with land management and other economic concerns, leaving administrative matters to the bureaucracy of the unwieldy obshchestva.[3]

For the sake of simplicity, this discussion will concentrate on the male-dominated commune and village assembly as the principal institutions of peasant Russia. Unlike the artificial sel'skoe obshchestvo, the commune was not an abstract concept for Russian peasants. It was a living social institution of all household heads who brought to the village assembly their individual interests and the collective wisdom inherited from past generations. When the term *community* is used in this study, it will not refer to the informal sel'skoe obshchestvo unless otherwise indicated, but to the informal social grouping of all villagers, regardless of age or gender.

The very existence of Russian peasant society demanded a complex strategy of survival. Peasant households had to produce enough to meet their own subsistence needs and the commune's numerous responsibilities to its own members and to the state. The creation of a strategy was in itself a daunting task, given the hostile environment in which Russian peasants lived. At the best of times, the short growing season of five and a half to six months in European Russia and the poor soils of the central industrial provinces, including Moscow, Tver, Iaroslavl', Kostroma, Nizhnii Novgorod, and Vladimir, limited crop yields. Even in the rich black earth areas—the central agricultural provinces of Voronezh, Kursk, Kaluga, Penza, Orel, Riazan, Tambov, and Tula—too much or too little rain, a late spring, a late frost, or a freak storm of hail in the summer could damage crops. Periodic poor harvests and fires that swept through the wooden villages forced peasants' backs to the wall.

A peasant of the village Kuzhutok in Nizhnii Novgorod district and province described the powerlessness he had felt in the face of fire:

> Need did not come to me suddenly; it crept up [on me] imperceptibly; it is a sly dog. At the beginning it came to me from the rear [and] entered through the back gates; it broke through them, then the yard, [and] from the yard [it went]

---

[2] Boris N. Mironov, "The Russian Peasant Commune after the Reforms of the 1860s," *Slavic Review* 44, no. 3 (Fall 1985): 441.

[3] Pearson, "Authority," pp. 6–9; Robinson, *Rural Russia*, pp. 69–70.

to the storage room and from the storage room into the hut. There is no way to drive the accursed thing out of the hut: it hid itself up on the rafters and sat there.[4]

Like innumerable peasants in his situation, this man had little choice but to build afresh and attempt to reap a living from the earth. At least he could depend upon his neighbors' help in rebuilding his home and outbuildings. The peasants of Kuzhutok were well aware of the indiscriminate nature of fire. They were fortunate this time: the fire was isolated to one farmstead; the next time they might not be so lucky.

Despite the natural odds against them, Russian peasants concentrated their attention on the land, maintaining a sacred, devotional attachment to it. Mother Earth was all-powerful, providing peasants with sustenance and definition of purpose.[5] She was a precious gift to peasants who were obliged to work and share in her produce equitably. Russian peasants believed that over the centuries they had been helpless bystanders as the Russian nobility robbed them of their treasure. Even the so-called emancipation had not restored to them all the land they believed to be rightfully theirs. Nevertheless, they readily clung to the notion of a future black repartition when all lands, both private and communal, would be redistributed equally among peasants. In the meantime they had to cope as best they could with what they had.

Through centuries of experimentation Russian peasants had devised ways of working the land, exerting some control, however fleeting, over the environment. One method was to apportion each peasant household some of the best and some of the worst lands. Since all peasants shared the task of maintaining families and owed similar obligations to commune and state, they believed that no peasant should be unfairly burdened with the worst lands. Russian peasants had also mastered extensive agricultural techniques, including leaving a third of the arable fallow in a given year, to mitigate the worst features of a short growing season, soil exhaustion, and erosion, and to provide a fairly reliable yield. More important, they firmly believed that collective efforts were far more effective than uncoordinated individual attempts. They charged the commune with overseeing the equitable distribution of both burdens and resources, coordinating peasant

---

[4] F. I. Marakin et al., "Kustarnye promysly Nizhegorodskoi gubernii: Nizhegorodskii uezd," *Nizhegorodskii sbornik* 7 (1887): 165, 111.

[5] All-knowing and just, Mother Earth even emerged as confessor or arbiter in land disputes. Arguments over land boundaries were fairly common. Part of the ritual in deciding the guilty party involved the contesting individuals' walking around the land allotment in question with earth on their heads. Before making a decision known, the judge also sought the earth's advice by eating some soil. Joanna Hubbs, *Mother Russia: The Feminine Myth in Russian Culture* (Bloomington, Ind., 1988), p. 57.

agricultural activities, and supporting nonagricultural activities to increase household revenues.

It was in the area of land allocation and usage that the commune played a primary role in the post-emancipation period. Concern for equality of burdens and obligations lay at the heart of the Russian repartitional commune, the predominant type of commune in central Russia. Through a complex division of communal arable into multiple strips, it guaranteed peasants equal access to both good and poor soils. Furthermore, it periodically redistributed these strips among households, apportioning a larger number to some and diminishing the holdings of others, to reflect changes in household composition, labor strength, and tax burdens. Households whose families had grown larger since the last repartition were compensated with more land at the expense of those in which death had claimed one or more family members. By making peasants collectively responsible for taxes and redemption payments, the state reinforced the notion of equality of burdens among the peasants. Only *podvornoe* (hereditary) communes, which were largely confined to the central agricultural province of Kursk[6] and the non-Russian western and southwestern regions, were legally exempt from repartition and communal control of land use. In these communes land was apportioned among households in hereditary, rather than temporary, tenure.

The lands of central Russian repartitional communes were divided into four sections over which the commune had differing degrees of control. The first involved farmstead or *usad'ba* land: there peasants erected their homes, barns, and storage sheds; there they cultivated their gardens and (in some areas) small orchards. According to law, peasants held the usad'ba in hereditary tenure.[7] This meant that the farmstead land was exempt from repartition. In practice, the majority of communes conformed to this pattern. However, communes that had repartitioned garden plots under serfdom continued that practice after 1861.[8] In all cases, the residential and

---

[6] In Kursk province 40.5 percent of communal land was held on hereditary tenure. Even here, however, peasants repartitioned the land. See K. Golovin, *Sel'skaia obshchina v literature i deistvitel'nosti* (St. Petersburg, 1887), p. 79.

[7] *Polnoe sobranie zakonov Rossiiskoi Imperii*, ser. 2, no. 35552, art. 110. Hereafter cited as *PSZ*.

[8] The commune of Torkhov in the central agricultural province of Tula, for example, repartitioned the cabbage, hemp, and potato gardens of the usad'ba at the same time that it redivided the arable. Communes in industrial Moscow province accommodated the needs of families for smaller or larger gardens because of changes in household size. Instead of repartitioning the gardens periodically, they sometimes required smaller households to compensate larger households with payments in cash or kind. At other times they enlarged or diminished a household's field allotments, offsetting the static size of household gardens. V. M. Borisov, "Torkhovskaia obshchina (Tul'skoi gub.)," in *Sbornik materialov dlia izucheniia sel'skoi pozemel'noi obshchiny*, ed. F. L. Barikov et al. (St. Petersburg, 1880), 1:177–78; and V. Orlov,

storage portion of the farmstead remained in the household's hereditary possession and consequently formed the focal point of peasant property devolution systems.

The second category of land in the repartitional commune involved allotments of arable. The emancipation statutes of 19 February 1861 and subsequent decrees of 1863 and 1866 gave all village communes the right of landownership upon redemption. The commune, in turn, apportioned allotments among individual households in strips scattered among three fields. These lands were subject to periodic repartition upon the agreement of at least a two-thirds majority of all household heads at the village assembly.[9] In other words, households farmed these strips at the commune's pleasure. They had no security in the possession of such land, which every few years had to be exchanged for allotments located in different areas within each of the three arable fields.

Communes throughout European Russia increasingly retained up to fifty and sixty *desiatinas* of arable for collective cultivation. Grain produced on that land served a variety of social, welfare, and community needs, including aiding poor households and landless widows; hiring doctors, teachers, herders, boatmen, and other rural employees; and repairing churches, bridges, and roads.[10] In this way collective farming shifted the heavy communal levies from individual households, leaving them to concentrate their efforts on fulfilling tax and redemption obligations to the state as well as sustaining themselves.

The third type of communal lands included natural pasturelands, meadows, woodland, and scrub. Except for the meadows, these areas remained undivided for the use of all communal members.[11] In order to facilitate collective use of meadows or hay fields, on the other hand, peasants often divided them into equitable sections. They apportioned each section to a group of households whose members collectively mowed the hay and then divided the harvest according to prior agreement or by lot.[12] Land leased by the commune as a whole, by individuals, or by groups of peasants constituted the final type of land within a commune's boundaries. Only land that the entire commune leased was subject to direct communal management and repartition.

Formy krest'ianskago zemlevladeniia (Moscow, 1879), in Sbornik statisticheskikh svedenii po Moskovskoi gubernii: Otdel khoziaistvennoi statistiki, vol. 4, pt. 1, p. 84.

[9] *PSZ*, ser. 2, no. 36662, arts. 113–14.

[10] Orlando Figes, "Collective Farming and the 19th-Century Russian Land Commune: A Research Note," *Soviet Studies* 38, no. 1 (1986): 89–97.

[11] Robinson, *Rural Russia*, p. 74.

[12] P. Tsypkin, "Obshchinnoe vladenie: Svod dannykh, dobytykh etnograficheskimi materialami pokoinago kniazia V. N. Tenisheva," *Zhurnal Ministerstva iustitsii* 15, no. 1 (January 1909), pt. 2, p. 151.

Continuing the traditions of serfdom, post-emancipation peasants normally apportioned communal land to households according to their labor strength, or number of *tiagla*. A tiaglo usually consisted of a married couple between the ages of eighteen and sixty. Sometimes communes chose instead to provide households with land based on a count of either the adult male members in each household or the mouths each had to feed. Each time a repartition took place, the number of allotments in a household's possession was readjusted to reflect changes in its composition. The system was reasonably just where complex family households were concerned.

Widows with small children, however, were disadvantaged by the allotment system. Since these women were no longer part of a tiaglo and landholding was a male prerogative, they risked forfeiting their communal allotments. In a complex household they could lean on other family members. In a nuclear family, however, the loss of communal allotments meant a loss of livelihood. That was the fate of the unfortunate Tifanova whose story introduced the book. The winter grain that she was allowed to keep as the fruit of her labors would in all likelihood have been barely sufficient to see her family through the spring. Although Tifanova came from a remote northern region, her situation was not uncommon in areas of central Russia. If a widow were lucky, the village assembly might give her a monthly apportionment of grain from the communal storehouse.[13] If that grain was inadequate for her family's or her own subsistence needs, however, she would be forced to leave the village to search for work in neighboring villages or towns.

Communes sometimes made exceptions for widows, allowing them to keep a full or partial communal land allotment until they remarried. A widow with young sons, for example, might be permitted to farm her land allotment temporarily as long as she had the necessary labor to do so. Once her eldest son became old enough to marry and assume the household headship, the allotment passed to his management. Even in such cases, however, village assemblies did not always protect widows from the encroachments of greedy male villagers who wished to expand their landholdings at the women's expense.

In the 1890s, the widow Aksin'ia Sazhina of the village of Korovino in industrial Iaroslavl' province was the victim of greed and collusion on the part of a fellow villager and local officials. A wealthy peasant named Shtykhin had his eye on the allotment of arable and farmstead land that the

---

[13] A widow of a village in Mtsensk district, Orel province, for example, was awarded one and a half *puds* of bread per month. See V. P. Vorontsov, *Krest'ianskaia obshchina: Obshchii obzor zemskoi statistiki krest'ianskago khoziastva* (Moscow, 1892), in Itogi ekonomicheskago issledovaniia Rossii po dannym zemskoi statistiki, ed. A. F. Fortunatov, 1:323; and *Sbornik statisticheskikh svedenii po Orlovskoi gubernii*, 3 vols. (Moscow and Orel, 1886–1887), 1:45.

widow Aksin'ia Sazhina cultivated with the help of her underage son. Wishing to extend his holdings, he bribed the village and cantonal authorities to seize the widow's land on the false pretext that it was not being farmed. The male-dominated village assembly, under pressure from the elder, granted Shtykhin the widow Sazhina's arable allotment and a large portion of her farmstead land. Shtykhin, however, was not satisfied with his victory and encroached upon the widow's remaining farmstead land by harvesting her garden crops. When Sazhina complained to the district land captain, he suggested that she take her protest up with the village elder and cantonal official (*starshina*). The elder and starshina in turn dismissed the widow's complaint and frightened her to such a degree that she let the matter rest.[14]

It is little wonder that Russian peasants lamented a widow's fate. According to popular sayings with a decidedly female voice, "It is bad for a field to be without a fence and a widow without defense." "To be widowed is to suffer always." "It is a bitter funeral when a wife buries her husband." "Without a husband a wife is always an orphan." "God takes care of the widow, but the people don't care for her." "A bad husband dies, and a good wife becomes a beggar."[15]

The commune's mutual responsibility for taxes and dues levied on all its lands was at the root of the way in which peasants apportioned land. Assigning land to labor units or tiagla was the best way of ensuring that the land would be worked to meet both peasant needs and tax obligations. A man in the fields was useless without a spouse to handle domestic affairs and help in the fields, and vice versa. Mutual responsibility for taxes and dues also explains the discriminatory practices against widows. If a widow was unable to work her land allotments and could not pay her taxes, other members of the commune had to make up the difference. Better to have the land in the possession of a productive household, rationalized the peasants.

At the same time, the yoke of mutual responsibility for taxes hampered the realization of complete equity in distribution of burdens. According to law, an entire commune was accountable for a household's default in its tax payments. In practice, village assemblies were selective in the aid they expended on debilitated households. Normally, they helped households struck by illness or sudden economic downturn due to such natural causes as fire or epizootics. They freed the household from some or all of its pay-

---

[14] Cited in V. V. Tenishev, *Administrativnoe polozhenie russkago krest'ianstva* (St. Petersburg, 1908), pp. 53–54.

[15] V. I. Dal', *Poslovitsy russkago naroda: Sbornik poslovits, pogovorok, rechenii, prislovii, shistogovorok, pribautok, zagadok, poverii, i proch.* (Moscow, 1862), p. 400; I. I. Illiustrov, *Sbornik rossiiskikh poslovits i pogovorok* (Kiev, 1904), pp. 157–60; and Elaine Elnett, *Historic Origin and Social Development of Family Life in Russia* (1926; reprint, New York, 1973), p. 120.

ments, by deferring payments or lending the capital interest-free. Wealthier communal households subsequently absorbed the costs of aiding their stricken neighbors.[16]

The temporary assistance which the commune extended to suddenly debilitated households reaffirmed the mutual aid that neighbors took the initiative to provide. It was not uncommon, for example, for villagers on their day of rest to form work parties and rebuild a hut destroyed by fire. They might plow or harvest a household's land as a way of offsetting a temporary crisis. The host was obliged only to provide them with food and drink after a hard day's work.[17]

Households in perpetual crisis, on the other hand, received neither communal nor neighborly aid. Communes could not justify maintaining repeated tax evaders, alcoholics, or those believed to be lazy, at the expense of other communal members. Instead they punished these tax delinquents by way of fines, arrest, or property confiscation and rewarded more reliable households with larger land allotments.[18]

Various repartitional practices allowed communes to augment or decrease households' land allotments according to the magnitude of the tax burdens, the reliability of households in meeting their obligations, and individual household needs. A general repartition, involving all a commune's households, was most common. The commune divided and apportioned the land in a complicated procedure that aimed at an equitable distribution of land among all households according to soil quality, flatness, moisture, and distance from the village.[19] Normally only one of the three fields of arable was reapportioned in a given year, the procedure usually taking more than a day.[20] First male peasants grouped themselves into tens for the purpose of sectioning off the field. A commune with 145 tiagla or work units entitled to allotments, for example, divided a field into fourteen and a half strips of land. The peasants then marked off the plots with the richest soils and those that lay closest to the farmsteads. These coveted strips were distributed by lot among the groups of ten. After this first distribution, the peasants identified the land with the next best soil quality, and once again each group cast lots to determine its share. They repeated the process until fourteen or more sets of lots had been cast. The household heads of each

[16] Mironov, "The Russian Peasant Commune," p. 460.

[17] For elaboration of forms of mutual aid, see M. M. Gromyko, "Obychai pomochei u russkikh krest'ian v XIX v. (K probleme kompleksnogo issledovaniia trudovykh traditsii)," *Sovetskaia etnografiia* (1981), nos. 4–5, pp. 26–38, 32–46; and her more recent study, *Traditsionnye normy povedeniia i formy obshcheniia russkikh krest'ian XIX v.* (Moscow, 1986).

[18] N. K. Brzheskii, *Nedoimochnost' i krugovaia poruka sel'skikh obshchestv: Istoriko-kriticheskii obzor deistvuiushchago zakonodatel'stva* (St. Petersburg, 1897), pp. 190, 200.

[19] "Prilozhenie," in *Sbornik statisticheskikh svedenii po Orlovskoi gubernii*, 2:70.

[20] A large commune with eight hundred revision souls needed three days to carry out the repartitional procedure. Orlov, *Formy krest'ianskago zemlevladeniia*, p. 31.

group of ten subsequently divided their group's lands among themselves on the basis of the number of tiagla, adult male laborers, or "eaters" (mouths to feed) in each household.[21]

At the end of a general repartition, each household was left with numerous strips scattered throughout the arable. These strips were divided, in some cases, by lanes for the passage of animals and plows and, in others, by boundary markings to identify each household's allotments.[22] Such dispersal of lands necessitated communal coordination of agricultural tasks to ensure that all households plowed, sowed, and harvested their crops and grazed their animals on the designated fallow at the same times.

A general repartition of the same land occurred at periodic intervals of anywhere from three to twenty-five or more years, depending upon regional variations in land quality, extent of manuring, and land values. Repartitions were more frequent in the northern forested areas of central Russia where soils were relatively poor and land burdensome. There heavily manured land allotments were sometimes excluded from the redistributive process. Peasants who had invested time and energy in endowing lands with a valuable, scarce commodity did not want to be robbed of that investment.

Peasants all over central Russia favored general repartitions immediately after emancipation when boundaries between lands belonging to former serfs and those of landlords were finally fixed and when former serfs were transferred from temporary obligation to redemption status. According to the emancipation statutes, peasants continued to owe their former owners feudal obligations for at least two years, after which time they remained "temporarily obligated" until both they and the landlords agreed to a date when the peasants would begin making redemption payments on their allotments. Those peasants who were still temporarily obligated by 1881 were automatically transferred to redemption status. With a decrease in redemption dues and a rise in land values in the 1880s, pressures for equalization of land allotments in line with production needs of individual households increased the frequency of repartition.

While the majority of communes repartitioned their arable on a fairly regular basis, approximately two-fifths of all communes in European Russia, including many located in the central Russian provinces of Tula, Orel, and Kursk, did not repartition their lands after the initial decade or so following emancipation. They fell into the category of communes that sub-

---

[21] "Prilozhenie," in *Sbornik statisticheskikh svedenii po Orlovskoi gubernii*, 2:70.

[22] P. N. Pershin, *Zemel'noe ustroistvo dorevoliutsionnoi derevni*, vol. 1: *Raiony: Tsentral'no-promyshlennyi, tsentral'no-chernozemnyi i severo-zapadnyi* (Moscow, 1928), p. 56; and N. Dobrotvorskii, "Krest'ianskie iuridicheskie obychai: Po materialam, sobrannym v vostochnoi chasti Vladimirskoi gubernii (uezdy Viaznikovskii, Gorokhovetskii, Shuiskii i Kovrovskii)," *Iuridicheskii vestnik* (October 1891): 198.

divided their lands only every twenty-five or more years, leaving the false
impression that the institution of the repartitional commune had atrophied
in these provinces. The infrequency of repartition often signified a victory
of larger households with more numerous land allotments over smaller and
poorer households in the village assembly vote on the question of repartition.[23] As village population grew and the number of tiagla or, in some
cases, persons in a household increased, wealthier households stood to lose
land in a repartition. They voted and coerced other communal members to
vote in the village assemblies against repartition. Poorer households were
not always able to win a battle for repartition. Some had to wait for the
upheaval of the revolutionary years of 1917–1918 when repartitional activity was resumed on a national scale.

In the quest for equality of burdens, Russian peasants also made use of
a series of partial repartitional systems in the intervals between general repartitions. These served to adjust landholdings of individual households
that had gained or lost labor strength and ability to pay taxes. *Svalki i navalki* or *skidki nakidki*, in which the commune took a land allotment away
from one household and apportioned it to another, was the most common
form of partial repartition, especially in the poor soil regions of the central
industrial provinces. Frequent repartitions of this type fragmented land
allotments into narrow strips dispersed haphazardly across the arable.
Households with fifteen to fifty strips were not uncommon. In the province of Tver isolated communes boasted an average of over one hundred
strips per household![24]

The endeavor to equalize burdens paradoxically impeded the proper ex-
ecution of agricultural tasks. Such highly fragmented landholdings increased the time peasants spent getting to their land and rendered the turn-
ing of a plow almost impossible in some areas. "Land that could have been
used for crops was taken up in boundary furrows and some parcels abandoned because they were too distant or because there was simply not the
labor available to work them all."[25]

Other forms of partial repartition became necessary to rectify the excessive fragmentation of land inherent in the practice of svalki i navalki. One
such method involved the casting of lots (*zhereb'evki*). Each peasant household head had his own lot, made out of birch or aspen twigs and marked
with a star, cross, notch, or other insignia, which he passed on to his son

[23] Moshe Lewin, "Customary Law and Russian Rural Society in the Post-Reform Era," *The Russian Review* 44, no. 1 (January 1985): 12.

[24] Pershin, *Zemel'noe ustroistvo*, p. 48.

[25] Judith Pallot, "The Development of Peasant Land Holding from Emancipation to the Revolution," in *Studies in Russian Historical Geography*, ed. James H. Bater and R. A. French, 2 vols. (London, 1983), 1:91.

upon retirement.[26] By casting lots for particular strips of land, the peasants simply redistributed land among households without changing the size or number of a household's land allotments. They altered only the location of the strips to improve land consolidation. Communes that did not practice svalki i navalki sometimes used this method of partial repartition for a more equitable distribution of land according to quality and distance from the farmstead core of their villages.[27]

Pereverstka or *peremerka* on an annual basis was yet another method of partial repartition. This time the total number and dimensions of land allotments remained the same, but their redistribution among households altered the number of allotments per household according to the number of males in each.[28] In still other communes strips were widened or narrowed (*v peredvizhku, v primerku*) to reflect alterations in household composition by moving the boundaries separating individual strips.[29] Households in communes that did not adopt any of these partial repartitions had to wait until the next general repartition to have their changes in labor strength or composition accommodated.

The periodic redistribution of land among peasant households, while equalizing landholdings and burdens as much as possible within the limitations set by mutual responsibility for taxes, deprived Russian peasants of secure rights of land possession. Although the emancipation legislation guaranteed the local customary inheritance practices of peasants, communal ownership of arable land severely limited those patterns.[30] Every household was expected to accept its share of the commune's arable, pay redemption dues and other taxes, and give up its allotments readily in a repartition. Peasants lacked the right to dispose of communal land until 1870 when for the first time it became possible for debt-free peasants to abandon their land and withdraw from communal membership. This provision had little effect, however, since a peasant without debts was a rarity in the post-emancipation countryside.[31]

Communal restraints on the land, together with limited peasant initiatives in land use, hampered the growth of notions of private property, this despite the fact that the emancipation statutes allowed repartitional com-

---

[26] Dobrotvorskii, "Krest'ianskie iuridicheskie obychai," p. 199.

[27] Vorontsov, *Krest'ianskaia obshchina*, p. 438.

[28] *Sbornik statisticheskikh svedenii po Saratovskoi gubernii*, 3 vols. (Saratov, 1883–1884), 1:61.

[29] Borisov, "Torkhovskaia obshchina," in Barikov, *Sbornik materialov dlia izucheniia sel'skoi pozemel'noi obshchiny*, p. 182; *Sbornik statisticheskikh svedenii po Orlovskoi gubernii*, 3:64; and Orlov, *Formy krest'ianskago zemlevladeniia*, p. 39.

[30] *PSZ*, ser. 2, no. 36657, art. 38.

[31] Robert Pepe Donnorummo, "The Peasants of Central Russia and Vladimir: Reactions to Emancipation and the Market, 1850–1900" (Ph.D. diss., University of Pittsburgh, 1983), p. 74.

munes to convert their collective land ownership to private ownership.[32] An insignificant number of communes took advantage of that clause, in part because of the peasants' weak understanding of private property. At least two-thirds of a commune's household heads had to agree to such a transfer. The following example of a commune that decided under pressure to adopt hereditary tenure illustrates how peasants retained a collective understanding of property ownership.

After 1861 frequent general repartitions had not been common among several communes of Perkinsk canton, Morshansk district, agricultural Tambov province. In fact, only one was carried out in the decade after emancipation. In 1870, a cantonal official, a rich timber merchant, tried to convince the peasants to take advantage of their legal right to transfer from communal ownership to hereditary land tenure. Relatively prosperous peasants with large landholdings, who stood to gain from the abolition of periodic redistributions of land, favored the proposal, which the majority of peasants opposed. These strong peasant households, supported by the cantonal official, succeeded in imposing private land ownership upon their weaker co-villagers. Theirs was a limited victory, however, for the Perkinsk peasants had become so accustomed to communal ownership and land repartition that they were unable to understand and take full advantage of private ownership. According to a local *zemstvo* statistician, peasants adamantly expressed their desire for a general repartition after completing the transfer to hereditary tenure.

> After personally interviewing the peasants of Perkinsk canton, we were entirely convinced that the peasants have a far from exact understanding of the separate proprietorship established for them. Without exaggeration one can say that one could leave Perkinsk canton without being aware that here the land was divided into private inheritable homesteads. . . . The peasants themselves were reluctant to admit that in their village private landownership is an established fact and that adjustment in land redistribution is not possible any more. At the present time most of the peasants . . . in the canton would like to have a redistribution of allotments according to the number of people in the household. The cantonal officer, of course, does not allow such redistribution of land, pointing out that . . . the land allotments have become private property. But the peasants are reproaching the officer for this situation, claiming that they never gave their approval to divide the land forever.[33]

Peasants believed "their collective function to be the management of land, not the mutual guarantee of individual rights."[34] A cantonal elder in

[32] *PSZ*, ser. 2, no. 36657, art. 12.
[33] Quoted in Sula Benet, ed. and trans., *The Village of Viriatino* (New York, 1970), p. 8.
[34] Yaney, *The Urge to Mobilize*, p. 171.

Vladimir district, Vladimir province, vocalized the Russian peasant attachment to repartition that equalized landholdings and burdens:

> If we were introduced to private ownership instead of collective ownership, ownership of scattered fields (*cherez-polozne*) would remain because of the disadvantages of independent farming. Certainly the field would be better manured and tilled, but on the other hand, the increase of the members of one family and the decrease in another and the expense of renting land from another, if possible, would cause even greater distinctions between most peasants and those that own private land, and [the land] would belong to one household instead of what we now have.[35]

Equalization of resources and obligations among all peasants was thus preferable to increased productivity for a minority.

Prosperous household heads who welcomed the abolition of repartitions and viewed their land allotments as inalienable family property rationalized their demands on grounds that did not contradict traditional notions of land.[36] Even under serfdom unfree peasants believed that the fruits of their labor belonged to them. And by virtue of their labor, they felt that they had as many or even more rights to the land than did gentry landowners. After emancipation in 1861 peasants who voted against repartition in their village assemblies continued to use the labor principle to justify their hereditary right to the land allotments at their disposal. They argued that they had worked the land for many years or "since time immemorial" and had met their communal taxes and redemption payments in full.[37] Had they been delinquent in their obligations to family, commune, and state, they would have found the commune justified in seizing their arable. This is a far cry from the Western belief in the sanctity of private property.

Regional Differences

Peasant communes in central Russia shared only three basic characteristics: the prevalence of the repartitional commune (with the exception of significant areas of Kursk province); the division of communal lands into

[35] Quoted in Donnorummo, "The Peasants of Central Russia," pp. 148–49.

[36] Some observers argued that these peasants' demands attested to a strong sentiment of private ownership pervading the Russian peasant psyche. See, for example, *Materialy po statistike narodnago khoziaistva v S.-Peterburgskoi gubernii*, 17 vols. (St. Petersburg, 1882–1895), vol. 6, pt. 2, p. 57.

[37] Ibid., pp. 51–52. In the 1880s in a commune in Orel district, Viatka province, prosperous peasants voted against repartition on the basis that their grandfathers and great-grandfathers had cleared the land. It was not their fault, they contended, that the forefathers of less prosperous peasants had been lazy. N. Dobrotvorskii, "Pozemel'naia obshchina v Orlovskom uezde, Viatskoi gubernii," *Russkaia mysl'* 5, no. 9 (September 1884), pt. 2, p. 36.

four categories (farmstead; arable; meadows, pasture, woodlands, and scrub; and leased land); and weak notions of private property. Before 1861 differences in topography, climate, and soil types elicited varying responses from peasants who struggled daily with the uncertainties of nature and landlords, whether private, state, or crown, who wished to exploit their peasant labor effectively. The non–black earth central industrial provinces of Vladimir, Kostroma, Moscow, Tver, and Iaroslavl' had evolved differently from their black earth counterparts of Voronezh, Kursk, Kaluga, Orel, Penza, Riazan, Tambov, and Tula to the south. The poorer soils in the north forced peasants to supplement their meager agricultural revenues with wages earned in trade and industry. Eager to tax these sources of income, serfowners abandoned corvée in favor of quitrent. On the other hand, the rich black soils of southern central Russia (with the exceptions of Tula and Riazan in which local trades and migrant labor were well developed) guaranteed the predominance of agricultural pursuits there. As pre-emancipation Russia became increasingly active in the international grain market, landlords in the black earth provinces demanded heavier corvée obligations from their serfs.

Emancipation merely exacerbated differences between north and south. Former serfowners wished to be compensated for the losses of peasant labor in the black earth belt and quitrent in the non–black earth region where "the person of the peasant had . . . a greater value than the land."[38] Consequently peasant redemption payments were set in excess of land values in both areas, but with greater consequences for peasants in the north. In the immediate post-emancipation years of 1863–1872 redemption costs in the non–black earth provinces exceeded market prices by an average of 90 percent; in south central Russia those costs were on average only 20.4 percent higher than market value. The general unprofitability of land in the central industrial provinces made the burden of these redemption costs more acute. Income generated from land fell significantly below total tax obligations. In Vladimir and Tver provinces, for example, taxes and dues on ex-serfs represented, respectively, 276 percent and 252 percent of estimated income from a desiatina of land.[39] Domestic industries and wage labor continued to be essential in the non–black earth belt to narrow the gap between taxes and farming revenues as well as meet peasant subsistence needs, whereas monocultural grain cultivation continued to characterize peasant economies in the south.

After emancipation increasing "land hunger" further diminished agricultural revenues, forcing peasants to seek supplementary income. The

[38] Robinson, *Rural Russia*, p. 83.

[39] Peter A. Zaionchkovsky, *The Abolition of Serfdom in Russia*, ed. and trans. Susan Wobst (Gulf Breeze, Fl., 1978), pp. 197–99.

emancipation legislation had reduced ex-serf allotments by just over 4 percent (in the black earth regions the percentage was much higher at 16). More than a quarter of all peasants in European Russia thereafter had insufficient land to meet their daily needs and fulfill communal and state tax obligations.[40] As the peasant population doubled in the second half of the nineteenth century, communes combated insufficient land resources by leasing and purchasing more and more land, and, in the black earth provinces, by extending the arable at the expense of pastures and meadows. By 1903 peasants were leasing almost half of the land belonging to the gentry. "For every six desiatinas of commune land the peasants held one desiatina of rented land."[41] Lands purchased by peasant communes and cooperatives climbed from 7.2 million hectares in 1877 to 25.7 million in 1905.[42] This expansion of arable, in the absence of universal adoption of intensive, as opposed to extensive, agricultural methods, did not, however, offset phenomenal population growth.

Land resources and labor strength remained acutely imbalanced in the poor soil areas of the central industrial region, forcing increasing numbers of peasants into domestic industries on either a seasonal or, in some cases, a full-time basis. Zemstvo studies in the late nineteenth and early twentieth centuries indicated that in European Russia "on average two workers per household contributed a non-agricultural income to the peasant budget."[43] In many central industrial provinces the average was much higher. Data from Nizhnii Novgorod province in the 1890s, for example, indicate that anywhere from 41.1 percent of household workers (in the better soil regions of that province) to 89.7 percent (in the poorer soils of the north) were involved in domestic industries.[44]

In the winter months peasants all over central Russia engaged in processing and manufacturing finished products from the flax and hemp they cultivated, woodworking, processing animal products, and, to a lesser extent, pottery and brickmaking.[45] Various specialized local trades, however, depended on the ready availability of raw materials and the existence of factories dependent on jobbers, small workshops, and cottage industry. Specialization was thus far better developed in the northern provinces of central Russia. Metal made possible the manufacture of chains, screens,

[40] Mironov, "The Russian Peasant Commune," pp. 464–65.

[41] Shanin, *The Roots of Otherness*, vol. 1: *Russia as a 'Developing Society,'* 136; and Pallot, "Development of Peasant Land Holding," p. 87.

[42] Peter Gatrell, *The Tsarist Economy 1850–1917* (London, 1986), pp. 114–15.

[43] Ibid., p. 84.

[44] M. A. Plotnikov, *Kustarnye promysly Nizhegorodskoi gubernii* (Nizhnii Novgorod, 1894), p. 17.

[45] R. Munting, "Outside Earnings in the Russian Peasant Farm: Tula Province 1900–1917," *The Journal of Peasant Studies* 3, no. 4 (July 1976): 429.

fences, and clothes hooks and eyes in certain villages of Moscow province; locks and keys, samovars, and accordions in areas of Tula province; and mesh, chains, hooks and eyes, sieves, and milk and tea strainers in some villages of Nizhnii Novgorod province.[46] Male peasants in Bogorodsk, Bronnitsy, and Kolomna districts to the east of Moscow found work in local mills and workshops that served large factories and plants. In the poverty-stricken nonindustrialized areas west of Moscow and the southeastern districts of Novgorod province, peasant women were attracted to the wet-nursing business as a way of increasing their household revenues.[47] Lace making and knitting were among the other exclusively female auxiliary trades in many areas of central Russia.

As domestic industries faced increasing competition from factories, however, more and more peasants were forced into migrant trades. The average number of internal passports issued annually to peasants in European Russia grew steadily from 1.29 million in the 1860s to 6.95 million in the 1890s.[48] Male peasants left their villages in the central industrial region and some areas of the central black earth provinces (notably Riazan, Tula, and Tambov) for major cities and towns. There they found work as carters, cabdrivers, carpenters, stonemasons, chimney sweeps, water carriers, stove makers, bakers, and factory workers. In areas of Moscow, Kostroma, and Nizhnii Novgorod provinces, it was not unusual for a migrant worker to be absent from the village for the better part of the year, year in and year out. During the summer scores of peasants, men, women, and children alike, departed the central agricultural provinces for New Russia and the steppe regions looking for paid work on gentry estates.[49] Major rivers such as the Volga, Desna, Don, and Dnieper beckoned male peasants from neighboring provinces to work as loggers, barge haulers, fishermen, steamboat operators, and raftsmen transporting pitch.

The role of the commune in domestic industries and migrant work was largely a supportive one. Extra-agricultural pursuits served the commune's interests by absorbing surplus village labor. Furthermore, revenues from local handicrafts and wages accumulated outside the commune flowed back into communal household coffers, making those households more reliable taxpayers. Thus it was unlikely for a commune to withhold a re-

[46] Anita B. Baker, "Deterioration or Development? The Peasant Economy of Moscow Province prior to 1914," *Russian History* 5 (1978): 16; Munting, "Outside Earnings," p. 429; and Plotnikov, *Kustarnye promysly*, p. 198.

[47] David L. Ransel, *Mothers of Misery: Child Abandonment in Russia* (Princeton, 1988), pp. 242ff.

[48] Gatrell, *The Tsarist Economy*, p. 89.

[49] See ibid.; and Timothy Mixter, "Of Grandfather-Beaters and Fat-Heeled Pacifists: Perceptions of Agricultural Labor and Hiring Market Disturbances in Saratov, 1872–1905," *Russian History* 7, pts. 1–2 (1980): 139–68.

quested passport from a migrant laborer, unless the head of the household from which the laborer originated refused to sanction his departure.

Despite the growth of migrant trades in the central industrial provinces, the land retained a tenacious hold on migrant laborers. These workers might normally have left their immediate families behind in the village to farm the households' land allotments. This reluctance to abandon the land stemmed partly from the restrictions that the commune imposed and partly from job insecurity and the difficulty of finding housing for families in the cities. Even industrial workers who left the village for more than six months in a given year or for several years running came back periodically to participate in the harvest or major festivals of the agricultural calendar. They returned permanently in their retirement years.

The maintenance of strong rural ties and *zemliachestvo* (living and working with co-villagers in the big city or factory town) among migrant workers reinforced traditional rural values and life-style and mitigated some effects of urban living. The parasols, leather boots, accordions, fine cloth, and other urban trappings that migrant workers brought back with them were eagerly welcomed by villagers but were in themselves insufficient to challenge village traditions. Returning workers, attuned to factory time, quickly accommodated themselves to the seasonal nature of an agricultural life. Their newfangled ways, including creeping individualism and greater dependence on money, did not have the same impact on village life as the onslaught of returning peasant soldiers would later have during the turbulent years of World War I and the Russian revolutions of 1917. These latter returnees brought with them a revolutionary message legitimizing the peasants' longing for more land.

The economy of the post-emancipation central industrial provinces was marked not only by better developed local and migrant trades, but also by agricultural diversification. The growth of cities and large towns acted as a powerful incentive for the development of market gardening, truck farming, dairy farming, and meat marketing in the hinterland. For example, market gardening on the non-black soils of Moscow, Kolomna, Bronnitsy, and Podol'sk districts in Moscow province and Pereslavl', Iur'ev, Suzdal', and Vladimir districts in Vladimir province became very profitable. Dairy farming and meat marketing also developed in Moscow district and other areas of the industrial belt.[50] Peasants increasingly engaged in the cultivation of hemp and flax, which they used as collateral—when necessity forced them to borrow grain and cash from local merchants—or worked into finished products for sale.[51] In some areas of Vladimir and Tver provinces

[50] Baker, "Deterioration or Development?" pp. 5, 14; and Donnorummo, "The Peasants of Central Russia," p. 27.

[51] Using hemp as collateral was a common practice among former serf communes in Orel province. Christine D. Worobec, "The Post-Emancipation Russian Peasant Commune in

and the central agricultural province of Tula, they even began growing various fodder grasses and clover. Of these crops, however, only flax was introduced into the three-field system. Peasants cultivated the other crops, including potatoes, on strips of land separate from the arable.[52]

The results of the diversification in agriculture and more intensive farming techniques in the central industrial region were mixed. On the one hand, they demonstrated the peasants' adaptability to market forces and ability to innovate. On the other hand, the peasants did not always act with good judgment. Flax cultivated within the traditional three-field system, for example, exhausted the soil. Nor were peasants, without heavy capital infusion from the state or gentry, able to revolutionize their way of farming. Wasteful, extensive farming methods, with a third of the arable given over to fallow, existed side by side with more intensive farming techniques.[53] This underscored the fact that Russian peasants were interested in the cultivation of industrial crops only insofar as they supplemented household income and facilitated the discharge of communal and state responsibilities. Surplus coins were not to be expended on anything other than the traditional staple of salt and such items as tea, matches, and kerosene, which by the end of the nineteenth century had become necessities. Any remaining coins were hoarded in dowry chests or valued as jewelry. Buying and selling for the sake of profit alone had not yet penetrated the peasant psyche.[54]

Fewer cities in the southern agricultural region of central Russia were able to compete successfully with the more urbanized and industrialized north in stimulating truck farming and introduction of new crops. The lack of diversification and capital eventually caused a general decline in per capita production in what had traditionally been European Russia's primary grain-producing area. By the end of the nineteenth century the steppe provinces of Ukraine and New Russia emerged as the largest per capita grain producers. This economic downturn in the central agricultural belt along with an ever-increasing population adversely affected peasant economic performance. The famine of 1891–1892 had its greatest repercussions in the central agricultural provinces, causing a sharp upturn in peasant indebtedness.[55]

Orel Province, 1861–1890," in *Land Commune and Peasant Community in Russia: Communal Forms in Imperial and Early Soviet Society*, ed. Roger Bartlett (London: Macmillan Press, in association with the School of Slavonic and East European Studies; New York: St. Martin's Press, 1990), pp. 100–101; this discussion appears here by permission of the publisher.

[52] Judith Pallot, "Agrarian Modernization on Peasant Farms in the Era of Capitalism," in Bater and French, *Studies in Russian Historical Geography*, 2:423–49.

[53] Ibid.

[54] Juliet du Boulay made the same observation of peasants living in an isolated Greek mountain community in the 1970s. See her *Portrait of a Greek Mountain Village* (Oxford, 1974), p. 37.

[55] S. G. Wheatcroft, "The Agrarian Crisis and Peasant Living Standards in Late Imperial

In addition to northern and southern central Russia's divergent economic patterns, the two areas were marked by differing peasant responses to the topographical and ecological environment. The north's poor soils and economic diversity encouraged relatively small villages averaging thirty to fifty households. Village size increased as one progressed southward to the better black soils of the central agricultural belt. The south boasted dense settlements of between fifty and two hundred households.[56]

Even village layout differentiated the north from the south. In the central industrial provinces peasant dwellings were situated perpendicular to the village street, while in the central agricultural region they faced each other, lining both sides of the street.[57] In the north it was common for the arable to extend around the farmstead core. In the south, on the other hand, rivers played an important role in shaping villages. Village lands were stretched along riverbanks in a narrow strip with the farmsteads normally located at one end. In many cases allotment lands were extended along several *versts* of a riverbank, making it inconvenient or even impossible for peasants to farm the farthest strips. Peasants had the choice of making periodic lengthy trips to these allotments, leaving the land fallow for extended periods, or leasing the allotments to other peasant villages at relatively low rates.

Even styles of residential and farm buildings varied from north to south in response to differing ecological conditions. In the extreme northern districts of Tver and Iaroslavl' in the central industrial belt, where winters were long and snows severe, dwellings and farm structures were combined into one long two-story log building under a common roof. The living quarters were raised some 1.5 to 3 meters off the ground because of harsh weather conditions. Peasants utilized the considerable space under the residential floor as storage for produce and utensils and shelter for fowl and small animals. As travelers progressed southward into Moscow, northern Riazan and Penza, and areas of Kaluga provinces, they saw smaller and lower huts with lower basements. Barns were no longer attached, but positioned either behind or to the side of huts, sometimes in an L-shaped design. Peasants in the more temperate southern black earth provinces built their huts with clay exteriors and thatched roofs right on the ground. The farm buildings were either scattered or grouped together in an enclosed area.[58]

Russia: A Reconsideration of Trends and Regional Differentiation" (Paper presented at the Conference on the Peasantry of European Russia, 1800–1917, University of Massachusetts-Boston, 19–22 August 1986), pp. 11–18.

[56] Pershin, *Zemel'noe ustroistvo*, pp. 2, 5, 149; and Basile H. Kerblay, *L'isba d'hier et d'aujourd'hui: L'évolution de l'habitation rurale en U.S.S.R.* (Lausanne, 1973), pp. 62–63.

[57] Kerblay, *L'isba d'hier*, pp. 62–63.

[58] See L. N. Chizhikova, "Dwellings of the Russians," *Soviet Anthropology and Archeology* 5, no. 1 (Summer 1966): 33–40.

Categories of Russian Peasants

The central Russian peasantry, besides being regionally diverse, was also heterogeneous because of historical circumstance, legal status, and resources. The pre-emancipation peasantry had been legally divided among serfs, state peasants, and crown peasants. The development of serfdom began in the late fifteenth century, finally culminating in the mid-seventeenth century. Over that time restrictions on peasant movement increased. Peasants who had fallen into debt to a gentry landowner were prohibited from leaving his estate at will. Those whom the state bestowed upon the gentry as an integral part of land grants also steadily lost their status as free persons. The categories of slave and serf gradually merged so that by the early eighteenth century Peter I was able to abolish slavery. Serfs owed a variety of obligations in both labor and kind to their owners as well as tax and military obligations to the state. They were little more than chattel under the guardianship of serfowners who interfered in their daily lives, administered rudimentary justice, and sold them at will. In order to maximize serf labor output, serfowners and their bailiffs forced peasants to marry young and maintain large households. Household serfs were the most exploited of unfree peasants, as they lived directly under the landowner's eye and were subject to his ever-changing whims.

Those peasants who remained on the so-called black lands, i.e., lands of the state patrimony which were not apportioned to gentry landowners, became known as state peasants. As the eighteenth century progressed and secularization as well as bureaucratization of the autocratic government increased, many social groups were merged into the state peasantry. Cossack farmers, former serfs on secularized monastic and ecclesiastical lands, and low-ranking military personnel who had served on garrison duty were drawn into this classification. Like serfs, state peasants paid a soul tax to the state and were subject to military recruitment. They were not, however, under the authority of individual landowners. Instead they had independent economies and paid a quitrent (*obrok*) directly to the state. According to the Tenth Revision or census of 1858, 36.76 percent of all peasants in Russia were state peasants and 57.23 percent serfs. The greatest concentration of state peasants was to be found in the empire's frontier regions, especially in the north. There were more state peasants in the central agricultural than central industrial regions, with a range from 17 percent to 66 percent of the peasant population. The remaining 6.01 percent of the 1858 peasant population were crown peasants who lived and labored on the crown demesnes.[59] By the end of the eighteenth century their situation

---

[59] N. M. Druzhinin, *Russkaia derevnia na perelome 1861–1880 g.g.* (Moscow, 1978), pp. 8–

approximated that of state peasants in terms of obligations performed and taxes paid to the state.

While in its emancipation legislation the imperial Russian government created one peasant estate, the goal of Russian peasant homogeneity was not realized. Serfs were freed in 1861, crown and state peasants not until 1863 and 1866 respectively. Glaring differences in obligations, land allotments, and land locations maintained disparities among former serfs and former crown and state peasants. In all respects ex-serfs were disadvantaged. They received smaller land allotments and lands of poorer quality than state and crown peasants. The problem was particularly acute in the central agricultural provinces where former serfowners wished to retain as much of the rich land as possible for their own exploitation. A nineteenth-century statistician argued that in the black earth region five desiatinas represented the minimum individual allotment necessary for subsistence; others cited three desiatinas per capita as the absolute minimum.[60] As table 1.1 demonstrates, average sizes of land allotments apportioned to former serfs did not come close to these minimums. Averages also mask tremendous variations among ex-serfs. For example, household serfs were liberated without land. Still other newly emancipated serfs chose to take the so-called beggar's allotment. One-quarter the size of the normal minimum allotment, the beggar's allotment was exempt from the redemption process. Insufficient arable guaranteed the continuing dependence of former

TABLE 1.1

Average Size of Land Allotments (1877–1878) per Taxed Revision Soul in Desiatinas in the Black Earth Provinces

	Former Status		
	Serfs	*Crown Peasants*	*State Peasants*
Tambov	2.44	—	4.98
Tula	2.63	5.26	4.23
Penza	2.52	—	4.96
Voronezh	2.39	4.67	5.65
Orel	2.95	3.81	4.13
Kursk	2.22	5.15	4.28
Riazan	2.74	3.06	4.08
Average	2.57	3.88	4.81

Source: N. M. Druzhinin, *Russkaia derevnia na perelome 1861–1880 g.g.* (Moscow, 1978), pp. 116–17, table 11.

9; and Jerome Blum, *Lord and Peasant in Russia: From the Ninth to the Nineteenth Century* (Princeton, 1972), p. 477.

[60] Cited in Zaionchkovsky, *The Abolition of Serfdom*, p. 161.

serfs upon estate owners. Necessity forced them to enter into sharecropping, rental contracts, or *otrabotka* agreements (where in return for working a portion of the landowner's estate the peasant received land usage or compensation in cash or kind).[61]

Ex-serfs also battled the chronic problem of having their land allotments dispersed in several locations and intermingled with lands belonging to gentry landowners or other peasant communes.[62] Under serfdom a landowner's arable had often bordered peasant farmsteads in order to make the owner's land readily accessible to serf labor. This meant that the peasants' arable was located beyond the serfowner's domain. Matters became even more complicated as landowner estates became subdivided through partible inheritance and sales of serfs with land. In implementing the emancipation provisions, designed to benefit former serfowners, peace arbitrators more often than not retained the intermingling of those lands.[63] As a result the lands apportioned to communes for redemption were often "awkwardly shaped and positioned."[64]

Land intermingling hindered peasant agriculture, forcing peasants to make a variety of accommodations with former serfowners and neighboring villages. Villagers of Grudnevo in Tambov district, Tambov province, for example, had to travel five versts through a landowner's stretch of land to reach their own arable. Rozhdestvennskaia peasants of Mtsensk district, Orel province, had their arable splintered by portions of land belonging to three separate landowners. In exchange for access to their allotments, they had to agree to work those landowner lands, a practice common in the post-emancipation era. Peasants in similar situations elsewhere sometimes chose to pay a transit fee for their animals and agricultural implements. In 1890 the commune of the village Pavlovki, Kasimov district, Riazan province, paid its neighboring landowner, Prince Golitsyn, 130 rubles for crossing privileges. In the same province villagers of Shopino had to pay a

[61] Steven L. Hoch, "Sharecropping and Peasant Tenancy Relations in Post-Emancipation Russia" (Paper presented at the Annual Convention of the American Association for the Advancement of Slavic Studies, November 1986), pp. 3–5.

[62] Former state and crown peasants were more fortunate in generally having all of their arable land in one location. Their hay fields and meadows, however, were sometimes inconveniently situated several versts from the village. For example, the state peasants of the village Krasnoe, Trubchevsk district, Orel province, had their three fields positioned around their farmstead lands, with the farthest allotment strips only three versts away from the village. The greater part of their hay fields, however, were situated across the Desna River at some distance from the village, because state officials chose to apportion hay fields to all state peasant communes of the district in one location. "Pribavlenie," in *Sbornik statisticheskikh svedenii po Orlovskoi gubernii*, 3:22; and Worobec, "The Post-Emancipation Russian Peasant Commune," p. 91.

[63] Pershin, *Zemel'noe ustroistvo*, p. 148.

[64] Gatrell, *The Tsarist Economy*, p. 73.

neighboring peasant commune a substantially lower figure of 30 rubles per annum for the same right. Elsewhere, Bogoslov villagers in Elets district, Orel province, were obliged to lease the five desiatinas of their former serf-owner's meadow, inconveniently situated amid their farmstead lands.[65]

Other forms of peasant dependence on landlords continued into the post-emancipation period as well. Former serfowners often retained valuable meadow, pasture, and forest lands that peasants desperately needed and were forced to lease in kind, cash, or labor.[66] In Orel province, which occupied an intermediary position between the non-black and black earth belts, peasants entered into a variety of leasing agreements. Peasants of the former serf commune of the village Uruch'e, Uruch'insk canton, for example, rented pasture from neighboring estates at 25 kopecks per head of cattle. In the same canton, the peasants of the hamlet Sosnovoe Boloto leased pasture and stubble on nearby estates for 50 kopecks per head.[67]

Some Orel peasant communes, on the other hand, rented land in return for labor. The former serfs of the landowner N. S. Salov, in the village Sosnovka, Uruch'insk canton, in exchange for access to Salov's pasture, had the onerous burdens of harvesting six desiatinas of Salov's meadow, delivering approximately 1,100 wagons of manure to his fields, and carting ten *sazhens* of wood for him. The peasants of the hamlet Aleksandrovki of the same canton in 1886 rented pastureland from two estates with the understanding that they would reap 48 shocks of rye on one estate and cart about 1,000 wagonloads of manure and 900 puds of grain a distance of thirteen versts for the other. Besides harvesting thirty desiatinas of grain and hauling 200 carts of manure for neighboring landowners in return for using their pastures, the peasants of the hamlet Sylenki, Prolysov canton, also had to provide forty men and forty women with spades and brooms in the event of a forest fire on the landowners' properties. The former serfs of the village Glinnoe of the same canton were also on fire duty, in addition to paying 90 rubles and providing 135 days of women's labor in exchange for the use of a landowner's pasture. Presumably peasant women were

[65] Pershin, *Zemel'noe ustroistvo*, pp. 30–32, 37–40, 177, 181–82; and Worobec, "The Post-Emancipation Russian Peasant Commune," p. 91.

[66] Upon emancipation in 1863 crown peasants received only land that had been registered in their names. Forests belonging to the crown, communal arable that had been heavily manured to produce excellent harvests, and rivers were not included in the post-emancipation allotments, forcing crown peasants to lease or purchase some of these lands outright. My study of serfs and crown peasants in Orel province suggests that the larger land allotments and development of auxiliary trades among crown peasants resulted in greater economic prosperity and the ability of crown peasants to purchase rather than lease these lands. See Worobec, "The Post-Emancipation Russian Peasant Commune," pp. 99–103.

[67] In the Sosnovoe example a head equaled either one cow, one horse, eight sheep, or six pigs. "Pribavlenie," in *Sbornik statisticheskikh svedenii Orlovskoi gubernii*, 3:39–41; and Worobec, "The Post-Emancipation Russian Peasant Commune," p. 99.

needed to work in the estate's hemp and potato fields and to process hemp.[68] Such onerous pasture rental in Orel province impeded the development of domestic industries and migrant trades among former serfs. Former state and crown peasants, not dependent upon landowners, were far freer to pursue those activities.

While glaring inequities divided various peasant subgroups, the survival strategy of individual communes within these groups was the same. Relative equality of resources and burdens within the parameters imposed by natural and human forces remained the underlying principle of peasant activity.

Awareness of a survival strategy, the commonality of the repartitional commune in central Russia, peasant attitudes toward land ownership, and the dichotomies between north and south, as well as different peasant categories, are essential to an understanding of post-emancipation peasant life. The commune was an important legal, social, and economic institution in post-emancipation peasant Russia. Its regulation of landholding and repartitional practices helped peasants to satisfy their own subsistence needs and obligations to community and state. Periodic repartitioning of lands redistributed resources and burdens to accommodate changes in composition and labor strength of individual households. Households with the requisite labor power received some of the poorest and some of the richest portions of land in the never-ending battle with the precarious environment. When natural disaster struck an individual household, its head could depend upon commune and village members to provide temporary assistance. Grain allotments from communal storehouses were dispensed to widows without means of support. In return for the "minimal subsistence insurance for villagers,"[69] each household had to carry its own share of responsibility by farming its allotments according to proven traditional methods and abiding by the village assembly's rules about the timing of plowing, sowing, harvesting, and grazing animals on the fallow. It also had to participate in collective labor on lands withheld from periodic redistribution. Any household head who defaulted in his responsibilities because of personal failings faced the undesirable consequence of losing that security cushion provided by commune and neighbors.

Redistribution and mutual aid reinforced a system that did not tolerate glaring inequities in economic standing among peasants. Indeed, relative prosperity in a Russian peasant commune was a fragile reward for a household that had successfully overcome the many obstacles to such an achieve-

[68] "Pribavlenie," in *Sbornik statisticheskikh svedenii Orlovskoi gubernii*, 3:45–46, 161, 173; and Worobec, "The Post-Emancipation Russian Peasant Commune," p. 100.
[69] James C. Scott, "Peasant Moral Economy as a Subsistence Ethic," in *Peasants and Peasant Societies: Selected Readings*, ed. Teodor Shanin, 2d ed. (Oxford, 1987), p. 306.

ment. An alteration in the weather, an uncontrollable epizootic disease, or a raging fire could suddenly obliterate that prosperity and drag the household to or below the subsistence line. Collective, rather than individual, enterprise was a far better surety for survival.

Russian peasants were highly suspicious of their few co-villagers whose relative prosperity seemed immune to normal environmental hazards. These prosperous types, they reasoned, came by their success either with the aid of supernatural forces or by subverting peasant ethics of collectivity and reciprocity. Since the likelihood of finding buried treasure was remote at best, they concluded that successful peasants more than likely achieved their wealth through usurious and unfair practices. It is little wonder that Russian peasants chose such pejorative names as *miroedy* (commune eaters/parasites) and kulaks to denote unethical wealthy peasants.[70]

Relative equalization of resources and burdens and personal accountability for one's actions were not confined to the commune alone. In fact, the Russian peasant's survival strategy encompassed more than the working of land, although land utilization remained at the foundation of peasant existence. Fulfilling subsistence needs was an insufficient guarantee for survival in a state that demanded redemption and tax payments. Whenever possible, peasants had to take advantage of other resources within and without the village through the establishment of domestic industries and migrant trades. Peasant survival, nevertheless, depended on more than economic strategies. The commune provided some, but not all social welfare functions. The extended Russian peasant family had to pick up where the commune left off.

Reproduction and devolution of property were essential factors in the perpetuation of Russian peasant families. Households needed an adequate amount of property to maintain the sustenance needs of nonlaboring and laboring members, as well as obligations to commune and state. The overriding principle of equality of responsibilities and burdens that informed the commune's repartitional practices found expression in the partible inheritance system and other property devolution patterns of individual households.

---

[70] For a discussion of the terms *miroed* and *kulak*, see Shanin, *The Roots of Otherness*, vol. 1: *Russia as a 'Developing Society,'* 156–58.

II

Family Rebirth: The Customs of Property Devolution

DEVOLUTION of property to heirs serves in agrarian societies to perpetuate the family as the fundamental economic and social unit within the framework of the community. The passage to family members of material wealth, either real (land) or movable (goods, chattels) property, guarantees the continuity of established families and, at times, the creation of new ones.[1] During both the pre- and post-emancipation periods the extended family household of Russian peasants functioned as both an economic component of the commune and a welfare institution that supported the elderly, infirm, or orphaned, as well as conjugal units disrupted by high mortality rates, conscription levies, and flows of migratory labor. Through partible inheritance, or the providing of equal shares to all sons, and the exclusion of endowed children from a further share of the family property, Russian peasants were able to retard the breakdown of extended families into smaller units and secure their pension rights as aged parents. Until alternative institutions could be created, the traditional extended family household was destined to remain the focal point of Russian peasant life. As such, it provided an element of stability in the countryside as Russia plunged into economic modernization.

Post-emancipation Russian peasant property devolution systems, among which partibility in the male line predominated, exhibited three notable characteristics. First, they demonstrated flexibility that accommodated not only the normative multiple family household but the simpler nuclear structure as well. Second, property devolution patterns displayed continuity over the nineteenth century despite emancipation. Third, civil law at times influenced customary inheritance practice. This chapter explores these characteristics, considering the property rights of both men and women. Although the general pattern of patrilineality excluded women from inheritance, women held their own inalienable property in the form of dowries and personal possessions and in certain cases were

[1] For general discussions of inheritance strategies among different societies, see Jack Goody, "Strategies of Heirship," *Comparative Studies in Society and History* 15, no. 1 (January 1973): 3–16; and idem, "Introduction," in *Family and Inheritance: Rural Society in Western Europe, 1200–1800*, ed. Jack Goody, Joan Thirsk, and E. P. Thompson (Cambridge, 1978), pp. 1–9.

entitled to a share of their husband's property. This chapter also examines the commune's role in limiting patterns of property devolution and the household head's authority in order to help maintain self-supporting, tax-paying households.

Both before and after 1861 Russian repartitional communes favored the multiple family household as the most viable economic unit. Periodic land reallocations on the basis of the number of married couples in a household, or tiagla, gave peasants an incentive for early marriage and encouraged increases in household size. The more able-bodied males a household had, the greater the chances of its being able to meet all its obligations. Thus, it was to a household head's advantage to welcome his son's bride into the household rather than lose that son's laboring power and land allotment. To encourage conjugal units to remain in the multiple family household, Russian peasants had devised an inheritance system that rewarded male kin according to their laboring capacities. Partible inheritance rested on the premise that each blood relation contributed his due share of labor. Entitlement to an equal share of property meant that young male peasants, unlike their contemporary Western European counterparts, were not immediately forced to migrate to urban centers to earn money that might one day enable them to return to the village, marry local peasant girls, and establish independent households. The patrilocal family household provided them with an immediate economic cushion, delaying their separation from the natal family for many years. Consequently, the multiple family household constituted the norm in both the pre- and post-emancipation periods.

Despite the predominance of the multiple family household, however, natural growth rates, periodic splintering of households into smaller units, and high mortality rates created a dynamic family life cycle. Over a period of years, individuals might live in a succession of household structures of the multiple (stem, joint, and complex joint) and nuclear family varieties. Inheritance strategies other than the normal devolution of property to all male heirs on an equal basis became essential to accommodate simple families, which became more numerous with the abolition of serfowner control in 1861. In the absence of direct male heirs, for example, a peasant household adopted an heir, usually a prospective son-in-law for an unmarried daughter, as a way to preserve the family patrimony and avoid its devolution to the commune. In return for fulfilling his labor and welfare responsibilities in the household, the son-in-law was rewarded as if he were a natural son. He received a property portion based firmly on his kin relationship to the household head. In nuclear families incapacitated by the premature death of the male household head, the principle of patrilineal inheritance was modified to permit devolution of property to females, at least on a temporary basis.

After emancipation the property that peasants passed on to their heirs was limited because of the commune's control of much of central Russia's arable. Only those real and movable items which remained outside the commune's jurisdiction could freely devolve to family members. These included the farmstead (usad'ba) and the residential and farm buildings erected upon it, privately owned land, plus all of the household's animals, farm implements, cash, agricultural produce, sown crops, and domestic items. According to the law, "the farmstead land of each peasant household remains in the hereditary possession of the family that lives in that household and devolves to its heirs in accordance with the customary order of inheritance in each locality."[2]

The commune held ownership rights to only escheated farmstead land and buildings.[3] When a household became extinct as a result of natural attrition and a lack of heirs, the commune could claim the farmstead land and its structures, unless a relative living elsewhere in the commune agreed to settle on the deceased's land. If that relative wished instead to remain living on his own farmstead, he had the option of transporting, at his own expense, the deceased's residential and farm buildings to that farmstead. By so doing, he forfeited the deceased's farmstead land to the commune. In the event that the relative lived in another commune and wished to take possession of the deceased's farmstead, he had to agree to surrender his own land allotments and farmstead land to his original commune, take up residence on the deceased's farmstead, and register as a new member of the deceased's commune.[4] These complicated procedures clearly favored the commune. By claiming escheated property the commune enlarged its own holdings, which it could then apportion to new households created as a result of the splintering of large households.

Patrilineal Partible Inheritance

The Russian lineage system rested on a patriarchal structure with the household head or *bol'shak* at its apex. Custom and law entrusted the bol'shak with managing the patrimony or collective familial property in the interests of both family and commune. He sometimes prepared a written or oral testament to prevent quarrels over property divisions or to uphold the property rights of a wife, adopted or illegitimate son, or son-in-law. A

---

[2] *PSZ*, ser. 2, no. 36662, art. 110.

[3] Ibid., art. 111.

[4] P. Zinov'ev, "Borokskaia obshchina (Pskovskoi gub.)," in Barikov, *Sbornik materialov dlia izucheniia sel'skoi pozemel'noi obshchiny*, p. 330; and A. M. Mikhalenko, "Zaozerskaia obshchina (Novgorodskaia gub.), s litografirovannym planom i 4-mia risunkami v tekste," in ibid., p. 297.

will might prevent immediate relations from encroaching upon the heir's rightful share. According to custom, all sons were to inherit equally, but a father had the right to bequeath one son a greater share of the real property if that son had to support his elderly mother, unmarried siblings, or other relatives. Custom and communal controls, however, prohibited the father from disinheriting a son unless extraordinary circumstances, such as debilitating illness or dissolute character, prevented him from managing the property.[5] A disinherited son was a potential burden for the commune. Wills were also designed to discourage more distant relatives from making property claims.

The household head possessed inviolable authority only as long as he guaranteed the economic functioning of the household and the perpetuity of the family. If he was a drunkard, squandered the patrimonial property, or prevented the household from fulfilling its communal obligations, it was not unusual for the commune to intervene. Either on its own authority or that of the cantonal court, the village administration might assign a guardian to the troubled household in an attempt to restrain the head's behavior. It might also transfer his authority to another family member, normally the eldest male in the household. If, however, all males in the home were underage, authority temporarily devolved to the household head's wife, the *bol'shukha*. The commune expected the wife to relinquish her duties to her eldest son when he came of age.

In the immediate post-emancipation period it was not unusual for village authorities, worried about the taxpaying capacities of individual households, to press charges against delinquent household heads in cantonal courts. For example, on 30 May 1871 in Mologa district, industrial Iaroslavl' province, an elected official of the village Kustova brought the Kriukov cantonal court's attention to the fact that the sixty-year-old peasant E. was both squandering his property and menacing his community. The official accused the household head of improperly seeding his field, constantly being drunk, and arguing with his hardworking son. Neighbors worried, the official reported, that if the delinquent E. continued to jeopardize his household economy, they would be held responsible for his tax arrears. The judges acted promptly to transfer E.'s headship to his industrious son and advised the son to report further fatherly wrongdoings to the appropriate authorities. They completed the defendant's humiliation by sentencing him to seven days in jail.[6]

By far the most common complaint against a delinquent household head was his inability to fulfill communal obligations because of a drinking

[5] V. F. Mukhin, *Obychnyi poriadok nasledovaniia u krest'ian: K voprosu ob otnoshenii narodnykh iuridicheskikh obychaev k budushchemu grazhdanskomu ulozheniiu* (St. Petersburg, 1888), pp. 63–69.

[6] *Trudy Kommisii*, 3:148–49, #19.

problem. In May 1871 the Kukarin cantonal judges of Mozhaisk district, Moscow province, acting upon a village elder's recommendation, likewise transferred the authority of a fifty-seven-year-old household head to his eldest son. They did so on the justification that the bol'shak was an alcoholic who, while squandering his household's property, could not pay his taxes. In yet another case, in June 1870, villagers in Rostov district, Iaroslavl' province, rather than entrust their complaint to a village official, personally appeared before the cantonal court to accuse three co-villagers of destroying their families and the community's tranquillity with their incessant drinking. The judges sentenced each defendant to twenty lashes and ordered that the commune appoint guardians over the delinquents' property to prevent the further disintegration of their households.[7]

Familial and communal constraints also limited a household head's activities regarding his control of family property. They prevented him from selling real property when household children were its rightful heirs. They also determined the type of property to be included in wills. A bol'shak could bequeath only movable property or, in the absence of direct descendants, the farmstead.[8] Furthermore, all testaments had to meet the requirements of the commune and peasant notions of equitable inheritance.[9]

Within these bounds, however, the bol'shak's authority was supreme. He functioned as administrator and decision maker for life. During his lifetime other family members had a right to live in the patrimonial home and be supported, in return for which they were expected to contribute to the household economy. They could use the common familial property as necessary but had no claim to its possession. Net revenues were put into a common pool over which the patriarch had undisputed control. These included wages family members earned as agricultural day laborers, as migrant workers, or in domestic industry. Since married sons were expected to live with their parents,[10] their separation from the household depended entirely upon the head's approval. Exceptions to that rule occurred in those rare instances in which the commune intervened to support the inheritance claims of partitioning sons.[11]

Upon the bol'shak's death his authority devolved to the most senior member of the family in the male line, either his eldest brother or his eldest son. It was at this point that other male family members had to decide whether to remain in the household or to split off from the household,

[7] Ibid., 2:264, #30; 3:264.

[8] Zinov'ev, "Borokskaia obshchina," in Barikov, *Sbornik materialov dlia izucheniia sel'skoi pozemel'noi obshchiny*, p. 328.

[9] *Trudy Kommisii*, 3:129.

[10] Mukhin, *Obychnyi poriadok*, p. 86.

[11] S. V. Pakhman, *Obychnoe grazhdanskoe pravo v Rossii: Iuridicheskiia ocherki*, 2 vols. (St. Petersburg, 1877–1879), 2:9.

taking their rightful shares of the patrimony with them. The first alternative was by far the simpler. If the household's occupants decided to remain
together as one family household, they divided the farmstead in theory but
in reality agreed to keep it intact as an economic unit, thus guaranteeing
the indivisibility of the patrimony.[12] Russian peasants rationalized this
practice with the saying "Although the inheritance is not divided, everyone
has to square his accounts."[13] In the second event, labeled by historians of
the family as postmortem fission, male heirs who wished to partition the
patrimonial household into two or more independent households had to
divide all real and movable property into equal portions for each heir.

In either case, the patrimony was usually divided on the basis of genea-
logical descent. Three married brothers in a joint family, for example,
would have each received a third of the real and movable property if the
family split into three separate units upon their father's death. Each brother's son was, in turn, entitled to an equal share of his father's property.
Thus, as in the case of the Serbian zadruga, "if in the next generation, one
brother had one son, the second had two, and the third had three sons,
these sons would receive, respectively, one-third, one-sixth, and one-
ninth" of the property.[14] Customary local practice, however, sometimes
departed from the strict generational breakdown of partible inheritance
when property devolved from an uncle to his nephew. The uncle's role in
his nephew's upbringing generally determined the nephew's right to patrimonial property. In many districts of industrial Moscow province, for
example, the generational principle was retained if a nephew was of age
when his father died and had subsequently helped his uncle in running the
household economy. The nephew was accordingly entitled to his father's
due share of the patrimony.[15] If, however, an uncle was left to bring up his
orphaned nephew, he had to be compensated for both the material expenses involved in raising a small nonlaboring child and the taxes and dues
that he had to pay on his deceased brother's allotment land.[16] The nephew
thus forfeited a portion of his father's share of the patrimony and inherited
equally with his male cousins.[17]

A number of rules had to be followed in the breaking up of a patrimonial
household upon a father's death (postmortem fission). Written law obliged

[12] Lutz K. Berkner found the same principle in preindustrial rural Germany. See his "Inheritance, Land Tenure and Peasant Family Structure: A German Regional Comparison," in
Goody, Thirsk, and Thompson, *Family and Inheritance*, p. 72.

[13] Dal', *Poslovitsy russkago naroda*, p. 413.

[14] Philip E. Mosely, "The Distribution of the Zadruga within Southeastern Europe," in
The Zadruga: Essays by Philip E. Mosely and Essays in His Honor, ed. Robert F. Byrnes (Notre
Dame, Ind., 1976), p. 63.

[15] *Trudy Kommisii*, 2:352.

[16] Mukhin, *Obychnyi poriadok*, p. 33.

[17] *Trudy Kommisii*, 2:352.

sons first to apply to the village assembly for permission.[18] In practice, peasants often bypassed this step; the assembly's approval, in any case, was usually automatic because of that body's reluctance to interfere in family affairs. Then the fissioning parties, with the aid of communal members, had to decide how to divide the property as equitably as possible. Community participation was necessary to validate the fission, to witness the property division in the event of later family quarrels, and to help maintain family tranquillity and unity.

A household division between two brothers, Aleksei and Artem Andreev, in the village Penkina, Smolensk province, demonstrates the complexity of the process and the rituals that Russian peasants attached to such a solemn event. The Andreev brothers' experience, while outside central Russia, was familiar to central Russian peasants. When their father died, the brothers decided to set up independent households. This meant dividing the patrimonial property of two farmsteads, three windmills, and numerous animals and agricultural implements. First the brothers summoned all the villagers, including relatives, to witness the division and to act as arbitrators if necessary. The negotiations proceeded inside the freshly swept patrimonial hut before a table laid with a holy icon and the traditional bread and salt. Lighted candles in the icon corner lent solemnity to the occasion. Then the division began. Aleksei and Artem Andreev agreed to take one mill apiece. Rather than share the third mill, Artem bought his brother's half of it for one hundred rubles. Aleksei, in turn, consented to leave the patrimonial farmstead in his older brother's possession, on condition that Artem also support their mother, and claimed the second farmstead. The communal allotment land was to be apportioned according to the number of males in each of the two families. The brothers divided the animals, agricultural implements, and outstanding family debts in half and drew lots to determine their respective shares. Since prior to fission Aleksei had contributed funds to cover the costs of his nephew's wedding, Artem was now required to give one of his nephews a comparable amount for his forthcoming marriage. Thus equity was observed in all matters. At the conclusion of the proceedings, to preserve family unity and guarantee future tranquillity, the Andreev brothers broke the ceremonial bread and embraced one another in farewell. Had Aleksei been required to build a new home for his family, his wife would later have carried a burning log from the patrimonial hearth to the new dwelling as a token of family protection. The commonality of fire from the ancestral hearth also emphasized the continuity of family unity.[19]

[18] *PSZ*, ser. 2, no. 36657, arts. 51–53, 57.

[19] The Andreev brothers' household division is described in S. V. Pakhman, "Ocherk narodnykh iuridicheskikh obychaev Smolenskoi gubernii," in *Sbornik narodnykh iuridicheskikh obychaev*, vol. 2, ed. Pakhman (St. Petersburg, 1900), pp. 72–73. Unfortunately, the source

Total equity in property division was also observed in an 1871 postmortem fission between two brothers in a village in Kurbsk canton, industrial Iaroslavl' province. However, this time, having received authorization from the village assembly for the fission, the brothers sought the cantonal court's aid in reaching an equitable decision. The judges apportioned one brother the house and yard; a half each of the shed, granary, barn, and icehouse; one cow, two sheep, and four lambs; a set of wheels (half of which were old and half new), the old woodcutters, and two of the new yokes. That brother was also held responsible for paying half the family's debt of 65 rubles. The judges gave the other brother possession of the remaining half of the enumerated buildings; one horse, one calf, two sheep, and four lambs; a set of wheels (half of which were old and half new), the new woodcutters, and the old yokes. He too was responsible for 32 rubles and 50 kopecks of the family debt. The judges awarded the solitary horse to the second brother as compensation for his not having received a house and yard in the property settlement. The subsequent physical division of property, as in the previous example, took place before community witnesses.[20]

Determining equity sometimes proved difficult in household divisions between brothers after a father's death, when one of the brothers was a retired soldier or a soldier on extended leave. Prior to the 1860s military recruits were conscripted for twenty-five years. That veritable lifetime sentence effectively cut soldiers off from village life and schemes of property devolution. Retirements and both temporary and unlimited leaves after the Crimean War, followed by reductions in the length of military service, however, inundated villages with returning soldiers.[21] These soldiers had to be incorporated into the partible inheritance system. Russian peasants generally acknowledged the debt they owed soldiers for taking on the burdens of military service, commonly asserting that recruits " 'served for their families, suffered in service, [and] fulfilled the tsar's service requirements.' "[22] They accordingly awarded soldiers full shares of their deceased fathers' property. Complications nevertheless arose between brothers if their father had died before the soldier's return home. Was that returning

concentrates on the property settlement alone. I have reconstructed the ritual aspect of a household division from other sources. See P. I. Astrov, "Ob uchastii sverkh-estestvennoi sily v narodnom sudoproizvodstve krest'ian Elatomskago uezda, Tambovskoi gub.," in *Sbornik svedenii dlia izucheniia byta krest'ianskago naseleniia Rossii: Obychnoe pravo, obriady, verovaniia i pr.*, ed. Nikolai Kharuzin, vol. 1 (Moscow, 1889), p. 147; O. P. Semenova-Tian-Shanskaia, *Zhizn' 'Ivana': Ocherki iz byta krest'ian odnoi iz chernozemnykh gubernii* (St. Petersburg, 1914), p. 85; and L. I. Min'ko, "Magical Curing (Its Sources and Character, and the Causes of Its Prevalence)," *Soviet Anthropology and Archeology* 12, no. 1 (Summer 1973): 21–22.

[20] *Trudy Kommisii*, 3:63, #56.
[21] See chap. III below.
[22] Quoted in Pakhman, *Obychnoe grazhdanskoe pravo*, p. 223.

soldier entitled to a share of the property his brother had in the meantime acquired by the sweat of his brow?[23]

When a nineteenth-century investigator of customary law posed that question to peasants in several cantons of Rostov district, industrial Iaroslavl' province, he found considerable variation in their answers. Some peasants replied that the former soldier was entitled to an equal share of all the property because he had served in the army on behalf of both his father and his brother. They made no distinction between the father's patrimony and the property that a son, in managing his deceased father's property, had accumulated on his own. Other peasants argued that the returning soldier had a right to only half the patrimony, which they defined as the property that had been under the father's direct management. They reasoned that property an individual acquired by his own labors should become the uncontested collective property of his own household, eventually devolving to his male heirs. Still other peasants contended that the resolution of the problem rested with the soldier's personal character. If he was a sober and honest fellow, he was entitled to an equal share of all the property. If, however, he was a drunkard, his potential as an upright member of the commune and reliable taxpayer was significantly reduced. In that event, they reasoned, the returning soldier should be allocated a smaller portion of his father's property than his brother.[24]

Customary local practice generally followed the above prescriptions concerning returning soldiers. When brothers divided their deceased father's property, they gave soldiers either an equal share of the patrimony or a slightly smaller portion. Sometimes the share was converted to a cash payment. Monetary settlements avoided the problems inherent in property division and prevented the disruption of working agricultural economies.[25]

While equity was generally followed in a postmortem fission, a son was entitled to a slightly larger portion, in the form of extra grain and animals, if he was responsible for looking after his mother, unmarried siblings, and perhaps other kin. In contrast to the normal principle of seniority, the youngest adult son usually remained on the patrimonial farmstead. He was obliged to provide for all family members and give his sisters dowries when they married.

Elder brothers who separated from their father's home, leaving a younger brother to support their mother and unmarried sisters, had to apply to the village assembly for new farmstead land. Usually those parcels were carved out of communal landholdings on the village outskirts, thus

---

[23] I. G. Orshanskii, "O pridanom," *Zhurnal grazhdanskago i torgovago prava* (December 1872): 185.

[24] Ibid.

[25] *Trudy Kommisii*, vol. 2.

reducing the commune's total amount of arable.[26] In some communes, the brothers had to purchase new farmstead land by selling the movables they had received in the property division.[27] If costs were prohibitive, they remained on the patrimonial farmstead, either building new homes or partitioning the old home into separate family units.[28] In certain cantons of Moscow province it was not uncommon for the youngest son to contribute funds from the common family coffers to his brothers' construction of new huts on the patrimonial farmstead. Once the building had been completed, all the brothers divided the agricultural implements, animals, and harvested grain equally among themselves but retained collective responsibility for working their land allotments.[29]

The apportionment of a greater property share to one son also occurred when some family members disrupted the family life cycle by splitting off from the patrimonial household during a household head's lifetime. Premortem fission became more frequent in the post-emancipation periods but in most cases did not disrupt the welfare function of the multiple family household. For reasons of age or illness household heads voluntarily transferred their headships to one son on condition that he support his parents, provisioning the remaining sons with property so that they could establish households of their own. Many Russian peasant proverbs stress reciprocal parent-and-child responsibilities: "To feed your father and mother is to repay an old debt."[30] "Feed your son for the time being; when the time comes your son will feed you."[31] "There is nothing harder than to pray to God, repay your debt, and feed your parents."[32] "Do not forsake your father and mother in their old age, and God will not forsake you."[33]

There was a variety of ways for a father to handle a household division. He sometimes partitioned the patrimony among his heirs but retained two portions for himself and his youngest son. The son would then be obliged to manage both portions, pay all taxes, and maintain his parents in the patrimonial residence.[34] In other cases the father apportioned household property equally among his sons on condition that they contribute an equal share, usually in the form of grain and clothing, for their parents'

[26] *Materialy po statistike narodnago khoziaistva v S.-Peterburgskoi gubernii*, 4:57.

[27] Mukhin, *Obychnyi poriadok*, p. 166n.

[28] *Materialy po statistike narodnago khoziaistva v S.-Peterburgskoi gubernii*, 4:57.

[29] *Trudy Kommisii*, 2:205.

[30] Aleksandr Evgen'evich Burtsev, *Narodnyi byt velikago severa: Ego nravy, obychai, predaniia, predskazaniia, predrazsudki, pritchi, poslovitsy, prisloviia, pribautki, peregudki, pripevy, skazki, priskazki, pesni, skorogovorki, zagadki, schety, zadachi, zagovory i zaklinaniia*, 3 vols. (St. Petersburg, 1898), 2:276.

[31] Dal', *Poslovitsy russkago naroda*, p. 410.

[32] Illiustrov, *Sbornik rossiiskikh poslovits*, p. 187.

[33] Elnett, *Historic Origin*, p. 129.

[34] *Trudy Kommisii*, 1:542.

maintenance. At times a rotational system was adopted in which parents boarded first at one son's home and then at another's. In all cases, equality of rights went hand in hand with equality of obligations, with village assemblies and cantonal courts upholding parents' claims to sustenance from their children.[35]

A case that came before a cantonal court in Mologa district, industrial Iaroslavl' province, in September 1870, illustrates well the equality of children in obligations to their parents. A dispute over filial duties had arisen between a father and his two sons. The eldest son had housed and provided for his quarrelsome father but after a short time refused to support him any longer. He believed that his younger brother should assume some responsibility for their father's welfare. The judges were able to persuade the brothers to reach an understanding. The younger brother agreed to look after his father in return for his elder brother's payment of ten rubles toward the maintenance costs. The rotational system of support and the ten rubles equalized the brothers' shares of responsibility in providing for their father.[36]

It was not unusual for a retiring household head to take legal action to ensure that his sons did not default on their obligations to him. As a Russian proverb warned, "One father will feed nine children sooner than nine children will feed one father."[37] Thus, if an elderly father chose not to live with his sons, he might draw up an agreement specifying the exact amount of sustenance and clothing, or their equivalent value in cash, they were required to provision him. Monetary settlements varied in sums from five to sixty rubles per annum, although the norm appears to have been in the range of eighteen to twenty-four rubles.[38] As early as 1860, a seventy-five-year-old father of Mozhaisk district, Moscow province, rather than simply have his son hand over a fixed sum of money, required him to provide three *chetverts* of rye per annum and to pay all taxes and dues.[39]

Fathers at least had documentary or oral evidence to buttress their customary claims to filial support if their sons did not live up to the support agreements. On 3 February 1871, in the Krestobogorodsk cantonal court, Iaroslavl' province, for example, a peasant charged his three sons with fail-

---

[35] Russian peasants were not unique in this respect. See Jack Goody, "Inheritance, Property and Women: Some Comparative Considerations," in Goody, Thirsk, and Thompson, *Family and Inheritance*, p. 32.

[36] *Trudy Kommisii*, 3:124–25, #9.

[37] Elnett, *Historic Origin*, p. 129.

[38] See Pakhman, "Ocherk narodnykh iuridicheskikh obychaev," in Pakhman, *Sbornik narodnykh iuridicheskikh obychaev*, 2:75. The averaging is based on cantonal court decisions found in the *Trudy Kommisii*, vols. 1–3.

[39] The judges of the Kukarin cantonal court in Mozhaisk district were informed of the contract's existence only in 1871 as a result of the son's having defaulted in his obligations. *Trudy Kommisii*, 2:266, #37.

ure to provide for him. The youngest son, a retired soldier, had not lived up to the conditions of a November 1868 contract in which he agreed to support his father, but had left the old man to fend for himself. All three sons were summoned before the court to account for their negligence. After hearing their testimonies, the judges ruled that the contract must be fulfilled and ordered the retired soldier to support his father in his home at his own expense. If, however, the second son wished to contribute to his father's maintenance, he was free to do so. The judges relieved the eldest son from any obligations to his father because he had not received any property when he separated from his father's household without the father's permission.[40] Furthermore, that son had enough difficulties supporting his own family out of his meager wages as an industrial laborer.

In the central industrial provinces it was not unusual for elderly fathers to be dependent on their migrant sons' wages. Support contracts at least provided them with a legal guarantee that obliged the sons to send money home. Nevertheless, when a migrant son defaulted in his obligations, the father found himself in a very precarious situation whether or not he had an agreement. He had to travel to the cantonal court at his own expense four or five times over a period of eight to ten months, if not more, and sign petitions, asking government officials to track down his son and force him to remit part of his wages. According to a land captain from Mozhaisk district, Moscow province, fathers had to depend on the judges' goodwill and did not always receive satisfaction.[41]

In an August 1871 case, judges of the Marinsk cantonal court, Mologa district, industrial Iaroslavl' province, sided with a father's complaint against his negligent migrant son even though a formal support agreement had never been drawn up. However the father's victory was won only after he had suffered personal misfortunes over several years. The father had launched his first petition in 1863 when old age and blindness had suddenly incapacitated him. He had to wait eight very long years for the authorities to track down his migrant son in St. Petersburg. When the son was finally brought before the cantonal court in 1871, the judges ordered him to cover expenses of ninety-six rubles (eighteen rubles for a household servant, fifty-four for food, twenty for clothes and linens, and four for small household expenditures), which his eighty-year-old father had incurred over the previous eight years.[42] Unfortunately, the document does not indicate how the father managed to care for himself while his case was pending. His having a household servant indicates that he may have had a fairly prosperous household economy. A father entirely dependent upon his mi-

[40] Ibid., 3:37–38, #8.
[41] *Trudy mestnykh komitetov o nuzhdakh sel'skokhoziaistvennoi promyshlennosti*, 58 vols. (St. Petersburg, 1903), 23:425.
[42] *Trudy Kommisii*, 3:137, #51.

grant son's wages would have been forced to rely on the Christian charity of his neighbors.

In addition to drawing up contracts and dividing property among his sons in return for support, a household head had the further option of formally bequeathing his property to his sons on condition that they provide for him and his wife until their deaths. For example, in 1861 a state peasant of the village Kazanovka, Usman' district, Tambov province, stipulated that his property was to devolve to his two sons only if they supported their parents and arranged memorial services for them when they died.[43] The demand that sons assume the additional Christian responsibility of interceding on behalf of their parents' souls was a common feature of peasant testaments. It pinpointed a strong linkage between the living and the dead in Russian peasant society and reassured parents that their memories would live on in their families.[44]

A peasant, I. I. Shch., of the village Studenka in Lipetsk district, agricultural Tambov province, composed a testament in which he immediately relinquished the household property to his son's management, with the understanding that the son would provide not only for his father and mother, but also for his sickly brother, widowed sister, and fatherless nephews.

> My wife E. is ill and old and my eldest son is ill and of poor intellect. Therefore, they cannot manage my property. I rewarded my middle son I. long ago and allowed him to live in a separate home. I am bequeathing to my youngest son G. a home, the yard buildings, an orchard, various pieces of furniture, animals, [and] birds. Neither of the other two sons has a right to the property. I hope that G. will treat me and my wife with filial respect. I ask him to look after his eldest brother and his sister who has small orphaned children.
>
> 14 September 1869[45]

The Studenka peasant could rest assured that his wishes would be honored because the testament was witnessed by the parish priest and several peasants. Normally a testament was also ratified before a village assembly meeting to ensure that it did not violate community needs dictated by mutual tax responsibility.[46] Registering a will with the cantonal administration created an additional safeguard that its provisions would be upheld.

Since Russian peasants expected their adult sons to live with them and perpetuate the family, they viewed premortem fissions with mixed feelings.

---

[43] Ibid., 1:557–58.

[44] Daniel H. Kaiser has stressed the importance of the linkage between the living and the dead in his "Death and Dying in Early Modern Russia" (Paper presented at the Kennan Institute for Advanced Russian Studies, Washington, D.C., 22 May 1986).

[45] *Trudy Kommisii*, 1:692.

[46] Ibid., 3:129.

The separation of a son from the household was entirely at the patriarch's discretion and usually depended on particular circumstances. If the family outgrew the farmstead resources, a father would usually agree to a premortem fission, granting his son the patrimonial share to which he was entitled. If, on the other hand, the son had not contributed his share of labor to the household economy, his father might cut him off with little or no property. A son who left his father's household without permission also did not receive any property.

The type of premortem division, with or without property, determined a son's claim to further inheritance and the extent of his filial obligations. If, for example, a father permitted his partitioning son to remain on the farmstead, either erecting a new hut for his conjugal family or dividing the patrimonial residence between them, the son usually continued to help his father and brothers work the household's communal land allotments. He was responsible for his share of the tax payments on the land and obliged to help support his parents when they retired. In return, the son retained rights to a share of the patrimony, minus whatever property he was given in the separation agreement. If, on the other hand, the provisions of a household division allowed a married son to stay on the farmstead but granted him his own share of the allotment land, which he then proceeded to farm independently, he was disqualified from further inheritance. By virtue of the property he received upon fission, however, he was expected to fulfill his obligations to his parents.

Once a contract had been drawn up for a household division, its provisions were legally binding on both parties. On 2 May 1871, a son charged his father and brother before the Borodinsk cantonal court in Mozhaisk district, Moscow province, with not upholding a separation contract endorsed by the village assembly. The agreement gave the son a share of the hut, half the barn, half the storage shed, and two storage bins. One winter had lapsed since the contract had been ratified, but none of its provisions had been fulfilled. The court upheld the son's claim and ordered the father and brother to hand over the property.[47] That ruling was enforced, but the son lost further rights to the patrimony.

A son automatically forfeited all further rights to inheritance when he moved away from his father's farmstead. If upon his departure he received a share of the patrimony, he still owed his parents his filial support. Only disinheritance freed a son from those obligations. In either case, the partitioned son, by virtue of his independent household economy, became totally independent of his father in property matters. The father lost all claims to the partitioned property and had no rights to any property that his sep-

[47] Ibid., 2:292, #64.

arated son acquired on his own.[48] These property restrictions also applied if a son established an independent household economy on his father's farmstead. Thus, in a case of November 1871 before the Dievo-Gorodishche cantonal court of industrial Iaroslavl' province, a partitioned son was fully justified in pressing charges against his father for infringing on his property rights. For two years since their legal separation the father had withheld his son's horse and harness. Although father and son continued to live in the same house, they managed separate agricultural economies. The court accordingly ruled that the father had no right to retain his son's property.[49]

In general, the village assembly and cantonal courts defended the patriarchal principle as being in the general community interest, almost invariably supporting petitioning fathers against sons who had left their households without their consent. They ordered the delinquents to return home, especially if the loss of their labors threatened to bankrupt their fathers' households. In June 1871, for example, the Borisoglebsk cantonal judges of Rostov district, Iaroslavl' province, admonished a son for refusing to abide by his father's wishes against a household division.[50] In another case in Kukarin canton, Mozhaisk district, Moscow province, the judges dealt more severely with a son who had left home without permission and subsequently refused to manage the family property or support his elderly father. They ordered him lashed and demanded that he return home.[51] The reasoning of the Sergiev cantonal court of Klin district, Moscow province, in December 1871, in barring a household division in which the father had agreed to provide his son with only a cow and sheep, reflects the court's desire to prevent the creation of an economically incapacitated household. The judges disallowed the fission because "family fissions lead to destruction and . . . if the boy is left without buildings and a horse he will abandon [agriculture] and will be a burden on the commune."[52]

In the absence of adequate statistical evidence it is difficult to determine the frequency of disinheritance. The 1873–1874 Liuboshchinskii Commission reports concerning the efficacy of cantonal courts, however, provide some clues. Peasants in only five of fifty-three surveyed Moscow provincial cantons referred to disinheritance of sons for failure to contribute to their fathers' household economies. In twenty-four cantons both judges and peasants stipulated that all sons inherited equal portions regardless of their labor input.[53]

Taking into account the margin of error generated by outsiders asking

[48] Mukhin, *Obychnyi poriadok*, p. 79n.
[49] *Trudy Kommisii*, 3:98.
[50] Ibid., pp. 269–70, #44.
[51] Ibid., 2:277, #23.
[52] Ibid., p. 585, #30.
[53] Ibid., vol. 2.

peasants questions about their daily lives and the fact that commission officials were not above standardizing peasant responses, one may still conclude that disinheritance occurred infrequently. Moscow was a province with a strong out-migration tradition. One would expect disinheritance cases to be relatively frequent here because of the importance of wage labor and the natural reluctance of sons to contribute their earnings to the common family coffers. However, because of communal constraints and prohibitive costs of housing in Moscow and St. Petersburg, married industrial laborers in the central industrial belt normally left their wives and children behind in their fathers' homes. Therefore they had a vested interest in sending money back home.[54] The regular flow of money from the city to the countryside somewhat eased the burdens of a father who maintained his son's wife and children and discouraged disinheritance. At the same time, the threat of disinheritance was a powerful weapon in a father's hands to deter sons from reneging on their obligations or leaving the household, unless the son had sufficient means of his own to set up an independent household.

Thus, time after time, the practices of partible inheritance reveal the vital importance of the multiple family household as a social and welfare as well as economic unit. The perpetuation of real and movable property through the male line helped a household fulfill its communal obligations, meet the needs of elderly parents, and look after dependent family members. Customary postmortem fission met those needs naturally. A son who was expected to look after his widowed mother, unmarried sisters, and other kin often received a slightly larger patrimonial share. In the event of premortem fission, however, a household head sought greater safeguards. While he too may have allotted one son a larger portion of the patrimony for old age care, he might also have drawn up a will or support agreement to ensure that his sons did not default on their obligations. The threat of disinheritance was a final deterrent to lazy or disobedient sons. Each son was expected to pull his own weight in the household economy and to repay his parents' investment by supporting them when they retired.

Alternative Inheritance Strategies

The inheritance strategy adopted when a family did not have heirs, a condition that affected about 20 percent of all families, demonstrates further

---

[54] See Johnson, *Peasant and Proletarian*. As late as 1908 a study of the highly skilled members of the Printers' Union of Moscow indicated that 52 percent of printers had their immediate families living in the countryside. Almost 90 percent of these men regularly sent home funds amounting to an annual average of one hundred rubles. Shanin, *The Roots of Otherness*, vol. 1: *Russia as a 'Developing Society,'* 118.

the welfare role of the Russian peasant household.[55] As early as the seventeenth century, Russian peasants, in the absence of direct male heirs, adopted a son—usually a prospective son-in-law for a marriageable daughter.[56] Adoption assured a household that its patrimonial property would be preserved intact for subsequent generations and would not devolve to distant relatives or, in the post-emancipation era, revert to the commune. An adopted son would, furthermore, provide necessary labor and meet the sustenance needs of the elderly.

In adopting a son-in-law a household head drew up a contract specifying the newcomer's obligations that, if fulfilled, earned him a right to the family property. In effect, an adopted son-in-law had all the responsibilities of a natural son: he was to support his adopted parents and their unmarried daughters, arrange the daughters' marriages and give them dowries, and provide for any household members incapacitated by the death of a male provider. In an 1871 agreement, registered in the industrial canton of Ivanovo, Shuia district, Vladimir province, a relatively prosperous father-in-law set three conditions for his son-in-law's taking over the management as well as proprietorship of his two-story stone house and farmstead allotment. The son-in-law was to give his in-laws the upper-floor back room of the house for their own use and a bottom-floor room for their unmarried daughter. He was also to provide sustenance for his in-laws. Finally, he was obliged to give his sister-in-law a hundred-ruble dowry when she married.[57] The last will and testament, dated 18 January 1864, of a peasant of Poddubrov canton in Usman' district, agricultural Tambov province, specified that the son-in-law was to look after not only his in-laws and their daughter, but the widow and three children of the household head's brother as well.

> I, the peasant Aleksandr Stepanov Pupynin of the village Otrozhki . . . , of sound mind and health, give this spiritual testament to my *natural [rodnoi]* son-in-law Anton Sil'verstov Lazukin, the state peasant of the village Demshino in the same canton, so that he . . . may have eternal ownership over my property, which I received in the fission with my brother, on condition that my son-in-law Anton feed and provide drink for me [and] my wife only until our deaths and our little girl, Ksen'ia, [whom he is] to give away in marriage. [He is] also [to support] my deceased brother Safronii Stepanov's wife Akilina Ivanova and her three small children until they reach maturity. If he, Anton, does not feed and provide

[55] Twenty percent is a rough estimation (based on a probability factor) of families without sons in European, including Russian, agricultural societies. See Goody, "Inheritance, Property and Women," pp. 10, 18.

[56] V. A. Aleksandrov, "Semeino-imushchestvennye otnosheniia po obychnomu pravu v russkoi krepostnoi derevne XVIII–nachala XIX veka," *Istoriia SSSR* (November–December 1979), no. 6, p. 46.

[57] *Trudy Kommisii*, 2:12–13, #83.

drink [for us] and does not obey me, he is not to have anything to do with my property.[58]

It is little wonder that Russian peasants remarked, "With a son-in-law in the household there are *pirogi* [stuffed dumplings] on the table."[59]

Although a son-in-law's contribution to the household economy naturally determined his ability to fulfill these obligations, he inherited the patrimony not for his labors per se, but for his kin relationship. As an adopted son he maintained the household, preserved the family patrimony, and perpetuated the family by providing male heirs. His acceptance of his new family's surname symbolized this relationship,[60] and his renunciation of all rights to his natal home sealed it. In fact, when a son departed for his bride's home he sometimes had to sign an agreement with his father, relinquishing any claim he might have to his natural father's property. One such contract, drawn up by a father and son in Zabelin canton, Vologda province, reads as follows:

We, Osip K. and [my] son Ivan K., mutually agreed upon the conditions, whereby I, Osip, with my son's permission, have freed my son Ivan from my family so that he might live in the home of the peasant Mikhail S. upon his marriage to Mikhail's daughter Ekaterina; I am giving him only one three-year-old ox from all the property . . . , but will not give him anything else, and refuse him everything except his clothing of which I am giving him full ownership. . . . Ivan has promised not to make a claim to any of his father Osip's property, both while he [the father] is alive and upon his death, and never to make a claim to and ask for a portion [of the property] from his brothers. On my part, I, Osip, will not ask or demand any help or sustenance from Ivan to support myself and my family.[61]

Had Ivan remained in his natal family, he probably would have inherited little of substance because he was one of several male children entitled to equal shares of the patrimony. Consequently he was a perfect candidate for an adopted son-in-law.

By renouncing claims to his natal family's property, a son-in-law became totally dependent upon his father-in-law; yet that relationship did not necessarily create a bond of trust between them. Russian peasant oral culture is rich in denunciations of adopted sons-in-law: "A son-in-law likes to take

---

[58] My emphasis. Ibid., 1:576.

[59] Illiustrov, *Sbornik rossiiskikh poslovits*, p. 196.

[60] P. A. Matveev, "Ocherki narodnago iuridicheskago byta Samarskoi gubernii," in *Sbornik narodnykh iuridicheskikh obychaev*, vol. 1, ed. Matveev (St. Petersburg, 1878), p. 30; and A. A. Titov, *Iuridicheskie obychai sela Nikola-Perevoz, Sulostskoi volosti, Rostovskogo uezda* (Iaroslavl', 1888), p. 47.

[61] Quoted in V. P. Shein, "Ocherki narodno-obychnago prava Vologodskoi gubernii," in Pakhman, *Sbornik narodnykh iuridicheskikh obychaev*, 2:137.

but not return." "He would not be a son-in-law if he did not have the reputation of a dog." "If you want a devil in your home—take in a son-in-law."[62] "Take in a son-in-law and get out yourself." "The father gave a ruble to have a son-in-law brought in; he'd give a ruble and a half to have him taken out." "There is no enemy like a son-in-law." "You cannot make bacon out of dog-meat; you cannot make a child out of a son-in-law."[63] "A son-in-law talks with his mother-in-law day and night, but obeys nothing."[64] These negative proverbs reflect, in part, cases in which sons-in-law did not meet their family obligations but nevertheless made claims on their in-laws' property.

Contracts between in-laws were broken for a variety of reasons. Sometimes the inability of a household head and his son-in-law to live together amicably resulted in the son-in-law's separating from the household. His departure invalidated the original contract but gave him the right to demand compensation for his labors. The extent of compensation depended on the number of years that he had lived and worked in his father-in-law's household. In Tver province, for example, if a departing son-in-law had been a member of his father-in-law's household for five years or more, he was normally entitled to one-third or one-half of the patrimony. If, on the other hand, he had lived in the household for less than five years, he received monetary compensation of between ten and twenty rubles for each year of residence, forfeiting his kinship right of parity with a natural son.[65] The same principle applied in other central Russian provinces; only the time intervals and amounts of compensation varied.[66]

Complications between a son-in-law and father-in-law also arose when the adopted son-in-law's wife (that is, the father-in-law's daughter) died, if the original contract had not made provision for such an event. In an 1868 case which came before the Mstera cantonal court in Viazniki district, industrial Vladimir province, a father-in-law asked that he be allowed to nullify an 1865 contract in which he had granted his son-in-law and daughter possession of half the farmstead. He justified his request on the grounds that since the drafting of the original contract, his daughter had died and the son-in-law had become disrespectful. The court sided with the plaintiff, denying the son-in-law his claim to the farmstead.[67]

[62] Illiustrov, *Sbornik rossiiskikh poslovits*, pp. 194–97.

[63] Elnett, *Historic Origin*, p. 130.

[64] Dal', *Tolkovyi slovar' zhivago velikorusskago iazyka*, vol. 4 (St. Petersburg, 1914), p. 763.

[65] Mukhin, *Obychnyi poriadok*, p. 298n.

[66] In an extreme case a contractual agreement stipulated that a son-in-law had to live and work in his mother-in-law's household a minimum of twelve years before he was entitled to a property share. That agreement was drawn up in 1890 in Polnov canton, Gdov district, St. Petersburg province. See "Materialy po obshchinnomu zemlevladeniiu," in *Statisticheskii sbornik po S.-Peterburgskoi gubernii 1897 god*, no. 4 (St. Petersburg, 1898), p. 63.

[67] *Trudy Kommisii*, 2:50, #8. Sometimes clauses were added in adoption agreements to

Nonfulfillment of contractual agreements is, however, only a partial explanation for Russian peasants' negative stereotyping of sons-in-law. Another explanation lies in elders' distrust of the younger generation. In premortem transfers of property peasants could not completely trust even their blood heirs, often having to resort to the legal guarantee of support contracts. From a son's point of view, looking after elderly parents was an additional burden in an unstable agrarian economy in which harvests were at nature's mercy, landed resources insufficient, and taxes and communal obligations onerous. If a natural son viewed his parents as burdens, that sentiment must have been stronger for a son-in-law whose tie to his in-laws was more tenuous. The negative appraisals of sons-in-law also stem from the stigma attached to adopting a surrogate son in a society that judged a man by the number of sons he could father.

An adopted son-in-law's position in the commune was not as secure as he might have wished. Complications arose with regard to use of land allotments if his adopted home was located in a different commune from that of his natal family and he had not been registered as a member of the new commune. Upon his father-in-law's death a son-in-law could continue farming his adopted family's land only until the next repartition, when the commune had the right to refuse him and his children an apportionment of arable.[68] Furthermore, a son-in-law often had to battle his deceased in-laws' direct female or lateral heirs over ownership of his father-in-law's property, even if he had fulfilled all the provisions of the adoption contract. Fortunately, the village assembly and cantonal courts invariably upheld the validity of such contracts. For example, in March 1872, the Bukholov cantonal judges of Volokolamsk district, Moscow province, denied two step-sisters shares of their parents' property, which their adopted brother-in-law had inherited. The brother-in-law provided proof, which was substantiated by the village elder and three household heads, that he was entitled to the contested property. The judges ordered the brother-in-law to carry out his promise to return the unmarried stepdaughter's dowry chest to her and to give her five rubles to remember her mother by. But he was freed

---

deal with the possibility of a daughter's death. In Vologda province, for example, a widowed mother-in-law, in the initial clauses of such a contract, agreed to award her prospective son-in-law half the residence and clothing if he agreed to enter her household and marry her daughter when she came of age. His possession of the remaining property, the contract continued, depended on his being obedient and respectful to the widow and fulfilling a promise to provide dowries for her two daughters when they married. The mother-in-law, however, inserted this restrictive clause: "If my daughter Anna dies before she marries K. [the prospective son-in-law], then I am obliged to pay him [K.] however much money he earned in my home." Quoted in Shein, "Ocherki narodno-obychnago prava," in Pakhman, *Sbornik narodnykh iuridicheskikh obychaev*, 2:132.

[68] F. A. Shcherbina, "Dogovornyia sem'i," *Severnyi vestnik* (September 1888), no. 9, pt. 2, p. 95.

from further obligations to the second daughter since he had already provided for her marriage.[69]

Women's Property Rights

So far this discussion has focused on the devolution of the patrimony to male heirs. The property rights of women must be discussed separately. These rights reflected influences of the written law that became stronger in the post-emancipation period with the increase in nuclear families and the introduction of cantonal courts to which women appealed to redress the injustices of customary law.

In the multiple family household real property, with one exception, did not devolve to women. The tendency toward universal marriage for women and patrilocality meant that daughters represented a poor investment. Proverbs underlining this sentiment were common: "A daughter is someone else's booty." "A daughter is someone else's laborer." "Feed a son and he will be of use to you; feed a daughter and you [will have] to give her to someone else."[70] "The son looks into the house, the daughter—out of the house."[71] A daughter, therefore, received support and protection only until her wedding day, at which time she became the responsibility of another household. Once a family provided a daughter with a dowry or trousseau as a reward for her labors, they excluded her from subsequent inheritance. Unmarried daughters inherited the patrimony only in the rare event that all male lineal and collateral heirs had died. The commune subsequently determined whether such women could retain the household's land allotments and maintain production on them.

When their fathers died, unmarried daughters found themselves dependent upon their brothers' goodwill.[72] In the Liuboshchinskii Commission reports of 1873–1874 peasants and cantonal judges occasionally stipulated the portions of movable property that brothers were to give their sisters. These varied from one-fourteenth to one-third.[73] This state of affairs mirrored the civil law code, the Digest of Laws, according to which daughters belonging to classes other than the peasantry had a right to a fourteenth share of their fathers' real property and an eighth share of the movable property. Wives, on the other hand, were entitled to one-seventh of their

[69] *Trudy Kommisii*, 2:348, #15.

[70] Illiustrov, *Sbornik rossiiskikh poslovits*, pp. 185–86.

[71] Elnett, *Historic Origin*, p. 127.

[72] In Lysogorsk canton, Tambov province, for example, brothers gave their sisters forty rubles and a fancy trimmed dress when they married. *Trudy Kommisii*, 1:15.

[73] Ibid., 1:124; 2:324, 389; 6:712, 723.

husbands' real and one-quarter of the movable property.[74] The confusion in peasant practice reflected the lack of customary law provision for daughters. Despite the marginal influence of the written law, peasants maintained their custom of endowing daughters with movable property only.

Dowries were deliberately modest, as was the case among Macedonian peasants, so as not to pose "a threat to the productive capital" of the receiving family. A bride had to depend on her new family's goodwill and her own labor capacity for rights to their property.[75] At the same time, she had responsibilities for her own conjugal unit, which she fulfilled using her dowry possessions. These included clothing, cloth, bed linens and chest, and sometimes cash, grain, or a few animals, as well as a loom or spinning wheel, depending on her natal family's resources. According to a popular saying, "[When] a mother puts aside a handwoven piece of linen and the father fifty kopecks for a daughter, they are amassing a dowry."[76]

Dowry contents, while insignificant compared to other forms of property, were a woman's inalienable possessions. As such they were a constant reminder of the intrusion of another kin group in the patrilocal household. Even in areas of Moscow, Tambov, Vladimir, and Nizhnii Novgorod provinces, where the dowry was relatively unknown,[77] the clothing and linens that were purchased with the bride-price (*kladka*, a sum of money which the groom's family gave to the bride's family to cover the wedding expenses and bride's trousseau) were considered a woman's personal property. The bride-price compensated the bride's family for the loss of a laborer and transferred the rights to a bride's reproductive powers from her natal to her conjugal family. All dowry or trousseau items were stored in a locked chest, the key to which dangled from the owner's belt, symbolizing the inalienability of that property.

In addition to the dowry, a wife's personal property consisted of the net revenues she earned selling mushrooms, fruits, milk products, eggs, vegetables, chickens, and woven and knitted items.[78] This income was usually

[74] *Svod zakonov Rossiiskoi Imperii*, 16 vols. (St. Petersburg, 1876), vol. 10, pt. 1, arts. 1127, 1148.

[75] The same applies to Macedonian peasants. See D. B. Rheubottom, "Dowry and Wedding Celebrations in Yugoslav Macedonia," in *The Meaning of Marriage Payments*, ed. J. L. Comaroff (London, 1980), pp. 233–34.

[76] Illiustrov, *Sbornik rossiiskikh poslovits*, p. 125.

[77] Outside of the central industrial and central agricultural provinces bride-price predominated in Samara, Penza, Saratov, Vologda, and Olonets provinces. See *Trudy Kommisii*, vols. 1–2; A. Smirnov, *Ocherki semeinykh otnoshenii po obychnomu pravu russkago naroda* (Moscow, 1877), 229; and Steven L. Hoch, *Serfdom and Social Control in Nineteenth Century Russia: Petrovskoe, A Village in Tambov* (Chicago, 1986), pp. 95ff.

[78] Dobrotvorskii, "Krest'ianskie iuridicheskie obychai" (May 1889): 265; and Matveev, "Ocherki narodnago iuridicheskago byta," in Matveev, *Sbornik narodnykh iuridicheskikh obychaev*, 1:22.

small but reflected a modicum of independence for a woman in her household economy. She had to travel to market to sell her goods, and the proceeds allowed her to help her daughters amass their dowries.[79]

Customary law protected the inalienability of a woman's personal property. If a husband or in-law encroached upon that property, its owner had the right to take the matter before an informal village court of elders who publicly considered the case against the offenders.[80] Repeat offenders were brought before cantonal courts, treated often as ordinary thieves, and sentenced to corporal punishment. On 17 January 1871, for example, the peasant woman Mironova of Elat'ma district, agricultural Tambov province, charged her brother-in-law T. Fedorov with breaking the lock of her dowry chest and stealing two rubles. The cantonal judges sentenced the defendant to the maximum punishment of twenty lashes and ordered him to repay the money. In June of the same year, the Prigorod cantonal judges of Borisoglebsk district, also in Tambov province, ordered that a husband be subjected to fifteen lashes for breaking into his wife's trunk and threatening to set her dowry linens on fire. For stealing his wife's shawl from her unlocked chest and selling it to buy vodka, a husband in Ziuzin canton, industrial Moscow province, had to spend three days in jail.[81]

Until a woman had children who became heirs to her personal property, she had the right to take that property with her if she abandoned her father-in-law's or husband's home. When a husband was called into the army, his family sometimes refused to provide for his childless wife and forced her to leave their home, underscoring how fragile was the link between a bride and her new family until she had children of her own.[82] Mutually agreed separations also allowed women to sever ties with their husbands' paternal households. In such cases the wives usually returned to their natal homes with their dowries and other personal property in hand.[83]

Indeed, the dowry continued to be associated with a childless woman's natal family. In the event of her death, her husband and in-laws were obliged to return her dowry to her closest surviving blood kin. Her spouse was entitled to some of the bedding and the icon with which the couple had been blessed on their wedding day. What remained constituted the inalienable property of the wife's parents. A woman could not bequeath

---

[79] Dobrotvorskii, "Krest'ianskie iuridicheskie obychai," p. 265.

[80] Ibid.

[81] *Trudy Kommisii*, 1:136, #8; 1:404, #26; 2:100, #26.

[82] A. Kh. Gol'mstem, "Dvadtsatiletniaia praktika Kremetskago (Valdaiskago uezda, Novgorodskoi gubernii) volostnago suda po voprosam grazhdanskago prava," in his *Iuridicheskiia izsledovaniia i stat'i*, 2 vols. (St. Petersburg, 1894), 1:55.

[83] See, for example, *Trudy Kommisii*, 3:69, #8; 52, #2.

any of her dowry property to her husband without her father's permission.[84]

Modifications of these general rules did occur in various areas of central Russia. Sometimes a husband returned his deceased wife's dowry to her kin only if their marriage had been of short duration, anywhere from less than two to less than ten years. Otherwise, the dowry contents, in all likelihood threadbare after several years of use, remained with the husband.[85] This practice was the exception in industrial Vladimir and Iaroslavl' provinces, but it was more readily adopted in industrial Moscow and agricultural Tambov provinces. In a few instances peasants of Moscow and Tambov stated that the dowry always remained with a childless wife's husband rather than reverting to her kin.[86]

While the inalienability of a wife's personal property applied equally to extended and nuclear family households, a widow's rights to her husband's property varied in the two structures to accommodate different support systems. The patriarchal multiple family household distinguished between widows with children and those without, making exceptions for the latter only if their marriages had been of significant duration. It provided a widow and her children shelter and sustenance, denying the widow a share of her late husband's patrimony unless he had specifically bequeathed her property in a testament. A recently married childless widow, on the other hand, received nothing but her dowry, clothing acquired during her marriage, and perhaps an item of her husband's attire as a token of remembrance. As far as her in-laws were concerned, she was not entitled to their support because they felt that she had contributed very little to the household economy and had failed to produce an heir. They expected her to return to her parents. Hence the Russian proverb: "When the husband has died the wife is not welcome."[87] Once the widow had observed a six-week period of mourning for her first husband, she was free to remarry.[88] If, however, she had been widowed after spending many years in her father-in-law's house, the father- or brother-in-law was obliged to support her. In the event that she wished to separate from the household, the in-law either voluntarily or involuntarily, upon the order of the village assembly or cantonal court, accorded her a hut and a measure of grain.

[84] See, for example, ibid., p. 230, #4.

[85] This was a point that Wendy Goldman made in her paper, "Alimony in the Peasant *Dvor*: Family Law and Soviet Life," presented at the Eighteenth National Convention of the American Association for the Advancement of Slavic Studies, New Orleans, November 1986.

[86] Peasants in six of eighteen districts of Moscow province and in twenty-two of forty-one districts of Tambov province distinguished between short and long marriages. *Trudy Kommisii*, vols. 1–2.

[87] Illiustrov, *Sbornik rossiiskikh poslovits*, p. 20.

[88] *Trudy Kommisii*, 1:185.

In a nuclear household, on the other hand, a widow was in a more precarious economic position and so received a portion of her late husband's patrimony to ensure her livelihood. Usually, she managed her husband's property either for life or until her sons reached maturity, at which time she received a patrimonial share for her maintenance or else became her sons' responsibility.[89] The influence of the written law can be discerned in the proportion of property that a widow was entitled to inherit. Normally she received between one-seventh and one-quarter of her late husband's real and movable property.[90] The same proportion applied to a childless widow, although if her husband did not leave behind any collateral heirs, she inherited all his real and movable property.

The following decision of a cantonal court underscores Russian peasant society's concern for a widow's maintenance, even if for no other reason than to prevent her becoming a burden on the community. In January 1871 the Chaplyzhensk cantonal judges of Bronnitsy district, Moscow province, awarded the elderly childless widow Irma her husband's property although her claim was contested by three stepdaughters. The judges argued that the stepdaughters were all married and provided for, while the sixty-year-old widow did not have children of her own or other relatives who could support her. Therefore she received her husband's hut, storage space, and shed. The horses, cows, plows, and harrows, on the other hand, were to be sold to settle the household's tax arrears and pay the deceased husband's funeral costs.[91] In all likelihood the judges assumed that the widow forfeited her deceased husband's rights to communal land allotments according to local custom. Consequently the sale of vital agricultural implements and draft animals would not have been burdensome to her. The judges also presumed she could support herself on her garden produce and whatever grain allowance the commune granted her. The childless widow also had a few other options. By adopting an adult son and bequeathing her property to him, she could avoid becoming dependent on communal charity, as the adopted son would be obliged to look after her. Or she might choose to take in a tenant to help her manage her household economy. With a male laborer, the widow might have retained some communal land allotments.[92] If none of these options was available, she would

[89] Aleksandra Ia. Efimenko, "Zhenshchina v krest'ianskoi sem'e," in her *Izsledovaniia narodnoi zhizni*, vol. 1: *Obychnoe pravo* (Moscow, 1884), p. 97.

[90] *Svod zakonov*, vol. 10, pt. 1, art. 1148. The practice of endowing a widow with a seventh share of her husband's property dates back to the pre-emancipation period. See Rodney Dean Bohac, "Family, Property, and Socioeconomic Mobility: Russian Peasants on Manuilovskoe Estate, 1810–1861" (Ph.D. diss., University of Illinois at Urbana-Champaign, 1982), pp. 191–92.

[91] *Trudy Kommisii*, 1:431, #1.

[92] "Materialy po obshchinnomu zemlevladeniiu," in *Statisticheskii sbornik po S.-Peterburgskoi gubernii 1897 god*, no. 4, pp. 125–26; and *Trudy Kommisii*, 1:411, #20.

be forced to employ herself as a village herbalist and midwife, or to leave the village for work elsewhere.

One childless widow of Podcherkov canton, Dmitrov district, Moscow province, who inherited her husband's home, yard, barn, and cow, left an extraordinary testament. The document is unusual by virtue of its completeness and expression of gratitude to a fairly large circle of kin and non-kin to whom the widow obviously felt indebted. It is also a rare example of a will composed by a woman. As such, it deserves quotation at length:

> In the name of the Father and the Son and the Holy Ghost, Amen. Having acquired my deceased husband D. T.'s (of the village Ochevo, Podcherkov canton) real and movable property and having been left a childless widow, I, being in [good] health and [having] complete recollection, have resolved to draw up . . . my spiritual testament.
>
> 1. I am asking my executors, named at the end of this testament, upon my death, to sell my home and yard with one cow, located in the village of Ochevo, Podcherkov canton. The net capital is to be placed in one of the credit institutions in the name of the holy Church servants of the *pogost* [graveyard] Cherno-griazh for the eternal memory of my and my husband's souls.
>
> 2. I am bequeathing my barn to my brother, the peasant V. I. of the village Volkovo, Aleksandrovsk district, Vladimir province.
>
> 3. I am bequeathing my cloth coat, silk shawl, cotton coat, one piece of linen, and cotton shirt to my niece, the peasant M. M. who lives in the parish of Danilovskoe.
>
> 4. I am bequeathing two pieces of linen to the poor and miserable.
>
> 5. I am bequeathing fifteen measures of rye to the peasant A. P. of the village Orudevo who did many good deeds for me during my lifetime.
>
> 6. I am bequeathing one piece of linen and a nankeen coat to my niece, the peasant D. M., who lives in the parish of the village Voronovo, the hamlet So-kolova.
>
> 7. I am bequeathing one piece of linen and a jacket to my brother's wife T. E., who lives in the village Volkovo.
>
> 8. I am leaving ten measures of rye to the Nikolopestush monastery for the remembrance of my and my husband's souls.
>
> 9. After my death my nephew, I. I. K., who is serving in the army, is to be given one ruble.
>
> 10. After my death my adopted son, [who is] also in military service, is to be given one ruble.
>
> 11. I am bequeathing my samovar to my nephew V. V. who lives in the village Volkovo.
>
> 22 August 1871[93]

---

[93] *Trudy Kommisii*, 2:525–26.

Thus the widow settled property on each of her surviving relatives, including her brother, two nieces, a sister-in-law, two nephews, and an adopted son. The tenacity of natal family ties, even though the relatives lived in another province, is striking. In accordance with the custom that daughters inherited their mother's dowry, the childless widow bequeathed the bulk of her dowry items to her nieces who were her closest female descendants. Furthermore, she endowed a neighboring church and monastery in order that prayers might be said regularly for her and her husband's souls unto eternity. In a charitable gesture she even bestowed some property on the poor. Clearly the widow was determined to die at peace with herself.

If husbands in nuclear family households wanted their wives to manage the patrimony after their deaths, they sometimes drew up wills to safeguard that property against the encroachment of direct and collateral heirs. On 17 March 1869 a rather wealthy peasant, Dmitrii Andreev Skachkov, of the village Petrov in Usman' district, Tambov province, made the following stipulations in his will:

> My children Stepan, Vladimir, and Aleksei are to respect and obey their mother, my wife Mariia Ivanova, and without her permission are not to divide my property. If one of my children does not obey her, I give her the right to deprive the disobedient son of his inheritance. If there remains money after my death it is to go to my wife Mariia Ivanova on condition that she bury me and have memorial services said for me in the Christian manner. . . . My wife Mariia Ivanova is to manage my leased land, but my children are obliged to help her in that task. My property is valued at one and a half thousand rubles.[94]

Complications over property devolution occurred when a widow remarried and took her children with her into her new household. As a mother, she did not forfeit her right to manage her first husband's property but usually made a will or an agreement with her second husband to ensure that that property devolved to her first husband's sons. Sometimes the commune appointed a guardian over the first husband's property to prevent the second husband and his relatives from encroaching upon it.[95]

The state peasant woman U. K. of Inokov canton, Kirsanov district, Tambov province, did not have the surety of a guardian after she remarried. Her first husband left behind a significant amount of property valued at 150 rubles. It included a hut, storage areas, a small unheated hut, an outbuilding, two horses, fourteen shocks of rye, one chetvert of ground rye, ten chetverts of barley, and various dishes. As manager of that property for her underage son and daughter, the widow U. K. was a lucrative catch for her second husband, M. K. For the first thirty weeks of marriage

[94] Ibid., 1:609–10.
[95] Ibid., p. 644, #7.

M. K. treated his new spouse and stepchildren well. Thereafter he began to beat them. As a result the remarried widow asked her son's grandfather to look after the boy. The stepfather then refused to give his stepson any of the patrimonial property to which the child was entitled. The remarried widow subsequently had to take the matter up with a cantonal and higher court to gain satisfaction.[96]

A childless widow sometimes forfeited the right to her first husband's property when she remarried. Dmitrii Ivanov of the village Zhivotno in Il'in canton, Dmitrov district, Moscow province, for example, stipulated in his spiritual testament of 8 August 1871 that upon his death his property was to be divided between his wife Natal'ia Prokof'eva and his nephew Ignatii Sergeev. He added the restrictive clause that if his wife should consider remarriage, then the entire property was to devolve to the nephew.[97] Ivanov thus prevented the patrimony from devolving to another kin group, assuming that his wife would receive all the shelter and sustenance that she required in her new family.

Difficulties often arose when a household head died leaving a second wife and children from two marriages. All natural male heirs were entitled to an equal share of property, but widows were often forced to fend for themselves and their children. On 17 October 1871 in Mozhaisk district, Moscow province, the peasant widow D. complained to the Kukarin cantonal court that her husband had recently died, leaving her with two underage sons and no property. The judges' decision once again underscored the strong community desire not to have members who could not look after themselves. The judges declared that they could not permit a widow with children to beg at strangers' doors. They ordered the family of one of the stepsons to support his stepmother and stepbrothers until the children came of age and could look after themselves as well as their mother.[98]

The partial property rights that a widow came to enjoy in the nuclear family had some effect upon the extended family household. While the woman's position in an extended family usually remained closer to the customary norm, by which she should not receive a portion of her husband's property, cantonal court judges sometimes awarded daughters-in-law one-seventh of their husbands' share of the patrimony if they departed from the households of their fathers-in-law. This created a precedent for women to appeal for legal redress for the injustices of customary law and their dependence on the goodwill of in-laws. Females were involved in a high proportion of litigation regarding inheritance claims. In the provinces of Vladimir, Iaroslavl', Moscow, and Tambov, for which cantonal court records

---

[96] Ibid., p. 533, #111.
[97] Ibid., 2:532.
[98] Ibid., p. 271, #8.

have survived, 64 percent of the inheritance cases that came before the courts involved women.[99]

Property Rights of Orphans

The discussion of welfare has thus far concerned the needs of the elderly and widows within varying family structures. The issue of orphans has not been addressed. Mention of adoption has been made only in instances in which peasants without male heirs adopted sons or sons-in-law to ensure the family's perpetuation or, at least, a childless widow's security. The question remains whether the Russian peasant family was sufficiently flexible to accommodate orphaned children with or without property of their own. The problem concerned the Russian imperial bureaucracy, which, in the emancipation provisions of 1861, endowed the sel'skoe obshchestvo or village community with tutelage powers over orphans. The government was, thereafter, not satisfied with the rural institution's performance in this capacity and recorded numerous cases in which guardians abused their authority by encroaching upon their wards' property.[100] Peasant customary practice of assigning the family, rather than the village administration, such welfare responsibilities may explain government discontent. Matters concerning orphans came to the attention of village officials only when familial support was not forthcoming or when a household's economic viability was jeopardized.

Russian peasants defined orphans far more broadly than did Western European societies. They considered any child who had lost one parent to be an orphan. This reflected the economic reality that household or family survival depended upon the labors of both spouses. As discussed earlier, communes normally assigned land allotments to a household on the basis of its number of tiagla or married couples.

When a parent died, orphaned children were naturally left in the care either of the living parent, in a nuclear family, or that of the bol'shak or household head in an extended family household. If the living parent or household head was male, the commune did not interfere in the management of the insignificant property that orphans inherited from their

---

[99] In Vladimir 19 of 43 property cases were instigated by women, in Iaroslavl' 35 of 76, in Moscow 62 out of 100, and in Tambov 105 (59 of which were brought against in-laws) out of 158 in the years 1869–1872. The majority of cases came before the courts in 1871, the year selected by the cantonal court commission as the most representative of the workings of the cantonal courts. *Trudy Kommisii*, vols. 1–3.

[100] See A. A. Rittikh, ed. *Krest'ianskii pravoporiadok* (St. Petersburg, 1904), pp. 269–70; and *Svod zakliuchenii gubernskikh soveshchanii po voprosam, otnosiashchimsia k peresmotru zakonodatel'stva o krest'ianakh* 3 vols. (St. Petersburg, 1897), vol. 2.

mother. In the event of a father's death in an extended family household, customary law dictated that the household head—the deceased's father, brother, or uncle—hand over the deceased's property share to the deceased's sons when they set up households on their own. The commune or cantonal count became involved only when abuses were brought to its attention. Matters were more complicated if the guardian was a woman in a nuclear family.

Peasant attitudes toward mothers as guardians varied on a regional basis. In the vast majority of areas in European Russia peasants considered mothers to be natural guardians of their children and believed that the village administration did not have a right to interfere in that guardianship. However, a mother's "guardian" rights were not always unconditional. When questioned by ethnographers, peasants in Odoev and Iukhnov districts in Tula and Smolensk provinces made economic security the overriding qualification for a mother to assume the role of guardian: "She [a mother] is always considered the natural guardian, if only she is in the position to carry on a household economy." The mother's ability to provide for her children in a nuclear family without help from in-laws or other relatives was of primary concern. Otherwise the family risked becoming a burden to the commune, whose resources were limited. In districts of Orel, Vladimir, and Kostroma provinces the village administration upheld the mother as the natural guardian of her orphaned children, but that body appointed a man from within the community to manage her household affairs and the property her orphaned sons inherited from their father. Economic considerations based on misogynist attitudes were uppermost in the minds of peasants in Karachev district, Orel province. They reasoned that a woman could not effectively manage property on her own because "it is a well known thing with a woman. Her hair is long but her mind short; in order to run a household you need intelligence, brains, reason, and one who turns away a ruble loses a ruble."[101]

As discussed earlier in the chapter, village administrations sometimes appointed guardians over "orphans'" property when mothers remarried. Guardians were to prevent stepfathers from encroaching upon the inherited property of their stepchildren. At the same time, however, village authorities were reluctant to place controls over a stepfather who agreed to support his stepchildren. Peasants in the eastern portion of Vladimir province, for example, noted that a stepfather had a right to use the profits (such as interest or animal offspring) which accrued from orphans' prop-

---

[101] In Griazovets and Krasnyi districts in Vologda and Smolensk provinces, peasants distinguished a mother's upright character as being the overriding qualification for guardianship. They commented that "she may be entrusted with guardianship, if she is pure in behavior; ... if she is a worthy woman." Tsypkin, "Opeka v krest'ianskom bytu," in Tenishev, *Administrativnoe polozhenie*, pp. 138–40.

erty if he maintained them in his household. "They [the orphans and step-father] warm themselves on top of the same stove [*pech'*]; they sit down together to eat at the same table—how are you going to keep accounts?" inquired the peasants.[102]

Instances in which a widowed mother married a man belonging to an-other commune further complicated matters. If she took her children with her to the other commune, their father's farmstead and communal land allotments passed into the hands of a male member of their original com-mune. That individual became responsible for meeting the redemption payments and taxes levied on the land, in return for which he received the produce of the land. The transfer of property was only temporary until the orphaned sons became adults. As long as the trustee met his payments, the village administration did not monitor the effectiveness of his manage-ment. Unfortunately, it was not unusual for farmstead buildings to fall into disrepair.[103]

Children who lost both parents, the so-called full (*kruglyi*) orphans, were in a less enviable position than those who had lost only one parent. An extended family household was naturally equipped to handle these or-phans, as the household head once again was expected to take on a guard-ianship role. The village administration did not hold him accountable for the way in which he managed his wards' inherited property. When, how-ever, orphaned children suddenly found themselves without a family, vil-lage elders normally appointed a guardian from among the children's clos-est relatives in the village.[104] If a relation could not be found, they appointed a non-kin communal member or sent the orphans out to learn a trade.[105]

Once the village administration selected a guardian for full orphans, it had to decide what to do with the deceased parents' property. The village elder and scribe inventoried the property and subsequently convened ei-ther a meeting of senior household heads or the entire village assembly to discuss which items were to be retained and which were to be sold. The village administration normally auctioned off property that could not weather the period of the orphans' childhood and adolescence. Buildings in need of constant repair, for example, fell into this category. The proceeds from the sale, together with any cash left by the orphans' parents, were placed in the safekeeping of the elder or in the village or cantonal treasury

[102] Dobrotvorskii, "Krest'ianskie iuridicheskie obychai," p. 276.

[103] N. K. Brzheskii, *Ocherki iuridicheskogo byta krest'ian* (St. Petersburg, 1902), p. 10.

[104] Tsypkin, "Opeka v krest'ianskom bytu," in Tenishev, *Administrativnoe polozhenie*, p. 142.

[105] A. A. Leont'ev, *Krest'ianskoe pravo: Sistematicheskoe izlozhenie osobennosti zakonodatel'stva o krest'ianakh*, 2d ed. (St. Petersburg, 1914), p. 347.

where it earned between 3 and 10 percent interest per annum.[106] By the end of the nineteenth century the newly appointed land captains and cantonal administrations increasingly took control of such funds.[107] The village administration placed any unsold property under the appointed guardian's management. Orphans were entitled to their full property shares when they reached the age of majority, which ranged between seventeen and twenty-four years, depending upon the region. Normally, the guardianship ended upon the ward's marriage.[108]

Government officials frequently complained that guardians abused their responsibilities, either squandering their wards' property or using it to serve their own interests. For example, a representative from Kursk province to the Witte Commission on Agricultural Needs complained that in 1897 a guardian in Markov canton, Ryl'sk district, sold a house belonging to his wards and with the proceeds purchased a piece of land in his own name. In 1898 in Muravlev canton, Kursk district, a guardian squandered forty-three rubles belonging to his wards. In 1900, yet another guardian in Sudzha district sold a portion of land belonging to orphans under her care to her own advantage.[109] Misappropriation of funds and property was a common charge against guardians in the cantonal courts as well. In spite of apparent greed, guardians' responsibility to support their wards at their own expense must be taken into account. Looking after an orphan was a considerable burden that peasants believed deserved compensation. Until an orphan could provide a full share of labor, he or she was simply another mouth to feed.

The notion that a guardian required recompense for looking after an orphan is graphically illustrated in cases in which orphans had little or no property to bring into their guardians' home. In Kozel'sk district, Kaluga province, when wards appeared too burdensome for a guardian, the cantonal administration sometimes demanded that the commune help the guardian. That aid took the form of two to three measures of potatoes or an equivalent amount of grain per annum. Communes in Kerensk district, Penza province, provided a maximum of 1 ruble 80 kopecks per month for a propertyless orphan. In Skopin district, Riazan province, the commune at times enticed a guardian into caring for poverty-stricken orphans by promising him an additional land allotment. In some cases these orphans were passed around from house to house on a rotational basis until they reached laboring age. In the worst of circumstances propertyless orphans

---

[106] Dobrotvorskii, "Krest'ianskie iuridicheskie obychai," p. 275.

[107] Brzheskii, *Ocherki iuridicheskogo byta*, p. 9.

[108] Tsypkin, "Opeka v krest'ianskom bytu," in Tenishev, *Administrativnoe polozhenie*, p. 159.

[109] Rittikh, *Krest'ianskoi pravoporiadok*, pp. 269–70.

were forced to beg for their food.[110] Peasants never refused bread to these young beggars, who were considered to be God's wards.[111]

The customary patrilineal partible devolution of property represented Russian peasants' response to the need to reallocate available land periodically and perpetuate the multiple family household, which met the requirements of the commune as a working economic unit. The system secured the economic viability of households by preserving the patrimony through the male line. In general, an affinal link was barred from inheriting the patrimony, except when a household was threatened with extinction by the absence of direct male heirs. Adoption of a son-in-law was preferable to lateral inheritance outside the household since in the latter case the farmstead land and communal land allotments would revert to direct communal ownership.[112]

Equally important, customary inheritance patterns provided a built-in welfare mechanism that protected family members in the event of illness, age-related debilitation, or the death of a laborer or parent. One of the main functions of the multiple family household was to provide security for parents in their retirement years. The family patriarch had at his disposal several means to ensure this security, including apportioning a greater share of property to one son, drawing up wills or support agreements, threatening disinheritance of a son, and, finally, adopting a son-in-law. The different needs of the more fragile nuclear family demanded a modification of the lineage system to recognize a widow's right to at least a portion of her husband's property.

The inheritance strategies of Russian peasants generated a significant degree of stability in the nineteenth-century countryside despite the abolition of serfdom and the growth of capitalism in the post-emancipation period. Peasants were able to cling to their traditional rhythms of life at a time when land resources were shrinking and the multiple peasant household was adapting to the demands of a changing economic environment. As land became more scarce, especially in the central industrial provinces, peasants turned increasingly to auxiliary trades in order to eke out a living. Nonetheless, the availability, however limited, of family resources for all sons continued to reinforce relatively early marriages and incorporation of new conjugal units into the patriarchal household until independent family

[110] Tsypkin, "Opeka v krest'ianskom bytu," in Tenishev, *Administrativnoe polozhenie*, p. 148.
[111] Ibid., p. 156; and Mukhin, *Obychnyi poriadok*, p. 172n.
[112] Normally a communal member could not have possession of two farmsteads. Mikhalenko, "Zaozerskaia obshchina," in Barikov, *Sbornik materialov dlia izucheniia sel'skoi pozemel'noi obshchiny*, p. 297.

units could be established. Until the state and other institutions could supplant the economic and welfare functions of the multiple family household—a structure with which the property devolution systems were inextricably tied—peasant traditionalism both impeded the impact of modernization and cushioned its effects.[113]

[113] The Russian peasantry was not unique in this respect. See, for example, Walter Goldschmidt and Evalyn Jacobson Kunkel, "The Structure of the Peasant Family," *American Anthropologist* 73 (1971): 1066–67; Robert Lee, "Family and 'Modernisation': The Peasant Family and Social Change in Nineteenth-Century Bavaria," in *The German Family: Essays on the Social History of the Family in Nineteenth- and Twentieth-Century Germany*, ed. Richard J. Evans and W. R. Lee (London, 1981), pp. 108–11; and Weber, *Peasants into Frenchmen*.

III

Family Life Cycle and Household Structures

THE FAMILY, as modern social historians view it, is dynamic rather than static. Through its natural life cycle it undergoes dramatic internal change. Births and deaths continually reshape household structure and the relationships of individuals within the family. A member's withdrawal from the main unit of consumption and production to establish an independent household also has a dramatic effect on household size and structure.[1]

In addition to changes in family membership, variations in age distribution and shifts in roles of family members distinguish a household's life

5. Peasant family. Reproduced from Francis B. Reeves, *Russia Then and Now, 1892–1917* (New York: G. P. Putnam's Sons, 1917), following p. 58.

[1] Jack Goody, "The Evolution of the Family," in *Household and Family in Past Time: Comparative Studies in the Size and Structure of the Domestic Group over the Last Three Centuries in England, France, Serbia, Japan and Colonial North America, with Further Materials from Western Europe*, ed. Peter Laslett and Richard Wall (Cambridge, 1972), p. 118.

cycle. A family household consisting of a young couple with two infant children and grandmother is very different fifteen years later when the grandmother has died and the children are adolescents. Upon the removal of the grandmother's influence over her grandchildren, through her role as a transmitter of traditional cultural values, parents begin acculturating their adolescent children in the responsibilities of an adult world.

In peasant societies the transition from childhood to adolescence is dramatic from the point of view of the family as an economic unit. Until the age of seven or eight, children are a drain on the household economy, demanding food and attention without contributing anything in return. Adolescents, on the other hand, are valuable laborers. When they reach adulthood, they must decide whether to leave the domestic hearth and establish their own households or to remain within the aging paternal household and support elderly parents. Property devolution patterns and community tradition shape their decision.

High fertility and mortality (particularly infant mortality) rates were characteristic of preindustrial societies. They severely regulated the number of persons surviving to adulthood and living out their adult years. Despite this similarity, however, preindustrial societies differed in the frequency and timing of household fission, that is, the point at which sons in particular left their natal families to set up independent households. The timing depended on the collective interests of family groups,[2] which, in turn, were largely defined by the nature of the economy, socioeconomic institutions that supported the economic base, and patterns of inheritance. Some societies sanctioned the partitioning of sons from the family household prior to the father's death. Others encouraged postmortem fission, division of the household after the father had died. Still others permitted fission only when the sons' children had reached full laboring age.[3] In societies with premortem fission, marriage was generally the precondition for partition, whereas in societies such as Russia, which favored postmortem fission, the marriage of sons strengthened the original household and encouraged multiple family household structures.

Extended families among Russian peasants promoted early ages at marriage and discouraged the setting up of new households. Sons brought their wives into their father's household, awaiting a time when they themselves could become household heads. Upon a father's death the household tended naturally to divide, as brothers and sons set up independent households with the property they took from the patrimonial household. The new households then went through a similar cycle of growth, equilibrium,

---

[2] Tamara K. Hareven, "Family Time and Historical Time," *Daedalus* 106, no. 2 (Spring 1977): 59.

[3] Goody, "The Evolution of the Family," p. 118.

and disequilibrium. Most Russian peasants thus experienced in the course of their lives a variety of household structures, ranging from the simple or nuclear to multiple family. They lived out the stages of childhood and adolescence, and a good portion of adulthood and parenthood, in the same household. Some even experienced grandparenthood in their father's household.

The Russian economist A. V. Chaianov was extremely sensitive to the various stages of the family life cycle among Russian peasants. He distinguished between small families consisting solely of newlyweds, those of parents and small children, mature families with laboring children, complex families of several related married couples, and lastly nuclear families containing elderly couples whose children had left the nest or died prematurely. At the end of twenty-five years, according to Chaianov, a family that had begun as a newly married couple would have grown to an optimum number (economically speaking) of eleven members, if high infant mortality were not taken into account. By that stage at least two or three children were ready for marriage.[4] A marrying daughter departed the paternal home for her in-laws', while a marrying son brought his new wife into his father's household, thus preserving its laboring strength. Eventually the household would increase in size and laboring power as the new daughter-in-law produced children.

The breakup of households upon the patriarch's death was a natural occurrence in the life cycle of the Russian peasant family in both the pre- and post-emancipation periods. These so-called *razdely* may be traced in Russian documentary records as far back as the early eighteenth century, and there is no doubt that they occurred even earlier.[5] Without these divisions, the typical household would have grown indefinitely to include kin more distantly related than first cousins.[6] Postmortem fission worked as a leveling mechanism. Large households that had attained economic stability and, in some cases, even prosperity were ready to divide into smaller units, each provisioned with the movable and real property necessary for economic survival.

Divisions of the patrimonial household prior to the patriarch's death, the so-called *vydely* and *otdely*, were not considered by contemporary ob-

[4] A. V. Chaianov, *A. V. Chayanov on the Theory of Peasant Economy*, ed. Daniel Thorner et al. (Homewood, Ill. 1966), pp. 56–57. For a more recent discussion of the household life cycle and fissions in the post-emancipation Russian village, see Cathy Frierson, "Razdel: The Peasant Family Divided," *The Russian Review* 46, no. 1 (January 1987): 35–51.

[5] E. N. Baklanova, *Krest'ianskii dvor i obshchina na russkom severe: Konets XVII—nachalo XVIII v.* (Moscow, 1976), pp. 165–66.

[6] Hoch, *Serfdom and Social Control*, p. 79; and Edgar Melton, "Proto-Industrialization, Serf Agriculture and Agrarian Social Structure: Two Estates in Nineteenth-Century Russia," *Past and Present* 115 (May 1987): 99.

servers of the nineteenth-century Russian peasantry as part of the family life cycle. A vydel, on the one hand, resulted when a son departed his father's household with the father's permission and his rightful share of the patrimony. Even if family tensions had been at the root of the son's departure, little or no acrimony was involved in the actual property division, as the family members stressed the importance of family unity and tranquillity. The ceremonial breaking of bread and transporting of fire from the natal hearth to the new household, described in the previous chapter, symbolized ongoing family unity. The otdel, on the other hand, occurred either on the patriarch's or his son's initiative as a result of irreconcilable dissension between father and son. Normally, a bol'shak kicked his son out with little or no property, or an independent-minded son chose to leave his father's household without first seeking permission, thus risking not only his father's displeasure but disinheritance. From the point of view of the commune, the otdely were the least desirable type of household division because they created unstable economic households. Nonetheless, Russian peasants undertook vydely as well as otdely in both the pre- and post-emancipation periods. With the abolition of serfowner controls in 1861, changes in military service after the Crimean War, and growth in nonagricultural employment, they resorted to them more frequently.

Many contemporary observers attributed the increase in premortem fission to growing individualism, influences of a developing cash economy, and a generational struggle that resulted in the weakening of patriarchalism in the post-emancipation Russian peasant village. In examining the reasons behind premortem and postmortem household divisions, the effects of emancipation, military reforms, and other government measures on the family, and regional differences in household size and structure, this chapter will endeavor to uncover the dynamics of the Russian peasant household after 1861.

Tensions in the Household

The previous chapter described the mechanics of fission in the post-emancipation period with regard to property division and the solemnity with which both family and community viewed the departure of a married son or brother from the natal home. Normally household members intent on splitting up their resources bypassed the village assembly and agreed to the fission on their own terms. They invited co-villagers to bear witness to the division and act as arbitrators in the event of a dispute. The illuminated sacred icon corner of the family hut, the traditional bread and salt of family hospitality, and the flickering flames of the family hearth enveloped the proceedings in an ambience of religious solemnity.

This picture of family unity was not entirely reflective of reality. The rituals surrounding household divisions were designed to restore peace to families whose members were often resentful of one another. Not all was harmonious within the Russian peasant hut. Disputes constantly arose over such matters as division of labor responsibilities, management of the household economy and resources, and a household head's arbitrary decisions. Generational conflicts between fathers and sons as well as mothers-in-law and daughters-in-law were endemic, at times resulting in the premature premortem division (vydely or otdely) of households. Together with these everyday tensions, the timing of household fissions was determined by such factors as the amount of land at a peasant family's disposal, a family's abilities to farm that land productively and meet state and communal obligations, and the capacity of preexisting living space to house new family members. At times, however, personal conflicts overrode the economic consequences of a household division, which in splitting a household's resources did not always guarantee the survival of the truncated original household or its offshoots.

In both pre- and post-emancipation Russia, peasant rationale for fissions remained constant. Enserfed and freed peasants attributed the splintering of households to large family size or, in slightly different terms, cramped living quarters, as well as family tensions. Eight out of ten surviving petitions from serfs on the Gagarin Manuilovskoe estate in Tver province during the first half of the nineteenth century complained of large family size.[7] Serfs on the Gagarin Mishino estate in Riazan province were more explicit, citing "constant fighting" and "disgraceful behavior" as causes of fission.[8] More than a century later peasants in Serenov canton, industrial Iaroslavl' province, echoed similar sentiments. There in 112 cases of household divisions between 1873 and 1883 peasants cited the following reasons for splintering a household:[9]

arguments among women	22.3%
arguments among brothers	17.9%
a stepmother	15.2%
a son's objectionable behavior	10.7%
large family size and small living space	9.8%
a father's objectionable behavior	5.4%
a brother's objectionable behavior	5.4%
a wish to leave the village for good to pursue a migrant trade	4.5%

[7] Bohac, "Family, Property, and Socioeconomic Mobility," p. 201.

[8] Peter Czap, Jr., "The Perennial Multiple Family Household, Mishino, Russia 1782–1858," *Journal of Family History* 7, no. 1 (Spring 1982): 22.

[9] Andrei Isaev, "Znachenie semeinykh razdelov krest'ian: Po lichnym nabliudeniiam," *Vestnik Evropy* (July 1883): 336–38.

large family size and the occurrence of fire	1.8%
large size of one brother's conjugal unit as opposed to another brother's that had no children	0.9%
unknown reason	6.3%

The peasants of Serenov canton evidenced the validity of the Russian say-ing which warned that "as families grow bigger, agreement occurs less fre-quently."[10] Over three-quarters of the reasons they gave for fission in-volved internal family tensions, with arguments among women heading the list. Generational conflicts and tensions between family members of the same generation appear to have been fairly evenly matched, suggesting the occurrence of both pre- and postmortem fission.

The high incidence of households' dividing after the death of a house-hold head in both the pre- and post-emancipation periods testifies to the insecure position of new household heads, whether uncles, brothers, or cousins to the deceased's offspring. For example, if a son became house-hold head upon his father's death, he could not command authority over his brothers as had his father, since all brothers were treated equally in the devolution of property. The other brothers were intent on being masters of their own households. In the 1880s in the village Romanovo, Kaliazin district, Tver province, for example, two brothers decided to split up their household, arguing that the present hut was too small for their joint fam-ily. When asked why a household division was necessary when a larger hut could easily be built to remedy the situation, one of the brothers replied, "I don't want to hear what is going on in the other hut; in another hut you can be your own master, the eldest."[11] Tensions between brothers arose also over distribution of laboring tasks within a large family unit. A father could delegate responsibilities and chores to his offspring yet, because of his age, not take on a full laboring share himself. The brother, however, as an equal among siblings had to lead by example to justify his headship position.[12] Even the relative size of each conjugal unit within a normal household created tension. A brother resented having to work twice as hard, or so he believed, because one of his brothers had twice as many children. A peasant complained to an outside observer, "One man has many mouths to feed while the other has only himself and his wife, or he

[10] L. S. Lichkov, "Krest'ianskie semeinye razdely," *Severnyi vestnik* (January 1886), no. 1, pt. 2, p. 102.

[11] *Sbornik statisticheskikh svedenii po Tverskoi gubernii*, vol. 5: *Kaliazinskii uezd* (Tver, 1890), p. 36, col. 1, n.2.

[12] V. P. Tikhonov, "Materialy dlia izucheniia obychnago prava sredi krest'ian Sarapul'skago uezda, Viatskoi gubernii: Chast' I," in Kharuzin, *Sbornik svedenii dlia izucheniia byta*, 3:75–76.

may have his own children; he doesn't want to have to work for someone else's children."[13]

The death of parents further encouraged household divisions by removing the need to provide for parents in retirement. Once a father died, sons looked to their own security, best met through household division and a new family life cycle in which children depended upon their father. "The ideal point for division fell when each married brother had working-age children to help him in his labors" and the large family household had sufficient capital in both real and movable property to sustain more than one economically viable household.[14]

Reasons for premortem fission that disrupted the natural family life cycle were varied. As in Serenov canton, Russian peasants often cited quarrelsome women as the cause of family tensions: "The wives do not get along." "Sisters-in-law are cunning when it comes to tricks, while daughters-in-law seek revenge."[15] Surely Russian peasant women were not more quarrelsome than men. Nevertheless, the constant interaction between women within the confined space of a peasant hut promoted conflict. Even in the best of circumstances relations between mothers-in-law and daughters-in-law were often tense. A daughter-in-law was subordinate to her mother-in-law in the running of the domestic household. She had to take orders, complaints, and sometimes beatings from her domineering mother-in-law and at times even sexual advances from her father-in-law. In an effort to exert some control over her life she might persuade her husband to set up a household independent of the directives of in-laws. When a household head's wife (bol'shukha) died, tensions sometimes erupted among the remaining women. If the function of bol'shukha passed from mother-in-law to sister-in-law, other sisters-in-law chafed in anger and frustration. Subordination to an equal was difficult to accept. Desirous of obtaining some independence and authority over her immediate family, a woman might press her husband to splinter from his father and brothers. Russian peasant women were not unique in disrupting multiple family households in favor of smaller family units over which they gained better control. Among Chinese peasants, Kay Ann Johnson has noted that "women, young women especially, can gain greater influence and freedom by undermining the larger kin unit in favor of the one in which they are emotionally and personally central. . . . Women may indeed be the worm in the apple of patrilocal domestic groups."[16]

---

[13] Lichkov, "Krest'ianskie semeinye razdely," p. 102.

[14] Melton, "Proto-Industrialization," p. 99.

[15] Lichkov, "Krest'ianskie semeinye razdely," p. 102; and Dobrotvorskii, "Krest'ianskie iuridicheskie obychai" (May 1889): 284.

[16] Kay Ann Johnson, *Women, the Family and Peasant Revolution in China* (Chicago, 1983), p. 20.

Tensions within a household were heightened if a father remarried upon his wife's death and brought a stepmother into the house to manage the household's domestic affairs and care for the children of his first marriage. Given the high mortality rate of women in childbirth, remarriages among widowers were frequent.[17] Children naturally distrusted their father's new wife and their stepsiblings. Mutual distrust sometimes resulted in premortem fission. Sons who remained in the household until their father died resented having to share their father's property with stepsiblings and look after their stepmother in her old age.

Generational conflicts between fathers and sons were also responsible for premortem household divisions. Russian peasants perennially complained of sons' disrespect for their elders: "The young want to be wiser than their elders." They also cited sons' laziness: "Today a father is in the field plowing while his son is on the *polati* [planking fixed between the ceiling and oven (pech')]."[18] Sons responded sarcastically to such complaints, noting that family harmony depended upon their suppressing their will.[19] They naturally resented having to take orders well into their thirties, forties, or even fifties before their fathers' deaths permitted them to ascend to the headship of the household. By that time they were well versed in the responsibilities of parenting. In some instances their children were approaching or had reached marriageable age; some indeed were already married. Under normal circumstances accession to a headship was, in essence, a reward for enduring the exigencies of adult life or, in Teodor Shanin's words, "a mark of maturity."[20] After they had married, however, impatient sons sometimes departed their fathers' homes and established independent households.

Wage labor, especially in the central industrial provinces, exacerbated strained relations between fathers and sons. Wage-earning sons resented having to contribute cash to the common family coffers. In the 1880s a villager in Kaliazin district, Tver province, refused to hand over to his father the wages he earned in out-migration. He was resentful of the fact that his father sat at home while he worked hard for a living. That resentment resulted in a household division.[21] Fission was not always the outcome of such quarrels, however. A migrant son sometimes depended upon

[17] O. V. Giliarovskii, a zemstvo doctor, reported that in Novgorod province in the 1860s approximately 59 per thousand women who had married over the age of twenty died in childbirth. See his *Izsledovaniia o rozhdenii i smertnosti detei v Novgorodskoi gubernii* (St. Petersburg, 1866), p. xv.

[18] Dobrotvorskii, "Krest'ianskie iuridicheskie obychai," p. 278.

[19] "How to live in a family is well-known: you keep your will under the bench," ran a Russian saying. Ibid., pp. 283–84.

[20] Teodor Shanin, *The Awkward Class: Political Sociology of Peasantry in a Developing Society, Russia 1910–1925* (Oxford, 1972), p. 86.

[21] *Sbornik statisticheskikh svedenii po Tverskoi gubernii*, p. 36, col. 1, n.3.

his father to look after his wife and children while he worked away from home. Furthermore, a father in the position of household head found it easier than a brother or uncle in the same position to contain those tensions with threats of disinheritance or partition with the barest of necessities.

External Limitations on Fission

In spite of the internal domestic reasons for household fissions, Russian peasants were not always free to decide the timing of such divisions. Beginning with serfdom and continuing into the second half of the nineteenth century, external constraints were placed on peasant household decisions in this matter, with differing results. Russian peasants had never had total control over their destinies. While the uncertainties of nature continually bent peasant will, landowners and government fiat intruded upon the natural rhythms of peasant life, at times shaping them to serve their own interests. Never was this more evident than in the era of serfdom.

Serfowners and the Ministry of State Domains warned of the negative effects of family fissions on peasant economies. By dividing economically viable households into two or more units, and dispersing material and human resources, they placed newly created households in precarious economic positions. The constellation of fewer male laborers, work animals, and agricultural implements, it was feared, would lead a family to economic ruin and undermine its capacity to pay landowner and state. In 1834 a new bailiff on a Gagarin estate in Borisoglebsk district, Tambov province, summed up this argument:

> Division among the peasants was permitted by the previous management. Everyone fulfilled his whims, which were carried to excess; nephew divided from uncle, brother from brother. And at the present time, the peasant who has a one-*tiaglo* family cannot carry out either his estate labor obligations or household field work, and such families will always be poverty-stricken.[22]

Fission, according to this reasoning, precluded any positive development in either household structure or economic well-being. Indeed, smaller family households tended to be poorer, sometimes too poor to meet their obligations. On the Sheremetev estate of Rastorg in Dmitriev district, Kursk province, poor families averaged only 5.1 members, solvent households 9.8. Only the larger households had sufficient labor to work their own lands as well as the serfowner's demesne.[23]

---

[22] Quoted in Steven L. Hoch, "Serfs in Imperial Russia: Demographic Insights," *Journal of Interdisciplinary History* 13, no. 2 (Autumn 1982): 240.

[23] Melton, "Proto-Industrialization," pp. 96–97.

Serfowners also believed that household divisions jeopardized the sanctity of patriarchal relations within families. In 1853 a landowner, Babarykin, with an estate in Nizhnii Novgorod district, Nizhnii Novgorod province, complained that fissions were leading to generational conflicts and a loss of children's respect for their parents. He was referring to cases in which sons set up their own households, departing from the normal practice of remaining in the patriarchal household to support their elderly parents.[24]

In response to the dangers of household divisions, serfowners instituted a variety of paternalistic measures to ward off fissions and maintain comparatively large and complex serf households. They ordered their bailiffs to curb peasant willfulness and independence and punish offenders who dared to set up new households without first seeking the bailiffs' permission.[25] The success or failure of such measures depended largely upon the ability of bailiffs to influence serf behavior on largely absentee landlord estates.

The published historical record regarding serfowners' effectiveness in stemming household fissions is limited to the experience of three Gagarin estates in the first half of the nineteenth century, which have been recently studied by Peter Czap, Jr., Steven L. Hoch, and Rodney D. Bohac. In cases of premortem fission on the Gagarin estates, the degree of an individual bailiff's control was a crucial variable. On the Petrovskoe estate in agricultural Tambov province the bailiff was particularly eager to fulfill his master's prohibition on fissions. His strict control of serf family life rendered premortem fissions an exception. On the Gagarin's Mishino estate in Riazan province, however, the bailiff was not as effective. Here sons were more successful in splintering off from their fathers' households. Such divisions accounted for 16 percent of all fissions. For the period extending from 1782 to 1858 the total number of households on the Mishino estate outstripped the estate's population growth by 15 percent, suggesting that peasants divided their households whenever necessary. Peasant demands for fission, voluntary peasant activity, the recruitment levy for the Crimean War, and impending emancipation also affected the frequency of household division and impeded total control by serfowners over peasant lives even on the more successful Gagarin estate of Petrovskoe.[26] Despite the

[24] V. Babarykin, "Sel'tso Vasil'evskoe, Nizhegorodskoi gubernii, Nizhegorodskago uezda," *Etnograficheskii sbornik* 1 (1853): 20.

[25] Hoch, "Serfs in Imperial Russia," p. 241; V. I. Semevskii, *Krest'iane v tsarstvovanie Imperatritsy Ekateriny II*, 2d rev. ed., 2 vols. in 3 (St. Petersburg, 1903), 1:321; and Czap, "The Perennial Multiple Family Household," pp. 12–13.

[26] Hoch, "Serfs in Imperial Russia," pp. 237–41; Bohac, "Family, Property, and Socioeconomic Mobility," pp. 166–67, 195; and Czap, "The Perennial Multiple Family Household," pp. 14–15, 21–22.

variation in the bailiffs' abilities to influence peasant activities, multiple three-generational family households predominated on all three estates.

The Ministry of State Domains followed the lead of serfowners and attempted to obstruct fissions in state peasant households by requiring peasants to petition for official permission for such action. That permission became increasingly difficult to obtain because officials feared that the smaller households resulting from fission would default in their military and tax obligations. Generally, fissions were permitted only when the original household was so large that the new units would have at least three male laborers each. Only atypically large and complex multiple family households could meet this demand.[27] However, state peasants were not closely supervised and, as a result, tended to split up households without first seeking official sanction.

Despite attempts to prevent household divisions, serfowners and government officials were unable to maintain artificially large complex households on the scale of the Serbian zadruga. Families with several conjugal units had largely disappeared among pre-emancipation Russian peasants. As early as the second half of the eighteenth century landlords nostalgically recalled a glorious past when the so-called big family predominated among the peasantry.[28] By the first half of the nineteenth century the typical household on the Gagarin estates of Manuilovskoe in Tver, Petrovskoe in Tambov, and Mishino in Riazan provinces had between 7 and 10 members. The average size of households in the central industrial regions was lower at 6.8 members, reflecting the prevalence of obrok (quitrent) rather than barshchina labor dues. On the Mishino estate four families, each with more than 30 persons at the beginning of the nineteenth century, underwent fission by 1814 and never reattained their former magnitude.[29] In the 1870s D. Ia. Samokvasov's discovery of an archetype of the zadruga on Russian soil in the 39-member Vorob'ev household economy (containing ten conjugal units) in Kursk district, Kursk province, represented an anomaly. Such large families had never been typical of Russian peasant society. Even the large Vorob'ev family splintered into four separate economic households a few years after the patriarch's death.[30]

While the Vorob'ev complex family was atypical in both the pre- and post-emancipation periods, different patterns of household division among Russian peasants, nevertheless, distinguished these periods. After

[27] Brzheskii, *Ocherki iuridicheskogo byta*, p. 103.

[28] Confino, "Russian Customary Law," p. 41.

[29] Bohac, "Family, Property, and Socioeconomic Mobility," p. 95; Hoch, "Serfs in Imperial Russia," p. 233; Czap, "The Perennial Multiple Family Household," pp. 11–12, 15; and Melton, "Proto-Industrialization," p. 98, 147n.

[30] D. Ia. Samokvasov, "Semeinaia obshchina v Kurskom uezde," in Matveev, *Sbornik narodnykh iuridicheskikh obychaev*, 1:11–15.

1861 fissions became more frequent and the incidence of premortem fission, in particular, intensified. Such changes resulted from the commune's displacement of serfowner control, introduction of military reforms, ineffective government regulation of peasant affairs, and an increase in non-agricultural opportunities for peasants in the central industrial region. The differences in fission patterns resulted in decreasing the size of post-emancipation Russian peasant family households.

Emancipation and Abolition of Serfowner Controls

In emancipating the Russian serfs the imperial Russian government had to deal with the immediate problem of filling the vacuum created by the removal of serfowners' authority. Thus it concentrated its efforts on extending the commune's powers, leaving peasants a good deal of freedom in managing their affairs. Only in the 1880s, when the government perceived a crisis among the peasantry, did it begin to interfere in peasant institutions, among which the family household figured prominently. The administration's initial laissez-faire attitude and subsequent stance of paternalistic concern, however, affected households in the same way, permitting peasants to decide for themselves their household composition.

From 1858, on the eve of emancipation, to 1886 the government merely sought to regularize household divisions and to provide them with an institutional foundation. The emancipation legislation of 1861 placed them under the village assembly's jurisdiction. A simple majority of the assembly's membership could accept a request for fission.[31] The commissioners knew that fissions, particularly among state peasants, had earlier been carried out without proper sanction, but the officials decided not to go beyond these cursory regulations. But when it became clear that peasants were failing to seek the village assembly's permission for household divisions, further government action was taken. The illegal fissions had caused difficulties in determining the military obligations of households and had to be rectified. The manifesto regulating the recruitment levy for 1863 declared that all fissions after 1 January 1863 were legitimate if verified by the village assembly. The law also empowered the village assembly to settle disputes arising from the selection of recruits from splintered households.[32] In September 1864 the government, also with the intent of deter-

---

[31] *PSZ*, ser. 2, no. 36657, arts. 51–53, 57.

[32] Ibid., no. 39799. These disputes were inevitable because the pre-1863 illegal status of newly formed households had made them responsible for the recruitment and tax obligations of the households from which they had separated. After 1863 it was difficult to sort out which obligations the newly legitimized fissioned households had already met.

mining households' military obligations, ordered village assemblies to record the dates of all fission agreements and the numerical compositions of the new households.[33] This was the last legislative measure concerning peasant household divisions until 1886.

The lifting of serfowner controls over household fissions, coupled with the concomitant bureaucratic effort to record them, gave Russian peasants greater independence in determining their households' composition. As a result, they began to use premortem fission more frequently to resolve family tensions. More sons and their wives refused to wait until the patriarch's death to leave the family household and set up on their own. However, premortem fissions did not suddenly overtake the postmortem variety. The partible inheritance system and peasant household support for elderly parents delayed fissions until after marriage and encouraged at least one married son to remain in his father's household to look after parents and unmarried siblings.

Data concerning household divisions in the immediate post-emancipation period are confined mainly to the impressionistic picture painted by the reports of the Liuboshchinskii Commission for Reforming the Cantonal Courts. The commissioners did not undertake a systematic counting of fissions but merely asked peasants about their frequency. Peasants responded that household divisions were quite common. Actual court cases recorded in the reports indicate that peasants often bypassed the village assembly and took their requests for household division to the cantonal courts. This occurred despite the courts' lack of jurisdiction over fission agreements, which were solely the prerogative of village assemblies. Peasants also appealed village assembly decisions regarding household division at cantonal courts and sometimes asked cantonal judges to sort out the property claims of fissioning parties.

The official commission report's random sampling of cantonal court cases in industrial Moscow and agricultural Tambov provinces regarding household division suggests a predominance of the postmortem variety. While not necessarily representative of the aggregate, they demonstrate the patterns of fission among post-emancipation Russian peasants. Since premortem household divisions were a departure from the norm, one would expect them to have predominated among the disputed cases coming before the cantonal courts. On the contrary, household division cases in Moscow and Tambov provinces in the early 1870s mainly involved disputes between brothers, uncles and nephews, and collateral relations. Fissions between fathers and sons (including stepsons and adopted sons) accounted

---

[33] Ibid., no. 41273; and G. A. Alekseichenko, "Prigovory sel'skikh skhodov kak istochnik po istorii krest'ianskoi obshchiny v Rossii vtoroi poloviny XIX veka. (Po materialam Tverskoi gubernii)," *Istoriia SSSR* (November–December 1981), no. 6, p. 124.

for only 17.72 percent of all fission petitions in the Moscow and 11.65 percent in the Tambov samplings.[34] These percentages are remarkably similar to those recorded on the pre-1861 Mishino estate. They also follow the household division patterns in agricultural Voronezh province, for which more reliable zemstvo data are available. Among former state peasants and serfs in Voronezh province over the extended period from 1849 to 1894, only 16.31 percent of a total of 141 fissions among 230 households were between fathers and sons. The overwhelming majority of fissions occurred between collateral kin.[35] The figures suggest that even in the pre-emancipation period peasants, if unencumbered by pressures from serfowners, sometimes resolved family tensions through premortem fission. At the same time, a strong cultural pattern of resisting premortem household divisions in favor of postmortem fissions persisted beyond the watershed of emancipation.

The cantonal court data for industrial Iaroslavl' province, on the other hand, indicate a relatively high incidence of household divisions between fathers and sons, accounting for 30.23 percent of all fission cases.[36] Statistics for Serenov canton, Iaroslavl' province, in the years 1873 to 1884 corroborate the unusually high rate of premortem fission in this province: 42, or 37.5 percent, of 112 observed cases were between fathers and sons. A high frequency of premortem household division would explain in part the relatively small mean household size of 4.9 persons by 1897 in Iaroslavl' province as a whole.[37] Abolition of serfowner control, however, can only partially explain the higher incidence of premortem fission there. The possibility of a modified cultural pattern, which had already appeared during serfdom and intensified after emancipation as a result of a growth in domestic industries and out-migration, must also be taken into account.[38] Sons could afford to ignore their fathers' threats of disinheritance given the option of pursuing nonagricultural employment.

The abolition of serfowner control, while having some effect upon premortem fission, may have had a greater impact upon the life cycle and composition of the multiple family household. Before 1861 serfowner pressure on the Gagarin estates regularized the household life cycle. By permitting periodic divisions among mainly complex family structures that retained

---

[34] Based on *Trudy Kommisii*, vols. 1–2.

[35] Based on F. A. Shcherbina, *Krest'ianskie biudzhety* (Voronezh, 1900). My calculations.

[36] *Trudy Kommisii*, vol. 3.

[37] Isaev, "Znachenie semeinykh razdelov," p. 337; and *Pervaia vseobshchaia perepis naseleniia Rossiiskoi Imperii, 1897 goda*, ed. N. A. Troinitskii, 89 vols. (St. Petersburg, 1899–1905), 50:iv.

[38] Peter Czap, Jr., " 'A Large Family: The Peasant's Greatest Wealth': Serf Households in Mishino, Russia, 1814–1858," in *Family Forms in Historic Europe*, ed. Richard Wall, Jean Robin, and Peter Laslett (Cambridge, 1983), pp. 148–49.

their complexity after fission, landlords artificially prevented a large variation in the size and structure of households and in this way helped secure their economic viability and taxpaying capacity.[39] "Fluctuations in a household's productive strength were minimized, and vulnerability to cyclical extremes of poverty and wealth due to changes in household composition were reduced."[40] Once peasant households were emancipated from direct serfowner control, changes were bound to occur. The more decisive cyclical economic fluctuation of peasant households and rural proletarianization in the second half of the nineteenth century are well documented, although the lifting of landowner control was only one of many reasons behind peasant responses to changing economic conditions.[41]

Changes in Military Service

The second change in household division patterns among Russian peasants in the post-emancipation period stemmed from a curtailment of military service requirements after the Crimean War. Discharge orders and a decree of 16 April 1866, which granted extended leave to all enlisted men in active service prior to 8 September 1859, brought the Nikolaevan soldier back to his native village. Subsequent decrees swelled the number of men on unlimited furlough. The release of 100,000 men between 1862 and 1870 created a new situation in most Russian villages to which households had to adapt.[42]

Before the Crimean War peasant recruits faced mandatory twenty-five-year periods of service, effectively severing them from their families and villages for life. Property devolution schemes reflected this by making no provision whatever for peasant-soldiers in their midst. Furthermore, returning soldiers were not entitled to communal land allotments. Having been absent during the census or revision of 1858 they would not have been registered as peasants with rights to such land. In the rare event that a soldier reached retirement age or was allowed to return to his village of birth or habitation because of physical disability, he was forced into a mar-

---

[39] Czap, "The Perennial Multiple Family Household," p. 24.

[40] Hoch, "Serfs in Imperial Russia," p. 242.

[41] See, for example, Vladimir I. Lenin, *The Development of Capitalism in Russia: The Process of the Formation of a Home Market for Large-Scale Industry* (Moscow, 1956); and Shanin, *The Awkward Class*.

[42] Forrestt A. Miller, *Dmitrii Miliutin and the Reform Era in Russia* ([Nashville, Tenn.], 1968), pp. 191–92.

ginal existence.[43] It is little wonder that some retired soldiers chose instead to settle on frontier crown lands.[44]

The regularization of army discharges and the post-Crimean leaves, however, forced peasants to make inheritance provisions for returning soldiers if they had been recruited after the reforms of the 1860s. They had been apportioned farmstead and allotment land on the basis of the 1858 revision before entering military service and could rightfully claim that land as theirs.[45]

The military reform of 1874, which introduced universal military service, had even greater impact upon peasant life. Reduction of obligatory service to a maximum of six years increased the need to accommodate returning soldiers into the household economy. Yet this very development produced tensions as well. If, for instance, a father died while his son was in service and another son had become household head, this second son would have worked and paid taxes on his soldiering brother's land allotment. He was unlikely to view his brother's return to the village with equanimity. As household head, this brother would also have been expected to provide for the other's conjugal family during the term of military service. Quarrels would sometimes break out over the management of the patrimony, leading to the returning solder's demand for a household division and his rightful share of the real and movable property.

The triggering effect of the new military provisions on fissions may be illustrated by zemstvo household budget studies pertaining to Voronezh province. There, in the years 1849 to 1894, nineteen, or 27.4 percent of sixty-nine fissions between brothers (in a sample of 230 households) resulted from quarrels that followed a brother's return from military service.[46] The direct effect of military discharge and leave may be further seen in a number of petitions for household divisions between brothers that came before the cantonal courts in Tambov province between 1870 and 1872. Of a random sampling of thirty-nine cases of fission between brothers, nineteen, or 48.7 percent, involved a brother who had served in the military. In Moscow province during the same period, 20.8 percent of petitions for fission between brothers involved a former soldier or a soldier on leave.[47] Thus the effect of the military changes in precipitating fissions

[43] Peter Czap, Jr., "Marriage and the Peasant Joint Family in the Era of Serfdom," in *The Family in Imperial Russia: New Lines of Historical Research*, ed. David L. Ransel (Urbana, 1978), p. 112.

[44] George Bolotenko, "Administration of the State Peasants in Russia before the Reforms of 1838," 2 vols. (Ph.D. diss., University of Toronto, 1979), 2:463.

[45] V. V. Ivanov, ed. *Obychnoe pravo krest'ian Khar'kovskoi gubernii*, 2 vols. in 1 (Khark'ov, 1896–1898), 2:59.

[46] Based on Shcherbina, *Krest'ianskie biudzhety*. My calculations.

[47] Based on *Trudy Kommisii*, vols. 1–2.

was significant, but due to the nature of documentation its magnitude is difficult to measure precisely.

Frequency of Fission

Beginning in the 1880s the government became increasingly concerned about the growing numbers of household divisions in the Russian countryside and decided to abandon its previous laissez-faire attitude in favor of stricter regulation of fission. According to data supplied by the County Administration for Peasant Affairs, 2,371,248 peasant households in forty-six provinces of European Russia had splintered in the twenty-year period since emancipation. The figures demonstrated that peasants generally ignored the law, dividing their households without first seeking permission from village assemblies. Only 12.8 percent of the estimated 2,371,248 fissions had been carried out with official approval. The data also indicated that in some provinces the number of households was growing at a faster rate than the population and that average peasant household size was decreasing. In the northern province of Olonets, for example, the number of households since the revision of 1858 had increased by 43.03 percent, whereas the population had grown by only 11.96 percent. Government officials attributed this dramatic increase in households to frequent fissions. The data indicated further that from 1858 to 1882, again as a result of household divisions, the average number of adult male laborers per peasant family in Olonets had decreased from 1.78 to 1.38. Similarly in Pskov province the number of households had increased by 50 percent between 1861 and 1880, while the population had grown only 20 percent; the average number of adult male laborers per household had dropped from 1.94 to 1.53.[48]

Reports from forty-three provincial governors supplemented the County Administration for Peasant Affairs statistics. These reports were limited to the shorter period of 1874 to 1884. They demonstrated that an average of 140,355 household divisions occurred per annum. This figure represented an increase of 20.76 percent over the annual average for 1861–1882. The growth over the ten-year period 1874–1884 in the number of households in twenty-two provinces was in the range of 21 percent. The high percentage of families without an adult male laborer or with only one—52.4 percent for thirty-seven provinces—was thought to reflect the negative effects of household divisions.[49] While a household with one

[48] Rittikh, *Krest'ianskii pravoporiadok*, p. 230; and Brzheskii, *Ocherki iuridicheskogo byta*, pp. 113–14.

[49] N. K. Brzheskii, "Krest'ianskie semeinye razdely i zakon 18 marta 1886 goda," *Russkoe ekonomicheskoe obozrenie* 4, no. 4 (April 1900): 65.

adult laborer could presumably be the outcome of fission, a household with none was the product of disaster, such as fire, illness, or death, perhaps preceded by fission.

The data suggest dramatic changes in the post-1861 countryside that had not been anticipated by the legislators of emancipation. Household fissions among peasants were occurring at a rapid rate, causing a significant increase in the number of households and a weakening of their laboring power. They also confirmed the worst fears of the minister of internal affairs, Count Dmitrii A. Tolstoy, that peasants were bypassing government-institutionalized administrative bodies, thus minimizing government influence over peasant society. He concluded that fissions were destroying the peasant household and urgently needed to be curtailed.[50]

Tolstoy had legitimate fears of a proliferation of nuclear family households with insufficient labor to take advantage of nonagricultural income, but the aggregate data on household fissions that he used to substantiate the need for government intervention in peasant life are suspect. Fissions had not been systematically counted until the 1880s, which raises doubts about the validity of figures submitted by various local government officials. Furthermore, the aggregate data were based on comparative analyses of the 1858 revision and population statistics compiled by the Ministry of Internal Affairs from police records and zemstvo censuses. The 1858 revision is a problematical source for comparative study, especially with regard to state peasants. Officials compiled their revision or census lists of state peasants using the previous revision as a guideline. They recorded which households had died out and which households had been added based on misleading information supplied by the peasants themselves. State peasants tended to ignore government sanctions against household fissions and divided their households, acknowledging their new composition only when emancipation was extended to them. Hence a considerable number of fissions attributed to the 1860s had in fact occurred earlier. The 1858 figures are thus inaccurate for state peasants, reducing the number of actual households and inflating both mean household size and the mean number of adult male laborers per household.[51]

The information supplied to the 1858 census takers by serfowners and their bailiffs regarding the serf population, on the other hand, was more reliable. According to N. Chernenkov, a zemstvo statistician of the late nineteenth century, fewer major discrepancies in household size appeared between the revision lists and subsequent population surveys. In keeping copious estate records serfowners served their own interests. They bene-

---

[50] I. M. Strakhovskii, *Krest'ianskiia prava i uchrezhdeniia* (St. Petersburg, 1903), pp. 185–87.

[51] N. Chernenkov, *K kharakteristike krest'ianskago khoziaistva*, vol. 1 (Moscow, 1905), pp. 57–63.

fited economically from large households with several conjugal units providing them with labor or cash payments. Large households also cushioned the effects of the loss of laborers to the military.[52]

The accuracy of the statistical data made available to Minister of Internal Affairs Tolstoy and the conclusions drawn from them were openly questioned at the time by Finance Minister M. K. Bunge. Other data assembled by officials in the Ministry of Finance suggested that household fissions were not detrimental to the peasantry's paying power. Bunge argued that the root of peasant impoverishment lay in the peasantry's heavy financial burdens, which he had undertaken to alleviate through a four-stage program, from 1883 to 1887, to abolish the soul tax.[53]

Government Interference: The Law of 18 March 1886

Count Tolstoy persuaded Alexander III of his claims regarding peasant impoverishment and won the ideological battle with Bunge. A triumphant Tolstoy then prepared legislation designed to curb sharply household divisions in the countryside. The law of 18 March 1886, which applied to settlements with communal land tenure only, required a peasant family desirous of fission to obtain the village assembly's permission. It authorized the assembly to examine the request only if the household head had agreed to the household division. The village assembly could overrule the patriarch's negative decision, but only in the face of positive proof that he did not have the interests of the entire household at heart. In other words, he had to be a spendthrift or an alcoholic, incapable of managing his own household properly. The 1886 law also provided that on receipt of a request for fission, the village assembly would determine its feasibility on the basis of explicit criteria: Were the reasons for fission legitimate? Would the newly formed households be able to carry on independent household economies? Would the amount of farmstead land for the new household or households meet government building standards? Were provisions adequate to discharge the original household's arrears, taxes, dues, and other obligations? If the proposed household division failed to meet any one of

[52] Ibid., pp. 64, 70n. Chernenkov's trust in the reliability of serfowner records is corroborated by recent studies of the Gagarin estate records by Peter Czap, Jr., " 'A Large Family' "; idem, "Marriage and the Peasant Joint Family"; idem, "The Perennial Multiple Family Household"; Steven L. Hoch, *Serfdom and Social Control*; and Rodney Dean Bohac, "Family, Property, and Socioeconomic Mobility."

[53] A. M. Anfimov and P. N. Zyrianov, "Elements of the Evolution of the Russian Peasant Commune in the Post-Reform Period (1861–1914)," *Soviet Studies in History* 21, no. 3 (Winter 1982–1983): 84. For a discussion of the argument between Tolstoy and Bunge, see Strakhovskii, *Krest'ianskiia prava*, pp. 185–87.

these, the 1886 law required that the village assembly deny the fission request. If the household did meet these requirements, a two-thirds majority of the assembly could permit the division. Then the assembly was empowered to divide the communal land allotments among members of the partitioning household and ensure that each new household received a farmstead, buildings, and movable property (especially agricultural implements and work animals) adequate to establish a viable household economy. In cases where the farmstead land in a family's possession was inadequate for its housing and farm buildings, the village assembly was to apportion sufficient land from vacant communal lands. The law also instructed the village assembly to apportion taxes, dues, arrears, and other obligations among the divided households. All members of the partitioned household retained joint responsibility for obligations such as military duty. Article 8 of the 1886 law stressed that fission "does not give the participating members . . . any new right concerning military duty."[54]

The law of 18 March 1886, in brief, clarified the commune's function as the administrative body responsible for household division, limited the acceptable reasons for fission, and buttressed patriarchal authority. In protecting multiple family households, it aimed to maintain economically viable units of production. The bureaucracy assumed that the village assembly would be able to discharge its responsibilities. Community interests, which might conflict with those of individual households, were not expected to enter the picture. Bureaucrats assumed furthermore that these legislative measures would suffice to deter peasants from bypassing village assemblies and undertaking household divisions on their own.

On a theoretical level, one might agree with V. I. Manotskov's harsh contemporary judgment that the March law "by suppressing individuality, upholding the patriarchal authority of the bol'shak [household head], interfering in the family life of peasant society . . . is repressive and consolidates the power of 'society' even more over individuality."[55] Yet practical experience demonstrated that by itself the new government regulation was unlikely to stop peasants from spontaneously dividing their households in response to changes and tensions within the family. Even the 1889 institution of the land captain to oversee village activity more closely had little effect on fissions. Peasants acted in accordance with what they perceived to be their best interests, a fact that bureaucrats faced more squarely during the implementation of the Stolypin reforms in the early twentieth century. Consequently, both before and after 1886, laws against voluntary household divisions had little if any impact on peasant behavior.

[54] *PSZ*, ser. 3, no. 5578.
[55] V. I. Manotskov, "Chto takoe krest'ianskii vopros?" *Vestnik Novgorodskago zemstva* 7, no. 20 (15 October 1905): 67.

Provincial governors' reports of the 1890s were almost unanimous in their negative assessment of the 1886 law's ability to curtail fission. Unfortunately, they provided little empirical data to support their conclusion. Only three reports from the central provinces offered statistical data to buttress their claims that the law was ineffective. The Tver provincial report noted that between 1866 and 1886 the number of households had increased by 30 to 40 percent. It related that increase to both legal and illegal fission. In Riazan province the governor reported that between 1887 and 1894 legal household divisions had increased on the order of 52 percent. The number of informal or illegal fissions over that period, on the other hand, decreased by only 18 percent. The governor of Riazan concluded that the March law of 1886, "created in part to limit informal family fissions, has in general had no influence on curtailing fissions."[56]

The provincial report from Orel province went much farther than the other two. It not only provided data concerning the frequency of household divisions but linked them to population growth and economic crises. Its findings also contradicted the view that fissions were a direct cause of peasant impoverishment:

> Statistical data demonstrate that the number of family fissions, in the majority of instances, is conditioned by the natural growth of the peasant population. . . . In 1892 all the peasants of Orel province numbered 1,843,925 souls of both sexes with 218,743 household heads; from this it is evident that the size of each family averaged eight persons. The village population for the years 1892 and 1893 increased by 45,405 souls. . . . With an average family size of eight the number of fissions should have been 5,675. In reality there were only 3,161 [fissions]. In 1892 with an increase of 13,280 souls there were 602 formal and 1,187 illegal fissions; in 1893 with an increase of 32,125 souls there were 478 legal and 894 illegal household divisions. Consequently, in the poor harvest and cholera year of 1892 the number of family fissions was almost double that of the good harvest year.
>
> Those figures demonstrate that first, population growth is more than sufficient to explain the reasons for family fissions; second, economic poverty does not lessen but increases the number of fissions; and third, no limitations can restrain the peasant population from dividing [their households] at will.[57]

Thus, the population in Orel province grew at a faster pace than the number of households. When household fissions occurred on an unprecedented scale, they represented peasant responses to famine and cholera. Orel's experience was very different from that of such diverse provinces as Tver, Nizhnii Novgorod, Tambov, and Voronezh, where the growth in number

---

[56] *Svod zakliuchenii gubernskikh soveshchanii*, vol. 2, pt. 2, pp. 197ff., 257, 232.
[57] Ibid., pp. 225–26.

of households more than doubled, in percentage terms, population growth.[58]

Clearly after emancipation the incidence of fission among Russian peasant households increased. The abolition of serfowner controls, changes in recruitment laws, population growth, growth in wage labor, and internal household tensions encouraged the partitioning of peasant households. Government action in 1886 to stem the frequency of fission proved ineffective because it ran counter to peasant interests and reactions to changing circumstances. Aggregate data shed little light on the specifics of fission, however. Which households were dividing? How often did they splinter? What were the economic consequences of household divisions? Zemstvo data reveal more concrete information about the mechanism of household divisions.

Case Studies of Fission

A sample of 230 Russian and Ukrainian households from agricultural Voronezh province provides a unique source for the study of the rhythms of the family life cycle and household fission.[59] The statistician F. A. Shcherbina compiled the sample at the turn of the century on the basis of thousands of zemstvo household budget studies that had been conducted within the ten-year period from 1887 to 1896. He selected households he judged representative of the entire province. By providing detailed information about family composition, ages and gender of family members, incidences of and reasons for fission, and the general economic well-being of a cross section of Voronezh peasant society, Shcherbina's compilation permits the historian to reconstruct the pattern of household divisions.

Between 1849 and 1894 fission affected 61.3 percent of the 230 households, resulting in a total of 141 household divisions (see table 3.1). In almost all cases these households splintered once in that forty-five-year period. Only two households underwent fission twice and one three times. The overwhelming majority of cases occurred after a household head's death. Almost 79 percent occurred between 1866 and 1890, peaking in

[58] By the 1880s and 1890s the peasant populations in key central industrial and agricultural provinces had increased between 25.6 and 37.3 percent since emancipation. Calculated on the basis of figures supplied by Z. M. Tverdova-Svavitskaia and N. A. Svavitskii, *Zemskie podvornye perepisi 1880–1913: Pouezdnye itogi* (Moscow, 1926): pp. 4–6 of tables. Chernenkov calculated that in three districts of Orel province the population of male souls increased 44.4 percent between 1858 and 1887, whereas the number of families grew only 30.1 percent for the shorter period of 1868 to 1887. He also provided statistics to demonstrate that the number of households in districts of Saratov province did not keep pace with population growth. See his *K kharakteristike krest'ianskago khoziaistva*, pp. 31–38.

[59] Shcherbina, *Krest'ianskie biudzhety.*

TABLE 3.1
Percentage Distribution of Fission by Kinship of Partitioning Parties in the Voronezh Sample of 230 Households, 1849–1894

	Total	Total Russian Family Fissions	Total Ukrainian Family Fissions
Between brothers	48.94	43.96	57.14
Between father and son(s)	16.31	21.98	6.12
Between uncle and nephew(s)	10.64	10.99	10.20
Between brother-in-law and widowed sister-in-law	2.84	1.10	6.12
Between cousins	1.42	2.20	—
Between father-in-law and widowed daughter-in-law	0.71	1.10	—
Between father-in-law and son-in-law	0.71	1.10	—
Unknown	18.44	17.58	20.41
Total	100.01	100.01	99.99

Source: F. A. Shcherbina, *Krest'ianskie biudzhety* (Voronezh, 1900). My calculations.
Note: Because the percentages have been rounded off to the nearest tenth, they do not add up to 100.

the period 1876–1885. The military reform of 1874 and increases in the repartitional activity of communes triggered the intensified activity of the late 1870s and early 1880s. Few household divisions (3.6 percent) occurred between 1891 and 1894 during and after the famine crisis of 1891–1892. Mergers were more likely than fissions to constitute peasant response to economic uncertainty at that time. In this respect the peasants of Voronezh responded quite differently to the famine than did peasants in Orel province, where the annual average of household divisions nearly doubled during the famine year.[60]

Confirming the reliability of the Shcherbina sample and revealing the same general pattern of fission, are 1886 data from seventeen villages in Endovishche canton, Zemliansk district, Voronezh province (see table 3.2). Every household in this canton splintered on average only once over a period of twenty to forty years. After several years households had become sufficiently complex to create the household composition and internal tensions that naturally caused fission. In twelve of the seventeen villages more than 30 percent of the household divisions occurred before 1866, suggesting that state peasants were acknowledging illicit household divisions which had taken place prior to emancipation. Except for upsurges in fission activity in a few villages between 1866 and 1876, another third or

---

[60] All calculations are based on ibid.

TABLE 3.2
Number of Fissions in Endovishche Canton, Voronezh Province, Pre-1866–1886

Village	Number of Households	Percentage of Households That Underwent Fission			
		1881–1886	1876–1881	1866–1876	pre-1866
Endovishche	381	24.15	17.85	16.80	41.21
Latanoe	201	25.37	14.43	21.90	38.31
Vyselki Latanskie	24	16.67	33.34	25.00	25.00
Tochil'nyi	57	21.05	7.02	40.35	31.58
Vyselki Tochilinskie	17	17.65	0.00	58.82	23.53
Voznesenskoe	249	20.48	21.69	22.09	35.74
Gubarevka	83	16.87	19.28	54.22	9.64
Ternovoe I	74	18.92	25.68	20.27	35.14
Gremiachii Kolodez	134	22.39	9.70	30.60	37.31
Minkin Kolodez	38	13.16	34.21	10.53	42.11
Ternovoe II	53	22.64	18.87	32.08	26.42
Bogoiavlenskoe	51	29.41	9.80	15.69	45.10
Min. Beduga	28	25.00	14.29	14.29	46.43
Losevo	99	11.11	26.26	15.15	47.47
Udobnoe	43	25.58	2.33	11.63	60.47
Gubarevo	51	19.61	13.73	62.75	3.92
Studenoe	60	21.67	13.33	8.33	56.70
Total	1,643				

Source: *Sbornik statisticheskikh svedenii po Voronezhskoi gubernii*, vol. 3, pt. 1: *Zemlianskii uezd* (Voronezh, 1886). My calculations.

Note: Because the percentages have been rounded off to the nearest hundredth, they do not always add up to 100.

more of the households in fifteen villages fissioned between 1876 and 1881.[61]

Shcherbina's data for Voronezh province exhibit a positive correlation between fission and the creation of nuclear families, consisting of only parents and children. Of the seventy-four nuclear family households in the sample of 230 households, forty-nine, or 66.2 percent, had been created directly because of fission. A majority of these household divisions involved brothers. The remaining twenty-five family households became nuclear as a result of family members' deaths.[62] The predominance of nuclear families among the newly created households marked a departure from the

[61] These conclusions are based on data in *Sbornik statisticheskikh svedenii po Voronezhskoi gubernii*, vol. 3, pt. 1: *Zemlianskii uezd* (Voronezh, 1886).

[62] Unfortunately Shcherbina's data are not sufficiently complete to determine the composition of both the original households or their partitioned units. I have been able to make my conclusions on the basis of the information supplied after the household divisions had taken place. Shcherbina, *Krest'ianskie biudzhety*.

days of serfdom, when serfowners permitted fissions only among families sufficiently complex that the new households were themselves complex in structure.

The division of the post-emancipation multiple family household into two or more units, however, did not always reduce household structures to the simplest nuclear family. Sometimes the original household retained complex structures. Of the thirty stem families in the Shcherbina sample, which had previously undergone division, ten had done so less than a decade prior to being inventoried. One of the seven extended families and eleven of the thirty-six joint families had undergone fission within the same period.[63]

Data from forty-five fission cases in the late 1880s in Kozlov canton, Sarapul' district, Viatka province, in northeastern European Russia, confirm that household divisions resulted in the creation of a variety of household structures. In this sample almost 70 percent of the household divisions involved a father and son or, as in one case, a stepfather and his stepson. The remaining fissions were between brothers (11), mothers and sons (2), and sisters-in-law (1). Prior to the divisions, the original household structures were complex, with over 85 percent having three generations. Two-thirds of the families were joint and almost one-quarter stem. After fission twenty or 44.4 percent of the original households became nuclear. The other twenty-five original households remained complex:

1 extended family remained extended
1 stem family remained a stem family because an already partitioned son agreed to return to his father's home after his brother had moved out
1 stem family became extended
2 joint families became extended
15 joint families became stem families
5 joint families remained joint

As in the Voronezh sample the new households created as a result of fission were overwhelmingly nuclear (36 out of 45). Two were solitaries, six extended, and one joint.[64]

The Shcherbina data for Voronezh province support the view that fission neither adversely affected household size in the long run nor destroyed the life cycle of the Russian peasant household, which tended toward the creation of multiple family units. At the time of the zemstvo study the mean household size of 8.26 persons among families who had earlier participated in fission was remarkably similar to the mean household size

---

[63] Ibid.

[64] Calculations are based on Tikhonov, appendix to "Materialy dlia izucheniia obychnago prava," in Kharuzin, *Sbornik svedenii dlia izucheniia byta*, 3:29–58.

of 8.47 persons among nonpartitioned families. This suggests that a nuclear household did not necessarily bring the household life cycle to a halt or extinguish a household. A household that included only an elderly bol'shak and his wife, whose children had already departed the parental nest, would have atrophied naturally. However, households with a young married couple or young parents and children were destined to follow the normal life cycle. New conjugal units would be incorporated within the household when sons married and, in the absence of male heirs, when a daughter married.[65]

Household divisions had mixed economic results. On the one hand, they did not always signify economic disaster for new households. Table 3.3 shows the dispersion of Voronezh fissions according to time period and household assets at the time of the household budget studies. Almost 48 percent of the households that were products of divisions within five years of the studies had assets in excess of five hundred rubles. This suggests that a significant percentage of the fissions during this period had occurred among the wealthiest households, which had sufficient property to establish independent households with viable economies. On the other hand, household divisions, as government officials and other observers of the peasantry feared, sometimes led to poverty. A significant 38.1 percent of households that had resulted from partitions within the same five-year period of the household budget studies had very low assets. Tensions within the original households had clearly overridden economic concerns. Smaller households with fewer laborers were more vulnerable to economic disaster if illness, death, poor harvests, or fire struck. Indeed, almost 30 percent of the Voronezh households that had been products of fission in the 1860s and 1870s were among the poorest in the 1890s. At the same time, household divisions were not always at the root of poverty. Table 3.4 distinguishes between the economic standing of households that had experienced or were products of fission and the standing of those that had not splintered. A remarkably similar percentage of households that had never undergone division were poor. Labor shortages in such cases may have been due to biological accidents such as the death of children in infancy or childhood or the premature death of a wife.[66]

Another sample corroborates the pattern in Voronezh province of the mixed economic results of household divisions. Of 112 cases of fission between 1873 and 1883 in Serenov canton, in industrial Iaroslavl' province, three-quarters of the original households retained their former economic status after members partitioned. A mere 3.6 percent improved their eco-

---

[65] Based on Shcherbina, *Krest'ianskie biudzhety*.

[66] Edgar Melton makes this point in reference to poor households before 1861. See his "Proto-Industrialization," p. 101.

TABLE 3.3

Incidence of Fission in Relation to Average Household Assets in the Voronezh Sample, 1887–1896

Assets in Rubles	Percentage of Households That Underwent Fission in the Previous						
	1–5 Years	6–10 Years	11–15 Years	16–20 Years	21–25 Years	26–30 Years	31 Years
1–250	38.10	47.05	20.83	8.70	35.71	21.05	—
250–500	14.29	17.65	25.00	34.78	7.14	21.05	—
500–1,000	23.81	20.59	29.17	30.43	35.71	26.32	66.67
Over 1,000	23.81	14.71	25.00	26.09	21.43	31.58	33.33
Total	100.01	100.00	100.00	100.00	99.99	100.00	100.00
(Number)	(21)	(34)	(24)	(23)	(14)	(19)	(3)

Source: F. A. Shcherbina, Krest'ianskie biudzhety (Voronezh, 1900). My calculations.

Note: Assets include the household residence, farm building, animals, agricultural and nonagricultural implements, and furniture. Because the percentages have been rounded off to the nearest hundredth, they do not always add up to 100.

TABLE 3.4

Percentage Distribution of Nonfissioned and Fissioned Households according to Average Household Assets in the Voronezh Sample of 230 Households, 1887–1896

Assets in Rubles	Percentage of Nonfissioned Households	Percentage of Fissioned Households
1–250	30.11	31.39
250–500	21.51	20.44
500–1,000	25.81	26.28
Over 1,000	22.58	21.90
Total	100.01	100.01
(Number)	(93)	(137)

Source: F. A. Shcherbina, *Krest'ianskie biudzhety* (Voronezh, 1900). My calculations.

Note: Assets include the household residence, farm buildings, animals, agricultural and nonagricultural implements, and furniture. Because the percentages have been rounded off to the nearest hundredth, they do not add up to 100.

nomic situations, while 21.4 percent deteriorated economically. Among the households created by fission, 54.5 percent maintained the economic performance levels of their original households, 9 percent surpassed them, and 26.8 percent fell. Taken together, slightly more than three-quarters of the households that participated in or were produced by fission either retained or improved on their prior economic situation. The overwhelming majority of household divisions thus occurred among the most prosperous family households whose property could sustain more than one viable economy. Almost one-quarter (24 percent), however, deteriorated economically. Illnesses, epizootics, and fires exacerbated the problems of their insufficient capital and labor capacity.[67] Such economic vulnerability would, in turn, have resulted in merger, extinction, or emigration.[68]

Family Size and Structure

The increase in household divisions after emancipation had a telling effect upon households by depressing their mean sizes. According to the 1897 national census (see tables 3.5 and 3.6) mean household size varied between 4.9 and 6.5 persons in central Russia. The industrial provinces of Iaroslavl', Nizhnii Novgorod, and Tver, and agricultural Kaluga province

[67] Isaev, "Znachenie semeinykh razdelov," pp. 338, 343–46.
[68] Shanin, *The Awkward Class*, p. 88.

TABLE 3.5
Mean Household Size in the Central Russian Provinces in 1897

Iaroslavl'	4.9
Nizhnii Novgorod	5.3
Tver	5.4
Kaluga	5.8
Tula	6.1
Moscow	6.3
Riazan	6.3
Orel	6.4
Kursk	6.5
Voronezh	6.5

Sources: *Pervaia vseobshchaia perepis naseleniia Rossiiskoi Imperii, 1897 goda*, ed. N. A. Troi-nitskii, 89 vols. (St. Petersburg, 1899–1905), vol. 9, bk. 2, p. ix; vol. 15, bk. 1, p. xii; vol. 20, p. xiv; vol. 25, bk. 1; vol. 29, p. xiv; vol. 35, p. iv; vol. 42, p. xvi; vol. 44, p. v; vol. 50, p. iv; and *Moskovskaia guberniia po mestnomu obsledovaniiu 1898–1900 gg.*, vol. 1 (Moscow, 1903–1904).

TABLE 3.6
Household Size on a Percentage Basis of the Total Number of Households in the Rural Areas of the Central Industrial and Central Agricultural Provinces in 1897

	2 Persons	3 Persons	4 Persons	5 Persons	6–10 Persons	11 and More Persons
Vladimir	12.5	13.9	15.7	16.0	38.1	3.8
Voronezh	6.8	9.7	12.8	14.7	45.1	10.8
Kaluga	8.4	10.7	13.6	15.0	43.9	8.5
Kostroma	11.0	13.5	16.2	16.9	39.8	2.6
Kursk	5.5	8.5	12.2	15.0	49.1	9.8
Moscow	14.1	15.7	16.9	16.0	34.1	3.1
Nizhnii Novgorod	12.7	14.0	15.5	15.7	37.8	4.3
Orel	6.1	9.0	12.9	15.1	47.6	9.3
Penza	8.3	11.5	14.7	15.7	42.9	6.9
Riazan	8.7	11.2	14.5	15.6	41.4	8.6
Tambov	7.0	9.7	12.9	14.4	45.5	10.5
Tver	10.0	11.7	14.7	16.3	43.5	3.7
Tula	7.7	10.5	13.8	15.4	44.9	7.8
Iaroslavl'	15.3	16.4	17.5	16.4	32.9	1.5

Source: *Pervaia vseobshchaia perepis naseleniia Rossiiskoi Imperii, 1897 goda*, ed. N. A. Troinitskii, 89 vols. (St. Petersburg, 1899–1905), vol. 6, bk. 2; vol. 9, bk. 1; vol. 15, bk. 1; vol. 18, p. x; vol. 20, p. xiv; vol. 24, p. xxv; vol. 25, bk. 1; vol. 29, p. xiv; vol. 30, p. iv; vol. 35, p. v; vol. 42, p. xvi; vol. 43, p. xi; vol. 44, p. vi; vol. 50, p. iv. My calculations.

Note: Because the percentages have been rounded off to the nearest tenth, they do not always add up to 100.

had the smallest households; industrial Moscow province and the agricultural provinces of Riazan, Tambov, Orel, Kursk, and Voronezh boasted the largest. Zemstvo data for individual districts of central Russian provinces (see table 3.7) between 1894 and 1905 confirm this pattern. They show mean household sizes ranging between 5.07 persons in Iur'ev district, Kostroma province, and 7.53 in Nizhnedevitsk district, Voronezh province. In general, households had grown smaller than pre-emancipation households. On the Gagarin serf estates, a mean of 8.0 persons was recorded in Mishino (Riazan province), 9.7 in Petrovskoe (Tambov province), and 7.7 in Manuilovskoe (Tver province). The pre-1861 central industrial regions had a lower mean of 6.8 persons.[69]

Household divisions account for the decreases in household size. The zemstvo data suggest that the stimulus to household divisions was strongest where the pressure on the land was weakest either because land was abundant or because a substantial portion of the population derived its income from nonagricultural pursuits. Accordingly, families tended to be smaller in the central industrial provinces (with the exception of Moscow) where almost every household was engaged in domestic industries. Population pressure on the land helped maintain fairly large households in Moscow province. Over the course of the nineteenth century (from 1811 to 1914) Moscow's population nearly quadrupled (3.79 times). This increase was substantially above the growth rates of other industrial provinces.[70] An 1893 study of Klin district indicates a significant increase of 12.2 percent in mean household size from 5.51 in 1878 to 6.18 persons in 1892 that was in step with a population increase of 11.8 percent.[71] Moscow province also boasted the highest population density of 83.1 persons per square verst in all of European Russia.[72]

The Shcherbina sample of 230 households for agricultural Voronezh province goes far beyond the aggregate data supplied by zemstvo censuses and the 1897 census in providing detailed information not only about household size, but about household composition.[73] It exhibits an inflated mean household size of 8.34 (standard deviation 5.01) persons. That size is significantly larger than the 1897 census count for Voronezh of 6.5 per-

[69] Czap, " 'A Large Family,' " p. 123; Hoch, "Serfs in Imperial Russia," p. 233; Bohac, "Family, Property, and Socioeconomic Mobility," p. 93; and Melton, "Proto-Industrialization, p. 98, 147n.

[70] A. G. Rashin, *Naselenie Rossii za 100 let (1811–1913 g.g.): Statisticheskie ocherki* (Moscow, 1956), p. 62, table 30.

[71] V. Davydov, "Materialy po krest'ianskomu khoziaistvu v Klinskom uezde, Moskovskoi gub.," in *Statisticheskii ezhegodnik Moskovskoi gubernii za 1893 g.* (Moscow, 1893), appendix, pp. 30–97.

[72] Rashin, *Naselenie Rossii*, pp. 77–79, table 45.

[73] All calculations pertaining to the 230 households are based on Shcherbina, *Krest'ianskie biudzhety.*

TABLE 3.7
Mean Size of Households in Relation to Allotment Size and Occupation in Domestic Industries for Several Central Russian Provinces, 1894–1905

District	Province	Census Year	Mean Persons per Household	Mean Allotment per Household	Percentage of Households Occupied in Domestic Industries
Iur'ev	Kostroma	1901	5.07	7.22	98.09
Rybinsk	Iaroslavl'	1898	5.16	8.04	89.47
Gorokhovets	Vladimir	1889	5.16	8.92	84.58
Makar'ev	Kostroma	1901	5.27	10.82	97.51
Bui	Kostroma	1898	5.28	7.05	91.01
Uglich	Iaroslavl'	1897	5.29	8.85	88.65
Iaroslavl'	Iaroslavl'	1901	5.32	7.37	86.70
Viazniki	Vladimir	1898	5.44	9.18	86.53
Myshkin	Iaroslavl'	1897	5.46	7.30	75.38
Soligalich	Kostroma	1900	5.49	9.38	94.33
Varnavin	Kostroma	1904	5.50	8.72	92.58
Galich	Kostroma	1902–4	5.52	8.01	94.44
Vladimir	Vladimir	1897	5.57	6.76	90.05
Moscow	Moscow	1899	5.57	—	—
Mologa	Iaroslavl'	1899	5.58	7.01	90.51
Sudogda	Vladimir	1898	5.66	9.68	91.68
Murom	Vladimir	1897	5.68	6.27	85.57
Pokrov	Vladimir	1900	5.70	8.48	96.16
Kologriv	Kostroma	1903–5	5.84	10.39	91.36
Suzdal'	Vladimir	1899	5.88	7.68	92.79
Melenki	Vladimir	1898	5.95	8.97	85.88
Aleksandrovsk	Vladimir	1900	5.98	10.90	90.10
Bogorodsk	Moscow	1899	5.99	—	98.12
Ruza	Moscow	1898	6.11	—	93.19
Kolomna	Moscow	1899	6.13	—	91.73
Pereslavl'	Vladimir	1900	6.15	10.64	91.77
Vetluga	Kostroma	1902–4	6.19	11.08	87.05
Zvenigorod	Moscow	1899	6.19	—	95.66
Orel	Orel	1894	6.26	6.41	54.95
Dmitrov	Moscow	1898	6.26	—	95.70
Bronnitsy	Moscow	1899	6.33	—	96.76
Volokolamsk	Moscow	1899	6.37	—	89.78
Podol'sk	Moscow	1900	6.37	—	96.82
Mozhaisk	Moscow	1898	6.38	—	91.54
Klin	Moscow	1899	6.49	—	95.14
Vereia	Moscow	1898	6.51	—	95.28
Kromy	Orel	1904	6.66	6.51	66.83
Zadonsk	Voronezh	1900	6.69	6.90	—

TABLE 3.7 (*cont.*)

District	Province	Census Year	Mean Persons per Household	Mean Allotment per Household	Percentage of Households Occupied in Domestic Industries
Serpukhov	Moscow	1900	6.73	—	99.74
Ostrogozhsk	Voronezh	1900	6.76	11.20	—
Sevsk	Orel	1894	6.78	8.18	60.99
Zemliansk	Voronezh	1900	6.92	8.08	—
Dmitrovsk	Orel	1901	6.96	6.48	66.15
Korotoiak	Voronezh	1900	7.11	11.24	—
Nizhnedevitsk	Voronezh	1900	7.53	10.98	—

Source: Z. M. Tverdova-Svavitskaia and N. A. Svavitskii, *Zemskie podvornye perepisi 1800–1913: Pouezdnye itogi* (Moscow, 1926). My calculations.

sons. The inclusion in the sample of twenty-six families with between fifteen and thirty members partly explains the inflation in household size. The 1897 census, as opposed to the zemstvo data, did not record laborers as residents of their village households. The inflation may also be attributed to the omission of one-member households from the random sample. Otherwise, there is a bunching of families with between two and ten members. Almost 78 percent of the sample's households fit that range. Forty-seven percent of the households had between two and four members. Because of that bunching, it is fair to conclude that the households in the sample were fairly representative, providing a general pattern of household structures in the central agricultural region.

More than two-thirds of peasant households (67.4 percent) in the Shcherbina sample were composed of extended families. Tables 3.8 and 3.9 use Peter Laslett's classifications to differentiate the households by structural type and kinship composition.[74] Fifty-seven percent were multiple family households with two or more conjugal units. The overwhelming majority (88.26 percent) contained either two or three generations in each, with a high proportion of daughters-in-law, grandchildren, and other affines and their children (see tables 3.10 and 3.11). The percentage (5.65) of *frérèches* (i.e., households made up of conjugal units of married brothers) in particular confirms the complex household structures of the Voronezh

[74] See Laslett, "Introduction," in Laslett and Wall, *Household and Family*, pp. 29–31; Eugene A. Hammel, Kenneth W. Wachter, and Peter Laslett, "Household Hypotheses," in *Statistical Studies of Historical Social Structure*, ed. Wachter, Hammel, and Laslett (New York, 1978), p. 40, exhibit 3.1; and Peter Laslett, "Family and Household as Work Group and Kin Group: Areas of Traditional Europe Compared," in Wall, Robin, and Laslett, *Family Forms*, pp. 520–21, table 17.2.

TABLE 3.8
Percentage Distribution of Household Structures in the Voronezh Sample of 230
Households, 1887–1896

Household Type	Percentage of Total Households	Percentage of Russian Households	Percentage of Ukrainian Households
Special	0.43	0.72	—
Nuclear	32.17	35.97	25.56
Extended:			
Lineal	6.09	2.88	11.11
Lateral	1.30	2.16	—
Lineal and lateral	3.04	1.44	5.56
Total extended	10.43	6.48	16.67
Stem:			
Multiple lineal	21.30	19.42	24.44
Multiple lineal and extended	1.30	1.44	1.11
Total Stem	22.60	20.86	25.55
Joint	20.43	22.30	18.89
Joint extended	3.04	4.32	1.11
Simple joint	6.52	4.32	8.89
Complex joint	4.35	5.04	3.33
Total joint	34.34	35.98	32.22
Total multiple family households	56.94	56.84	57.77
Total Number	230	139	90

Source: F. A. Shcherbina, *Krest'ianskie biudzhety* (Voronezh, 1900). My calculations.
Note: Because the percentages have been rounded off to the nearest hundredth, they do not always add up to 100. One of the 230 households was of German descent and therefore was not included among either the Russian or Ukrainian households.

sample and the continuity of strong cultural patterns over the 1861 dividing point. On the Gagarin Manuilovskoe estate in Tver province in the pre-emancipation period, frérèches accounted for between 4.1 and 14.6 percent of all households and on the Gagarin Mishino estate in Riazan province for almost 9 percent. In preindustrial western and northern Europe where the nuclear family predominated, frérèches were virtually unknown.[75]

[75] Bohac, "Family, Property, and Socioeconomic Mobility," p. 134, table 5.1; and Laslett, "Family and Household," pp. 520–21, 533.

TABLE 3.9
Percentage Distribution of Household Structures in the Voronezh Sample, 1887–1896, on the Basis of Laslett's Classification of Households by Type and Kinship Composition

Household Type	Class	Number of Households	Proportion of Households (%)
1. Solitaries (singletons in households)	1a. Given as widowed		
	1b. Given as nonmarried or of unknown marital status		
2. "No family" households (co-residents among whom no conjugal unit can be discerned)	2a. Co-resident siblings	—	—
	2b. Other co-resident relatives	1	0.43
	2c. Co-residents with no familial relationship given	—	—
3. Simple family households (conjugal family units only)	3a. Married couples without offspring	14	6.09
	3b. Married couples with offspring	56	24.35
	3c. Widowers with offspring	1	0.43
	3d. Widows with offspring	3	1.30
	Subtotal	75	32.60
4. Extended family units	4a. Extension upward (of which 2 have fathers, 1 father-in-law, 1 stepfather, 8 mothers, 1 mother-in-law)	13	5.65
	4b. Extension downward (of which 1 has grandchildren only)	1	0.43
	4c. Extension sideways (of which 2 have brothers only and 1 sisters only)	3	1.30
	4d. Combinations of 4a–4c, or any other form of extension	7	3.04
	Subtotal	24	10.42
5. Multiple family households	5a. Households with secondary units disposed upward from head (of which 1 extended)	1	0.43
	5b. Households with secondary units disposed downward from head (of which 13 extended)	94	40.87

TABLE 3.9 (*cont.*)

Household Type	Class	Number of Households	Proportion of Households (%)
5. Multiple family households	5c. Households with secondary units disposed sideways from head, member of parental generation being present (of which 1 also extended in other directions)	7	3.04
	5d. *Frérèches*: households with secondary units disposed sideways from head; no member of parental generation (of which 0 also extended)	13	5.65
	5e. Combination of 5a–5d, or any other multiple household arrangement (of which 7 also extended)	16	6.96
	Subtotal	131	56.95

Source: F. A. Shcherbina, *Krest'ianskie biudzhety* (Voronezh, 1900). My calculations.
Note: Because the percentages have been rounded off to the nearest hundredth, they do not add up to 100.

The Shcherbina data demonstrate not only the complexity of households in an agricultural province, but the economic incentives for maintaining such large households. Given the commune's practice of awarding land to households on the basis of their number of tiagla, or laboring married couples, larger households had more land to farm (see table 3.12). Assets also tended to increase as a household's structure became complex (see tables 3.13 and 3.14). Smaller households were involved in nonagricultural activities (see table 3.15). They had a greater concentration of nuclear and extended families than larger households mainly occupied in farming. Households whose members were employed as agricultural and industrial wage laborers had the smallest mean size of 5.61 persons. Families pursuing domestic industries and local trades had the next highest mean household size of 6.29. Nuclear and extended families predominated in both groups. The largest families of between 8.44 and 10.64 persons were involved either solely in agriculture or in a combination of agricultural and industrial paid work, domestic industries, and local trades. These families had the largest percentages (between 56.44 and 78.57) of multiple family households. Despite the disparities in household size and composition, however, all the groups evince the same cultural pattern, favoring multiple family households.

TABLE 3.10
Percentage Distribution of Households in the Voronezh Sample of 230 Households by Number of Conjugal Units and Number of Generations in Each, 1887–
1896

Number of Marital Units	
None	0.43
One	41.30
Two	32.61
Three	16.52
Four	3.91
Five or more	5.22
Total	99.99
Average number of units	2.01
Number of Generations	
One	6.52
Two	42.17
Three	46.09
Four	5.22
Total	100.00
Average number of generations	2.50

Source: F. A. Shcherbina, *Krest'ianskie biudzhety* (Voronezh, 1900). My calculations.
Note: Because the percentages have been rounded off to the nearest hundredth, they do not
always add up to 100.

Data from seventy-eight households in four villages of Kaziul'kin canton, Odoev district, agricultural Tula province, corroborate the correlation
in the Voronezh sample of household size and composition with economic
activities. The largest households pursued a variety of economic opportunities both within and outside their villages. The population of the four
villages of Bol'shoe and Maloe Triznovo, and Staroe and Novoe Rusanovo
combined farming with manufacturing of harrows and migrant trades to
differing degrees. The average of 7.26 persons in the thirty-four households in Bol'shoe Triznovo was noticeably larger than the 4.85 average in
Maloe Triznovo. The latter village did not contain any migrant laborers,
while seventeen households of the former had twenty-six, suggesting that
only the largest families could expend surplus labor for nonagricultural
pursuits outside the village. In all likelihood more families in Maloe Triznovo were exclusively involved in domestic industries. In Staroe Rusanovo
and Novoe Rusanovo households averaging 6.75 and 6.26 persons were
more economically diverse. They were involved not only in farming and

TABLE 3.11
Kins and Affines of Household Heads in the Voronezh Sample by Category and
Gender, 1887–1896

Males			Females		
	Number	*%*[a]		Number	*%*[a]
Son[b]	396	23.5	Daughter[d]	257	15.3
Grandson	172	10.2	Wife	206	12.2
Nephew	60	3.6	Daughter-in-law	160	9.5
Brother	44	2.6	Granddaughter	155	9.2
Father	13	0.8	Sister-in-law	43	2.6
			Niece	40	2.4
			Mother	30	1.8
Other[c]	19	1.1	Other[e]	36	2.1
Indeterminate	26	1.5	Indeterminate	27	1.6
Total	730	43.3	Total	954	56.7

Source: F. A. Shcherbina, *Krest'ianskie biudzhety* (Voronezh, 1900). My calculations are
based on the format of a table in Peter Czap, Jr., " 'A Large Family,' " in *Family Forms in
Historic Europe*, ed. Richard Wall, Jean Robin, and Peter Laslett (Cambridge, 1983), p. 135.

Note: The household heads group includes 206 married males, 21 widowers, 1 unmarried
male, and 2 widowed females.

[a] Percentage of 1,684 (equals total population less 230, the number of household heads)
[b] Includes 2 adopted sons and 4 stepsons
[c] Includes great-grandsons, grandnephews, sons-in-law, stepfathers, cousins, fathers-in-
law, grandfathers, and orphans
[d] Includes 1 stepdaughter
[e] Includes sisters, mothers-in-law, granddaughters-in-law, grandnieces, aunts, spouses of
nephews

domestic industries, but in out-migration as well. Three families in Staroe
Rusanovo had a total of five migrant laborers while four families in Novoe
Rusanovo each had one.[76]

Concrete data on household size and composition are not as readily
available for a central industrial province. However, D. N. Zhbankov did
record household membership in four villages of northwestern Kostroma
province heavily involved in out-migration. The land in Soligalich and
Chukhloma districts was so poor that adolescent and adult male laborers
frequently abandoned the village for the greater part of the year to pursue
work in far-off St. Petersburg as painters, potters, stove builders, coopers,
coach makers, carpenters, bakers, and butchers. They left women and the
elderly behind in the village to work the land. The average household in
the four villages contained only 5.0 persons (standard deviation 2.37), but

[76] N. Nechaev, "Kustarnaia promyshlennost' Odoevskago uezda," in *Trudy kommisii po
izsledovaniiu kustarnoi promyshlennosti Rossii*, vol. 7 (St. Petersburg, 1881), pp. 1078–83.

TABLE 3.12

Mean Household Size and Percentage Distribution of Household Structures according to Amount of Land per Household in the Voronezh Sample, 1887–1896

Land Allotment (in Desiatinas)	Mean Household Size	Percentage of Family Households within Each Landed Category				
		Special	Nuclear	Extended	Stem	Joint
Landless	5.00	16.67	33.33	33.33	16.67	—
Less than 5	4.77	—	63.64	16.67	12.12	7.58
5–15	7.70	—	30.95	9.52	28.57	30.95
15–25	10.98	—	6.12	6.12	24.49	63.27
More than 25	15.16	—	4.00	—	28.00	68.00
Total 230 families	8.34	0.43	32.17	10.43	22.60	34.34

Source: F. A. Shcherbina, *Krest'ianskie biudzhety* (Voronezh, 1900). My calculations.

Note: Because the percentages have been rounded off to the nearest hundredth, they do not always add up to 100.

TABLE 3.13

Percentage Distribution of Households within Structural Type According to Amount of Assets per Household in the Voronezh Sample, 1887–1896

	Household Assets (in Rubles)			
	1–250	250–500	500–1,000	Over 1,000
Special	—	—	100.00	—
Nuclear	62.16	21.62	13.51	2.70
Extended	50.00	37.50	8.33	4.17
Stem	17.31	23.08	36.54	23.08
Joint	5.06	15.19	34.18	45.57

Source: F. A. Shcherbina, *Krest'ianskie biudzhety* (Voronezh, 1900). My calculations.

Note: Assets include the household residence, farm buildings, animals, agricultural and nonagricultural implements, and furniture. Because the percentages have been rounded off to the nearest hundredth, they do not always add up to 100.

the smaller household size masks the general complexity of household composition. While nearly 47 percent of the households were nuclear, almost the same percentage were of the extended, stem, or joint varieties. This breakdown suggests once again that the nuclear family was but an interim stage in the household life cycle. A significant proportion of households contained daughters-in-law and grandchildren, although the number of affines and their offspring was far fewer than in the Voronezh sample (see table 3.16). The large percentage of stem families (27.42 percent) in the sample as opposed to the smaller percentage of joint families (11.29 percent) indicates that only one married son generally remained in the pat-

TABLE 3.14
Percentage Distribution of Households within Structural Type according to
Amount of Assets per Capita in the Voronezh Sample, 1887–1896

	Household Assets (in Rubles) per Capita				
	1–50	50–100	100–150	150–200	Over 200
Special	—	—	—	—	100.00
Nuclear	52.70	29.73	6.76	5.41	5.41
Extended	45.83	41.67	8.33	4.16	—
Stem	26.92	38.46	26.92	3.85	3.85
Joint	27.85	46.84	16.46	5.06	3.80

Source: F. A. Shcherbina, *Krest'ianskie biudzhety* (Voronezh, 1900). My calculations.

Note: Assets include the household residence, farm buildings, animals, agricultural and nonagricultural implements, and furniture. Because the percentages have been rounded off to the nearest hundredth, they do not add up to 100.

rilocal household to look after elderly parents. Other sons and brothers generally left the household sometime after marriage.[77]

During both the pre- and post-emancipation periods, the Russian peasant family household was neither a static entity nor as complex as the Serbian *zadruga*. Births, deaths, and the aging of family members changed the composition of households and the responsibilities of family members. Sons who had once been completely dependent upon parents were obliged to support retired parents. This duty, coupled with the communal system of apportioning land to tiagla, the partible inheritance system, and peasant demand for labor in the household economy favored postmortem fission. Sons who married did not automatically depart their parents' home to set up independent households but often remained until their father's death. At that time they equitably divided the patrimony among themselves and set up new households in which their own children were exclusively dependent upon them and would in turn maintain them when the time came. These partitions had a leveling effect on the economic status of the households involved. The largest as well as wealthiest tended to undergo fission and the splintering of their resources. Premortem fissions occurred when family tensions disrupted a household. Daughters-in-law and sons sought to escape the domineering and oppressive authority of their seniors by setting up independent households even if that meant renouncing aid from parents.

Household divisions, particularly the premortem variety, increased after emancipation due to the abolition of serfowner controls, the ineffective-

[77] Based on the appendix in D. N. Zhbankov, *Bab'ia storona: Statistiko-etnograficheskii ocherk* (Kostroma, 1891).

TABLE 3.15

Household Structure and Size according to Economic Pursuits in the Voronezh Sample, 1887–1896

Structural Type	Percentage of Total Number of Households within Each Grouping				
	Agriculture (163)	Prosperous Agriculture (28)	Agricultural and Industrial Wage Labor (18)	Domestic Industries and Local Trades (17)	Involved in Both of Latter Two Categories (4)
Special	—	—	—	5.88	—
Nuclear	31.90	14.29	44.44	52.94	25.00
Extended	11.66	—	16.67	11.76	—
Stem	20.25	28.57	33.33	17.65	50.00
Joint	25.15	39.29	—	5.88	25.00
Simple joint	6.75	10.71	5.56	—	—
Complex joint	4.29	7.14	—	5.88	—
Mean household size	8.44	10.64	5.61	6.29	8.50
Standard deviation	4.58	6.56	2.25	6.47	3.70
Coefficient of variation for household size of each subset	54.27	61.65	40.11	102.86	43.53

Source: F. A. Shcherbina, *Krest'ianskie biudzhety* (Voronezh, 1900). My calculations.

Note: I have divided the strictly agricultural households into self-sufficient and prosperous. The latter are involved in selling grain on the market, hiring day laborers, and leasing large tracts of land. Because the percentages have been rounded off to the nearest hundredth, they do not always add up to 100.

ness of government regulation of peasant daily life, and significant changes in military service. Marked population growth and increases in opportunities for wage labor also contributed to a surge in premortem fission and growth in nuclear family households, with mixed economic results. Both before and after 1861 units of young couples and their children, however, represented but interim stages in the life cycle of the Russian peasant family if death or disaster did not intervene. As a young family developed over the years, sons matured, married, and brought their young brides into their parents' household. Nuclear households of elderly couples, on the other hand, were destined to die out.

Russian peasant families were generally larger and more complex in structure in the traditional grain-growing central agricultural provinces than in the central industrial provinces. Such differences had already appeared during serfdom, but they became more pronounced after its abolition. Household size and structure affected peasants' economic options.

TABLE 3.16
Kin and Affines of Household Heads by Category and Gender in Four Villages of Kostroma Province

	Males			*Females*	
	Number	%[a]		Number	%[a]
Son	70	28.6	Daughter	49	20.0
Grandson	22	9.0	Wife	38	15.5
Nephew	2	0.8	Daughter-in-law[b]	24	9.8
Brother	3	1.2	Granddaughter	20	8.2
Father	0	0.0	Sister-in-law	2	0.8
Son-in-law	1	0.4	Niece	1	0.4
			Mother	1	0.4
			Other[c]	10	4.1
			Indeterminate	2	0.8
Total	98	40.0	Total	147	60.0

Source: D. N. Zhbankov, appendix in *Bab'ia storona: Statistiko-etnograficheskii ocherk* (Kostroma, 1891). My calculations are based on the format of a table in Peter Czap, Jr., " 'A Large Family,' " in *Family Forms in Historic Europe*, ed. Richard Wall, Jean Robin, and Peter Laslett (Cambridge, 1983), p. 135.

Note: The household heads group includes 38 married males, 1 widower, 22 widows, and 1 spinster.

[a] Percentage of 245 (equals total population less 62, the number of household heads)
[b] Includes 1 common-law daughter-in-law
[c] Includes a mother-in-law, grandmother, sisters, aunts, and a cousin

The smallest households had limited opportunities. They were involved strictly in wage labor, whether in the industrial or agricultural sectors of the economy. Those occupied in domestic industries were larger than their wage-laboring counterparts. The largest households were the most fortunate, having enough labor to pursue either farming alone or a combination of agriculture and domestic industries. Areas of heavy male out-migration, such as northwestern Kostroma where soils were too poor for adequate agricultural incomes, were characterized by small families in which agricultural tasks were delegated solely to women and the elderly. Men abandoned the land for work in St. Petersburg. A higher percentage of these households was composed solely of nuclear families than was the case for households in areas with better soils. However, even here, the nuclear family did not dominate. Almost half the households were composed of extended, stem, or joint families. Their structures indicate that usually only one son remained in the patrilocal household to look after elderly parents.

This and preceding chapters have on several occasions referred to marriage and age at marriage. It has been suggested that early marriage was encouraged and that newlyweds generally entered the groom's parents' home rather than set up an independent household. The discussion now turns to these matters. Marriage was one of the most important moments in a peasant's life. Through courtship and marriage rituals the community and family joined together to support mutual interests and maintain well-defined behavioral norms. While the commune may have hesitated to interfere directly in family squabbles that might result in household divisions, it played a supportive and complementary role in courtship and marriage.

IV

New Players, Old Games: Courtship under the Community's Watchful Eye

May God permit me to marry once,
be baptized once, and to die once.

A person undergoes three wonders: when he
is born, when he marries, and when he dies.

A goose without water is like a peasant
without a wife.

Without a husband is the same as without a
head; without a wife the same as without a
brain.
  (*Russian proverbs*)

6. Young girls threshing at a working bee in Mikhailovskoe village, Penza province, 1898. (Notice their holiday attire.) Photograph from NOVOSTI from SOVFOTO.

OTHER THAN birth and death, marriage constituted the most important event in the lives of Russian peasants.[1] It introduced young men and women to a world of responsibilities, social status, and respect within the peasant community that had been closed to them in their childhood and adolescence. The tiaglo, or married couple, was, after all, the primary labor unit within the commune. As such, it was entitled to a land allotment. Besides their economic function, a husband and wife also had the social obligations of producing children and acculturating them in the values and norms of society as a whole.

Despite the change and elevated status that marriage commonly conferred on young people, the meaning of marriage differed for men and women in a patriarchal society where functions were strictly delineated along gender lines. A young man derived his legitimacy as a full-fledged communal member from marriage. "Without a wife and family a peasant is not a peasant," reasoned a popular Russian peasant saying.[2] In the repartitional commune bachelors were not "peasants" precisely because they were not entitled to land allotments. A peasant in Elat'ma district, Tambov province, elaborated further on the disadvantages of bachelorhood: "What kind of life is it [to remain a bachelor]? You forever remain a landless peasant; no one will say a kind word to you; you will have no one to look after you in your old age, and when you die there will be no one to bury you!"[3] Thus marriage not only provided a man with land and an essential laborer to run the household, but children who would later repay their father for bringing them up by supporting him in his old age. And with full communal membership, a newly married man could take his rightful place among male elders in the home, at the local taverns, church, and community festivities. No longer did he have to sit mum, patiently listening to the men telling their stories of fantasy and experience. Now he had the opportunity to contribute his words of wisdom to the community treasury of oral culture. Eventually he might also be accorded political rights in the village assembly as head of his own household.

Marriage was an even more dramatic event for a young girl. The rewards that she received as wife and later as mother were tempered by the adjustments that she had to make in her spouse's household. With patrilocal res-

---

[1] The proverbial epigraphs underlining this assertion are quoted from V. N. Dobrovol'skii, comp., *Smolenskii etnograficheskii sbornik*, vol. 3 (St. Petersburg, 1894), p. 8; Illiustrov, *Sbornik rossiiskikh poslovits*, p. 140; Burtsev, *Narodnyi byt velikago severa*, 2:282; and Elnett, *Historic Origin*, p. 119.

[2] In Sarapul' district, Viatka province, the peasants referred to a bachelor as a *kholostezh*, which had a derogatory connotation of "loafer" or "good-for-nothing." See Tikhonov, "Materialy dlia izucheniia obychnago prava," in Kharuzin, *Sbornik svedenii dlia izucheniia byta*, 3:77.

[3] A. P. Zvonkov, "Sovremennye brak i svad'ba sredi krest'ian Tambovskoi gubernii Elatomskago uezda," in Kharuzin, *Sbornik svedenii dlia izucheniia byta*, 1:80.

idence the norm, marriage celebrations constituted a rite of passage during which a bride made the transition from the security of her natal family to the insecurity and uncertainty of her new husband's family. It is little wonder that as an intruder into the established rhythms of a tightly knit family household, a bride viewed her new life with trepidation. No longer could she count on the support of a loving father and mother. Instead she had to cultivate potentially hostile in-laws who might harass her verbally, physically, and sexually. Through labor, obedience, and, most important, the bearing and raising of children, she would slowly create bonds with them. These links were, nevertheless, fragile, as the untimely death of her husband could make her an unwanted guest in her in-laws' home.

As it did for a man, marriage also initiated a woman into the larger community. However, that community was more narrowly defined to include only married women, whose authority was confined to the domestic household. A bride's symbolic entry into this group involved her abandoning the maidenly single braid for the two braids of a married woman and donning a traditional headdress that completely covered her sexually enticing hair.[4] Visually undifferentiated from other married women, the young novice joined her new peers in gossip across the yards, laundry sessions at the rivers, and local festivities. The collective of married women helped her understand her subordinate position in life and showed her how to carve a niche for herself in the patriarchal system.

Thus marriage was not simply a personal union of two individuals, but a union of families and the initiation of a bride and groom into community membership. Accordingly, it was a tightly controlled family and community affair, beginning with the courtship stage and ending with the marriage's consummation. Elaborate rituals, emphasizing the social and economic responsibilities of marriage and the subordination of women, guided a couple through this complex rite of passage.

The economic underpinnings of marriage meant that the individual feelings of the bride and groom were of little consequence in the overall scheme of things. Indeed, a suitor and his bride-to-be were mere spectators in the events that sealed their fates for life. While greater freedom in choice of marriage partner in the decades following emancipation began to challenge the traditional practice of arranged marriages, the utilitarian criteria for selecting a spouse in a largely subsistence economy remained the same. Sobriety, diligence, and physical strength and well-being were far more important characteristics of a future workmate than looks and personality. After a selection had been made, the couple became passive observers in a

---

[4] For a discussion of the regional variations of headdresses among Slavic women in the Great Russian, Belorussian, and Ukrainian provinces, see D. K. Zelenin, "Zhenskie golovnye ubory vostochnykh (russkikh) slavian," *Slavia* 5 (1926–1927): 303–38, 535–56.

highly ritualized drama of negotiation, property transfer, and union of kin. A matchmaker initiated the betrothal discussions, the parents of the betrothed sealed the marriage contract and arranged the wedding festivities, and male and female peer groups performed rituals, often acting as intercessors for the bride and groom.

In the last decades of the nineteenth century economic changes and influence of urban ways also failed to disrupt the ultimate control of family and community over courtship and marriage. Economic necessity sometimes forced the suspension of some of the more elaborate traditional wedding rituals, but the meaning of courtship and marriage remained the same. Cash and factory-produced fabrics and garments increasingly became part of a bride's dowry. However, the new contents did not alter the traditional concept of a dowry as a woman's inalienable property. Lastly, urban cultural trappings such as the quadrille, *chastushka* (a spontaneously composed song of rhyming couplets), and the accordion made their way into courtship and wedding festivities without diminishing the tight controls of family and community.[5] As long as a household's productive functioning retained utmost importance in the maintenance of rural life, peasants adopted only those changes which did not threaten their traditions and, ultimately, their survival.

Family and community contraints were strongest in the area of morality. Russian peasants had developed a variety of shaming practices to punish delinquents and deter others from stepping outside the bounds of behavioral norms. Rituals highlighting moral standards were not outdated and "meaningless charades" performed "through force of habit."[6] Nor were they the preserve of the older generation. Their constant repetition in courtship and marriage festivities and their many connotations, especially with respect to a girl's virginity, set important guidelines for individual behavior, even if they were not totally determinant.[7] Transgressions of the moral code among youths did occur, but their occurrence was not testimony to the rejection of that code. Rather, "deviance helps a society to define the limits of acceptable behavior."[8]

This chapter concentrates on post-emancipation Russian peasant courtship practices and the criteria that peasants used in selecting prospective

[5] Matti Sarmela found the same adoption of urban elements occurring in rural Finland. See his *Reciprocity Systems of the Rural Society in the Finnish-Karelian Culture Area with Special Reference to Social Intercourse of the Youth* (Helsinki, 1969), pp. 232–38.

[6] Diana Leonard makes this perceptive point in her discussion of ritual in *Sex and Generation: A Study of Courtship and Weddings* (London, 1980), p. 2.

[7] Gail Kligman, "The Rites of Women: Oral Poetry, Ideology, and the Socialization of Peasant Women in Contemporary Romania," in *Women, State, and Party in Eastern Europe*, ed. Sharon L. Wolchik and Alfred G. Meyer (Durham, N.C., 1985), p. 343.

[8] Eve Levin, *Sex and Society in the World of the Orthodox Slavs, 900–1700* (Ithaca, N.Y., 1989), p. 15.

marriage partners. From an early age mothers emphasized the importance of domestic work for their daughters, teaching them the basic skills that would make them excellent housekeepers and agricultural laborers when they married. As young women and men approached marriageable age, they found themselves more and more under the scrutiny of the village community, in general, and males and females of their own age, in particular. A variety of labor and social settings provided them with opportunities to meet each other, to practice their work skills and examine those of others, and to initiate personal associations with members of the opposite sex. Adults often supervised or were spectators at these gatherings, providing behavioral guidelines and examining prospective mates for their children and other kin. Dances, folktales, and songs about love, responsibilities of marriage, sexual mores, and anxieties about the future were an integral part of the gatherings. In areas where bundling was practiced, supervision passed from the older to the younger generation, who generally upheld the moral code of the community as a whole, punishing deviants as well as pranksters who falsely questioned a young woman's reputation. Given men's domination of women, it is not surprising that Russian peasants maintained a double standard of behavior for men and women. Young women, far more than young men, were the targets of peer and community censure.

From approximately age eight or nine to sixteen or seventeen, Russian peasant girls were taught the responsibilities of a bride-to-be, wife, and mother. Mothers schooled their young apprentices in the arts of preparing flax and hemp, spinning, weaving, embroidery, cooking, baking bread, gardening, animal tending, and threshing, all the chores that would eventually become theirs in married life. At a fairly early age, daughters were also introduced to domestic industries. This might involve learning how to knit, make gloves or lace, or roll cigarettes, depending on the village's specialization and proximity to markets. As young girls matured, they used these skills to amass their dowries or trousseaux. It was not unusual for them to labor as nannies or agricultural workers for wages in money and kind during the peak growing and harvesting seasons, which began on 23 April (Egor'ev Den') and ended on 1 October (Pokrov, a holiday in honor of the Protection or Intercession of the Virgin).[9] In the fruit-growing areas, young girls were allowed to pick the family fruit and sell it at the nearest market; elsewhere they sold wood and produce from their own corner

[9] T. A. Bernshtam, "Devushka-nevesta i predbrachnaia obriadnost' v Pomor'e v XIX–nachale XX v.," in *Russkyi narodnyi svadebnyi obriad: Issledovaniia i materialy*, ed. K. V. Chistov and T. A. Bernshtam (Leningrad, 1978), pp. 49–51. Pokrov commemorates the day upon which Mary, according to legend, saved Constantinople from the Saracens by draping the city with her veil. Linda J. Ivanits, *Russian Folk Belief* (Armonk, N.Y., 1989), p. 23.

of the family's garden. It was also customary for them to weave, sew, and knit for cash or payment in kind, adding the proceeds or items to their dowries.[10]

During the idle winter months a young girl, in addition to the aid she gave her family in domestic industries, wove and embroidered numerous items for her trousseau. This work both served a practical purpose and provided a profile of the girl's character. The trousseau included clothing and linens for a bride and her husband, as well as towels, shirts, and ker-chiefs that a bride presented as wedding gifts to her new relatives and hon-ored guests. Equally important, a girl's "diligence, abilities, and tastes were judged by the number of articles prepared, the perfection of patterns wo-ven and embroidered, and the harmony of colors she used."[11] Young girls had to select colors and intricacies of embroidery patterns in accord with local styles. Bright red threads characterized the embroideries of the north. In the south brilliant colors of scarlet, blue, green, gold, and violet blended together in a tableau of exquisite beauty.

The stories that the embroidery patterns told also enhanced a young girl's reputation and introduced her to the worldview of Russian peasant women. Stylized designs of geometric and floral motifs, and depictions of birds, animals, goddesses, and men on horseback were passed on from one generation of women to another. Each girl could add her own signature to those designs by telling her personal story. Consequently no two patterns were ever exactly the same. Yet "the harmonious balance between man and woman" and men's reverence of women remained dominant embroidery themes. On the one hand, they reflected the living union of husband and wife and re-creation of life and, on the other, a reversal of the painful reality of female subordination in a misogynist patriarchal society.[12] The powerful image of the fertility goddess, at times personifying the tree of life, on ritual towels and head coverings reflected Russian peasant women's collec-tive definition of the importance of their sex to the perpetuation of their society. The goddess these women lovingly depicted was also the protector of family and community. Joanna Hubbs has gone so far as to argue that through their goddess worship women made a strong political statement denying "the hegemony of the masters and political rulers and declar[ing] the subordination of the social order to the feminine cosmic one."[13] Em-broidery provided women with an avenue of passive resistance to a male-

[10] Wages in kind might have included kerchiefs, shawls, embroidery thread, soap, material for a blouse or jumper (*sarafan*), and luxury items of tea and sugar. Efimenko, "Zhenshchina," in her *Izsledovaniia narodnoi zhizni*, 1:77; and Bernshtam, "Devushka-nevesta," p. 50.

[11] Nina T. Klimova, *Folk Embroidery of the USSR* (New York, 1981), pp. 10–13, 22.

[12] Netting, "Images and Ideas," pp. 63–64.

[13] Hubbs, *Mother Russia*, pp. 25–26.

dominated world that excluded them from village politics and decision making.

As young men and women approached the age of marriageability in their midteens, their world of learning expanded outside the peasant hut to include socialization with and labor among their peers. These activities were aimed at helping adolescents and their parents scrutinize and select future spouses within a reasonable period of time. Community pressure for early and universal marriage was considerable.

The disdain with which Russian peasants treated men and particularly women who for one reason or another did not wed carried very strong messages for youths. Peasants perceived the unmarried not only as exceptions to the rule, but as potential idlers and parasites, especially in the predominantly agricultural provinces of central Russia where nonagricultural pursuits were limited. A popular proverb noted, "A man who is not clever at twenty, not married at thirty, and not rich at forty, is good for nothing."[14] In a variety of pejorative names and proverbs Russian peasants blamed spinsters for their own circumstances, accusing them of failing to accept their social and economic responsibilities as wives and mothers. "Soured bride," "homely girl," "homebody," *vekovusha* (an age-old girl), and "one-braided one" (*odnokosaia*—a spinster had to wear the single braid of a maiden as opposed to the two worn by married women) were mild slurs compared to "privateers," "wolfish women," and "hypocrites."[15] Popular folk sayings were particularly derisive of unmarried women: "There is nothing worse than a priest's dog, a retired soldier, and an old maid." "An old maid is a family ulcer."[16] "The bee flies to a pretty flower, but even the devil would not look at an old woman." "An old maid and a torn sheepskin coat smell alike."[17] Only unmarried women who assumed a religious vocation, so-called *chernichki*, were accorded community respect.[18]

Low mean ages at first marriage and a very high incidence of marriage

[14] Ia. Kuznetsov, "Semeinoe i nasledstvennoe pravo v narodnykh poslovitsakh i pogovorkakh," *Zhurnal Ministerstva iustitsii* 16, no. 6 (June 1910), pt. 2, p. 211. Translated in Elnett, *Historic Origin*, p. 107.

[15] Titov, *Iuridicheskie obychai*, p. 31. A. Balov, S. Ia. Derunov, and Ia. Il'inskii, "Ocherki Poshekhon'ia," *Etnograficheskoe obozrenie* 10, bk. 39, no. 4 (1898): 88; and V. N. Bondarenko, "Ocherki Kirsanovskago uezda, Tambovsk. gub.," *Etnograficheskoe obozrenie* 2, bk. 7, no. 4 (1890): 3.

[16] N. A. Ivanitskii, "Materialy po etnografii Vologodskoi gub.," in Kharuzin, *Sbornik svedenii dlia izucheniia byta*, 2:54.

[17] Elnett, *Historic Origin*, pp. 107–8.

[18] Too poor to enter a convent, these women religious often lived together at the edge of a village and performed spiritual services for communal members. They washed, dressed, buried, and mourned the dead and sometimes even taught children to read. For more information, see Balov, Derunov, and Il'inskii, "Ocherki Poshekhon'ia," p. 88; Bondarenko, "Ocherki Kirsanovskago uezda," pp. 2–5; Gromyko, *Traditsionnye normy*, p. 103.

reflected community norms. In 1897 in the Russian populated areas of European Russia 20.4 was the mean age at first marriage for women.[19] Variation occurred among regions, depending upon custom and economic circumstances. In the 1880s the central industrial regions were marked by higher average ages at marriage than the central agricultural provinces because of greater urbanization and widespread migrant trades (see table 4.1). Urban dwellers out of necessity postponed marriages until they could accumulate sufficient capital to establish new households and support families. Provinces with the highest ages at marriage for males, including Iaroslavl', Moscow, Kursk (a black earth province), Tver, Kostroma, northern Orel (an intermediary province between the black and non–black earth provinces), and Vladimir, had well-developed male migrant trades. A majority of males in these regions waited until they were between 21 and 25 years of age before being wedded, and some did not marry until they were between 26 and 30. This contrasted sharply with the pattern in the purely agricultural provinces of Voronezh, Tambov, Tula, Kaluga, and Riazan, and in the mixed agricultural and domestic industrial economies of the Volga regions of Nizhnii Novgorod and Penza. There a significant percentage of men married before their twenty-first birthday. This suggests that in the non–black earth regions meager land resources and revenues

TABLE 4.1

Average Age at Marriage for the Orthodox Population of the Central Russian Provinces, 1882–1886

	Males	Females
Vladimir	24.0	21.8
Voronezh	22.7	19.0
Kaluga	22.7	19.3
Kostroma	24.3	22.0
Kursk	25.1	21.1
Moscow	25.8	22.7
Nizhnii Novgorod	22.9	19.7
Orel	24.2	20.1
Penza	22.2	19.4
Riazan	22.4	18.8
Tambov	22.2	19.0
Tver	24.5	21.6
Tula	22.7	18.7
Iaroslavl'	26.0	23.4

Source: Statistika Rossiiskoi Imperii, vol. 18 (St. Petersburg, 1891), p. 30.

[19] Ansley J. Coale, Barbara A. Anderson, and Erna Härm, Human Fertility in Russia since the Nineteenth Century (Princeton, 1979), p. 136.

from domestic trades were insufficient to support a new laboring unit. Young men had to leave the village in search of paid employment to expand the resources of their fathers' household economies. In some areas part of their wages was also set aside for the bride-price and, in some cases, the setting up of an independent household not too long after marriage.[20] Young women were often attracted to these migrant workers, especially the so-called *Pitershchiki* (laborers who found work in St. Petersburg),[21] because they were more likely to build homes away from their fathers'. A young bride would thus be mistress of her own home, free from the authoritarian rule of in-laws.

Early ages at first marriage for both men and women characterized the agricultural belt of the center and Volga regions. Here, resource accumulation as a prerequisite for matrimony was unnecessary. Equal partible inheritance, the apportionment of full communal land allotments to married men alone, the incorporation of new conjugal units into existing patriarchal extended family households, and supplementary incomes from domestic industries encouraged men and women to wed early. In Riazan, Kursk, and southern Orel provinces girls as young as twelve through fifteen were at times favored catches on the matrimonial market. Peasant petitions to ecclesiastical authorities for permission to marry female minors (under the age of sixteen) cited the need for an extra laborer or mistress of the home as justification.[22] As popular sayings advised: "The earlier the marriage, the more profit for the house." "If you rise early you will do more, if you marry young you will have help sooner."[23]

Even in areas of the central industrial provinces where the amount of communal land at a household's disposal depended upon the number of laboring couples, relatively early marriages were still encouraged, until land hunger drove more young men into migrant trades. Unmarried women in the central industrial provinces, on the other hand, were more likely to stay in the village than become migrant laborers. Accordingly, their marriage ages remained relatively low. The highest ages at marriage for women characterized those districts of Vladimir, Kostroma, Moscow, Tver, Nizhnii Novgorod, and Iaroslavl' provinces where domestic industry grew increasingly important as the returns on land allotments became in-

[20] Part of young men's wages went toward the bride-price even in a central agricultural province like Tambov. See Zvonkov, "Sovremennye brak i svad'ba," in Kharuzin, *Sbornik svedenii dlia izucheniia byta*, 1:104.

[21] Zhbankov, *Bab'ia storona*, p. 16; and Barbara Alpern Engel, "The Woman's Side: Male Out-Migration and the Family Economy in Kostroma Province," *Slavic Review* 45, no. 2 (Summer 1986): 264.

[22] Boris N. Mironov, "Traditsionnoe demograficheskoe povedenie krest'ian v XIX–nachale XX v.," in *Brachnost', rozhdaemost', smertnost' v Rossii i v SSSR: Sbornik statei*, ed. A. G. Vishnevskii (Moscow, 1977), p. 92.

[23] Elnett, *Historic Origin*, p. 107.

sufficient to meet a family's subsistence needs. Since daughters were important assets as laborers in household economies engaged in local trades, parents either discouraged early marriages or expanded the household's labor capacity by adopting a son-in-law.

In spite of the differences in ages at marriage between the industrial and agricultural regions of central Russia, both areas experienced a marked increase in average marriage age for men over the course of the nineteenth century. In mid-nineteenth century agricultural Riazan, for example, men wed fairly early at age 20.[24] By the 1880s (see table 4.1) that average had risen to 22.4. A similar pattern emerged in the village Borisoglebskoe, Poshekhon'e district, industrial Iaroslavl' province. There the number of males who wed before their twenty-second birthday declined from 51 percent in 1865 to 30 percent in 1885 (with temporary increases to 71 percent in 1867 and 55 percent in 1869).[25] The later ages at marriage for men may be explained by the 1874 military reform, requiring all able-bodied peasant males to serve between four and six years in the army. Young men began postponing marriage until after they had completed their military service. Thus, in 1874 only 38.4 percent of the new recruits from all across European Russia were married. By 1878 that percentage had dropped to 32.0.[26] The military reform thus artificially raised the average male marriage age.[27]

Even though Russian peasant men married later in the last quarter of the nineteenth century, the general marriage pattern of central Russian peasants remained non-European. The average marriage ages were well below those characterizing the preindustrial Western European pattern of late marriages for both women and men (25 years or more for women and 27 years for men).[28] Russian practice also diverged from the European in the near universality of marriage for both sexes. A very high proportion of women in preindustrial Western Europe did not wed: "Between two-fifths and three-fifths of the women of childbearing age 15–44" were single. Under 40 percent of women aged 20 through 24 were married; by age 50, 10

[24] Czap, "Marriage and the Peasant Joint Family," pp. 110–11.

[25] A. V. Balov, "Ocherki Poshekhon'ia," *Etnograficheskoe obozrenie* 9, bk. 35, no. 4 (1897): 59.

[26] Regional variation was still considerable, reflecting once again disparities between north and south. Among recruits from the agricultural provinces of Tambov and Penza, 65.5 percent and 65.4 percent were married. Rashin, *Naselenie Rossii*, p. 172.

[27] Mironov, "Traditsionnoe demograficheskoe povedenie," p. 92; and idem, "Russkaia sel'skaia obshchina posle reform 1860-kh gg. (Reformi sverkhu i sotsial'nie izmeneniia vnizu)" (Unpublished paper, 1983), p. 37. A translation of an abridged version of this paper appeared as "The Russian Peasant Commune after the Reforms of the 1860s," *Slavic Review* 44, no. 3 (Fall 1985): 438–67.

[28] J. Hajnal, "European Marriage Patterns in Perspective," in *Population in History: Essays in Historical Demography*, ed. D. V. Glass and D.E.C. Eversley (London, 1965), pp. 101–43.

percent or more remained unmarried.[29] In marked contrast, 65.1 percent of the post-emancipation Russian population over the age of fifteen was married.[30] According to the 1897 census well over 60 percent of central Russian peasant women in the age cohort of 20 to 29 were married.[31] The percentage of single women in the age group 40 to 59 was a relatively low 6.91 in Moscow and 7.11 in Kaluga provinces. Percentages of bachelors in this age cohort in Moscow and Kaluga provinces were even lower, at 3.17 and 4.48 respectively. In Penza province 94.5 percent of men and 90.2 percent of women between the ages of 30 and 40 were married; 1.9 and 4.6 percent of men and women in this age cohort were already widowed. Similar percentages were true of other central Russian regions.[32]

In encouraging early and universal marriage, Russian peasant communities provided marriageable men and women with a variety of courting opportunities closely tied to the agricultural calendar. Spring and fall were important seasons for youth gatherings, the spring featuring dances and promenades on holidays and Sundays, the fall work-intensive as well as purely social gatherings called *posidelki*. Some of these activities were reserved for young women alone, others for both women and men. Normally they were confined to the youth of one village, but on special occasions youths from several neighboring communities came together, broadening the pool of prospective suitors.

The most important formal village festivities for bringing together prospective marriage partners occurred in the spring and early summer in preparation for the busy postharvest wedding season. *Khorovody*, or round dances, began either on the first two days of Easter or on Krasnaia Gorka, the first Sunday after Easter, and usually ended with Petrov Den' (29 June).[33] They were held on all formal holidays and, in some areas, on Sundays as well, on the village street, in wooded glades close to the village, or in fields or meadows. In the event of inclement weather, dances were moved to a large barn or shed. The khorovody occurred either at midday for three or four hours or in the late afternoon until ten or eleven o'clock in the evening or sometimes until dawn.[34]

In some localities only girls participated in the round dances; in others

---

[29] E. A. Wrigley, *Population and History* (New York, 1976), p. 90; Coale, Anderson, and Härm, *Human Fertility*, pp. 136–38.

[30] Mironov, "Traditsionnoe demograficheskoe povedenie," pp. 89–91.

[31] Coale, Anderson, and Härm define the Eastern European marriage pattern in the following terms: "At 20–24 the proportion of women ever-married is more than 60 percent and fewer than 5 percent are still single at age 50." See their *Human Fertility*, p. 138.

[32] *Pervaia vseobshchaia perepis*, vol. 15, bk. 2, p. vii; 24:xxviii; 30:x.

[33] Krasnaia Gorka was reserved for matchmaking throughout the Great Russian area. S. V. Maksimov, *Nechistaia, nevedomaia i krestnaia sila* (St. Petersburg, 1903), p. 421; and Gromyko, *Traditsionnye normy*, pp. 168–69.

[34] Balov, "Ocherki Poshekhon'ia," p. 67; Gromyko, *Traditsionnye normy*, p. 170.

both boys and girls took part. Some khorovody for girls alone were occasions for presenting marriageable girls (*nevestki*) from one or several villages. Others, held in the flax or hemp fields, were part of a fertility rite providing sympathetic magic to help the crops grow. Sometimes dances for women alone occurred in areas of heavy seasonal male out-migration. For example, in the village Barmin, Egor'evsk district, Riazan province, all single men aged fifteen and upward were away from the village for much of the spring working as carpenters fifty to a hundred versts away. During their absence single women continued to assemble for dances. In other areas, including villages in Kozel'sk and Medynsk districts, Kaluga province, girls and recently married women began the khorovody. Later they were joined by eligible bachelors, at which point very young girls and married women departed.[35] The youths were left to sing, dance, and pair off under the watchful eye of community members.[36]

The mood of the khorovody and the themes of the songs that accompanied the dancing were based on the composition of the participants. Assemblages of girls were generally somber occasions, during which the participants commiserated about the lot that awaited girls in marriage. Many songs contrasted a maiden's freedom, her enviable position, and her mother and father's protection with the loss of freedom she would endure in a strange home with a husband and hostile in-laws. Images of a domineering husband who scolded and beat his wife were common.

Do not wait girls . . .
Dance now,
They will give you away in marriage in the fall,
They will not give you such freedom.
Your good-for-nothing husband will bring all his weight
down to bear on [you].
[He] will scoff at you.
. . . [He] will taunt,
[And] abuse me for everything.[37]

I lived at my father-in-law's,
I created three misfortunes.
Here is the first misfortune:
I cooked some *shchi* [cabbage soup]—and spilled it;
Here is the second misfortune:
I made *pirogi* [dumplings]—and burned them;
The third misfortune:

---

[35] Gromyko, *Traditsionnye normy*, pp. 172–75.
[36] Bernshtam, "Devushka-nevesta," p. 53.
[37] Quoted in Semenova-Tian-Shanskaia, *Zhizn' 'Ivana,'* p. 44.

I did not lie down to sleep with my husband.
[And] how my husband beat me,
He avidly beat me.
I had to take to my bed
From that beating;
I was in bed for three weeks.[38]

Another popular song suggested to the contrary that a husband was the only friend that a daughter-in-law could expect in her in-laws' home, as

Neither her father-in-law nor mother-in-law,
Neither her brother-in-law nor sister-in-law

loved her.[39]

The mood at the mixed khorovody was more jovial. Here songs sometimes overstepped the normal social barriers prohibiting open discussion of sexual matters.[40] They touched on the purely sexual aspect of love and first sexual encounters by juxtaposing images of girls' sowing and growing flax with boys' trampling it down.[41] In such fashion did communities sanction and guide young couples in preparation for the ideal of romantic love and intimate relations within their future marital unions.

Youth socialization continued into the summer and fall but took on an increasingly labor-oriented function. During the busy agricultural months marriageable men and women planted vegetables, carted wood, delivered manure to the fields, built new huts and clay ovens, and repaired roofs. They worked in groups for the benefit of the community at large or of individuals within the community who, because of dire economic circumstances, needed village aid. These activities also provided opportunities for youths to scrutinize the skills and diligence of prospective marriage partners. The formal fall posidelki or gatherings of youths beginning at the end of the August fast period and the inauguration of the wedding season continued to emphasize labor. The initial posidelki involved harvesting and pickling cabbage. This task was done on a rotational basis for households in the village that required the collective labor of village youths. Young women did all of the physical work, while the young men provided entertainment. At the end of the workday, the household for which the cabbage had been prepared treated the youths to dinner, after which they sang,

---

[38] Zelenin, "Iz byta i poezii krest'ian Novgorodskoi gubernii," *Zhivaia starina* 14, nos. 1–2 (1905): 17.

[39] Dobrovol'skii, *Smolenskii etnograficheskii sbornik*, 4:308.

[40] Vera St. Erlich, *Family in Transition: A Study of 300 Yugoslav Villages* (Princeton, 1966), p. 145.

[41] N. I. Kostomarov, "Velikorusskaia narodnaia pesennaia poeziia: Po vnov' izdannym materialam," in *Sobranie sochinenii N. I. Kostomarova: Istoricheskiia monografii i izsledovaniia*, 21 vols. (1903–1905; reprint, The Hague, 1967), bk. 3, 13:525.

played games, and danced until morning.[42] This set the pattern for later posidelki, some having a distinct labor component for marriageable young women and others specifically designed for socializing with members of the opposite sex.

The labor-intensive posidelki, or working bees, which were widespread in Western Europe, were extensions of women's labor groups that helped households with insufficient female labor to prepare flax and hemp for making thread.[43] Beginning in the evenings or during the days of early October working bees brought marriageable peasant girls together on a threshing floor or in a yard to brake, scutch, and comb the year's harvest of flax or hemp. That work completed, the girls met to spin flax and hemp, knit stockings, make lace or gloves, and weave cloth. Normally, they worked for themselves, adding the finished products to their dowry chests or selling them for cash.

Marriageable village girls were responsible for organizing the posidelki. They divided themselves up into groups of between five and fifteen, according to age or wealth. Each of the groups then looked for a villager's hut or bathhouse for its gatherings. Normally a group of girls rented a hut belonging to a small family or landless widow who welcomed the payment in kind and labor. The girls promised to heat the hut for the entire winter with their own wood, clean the hut for all major holidays, and present the woman of the house with a share of the flax or hemp they had worked, a kerchief, and some tea and sugar. Rent was forwarded collectively or, in cases where each girl took her turn in meeting the obligations, by rotation.[44]

At least one older married woman, often the owner of the rented hut, supervised a posidelka. By interpreting the songs that the girls sang and telling the girls' fortunes, she ensured community control over such meetings.[45] She also told tales that underlined the maidens' future responsibili-

[42] For more information about the collective labor parties, see Gromyko, *Traditsionnye normy*, pp. 39–57.

[43] Gromyko, *Traditsionnye normy*, pp. 53, 57. For a discussion of veillées in Western Europe, see Weber, *Peasants into Frenchmen*, pp. 413–18; Emile Violet, *Les Veillées en commun et les réunions d'hiver* (Mâcon, 1942); Sarmela, *Reciprocity Systems*; Edward Shorter, *The Making of the Modern Family* (New York, 1975), pp. 124ff; idem, "The 'Veillée' and the Great Transformation," in *The Wolf and the Lamb: Popular Culture in France from the Old Regime to the Twentieth Century*, ed. Jacques Beauroy et al. (Saratoga, Calif., 1976).

[44] Balov, "Ocherki Poshekhon'ia," pp. 67–68; Dobrotvorskii, "Krest'ianskie iuridicheskie obychai" (November 1891): 355–57; Father Raikovskii's 1851 account of working bees in Semenov county, Nizhnii Novgorod, cited in D. K. Zelenin, *Opisanie rukopisei uchenago arkhiva Imperatorskago russkago geograficheskago obshchestva*, 3 vols. (Petrograd, 1914–1916), 2:825; Bernshtam, "Devushka-nevesta," pp. 57–58; and Josephine Calina, *Scenes of Russian Life* (London, 1918), pp. 139–40.

[45] Ibid.

ties as wife, daughter-in-law, and mother, complementing the education
the girls had received from their mothers. At one and the same time she
welcomed the young women in advance to the fold of wedded women.

Whether or not young men socialized with young women at the labor
posidelki depended on local custom. In Nizhnii Novgorod district, for example, prospective suitors attended the working bees after the marriageable girls had processed the hemp and flax. Together with the girls they
made fishing nets. Boys in Vladimir province also arrived at the working
bees later in the evenings, bringing food and drink with them.[46] Generally,
however, visiting with the opposite sex was reserved for the social posidelki, when girls put aside their handiwork. Those gatherings were held
only in the evenings, usually on holidays and weekends, in the same huts
rented for the working bees. The boys and girls of the village and, at times,
of the surrounding hamlets partied from six or seven o'clock in the evening
until the early hours of the morning.[47] The girls provided food and refresh-
ments, the boys entertainment. By the end of the nineteenth century the
urban accordion became an indispensable feature of these evening socials.

Youth socialization at the khorovody and posidelki was not without its
formal rules and regulations. As gatherings specifically intended to provide
marriageable youths with opportunities to pair off and become better acquainted with one another before formal betrothal negotiations began,
they were carefully regulated by family and community. Community
norms and values as well as parental guidance limited the selection of a
partner or prospective spouse at the mixed khorovody. Before and during
the courting seasons parents made discreet inquiries, often through matchmakers, about the families, kin groups, wealth, and capacity for labor of
marriage prospects, especially those from surrounding villages. Since a
male suitor's parents ultimately initiated formal betrothal proposals, the
male voice dominates the record of the oral culture, outlining the proper
characteristics of a future wife.

In deciding upon a suitable bride for their son, parents first had to ensure
that kinship taboos were enforced. "Choose a cow by its horn, a maiden
by her kin," a popular saying enjoined.[48] In Elat'ma district, Tambov province, for example, it was only permissible to marry a relative beginning
with the fourth degree. If a father had to choose between two girls for his
son's bride, one of whom was distantly related and the other not, he generally preferred the former. The time-honored saying "Better the devil you

[46] Marakin, "Kustarnye promysly nizhegorodskoi gubernii," p. 71; and Dobrotvorskii,
"Krestian'skie iuridicheskie obychai," pp. 355–57.

[47] Balov, "Ocherki Poshekhon'ia," p. 71.

[48] P. S. Efimenko, comp., *Materialy po etnografii russkago naseleniia Arkhangel'skoi gubernii,*
Izvestiia Imperatorskago obshchestva liubitelei estestvoznaniia, antropologii i etnografii 30,
nos. 1–3 (1878): 244.

know than the one you don't know" may have prompted his choice.[49] The relatively limited pool of girls whose families were not related to everyone else in the small villages of the central industrial regions prompted searching for a bride in a neighboring village.[50] This explains why a number of popular sayings cautioned against marrying a neighbor's daughter: "Do not buy a horse or marry a daughter of your neighbor: both will run away." "Get a wife from afar, buy a cow near." "Even an owl, but from a different village." "A girl is like a willow; she'll take root wherever she is planted."[51] A girl too close to her parents' home was also undesirable because she would be more likely to run there whenever she faced problems in her new life as wife and daughter-in-law.

In addition to kinship considerations, Russian peasants also selected brides on the basis of their personal attributes. They prized a woman's strength and diligence in work above physical beauty. Many sayings cautioned against the seductive attraction of a woman's looks: "Choose a wife not with your eyes, but with your ears." "Do not look for beauty, look for goodness."[52] "Choose a bride not at a round dance but in the garden." "Do not praise a wife's body, but praise her work."[53] "Beauty is good only for lovers." "Choose between a wife who will pull the wagon and one who will ornament your yard."[54] Russian peasants also highly prized a maiden's virginity. A male suitor's family put a premium on a prospective bride's reproductive capacity and purity of bloodline. By producing male heirs a woman perpetuated "the family and its honor."[55] Young men in Poshekhon'e district, industrial Iaroslavl' province, went so far as to test their girl-friends' sexual purity by requesting them to cast rye kernels in a nearby river. They certified the young women as virgins if the grain remained afloat. One may assume that boys cast aside girls whose rye kernels sank.[56]

[49] Zvonkov, "Sovremennye brak i svad'ba," in Kharuzin, *Sbornik svedenii dlia izucheniia byta*, 1:90–91.

[50] A physician in the late nineteenth century remarked that in the smallest villages everyone was related to everyone else. Sometimes all villagers bore the same family name. Cited in Laura Engelstein, "Morality and the Wooden Spoon: Russian Doctors View Syphilis, Social Class, and Sexual Behavior, 1890–1905," *Representations* 14 (Spring 1986): 178. Moshe Lewin suggests that the marriage market extended to within a 6.2–mile radius of the village. "Data from the turn of the century in European Russia, Moscow guberniia, show the radius of matrimonial relations of no more than 10 km. and 80 percent of the new families were created inside this confine (years 1861–1901)." See his "The Obshchina and the Village" (Paper presented at a Conference on the Peasant Commune and Communal Forms in Russia, School of Slavonic and East European Studies, University of London, July 1986), p. 21.

[51] Elnett, *Historic Origin*, p. 105.

[52] Kuznetsov, "Semeinoe i nasledstvennoe pravo," pp. 233–35.

[53] Illiustrov, *Sbornik rossiiskikh poslovits*, p. 118.

[54] Elnett, *Historic Origin*, p. 105.

[55] Kligman's observations about the beliefs of the Romanian peasants apply to those of the Russian. See her "The Rites of Women," p. 329.

[56] Balov, "Ocherki Poshekhon'ia," p. 71.

The bride's family used similar criteria, with a few modifications, to judge the character of a prospective suitor. Responsibility and diligence were highly valued qualities of a husband. "A handsome husband," Russian peasants warned, "brings sin."[57] Delinquent and irresponsible young men were to be scrupulously avoided since they had clearly lost all fear of God and of their parents.[58] Nor could they be relied upon as responsible, hardworking members of the community. Parents also placed great stock in a suitor's social status, wishing their daughters to marry into more prosperous families. The following courtship song exemplifies the norm whereby girls were to refuse advances from potential suitors of a lower social station:

> My love is ill, ill,
> Extremely unhealthy.
> They say that he caught a chill
> At the evening dance.
> At the posidelka dance
> The fellow embraced a girl.
> The girl became embarrassed,
> [And] began to cry and sob.
> The young fellow became wretched,
> He began to calm the girl down:
> "Don't cry, girl, don't cry, my beauty,
> I am a bachelor, not a married man:
> When I decide to marry
> I will ask for your hand."
> "You are poor, I am rich—
> I cannot be your girl."
> "You are rich, but I am poor,
> I am handsome compared to you."[59]

The amount of land, labor, cattle, grain, and cash a household had at its disposal determined its economic standing in the village. With the balance between subsistence and utter destitution so precarious, it was only natural for peasants to maintain social differentiations when looking for prospective spouses.

In addition to physical strength, personal attributes, and economic standing, parents also considered prospective spouses' ages. The community as a whole generally expected a husband and wife to be close in age. Peasants advised their children that "to live with an old one is to spoil your life; to live with too young a one is to suffer; to live with your equal is to

[57] Elnett, *Historic Origin*, p. 105.

[58] Zvonkov, "Sovremennye brak i svad'ba," in Kharuzin, *Sbornik svedenii dlia izucheniia byta*, 1:80.

[59] Burtsev, *Narodnyi byt velikago severa*, 3:302.

enjoy life."[60] They particularly frowned upon young men marrying significantly older women. According to popular sayings: "When a young man marries an old woman, it is the same as when a young horse is hitched to an old wagon: he will soon break the wagon." "Here's a lesson for you, grandma; don't marry your grandson."[61] This disdain for older women may be explained by the fact that these women were normally widows with claims to a share of their first husbands' property. Their marriages to young men threatened the patriarchal power structure of peasant society since they were more likely to reverse the traditional patterns of virilocal residence and subordination of wife to husband. Once again, peasant wisdom warned, "To take an old one is to have trouble too often." For a young girl to marry an old man, on the other hand, was perfectly acceptable if the alternative was for her to remain a spinster: "Better an old man than to remain an old maid."[62]

While families played a significant role in selecting spouses for their children, changes in the post-emancipation period with the abolition of serfdom suggest that ideally love, and presumably free choice, entered into the picture as well. Emancipation facilitated greater freedom of choice in marriage among former serfs. Previously serfowners' and bailiffs' dictatorial powers circumscribed peasant choice. Serfowners were interested in the creation of new tiagla or labor units as additional sources of income and consequently pressured peasants to marry early. If families had not married off their children by the appropriate age, forced marriages sometimes resulted. Stories of landowners' compelling women to wed young boys of eleven or twelve are familiar enough.[63] Arranged marriages often meant that the betrothed met one another only at the engagement ceremonies. Once emancipation abolished serfowner interference, the emphasis on courtship institutions accorded a suitor or a bride-to-be some choice in selecting a spouse.

Courtship songs such as the following challenged traditional emphases on a family's reputation and wealth in deciding upon a suitable mate for life:

[60] Elnett, *Historic Origin*, p. 107.

[61] Kuznetsov, "Semeinoe i nasledstvennoe pravo," pp. 212–13.

[62] Elnett, *Historic Origin*, p. 107. Data concerning the ages of 433 married couples in various villages of Voronezh province at the end of the nineteenth century suggest that the desideratum of closeness in age was often achieved. Of the sample, 26.56 percent of wives were exactly the same age as their husbands, 69.28 percent were younger, and only 4.16 percent were older than their husbands. An overwhelming majority (81 percent) of the younger wives were within one to five years of their husbands' ages. Of the older wives, over 83 percent were senior to their husbands by only one to two years. Based on Shcherbina, *Krest'ianskie biudzhety*. My calculations.

[63] For an account of pressures that landlords exercised on their serfs to promote early ages at marriage, see Semevskii, *Krest'iane v tsarstvovanie Imperatritsy Ekateriny II*, 1:308–14.

Love me girl,
Love me beauty,
Not for my kin, not for my ancestry,
Not for gold, not for silver,
Not for a daring youth,
[But] solely for a tender love.[64]

Still others noted conflicts between parents and their children when children were guided by notions of romantic love rather than utilitarian considerations. A chastushka from a late nineteenth-century Novgorod village underscored that conflict well:

Things were very difficult for me last night.
When my mother beat me;
She beat me and told me,
To forget my sweetheart.
However you beat me, mother,
I will not listen to you
Neither to you nor to father—
I will love my young man![65]

Even with greater freedom of choice in marriage partner in the post-emancipation period and the existence of some conflict between parents and children, romantic love remained largely an ideal. Generally a bachelor or maiden's criteria for selecting a spouse did not vary from those of their parents. The fragility of peasant household economies and the need to supplement meager agricultural incomes with domestic industries or migrant trades inclined a suitor to choose his bride for her physical strength to bear many children and do the heavy labors in and around the home. Likewise, a maiden observed her prospective suitor's character, considering sobriety and conscientiousness as prerequisites for a respectable husband. The social and economic status of the respective families within the community constituted another important factor in the selection of a mate. Parental approval of a prospective spouse as a precondition for matrimony in the post-1860 period further limited youth rebelliousness. A chastushka of the late nineteenth century in which a girl lamented,

I will not dance any more,
Buy me a black coffin
And write on the lid:
Died of love,

---

[64] Burtsev, *Narodnyi byt velikago severa*, 3:312.
[65] D. K. Zelenin, "Sbornik chastushek Novgorodskoi gub. (Po materialam iz bumag V. A. Voskresenskago)," *Etnograficheskoe obozrenie* 17, bks. 65–66, nos. 2–3 (1905): 190.

implied parental retention of control.[66] Few youths were willing to challenge their parents outright and risk losing their family's favor. Parental blessing of a marriage, symbolized in numerous rituals, was an integral part of wedding festivities. Without that blessing, a couple was forced to forgo elaborate wedding celebrations involving community participation and faced ostracism from both family and community.

To ensure the proper selection of mates, parents and community controlled courtship activities in a variety of ways. Mention has already been made of elders' observing the khorovod activities and at least one married woman's supervision of the labor-intensive posidelki. Adults were also often present at the purely social posidelki, overseeing not only the pairing off of couples but relations between the sexes. The high value that peasants placed upon a maiden's virginity reinforced community and family efforts to regulate the ways in which marriageable youths interacted with one another. While community values could not be entirely determinant, they effectively constrained individual behavior. In areas of both the industrial and more backward agricultural provinces of central Russia parents who supervised the posidelki allowed courting couples a degree of restrained intimacy. For example, in Poshekhon'e district in Iaroslavl' province, Soligalich and Chukhloma districts of Kostroma province, all in the central industrial belt, older women and men customarily frequented the evening socials as spectators. They sat at the back of the huts under the berths while the young folk sang songs and played games, including kissing games. It was not unusual for girls to sit in boys' laps.[67] Kissing games were also permitted in Skopin district, Riazan province; Medynsk district, Kaluga province; and Maloarkhangel'sk district, Orel province.[68] In Kirsanov district in the central agricultural province of Tambov, it was taboo for young people to caress one another in public at the khorovody or round dances, but permissible for them to do so at the posidelki, specifically designed for greater intimacy.[69] Participants and spectators ensured that everyone was paired off into couples, considering it dishonorable for a girl not to have her own boyfriend.[70]

In some areas, relationships between boys and their girlfriends were more intimate, as couples were permitted to become acquainted in private. In the northern provinces of Novgorod and Pskov, for example, an eyewitness reported that when the socializing at the posidelki came to an end

[66] V. I. Stepanov, "Derevenskiia posidelki i sovremennyia narodnyia pesni-chastushki," *Etnograficheskoe obozrenie* 15, bk. 59, no. 4 (1903): 95.

[67] Balov, "Ocherki Poshekhon'ia," p. 72; and Zhbankov, *Bab'ia storona*, p. 76.

[68] Gromyko, *Traditsionnye normy*, pp. 236–37.

[69] Bondarenko, "Ocherki Kirsanovskago uezda," bk. 6, no. 3, p. 79.

[70] Balov, "Ocherki Poshekhon'ia," p. 68; and Smirnov, "Ocherki semeinykh otnoshenii," *Iuridicheskii vestnik* 9, nos. 1-2 (January–February 1877): 58.

the "fellows abducted their girlfriends." This is presumably a reference to bundling. An account of courtship practices in the province of Perm makes clearer nocturnal intimacy between courting couples. There an outside observer noted that during the warm summer months young marriageable girls were allowed to sleep in unheated granaries or small huts, separate from the family residence. The physical separation of these girls from the collective family room, a combined dining- and bedroom, confirms that girls and their boyfriends were encouraged to court one another in private.[71] A chastushka from Borovichi district of Novgorod province was teasing and suggestive:

> My dear don't be naughty,
> Don't kiss me in front of people!
> Kiss me in private,
> So that it would be pleasant for me.[72]

Bundling was not unique to Russian peasants. It was common among preindustrial Welsh, Dutch, German, and Scandinavian peasants, as well as courting couples in eighteenth-century New England and the American middle colonies. In all of these areas parents had given their approval to this opportunity for limited physical intimacy between courting couples. Couples could spend the night together as long as they observed certain restrictions. In colonial America parents expected them to be fully clothed and in some cases to have a " 'bundling board' between them." Among Scandinavian couples strict regulations governed "what clothing needed to be left on, what body parts might touch, and so on."[73] Russian peasants had similar rules, which again varied from district to district. In Cherepovets district, Novgorod province; Melenki district, Vladimir province; and Egor'evsk district, Riazan province, lads were allowed to go as far as to fondle maidens' breasts and in Melenki to clutch at their genitals.[74] In other

---

[71] Smirnov, "Ocherki semeinykh otnoshenii," pp. 58–59.

[72] Zelenin, "Sbornik chastushek," p. 182.

[73] John D'Emilio and Estelle B. Freedman, *Intimate Matters: A History of Sexuality in America* (New York, 1988), p. 22; and Ellen Ross and Rayna Rapp, "Sex and Society: A Research Note from Social History and Anthropology," in *Powers of Desire: The Politics of Sexuality*, ed. Ann Snitow, Christine Stansell, and Sharon Thompson (New York, 1983), p. 59. For further information about Scandinavian bundling practices, see also Orvar Löfgren, "Family and Household among Scandinavian Peasants," *Ethnologia Scandinavica* 4 (1974): 1–52; and Shorter, *The Making of the Modern Family*, pp. 102–5. Bundling in which fondling stopped short of sexual intercourse was also reported among seventeenth- and eighteenth-century French peasants. See Martine Segalen, *Historical Anthropology of the Family*, trans. J. C. Whitehouse and Sarah Matthews (Cambridge, 1986), p. 129.

[74] Barbara Alpern Engel, "Peasant Morality and Pre-Marital Relations in Late 19th Century Russia," *Journal of Social History* 23, no. 4 (Summer 1990): 700.

words, peasants there considered it permissible for young men to let off pubescent steam.[75] In all areas of preindustrial Europe, America, and Russia both youths and parents shared the expectation that such caressing and fondling would not lead to sexual intercourse.

Any impropriety among bundling couples quickly became the common knowledge of tightly knit rural communities. In Rostov district, Iaroslavl' province, males were accompanied by their peers to their girlfriends' homes where they spent the night. Presumably they were required to report back to their circle of male friends. At other times groups of girl-friends and boyfriends engaged in bundling, keeping a watchful eye on the activities of others.[76] If couples overstepped the bounds of acceptable behavior, the young woman found herself subjected to public humiliation and the young man found himself obliged to marry his dishonored girl-friend.

Sexual taboos were inextricably tied to community mechanisms of control over morality, as community direction of premarital relations went far beyond providing a social framework for courtship. Russian peasants jealously monitored the behavior of their fellow villagers to uphold community respectability and honor. Delinquents drew the community censure of ritual shaming or charivaris upon themselves and their households.[77] Public humiliation was designed not only to punish delinquents but to deter others from breaking the moral code.

Some incidents of ritual shaming involved the entire community. An 1870 example from Semenov district, Nizhnii Novgorod province, demonstrates an attempt by family and community to discourage rebellion among the younger generation. In this case, the crime was not of a sexual nature. Instead, the public shaming was to prevent the marriage of a couple who had not sought parental approval and who were not of the same social standing. The richly detailed eyewitness account is worth presenting in full. A Semenov priest explained that around midnight one evening he was passing by a village when he heard a great racket:

Passing the crossroads of the village I saw a crowd of peasants who had gathered near a dilapidated and humbly tilting entrance to a hut: some of them shouted

---

[75] This is a point that I make in my article "Temptress or Virgin?" p. 233.

[76] Titov, *Iuridicheskie obychai*, p. 26.

[77] There is a well-developed literature on the charivari in Western European societies. See, for example, André Burguière, "The Charivari and Religious Repression in France during the Ancien Régime, in *Family and Sexuality in French History*, ed. Robert Wheaton and Tamara K. Hareven (Philadelphia, 1980), pp. 84–110; Natalie Zemon Davis, "The Reasons of Misrule," in *Society and Culture in Early Modern France* (Stanford, 1975), pp. 97–123; Jacques Le Goff and Jean-Claude Schmitt, eds., *Le Charivari* (Paris, 1981); and Edward P. Thompson, "Rough Music: le charivari anglais," *Annales: Economies, Sociétés, Civilisations* (March–April 1972): 285–312.

with rage and banged on the windows; others banged the gates, doing every type of mischief possible; and still others crawled along the roof of the farmstead buildings, trying to get inside the hut.

After making some inquiries, the priest learned that a father and his neighbors were shaming a poor villager who had had the audacity to ask a girl to marry him without first seeking her father's permission. The father explained that his daughter had willfully accepted the proposal of Vas'ka Gribanov, a poor peasant "with neither house nor home." "His whole family is worthless!" exclaimed the father. "At a social gathering he seduced my Dun'ka with his cunning and forcibly took her ring off her hand, and pulled a ribbon out of her hair [as a pledge of their engagement]." The father further explained that although his daughter had already dishonored herself and her family, he was trying to save face by preventing her from going through with the marriage; hence the community charivari. Public shaming of this order had the intended effect, according to the priest, of deterring a number of young women in Semenov district from marrying against community-reinforced parental wishes.[78]

Public humiliation of individuals who broke the rules of moral conduct was common in the Russian countryside. In the case of premarital sex, censure fell squarely on the shoulders of young girls. Russian peasants, like other patriarchal societies, held double standards. They held young women responsible for either enticing their suitors into having sexual intercourse with them or acquiescing in young men's advances because of their moral weakness. As the Russian populist Praskovia Ivanovskaia noted, in the summer of 1876, of Ukrainian migrant agricultural workers in Tavrida province: "But should a girl get pregnant, it was generally she alone who was censured by those around her, cruelly and categorically, for her weakness and inability to protect herself. The girl bore all the consequences of the couple's mutual sin."[79] A young girl in a Russian chastushka expressed the community's assumption that the burden of guilt for sexual impropriety was hers alone:

[78] The priest surmised that the real reason for the father's discontent may have been his reluctance to allow his daughter to marry anyone in the face of his need for her valuable labor. Cottage industry made all family workers, male and female, assets to household economies. Dun'ia's labors were particularly important in her father's household because his other children were still minor. A. Kordatov, "Samokrutka," *Nizhegorodskii sbornik* 3 (1870): 141–47.

[79] Translated in Barbara Alpern Engel and Clifford N. Rosenthal, eds. and trans., *Five Sisters: Women against the Tsar* (New York, 1975), pp. 108–11. For information about courtship practices among nineteenth-century Ukrainian peasants in the Russian Empire, see Oleksa Ripets'kyi, "Parubochi i divochi zvychai v seli Andriiashivtsi, Lokhits'koho povitu na Poltavshchyni," *Materialy do ukrains'koi etnol'ohii* 18 (1918): 155–69; Khvedir Vovk, *Studii z ukrains'koi etnohrafii ta antropolohii* (Prague, [1926]); and Worobec, "Temptress or Virgin?" pp. 233–38.

I was sitting in the shack,
People said that I was with Jack;
I thought of life and all I missed,
People said we sat and kissed;
I leaned against the window pane,
People said with Jack I'd lain.[80]

Public shaming of disreputable girls took various forms. In the pre-emancipation period elderly village women punished a girl whose sexual liaison with a man had been discovered by shearing her braid or plaiting her hair into the two braids worn only by married women and covering it with a kerchief. They expected her to continue dressing her hair in this fashion as public demonstration of her moral depravity.[81] In Orel district, Orel province, a customary shaming practice involved cutting a disreputable girl's maidenly braid, tarring her shirt, and parading her, naked to the waist, about the village.[82] In the latter half of the nineteenth century such harsh public shaming appears to have died out; the parading practice came to be reserved for the greater transgressions of adultery and petty theft.[83] However, tarring the gates and breaking the windows of a home that sheltered a girl whose purity was in question were common practices.

Charges of impurity and sexual promiscuity against an unmarried woman were extremely serious. A young girl might find herself not only ostracized from the social gatherings of her peers, but shunned as a marriage partner. In the northern village of Maripchelki in Velikie-Luki district, Pskov province, where bundling was permitted, suitors shunned unwed mothers as marriage partners.[84] In several areas of central industrial Moscow province young men also purposely avoided as prospective wives young women who had sullied reputations.[85] Further south, in Elat'ma district in agricultural Tambov province, a girl continuously in and out of love fell victim to her own capriciousness. She became the object of scorn among her friends and the entire community. If she went so far as to indulge in sexual intercourse, all men, including widowers, refused to con-

[80] Translated in Alex E. Alexander, *Russian Folklore: An Anthology in English Translation* (Belmont, Mass., 1975), p. 394.

[81] St. fon-Nos, "Pokrytka," *Kievskaia starina* 1, no. 2 (February 1882): 427–29.

[82] Tenishev, *Pravosudie*, pp. 46–47; E. Vsevolozhskii, "Ocherki krest'ianskago byta Samarskago uezda," *Etnograficheskoe obozrenie* 7, bk. 24, no. 1 (1895): 6; and I. N. Shmakov, "Svadebnye obychai i prichitaniia v seleniiakh Terskogo berega Belogo moria," *Etnograficheskoe obozrenie* 15, bk. 59, no. 4 (1903): 56.

[83] E. I. Iakushkin, *Obychnoe pravo: Materialy dlia bibliografii obychnago prava*, 3 vols. (Moscow, 1896–1910), 2:167; Titov, *Iuridicheskie obychai*, p. 102; and Semenova-Tian-Shanskaia, *Zhizn' Ivana,'* p. 47.

[84] M. Uspenskii, "Maripchel'skaia krest'ianskaia svad'ba. (Bytovoi ocherk)," *Zhivaia starina* 8, no. 1 (1898): 81.

[85] Smirnov, "Ocherki semeinykh otnoshenii" (May–June 1877), nos. 5–6, p. 93.

sider her a possible marriage partner.[86] In the village Meshkovo, Orel province, young men admitting to having questioned a young woman's reputation without any basis noted the likelihood that she would have remained unmarried if she had been guilty. "Forgive us, for God's sake," they beseeched their victim, "you are not guilty, but we laughed at you and thought that you would remain single."[87]

This scorn of premarital pregnancies was not, however, universal. For example, in Vologda province, where average ages at marriage were relatively high (26.8 and 23.7 for men and women), peasants did not censure a girl who had a son out of wedlock. In fact she had a greater chance for an early marriage since she had demonstrated her fecundity: "It is not a vice for a maiden to have a son, but it is a vice if a maiden has three daughters."[88]

Understandably, given the general consequences of ostracism and possibly spinsterhood for engaging in premarital sex, young girls were careful to preserve their reputations, a fact reflected in the low incidence of illegitimate births. In all of European Russia "the contribution of the nonmarried to overall fertility was . . . only 1.9 percent in the rural population." In central Russia, the highest rates were in the industrial provinces, with Moscow at 4.0 percent taking the lead, and the lowest rates (under 1.0 percent) in the agricultural belt (see table 4.2).[89] These figures are comparable to illegitimacy rates recorded in other preindustrial societies. In England and Europe before the eighteenth century illegitimate children accounted for between 1.0 and 2.0 percent of all births, while in colonial America before 1750 the percentages ranged between 1.0 and 3.0 percent.[90]

---

[86] Zvonkov, "Sovremennye brak i svad'ba," in Kharuzin, *Sbornik svedenii dlia izucheniia byta*, 1:67–68. Widowers considered girls who had lost their virginity to be bad risks as mothers and housekeepers. Gromyko, *Traditsionnye normy*, p. 232.

[87] Gromyko, *Traditsionnye normy*, p. 98.

[88] *Statistika Rossiiskoi Imperii*, 90 vols. (St. Petersburg, 1887–1914), 18:30; and Ivanitskii, "Materialy po etnografii Vologodskoi gub.," in Kharuzin, *Sbornik svedenii dlia izucheniia byta*, 2:63. A correlation between high ages of marriage and more tolerant moral norms did not always exist. In some other areas, north of central Russia, sexual intimacy in courtship was strictly controlled. There was some interregional variation, associated with the sway of Orthodox or of Old Believers in one or another district. In the Pomor'e region, for example, kissing games at the posidelki were acceptable in the villages close to Onega. On the other hand, in Kemo and Vygostrovo of the same region girls conducted themselves in a formal, ceremonial fashion, careful not even to raise their heads while they danced. There, as in Shenkura district of Archangel province, kissing at the posidelki automatically tarnished a girl's reputation. Bernshtam, "Devushka-nevesta," p. 58; and Smirnov, "Ocherki semeinykh otnoshenii" (March–April 1877), p. 125.

[89] Coale, Anderson, and Härm, *Human Fertility*, pp. 251–53.

[90] Edward Shorter, "Illegitimacy, Sexual Revolution, and Social Change in Modern Europe," in *Marriage and Fertility: Studies in Interdisciplinary History*, ed. Robert I. Rotberg and

TABLE 4.2
Contribution of the Nonmarried to Overall Rural Fertility in Percentages for Selected Provinces of European Russia, 1897

Pskov	4.8
Perm	4.7
Moscow	4.0
Novgorod	2.9
Iaroslavl'	2.8
Kaluga	2.6
Nizhnii Novgorod	2.3
Kostroma	2.3
Vologda	1.7
Tver	1.5
Vladimir	1.5
Orel	0.8
Tambov	0.7
Tula	0.7
Kursk	0.6
Riazan	0.5
Voronezh	0.5

Source: Based on table C.1 in Ansley J. Coale, Barbara Anderson, and Erna Härm, *Human Fertility in Russia since the Nineteenth Century* (Princeton, 1979), pp. 252–53.

Several factors may help explain the low illegitimacy rates among post-emancipation Russian peasants. The public humiliation of women suspected of disreputable behavior certainly had its effect in psychologically terrorizing young women, making them very reluctant to transgress the norm of premarital chastity. The charivaris, directed mainly at women, however, could not regulate the behavior of young men who pressured girlfriends for sexual favors. Public shaming was not totally determinant of behavior. Other reasons must be adduced to explain low illegitimacy. While infanticide may have contributed to the underreporting of illegitimate births, two other practices suggest that illegitimacy rates were minimal. First, early ages at marriage for women helped to depress the incidence of illegitimate births. The eminent anthropologist Jack Goody has pointed out that "when women marry young, the code of honor can be more easily sustained, the breaches being both less frequent and more serious."[91] Second, while Russian peasants frowned on premarital sex and

Theodore K. Rabb (Princeton, 1980), p. 92; Cissie Fairchilds, "Female Sexual Attitudes and the Rise of Illegitimacy: A Case Study," in Rotberg and Rabb, *Marriage and Fertility*, p. 163; and D'Emilio and Freedman, *Intimate Matters*, p. 33.

[91] Goody found this to be a general pattern in his examination of various European societies. See his *Development of the Family and Marriage in Europe* (Cambridge, 1983), p. 212.

treated pregnant unmarried women with disdain, they also held young men responsible for marrying their pregnant girlfriends if they had previously made promises of marriage. Normally, young women agreed to engage in sexual intercourse when such promises, symbolized by the exchange of gifts, had been made. The girl wove a belt or embroidered a towel for her boyfriend; the young man gave her a kerchief or ring or, more often, carved a *prialka* (spinning distaff) for her.[92] In Rostov district, Iaroslavl' province, if a young man had sexual intercourse with a girl on the pretext that he was going to marry her, the community pressured him to fulfill his promise. The village priest supported community attitudes by refusing to marry him to another.[93] Given the pattern of near universality of marriage and the peasants' reticence to have unproductive villagers in their midst, pressure of this kind must have been considerable.

The frequency of prenuptial pregnancies would help determine definitively the extent to which youths abided by the village moral code that frowned on premarital sex. Unfortunately, until Western scholars have complete access to nineteenth-century parish records that can illuminate the number of months between the wedding day and birth of the first child, statistics for post-emancipation Russian village practice will be unavailable. Colonial American patterns suggest that rates of illegitimacy and prenuptial pregnancies are closely related. When one is low, so is the other. Thus, at the beginning of the eighteenth century when illegitimacy rates were between 1.0 and 3.0 percent, the rate of prenuptial pregnancies was a relatively low 10.0 percent of all births.[94] A similar pattern may have existed in the post-emancipation Russian countryside.

Higher illegitimacy rates in some provinces may be attributed both to rural practices and to changes outside the village. Bundling certainly helped increase the possibility of premarital sex. Pskov and Perm provinces, which were outside central Russia, both practiced bundling and had higher rural illegitimacy rates—4.8 percent and 4.7 percent—than Moscow province. As in Western Europe, the higher illegitimacy rates in the

---

The late onset of menarche (ages fifteen to seventeen) among Russian women may also have contributed to a low illegitimacy rate and masked premarital sexual activity. See A. Muratov, synopsis of N. I. Grigor'ev, "O polovoi deiatel'nosti zhenshchin Myshkinskago uezda, Iaroslavskoi gubernii (*Vracheb. Ved.* (1883) nos. 21–23)," *Meditsinskoe obozrenie* 20 (July 1883): 107; and A. O. Afinogenov, *Zhizn' zhenskago naseleniia Riazanskago uezda v period detorodnoi deiatel'nosti zhenshchiny i polozhenie dela akusherskoi pomoshchi etomu naseleniiu: Mediko-statisticheskoe izsledovaniia* (St. Petersburg, 1903), pp. 19–23; Mironov, "Traditsionnoe demograficheskoe povedenie," p. 94; and Engelstein, "Morality and the Wooden Spoon," p. 179.

[92] Pavel Levitskii, "Cherti nravov krest'ian Totemskago uezda," *Etnograficheskii sbornik* 5 (1892): 57. The carvings of the prialki are described in Netting, "Images and Ideas," pp. 48–68.

[93] Gromyko, *Traditsionnye normy*, p. 224.

[94] D'Emilio and Freedman, *Intimate Matters*, pp. 22, 41, 46–47, 73.

industrial and northern provinces also reflect growing mobility and the
increase in unskilled workers in urban and rural areas, resulting in the
greater vulnerability of women.[95] Russian peasants themselves blamed
what they believed to be a rise in promiscuity on the effects of migrant
trades and the lures awaiting women and men in towns far from the community controls of the village. Villagers in Cherepovets district, Novgorod
province, for example, complained that young girls who traveled to St.
Petersburg or Moscow to find employment returned sexually impure. They
commented, "You will find wild strawberries growing in moss faster than
you will find a chaste girl among us."[96] In 1897 the extremely high rates of
illegitimacy of 26.4 percent and 22.2 percent of all births for the cities of
Moscow and St. Petersburg reflect a higher incidence of premarital sex or
at least a greater number of premarital pregnancies that did not result in
marriage.[97] Barbara Alpern Engel, in her examination of the personal and
social characteristics of prostitutes in St. Petersburg, agrees with the peasants' negative assessment of urban life but attributes this rise in premarital
sex to the vulnerability of women in the urban environment. She notes that
"when she moved from village to city, the marriageable woman left behind
a patriarchal way of life that not only protected her from the vagaries of
the marketplace, but also controlled her sexual behavior by keeping her
close to home." Russian peasant women were not more promiscuous in
large cities. Rather, they were sometimes forced to turn to prostitution as
a result of sexual exploitation on the job or an inability to make a decent
wage in the service industries. Just over 40 percent of St. Petersburg prostitutes had formerly worked as maids, nurses, and cooks. Still others had
agreed to violate the norm of premarital chastity on the basis of a false
promise of marriage.[98]

   The greater growth in migrant trades for men in the post-emancipation
period had its effects upon sexual practices among the rural youth as well.
Olga Semenova-Tian-Shanskaia, a contemporary observer of late nineteenth-century Russian peasant life, complained about the pernicious influence of a growing population of migrant laborers who worked on the
large estates of the central agricultural provinces. She attributed a loosen-
ing of community and family control over moral behavior to the influx of
these men into villages, noting that they infused the normally quiet peasant

[95] For an excellent discussion of how women were affected by industrialization and urbanization, see Louise A. Tilly, Joan W. Scott, and Miriam Cohen, "Women's Work and European Fertility Patterns," in Rotberg and Rabb, *Marriage and Fertility*, pp. 219–48.
[96] V. Antipov, "Poslovitsy i pogovorki (Novg. g. Cherepov. u.)," *Zhivaia starina* 15, no. 1
(1906), pt. 2, p. 72.
[97] Coale, Anderson, and Härm, *Human Fertility*, pp. 252–53.
[98] Barbara Alpern Engel, "St. Petersburg Prostitutes in the Late Nineteenth Century: A
Personal and Social Profile," *The Russian Review* 48 (1989): 22, 27–28.

streets with an alien and boisterous element. A migrant worker who got a village girl pregnant could escape the area at a moment's notice.[99]

Despite early signs of change in illegitimacy rates inherent in the encroachment of capitalism on the central Russian village, peasants continued to treat the questioning of a marriageable peasant woman's reputation very seriously. Since a single woman faced ostracism from her peer group and, in the extreme, spinsterhood, as well as the dishonor of her entire family, only positive proof of her sullied reputation was acceptable as the motive for a public shaming. Women and their families had some recourse against false accusations.

New Year's Eve was traditionally the time when peasants used fortune-telling and omens to prognosticate their destiny for the coming year. A disgruntled or spurned suitor sometimes chose this occasion to wreak vengeance on a family by smearing the household's windows and gates with a thick layer of thawed-out dung.[100] Similar pranks also occurred at other times of the year. Village assemblies and cantonal courts harshly punished these delinquents. The culprits were required to compensate their victims for having cast aspersions on their characters. They were obliged as well to treat village assembly members to vodka, which amounted to a public apology and gesture of reconciliation.[101] On 10 October 1870, for example, a peasant of Kozlov district, agricultural Tambov province, complained to the cantonal court of Zhidilov that his daughter's reputation had been unfairly tarnished. He related that one evening two peasants visited him. One of them threatened his host after being refused a second glass of vodka. The plaintiff ignored the threat but in the morning found his gates, door, and shutters tarred. Outraged by the public defamation of his daughter's character, he immediately informed the village elder. The elder investigated, discovering drops of tar in the yard of the peasant who had made the threat on the previous evening. With such evidence in hand, the can-

[99] Semenova-Tian-Shanskaia, *Zhizn' 'Ivana,'* p. 41. The linkage between migrant work and extramarital sex has been made in the context of the virulence of syphilis in the late nineteenth-century countryside. Timothy Mixter's examination of migrant workers in the southern agricultural belt demonstrates the ready availability of prostitutes in the hiring market and the higher incidence of syphilis among migrants than among the sedentary population. Migrant workers, miners, and carpenters brought syphilis back to villages in Tambov province. Timothy Mixter, "Women Migrant Agricultural Laborers in Russia, 1860–1913" (Unpublished paper), pp. 14, 17. Soviet ethnographers noted that migrant workers, miners, and carpenters from Tambov province brought syphilis back to their villages when they returned home during the off-season. See Benet, *The Village of Viriatino,* p. 145. For an excellent discussion of syphilis in post-emancipation rural Russia, see Engelstein, "Morality and the Wooden Spoon," pp. 169–208.

[100] V. I. Čičerov, "Some Types of Russian New Year Songs," in *The Study of Russian Folklore,* ed. Felix J. Oinas and Stephen Soudakoff (Bloomington, Ind., 1971), p. 122.

[101] Stephen P. Frank, "Popular Justice, Community and Culture among the Russian Peasantry, 1870–1900," *The Russian Review* 46, no. 3 (July 1987): 255.

tonal judges found the twenty-three-year-old accused guilty, sentenced him to twenty lashes, and ordered him to pay the plaintiff four times the amount of annual village dues levied on a soul, some 35 rubles and 76 kopecks, to indemnify the plaintiff for having his daughter's reputation impugned.[102] In Orel district, Orel province, at the end of the nineteenth century village assemblies levied a fine of 50 rubles against men who falsely accused women of having sexual intercourse with them and even exiled them from the village for an entire year.[103]

Village authorities also dealt harshly with young girls who smeared another girl's reputation without just cause. In 1887, in the hamlet of Iazykova in Petrovsk district, Saratov province, the gates to two homes in which marriageable girls lived had been tarred. The girls' parents informed the village assembly that they suspected three village girls with whom their daughters had quarreled over suitors. Since the quarrel was common knowledge in the community, the assembly held the parents of the accused partly responsible for their daughters' actions and ordered them to treat the assembly members to fifteen rubles' worth of vodka. Moreover, each of the guilty girls was shamed publicly by having a tarred piece of string tied round her neck. A crowd then led them to the tarred gates and forced the girls to kiss them. Such public humiliation weakened the offenders' chances for making ideal marriage matches.[104]

Even suggesting in public that a girl was impure provoked strong censure if the accusation was false. Thus on 20 September 1871 in Rostov district, industrial Iaroslavl' province, a peasant girl complained to the Primkov cantonal court that three young men, during an outdoor fete in the village of Strely, called her disgusting names. A witness confirmed the charge. The defendants admitted their guilt and begged the plaintiff for forgiveness. The girl agreed to forgive them on condition that they each compensate her with five rubles. The judges approved the settlement but admonished the young men to refrain from such behavior. In another case, before the same court on the same day, the eighteen-year-old defendant Katalov, with whom the reader became acquainted in the Introduction, was treated more harshly. The judges sentenced him to the maximum punishment of twenty lashes for publicly insulting a fifteen-year-old peasant girl. They also ordered him to appear before the village assembly and, in the presence of the offended girl and her father, declare that he had falsely shamed the girl. The judges were clearly sensitive to the fact that without

[102] *Trudy Kommisii*, 1:322, #85.
[103] Gromyko, *Traditsionnye normy*, p. 99.
[104] "Obrashchik krest'ianskago suda," *Moskovskiia vedomosti*, 19 July 1887, p. 2, col. 6. Also cited in Iakushkin, *Obychnoe pravo*, 2:66, #610.

the public apology, the reputations of the victim and her family remained in doubt.[105]

Falsely accusing a girl of being pregnant out of wedlock constituted a particularly odious breach of neighborly conduct and was punished accordingly. In May 1871 the Ivanovo cantonal court of industrial Vladimir province sentenced a male peasant to three days in jail for falsely accusing a neighbor's unmarried daughter of having delivered a baby. A month later the Kulevatov cantonal court of agricultural Tambov province fined the peasant Katerina Borodina for publicly and falsely attributing a young unmarried girl's illness to a secret birth.[106]

While community members and cantonal judges were sympathetic to the plight of an unwed woman whose reputation was falsely slandered, their misogynist attitudes toward women placed the burden on victimized women to prove their innocence. At the cantonal court it was common to summon character witnesses on behalf of the victims. At the village level more extreme measures were sometimes taken. For example, in 1899 in the village Meshkovo, Orel district, a young woman falsely accused of not being a virgin confronted her accuser at a village assembly. The assembly required that she undergo a humiliating physical examination to prove her virginity. Once the village midwife proclaimed her chaste, the eligible bachelors of the village publicly asked the victim for forgiveness. The prankster who had tarred the gates to her parents' home had to pay a fine and was at the mercy of the girl's relatives, who might choose to exact further retribution by beating him up. The village officials hung a sign and made a white mark beside the tar on the victim's parents' gates, announcing to the community that the girl had been "acquitted."[107] That acquittal could not, however, make up for the humiliation the girl suffered in being subjected to a physical examination to determine whether her hymen was intact.

Much of the ritual shaming described thus far has involved young men and women punishing marriageable women suspected of promiscuous behavior. Young men also subjected intruders into the local marriage pool to public humiliation or, in some cases, physical violence. For example, in an unusual incident in 1888 in the village Kosovo, Sviiazh district, Kazan province, village bachelors subjected a widower to a charivari. They pelted the widower with pairs of worn-out bast shoes as he left the church with his bride on his wedding day. Several of the youths unsuccessfully attempted to hang a string of shoes round the widower's neck. The harassment continued even after the newlyweds reached their home. The victim

[105] *Trudy Kommisii*, 3:280, #14, #25.
[106] Ibid., 2:12, #23; 1:51, #5.
[107] Gromyko, *Traditsionnye normy*, p. 98.

had trangressed two norms. First, as a widower without children he had
no right to remarry. The assumption was that a widower needed a caretaker for the children of his previous marriage, not a personal companion.
Second, by marrying a young village girl he decreased the pool of marriageable maidens. The charivari's message was clear: widowers were to
stay away from maidens, who were the preserve of the village's young men,
and if they had children, were to confine their search for marriage partners
to widows.[108]

Similar hostility to outsiders was sometimes demonstrated in khorovody
or posidelki frequented by migrant laborers or young men from surrounding villages. According to protocol, outsiders gained entry to one of these
gatherings only by invitation of the host village. The hosts then had a responsibility to ensure that their guests had local partners when the dancing
commenced. On other occasions the guests reciprocated the hospitality
and invited their former hosts to one of their functions. Ugly incidents did,
however, sometimes occur when uninvited young men appeared at the festivities, causing quarrels and fistfights. A correspondent from Nikol'sk district, Vologda province, noted that if an uninvited young man wished to
court a local girl at the games and dances, he had first to buy off with vodka
the local boys whose circle of prospective brides was being threatened.
Otherwise the local suitors ganged up and beat him. It was not unusual for
the injured party to seek revenge by rounding up friends from his own
village, treating them to vodka, and then leading them in a fight with the
young men in the host village. If the host villagers won, they were permitted to participate in the social events of the outsiders' village free of charge;
if they lost the fight they had to treat the victors to vodka at future local
dances.[109] Fistfights among contending suitors, both local and distant, also
characterized social gatherings in agricultural Tambov province into the
twentieth century.[110]

Bachelor solidarity against outsiders, whether widowers or strangers to
the village, was designed to protect the circle of prospective local brides
against such would-be suitors. In other words, local boys jealously guarded
their right to have first choice. When they had chosen their girlfriends it

[108] Iakushkin reported that from 1879 to 1886 in forty-six out of every one hundred weddings involving widowers in Orthodox European Russia, the bride was a widow. See his
"Zametki o vliianii religioznykh verovanii i predrazsudkov na narodnye iuridicheskie obychai
i poniatiia," *Etnograficheskoe obozrenie* 3, bk. 9, no. 2 (1891): 6–7.

[109] I. G. Orshanskii, *Izsledovaniia po russkomu pravu obychnomu i brachnomu* (St. Petersburg,
1879), p. 43; and Maksimov, *Nechistaia, nevedomaia i krestnaia sila*, pp. 295–96. Titov observed the same practice in Rostov district, Iaroslavl' province, in his *Iuridicheskie obychai*, p.
27. For a description of gang fights in Kovrov district, Novgorod province, see Anne Louise
Bobroff, "Working Women, Bonding Patterns, and the Politics of Daily Life: Russia at the
End of the Old Regime," 2 vols. (Ph.D. diss., University of Michigan, 1982), 1:239n.

[110] Benet, *The Village of Viriatino*, p. 139.

was permissible for outsiders to enter the ranks of the privileged suitors, but at a price—vodka for the local boys and maintenance of local protocol. An outsider could not compete with a local boy for a girl's affection without suffering consequences. He was only permitted to court a girl who was not coveted by a local fellow.

Bachelor solidarity to protect the local pool of marriageable women from outsiders and the controlled intimacy of prospective spouses bear witness to increasing freedom in post-emancipation marriage. All of the courtship practices examined here indicate that the community and family expended a considerable amount of time acquainting marriageable young people with one another and encouraging them to pair off according to personal inclinations, however these were limited by considerations of kinship, status, and wealth. A degree of intimacy and in some areas bundling allowed prospective marriage mates to test their compatibility.

Nevertheless community and family supervision of courtship and individual behavior lessened the potential impact of a greater freedom of choice in marriage. Community members attended the social functions of marriageable youth, closely watching behavior to maintain norms. At least one matron participated in the labor-intensive posidelki and interpreted the songs and stories that accompanied the maidens' work in accordance with community values. Ritual songs of courtship praising a maiden's purity and public shaming of girls suspected of deviant behavior continued to control premarital sex in the second half of the nineteenth century. Even though rigorous shaming practices were dying out, the threat of public shaming was still very much present. Through regulation of the marriage market and private courting practices young people complemented traditional community and family institutions. These controls could not eliminate premarital sex but together with early and universal marriage helped maintain low illegitimacy rates. Increased mobility in some areas of the late nineteenth-century countryside began to challenge the effectiveness of these limitations, which could not protect individuals outside the village. Within the village, however, peasants of the younger and older generations continued to imprint their stamp on individual behavior during not only courtship, but the betrothal and wedding stages of marriage as well.

V

Marriage: Family and Community Renewal

CONTINUING family and community controls over marriage in the post-emancipation Russian village manifested themselves most clearly in wedding arrangements and festivities. Once a marriage partner had been selected, the suitor and his prospective bride played a passive role in the betrothal and marriage preparations. From that point onward a complex ritual drama under the direction of the couple's parents and kin groups forged the links of a marital union. Traditional premarriage, wedding, and postmatrimonial festivities involved symbolic rituals in which all community members participated. The community focused attention on the bride's character, chastity, and subordination to husband and in-laws as it blessed the alliance of two kin groups. The elaborateness of ceremonies varied according to region and wealth of the kin groups involved. At the formal engagement ceremony, kin groups sealed the marriage contract. At the *devishnik* the bride bade farewell to her maidenhood among her girl-friends and participated in the ritual bath. The marriage ceremony, the main wedding feast in the groom's parents' home, the consummation of the marriage, and the feast provided by the bride's mother thereafter involved the community in the joining of two kin groups and the transformation of "strangers into in-laws." The movement of the wedding party and guests between the homes of the bride's and groom's parents symbolized the new alliance as well as the final departure of the bride from her father's to her in-law's home.[1] An examination of the various components of the marital drama will illuminate the supportive roles of family and community in the institution of marriage.

The timing of weddings depended largely on the agricultural and church calendars. Almost all weddings took place between Christmas and Shrovetide in January and February, in the spring months following Lent, or during the late fall in October and November (see table 5.1). Peasants generally avoided marrying during the busiest spring, summer, and early fall months when hard field labor left little time for marriage festivities. The Orthodox Church forbade marriage during Advent, Lent, and Assumption fast periods. The close conformity of the nationwide European Russian

---

[1] For an analysis of the elaborate rituals of a French peasant marriage, which exhibited the same supportive relationship between family and community, see Segalen, *Historical Anthropology*, pp. 127ff.

marriage pattern to the rural pattern, as exemplified in table 5.1, demonstrates the overwhelmingly rural character of the total population and the strength of church prohibitions.

Marriages occurring outside the traditional wedding months faced popular censure because of the disaster peasants believed would befall a married couple who disturbed the natural rhythms of agricultural life: "To marry on Pestraia [a week prior to Maslenitsa, that is, Carnival] is to court trouble." "Be patient—to marry in May is to waste your whole life." "[He] who marries in the summer will have no good come of it."[2] Marriages that took place during those unlucky times were normally a product of necessity. The death of a wife in a family with several underage children and no female laborers might prompt a speedy remarriage, or a premarital pregnancy might advance the wedding date. Weddings of this kind were celebrated and consummated without the elaborate ceremonies and festivities reserved for fall and winter weddings when time, food, and cash were not at a premium.[3]

Betrothal initiated the marriage cycle. This also occurred outside Lenten periods and the busy agricultural months. Once a suitor and his parents in counsel with other family members had chosen a marriage partner, they selected a *svakha* or matchmaker to initiate the bargaining rituals and seal the marriage contract with the bride-to-be's kin. More often than not, a married female was cast in the matchmaking role. "An unmarried matchmaker is not sent out," peasants affirmed.[4] They considered a married woman the best matchmaker because her own successful marriage and experience as wife and mother portended well for any forthcoming match. Often the groom's mother, married sister, or aunt was chosen as matchmaker. A non-kin acquaintance could also fill that position. In some areas the suitor's godfather accompanied the matchmaker to the home of a prospective bride.[5]

The matchmaker played a vital role in the betrothal process. Popular wisdom advised; "Don't choose a bride, but a matchmaker." An experienced svakha, versed in ritual and bargaining mechanisms, procured not only a good marital match but also a satisfactory arrangement concerning matrimonial celebration costs. In areas where the dowry predominated, the matchmaker was not concerned with obtaining a lucrative marriage

[2] Illiustrov, *Sbornik rossiiskikh poslovits*, pp. 138–39. In nineteenth-century Western Europe, May was not a popular month for weddings because it was the month of the Virgin Mary. See Segalen, *Historical Anthropology*, p. 112.

[3] V. N. Mal'kovskii, "Svadebnye obychai, pesni i prigovory: Zapisany v Rybinskoi volosti, Bezhetskago uezda, Tverskoi gub. v 1903 godu," *Zhivaia starina*, 13, no. 4 (1903): 426.

[4] Burtsev, *Narodnyi byt velikago severa*, 2:282.

[5] Smirnov, *Ocherki semeinykh otnoshenii*, p. 229.

TABLE 5.1

Seasonal Variation of Marriages (Monthly Breakdown) on a Percentage Basis for European Russia, 1867–1887

	Jan.	Feb.	Mar.	Apr.	May	June	July	Aug.	Sept.	Oct.	Nov.	Dec.
1867–71	22.30	14.23	1.02	5.17	8.13	4.35	5.00	1.83	4.28	17.10	15.87	0.73
1876	27.66	11.46	1.00	6.08	9.84	2.06	4.74	1.74	4.33	18.23	12.17	0.70
1877	32.20	12.30	1.28	7.63	8.88	1.94	5.79	1.56	3.46	17.23	6.71	1.02
1878	18.75	20.30	1.03	3.51	6.06	4.73	4.15	1.58	3.80	19.12	15.96	1.01
1800[a]	20.91	24.60	—	1.93	5.94	5.95	3.33	1.25	3.74	16.52	14.54	—
1887[b]	25.49	12.72	0.90	4.80	9.00	2.04	3.81	1.46	4.04	17.63	17.30	0.82
1887	24.84	12.54	0.99	5.02	8.99	2.15	4.19	1.88	4.39	17.20	16.89	0.92

Sources: Statistcheskii vremennik Rossiiskoi Imperii, ser. 3, vols. 7, 25 (St. Petersburg, 1887, 1890); and Statistika Rossiiskoi Imperii, vol. 1 (St. Petersburg, 1887), pp. 36–37, vol. 18 (St. Petersburg, 1891). My calculations.

Note: Because the percentages have been rounded off to the nearest hundredth, they do not always add up to 100.

[a] Orthodox population (and dissenters) only

[b] In the countryside only

settlement. The dowry was not transferred to the ownership of the suitor and his family but remained the inalienable property of the wife and ultimately of her consanguineal kin. Peasants warned against the evils of large dowries: "A large dowry does not make a husband." "Take a rich bride and think about how to feed your family." "It is better not to take a rich wife than have her boss her husband."[6] In areas where the suitor's family paid a bride-price to the bride's family, the matchmaker had to get a sense of the bridal family's expectations and perhaps lower those expectations. Since the suitor's family paid a substantial portion of the wedding expenses, keeping costs within a reasonable range was also desirable.

The bargaining mechanisms for sealing a marriage contract, the private counterpart of a civil contract, involved the matchmaker's clever manipulation of the situation at hand. She naturally tried to present the suitor in the best possible light.[7] To stress the suitor's advantages, the matchmaker acted as a broker in a transaction akin to purchasing a major item on the open market. She usually began the bargaining at the prospective bride's home, amid the girl's relatives, with a line such as, "We heard that you have some merchandise, while we have a buyer,"[8] or "We will find an overseas [foreign] merchant for your goods."[9] After 1861 greater freedom of choice in selecting a marriage partner and greater canon and civil law influence, defining marriage as a special conjugal relationship between two individuals, somewhat mitigated the tradition of bride purchase.[10] Nevertheless, the retention of marriage contracts stressed the continuing importance of marriage as a union of kin groups involving property transfer, in the form of the bride-price and rights over the bride's labors and reproductive powers.[11]

After an initial proposal, the matchmaker asked to examine the prospective bride to determine her physical stamina. Good health and strength were prerequisites for a laborer and mother. The matchmaker also had the right to ask the young woman to demonstrate her domestic skills of weaving, sewing, and cooking.[12] In most cases this examination was pro forma, since a girl's skills had already been demonstrated during the posidelki and

[6] Illiustrov, *Sbornik rossiiskikh poslovits*, pp. 101, 127–28.

[7] Aleksandra Ia. Efimenko, "Narodnyia iuridicheskiia vozzreniia na brak," in her *Izsledovaniia narodnoi zhizni*, :9–11.

[8] Recorded by P. V. Shein in the village of Verkhniaia Zalegoshch', Novosil district, Tula province, in his *Velikoruss v svoikh pesniakh, obriadakh, obychaiakh, verovaniiakh, skazkakh, legendakh i t.p.*, 2 vols. (St. Petersburg, 1900), 1:565.

[9] Kuznetsov, "Semeinoe i nasledstvennoe pravo," p. 221.

[10] Efimenko, "Narodnyia iuridicheskiia vozzreniia," in her *Izsledovaniia narodnoi zhizni*, 1:31–33.

[11] Iakushkin, *Obychnoe pravo*, 2:xvii.

[12] D. Azarevich, "Russkii brak," *Zhurnal grazhdanskago i ugolovnago prava* 10, no. 6 (December 1880): 124.

agricultural labors of youth parties. A matchmaker's opinion could, nevertheless, enhance or color a maiden's reputation. Such an examination took on added importance if the prospective bride lived in another village. If satisfied with the inspection, the matchmaker then proceeded to enumerate the grain, animals, and other movable property at the suitor's disposal. Should the bride-to-be's father or guardian consider the match desirable, he then provided a comparable listing of items to be included in the dowry (in areas in which the dowry predominated).

The prospective bride's family also had the option of rejecting the suitor's proposal of marriage, thereby humiliating both suitor and matchmaker. In the event that the suitor was unacceptable, the prospective bride's father might have answered the matchmaker's proposal with words such as, "It is too early: this girl is too young," or, "Thank you for [your offer of] love, matchmaker; we do not wish to give away our young girl."[13] Once a refusal had been voiced, the matchmaker had to follow local protocol and decline all offers of food and drink from the girl's relatives. A spurned matchmaker sometimes had to bear the indignity of having a harrow displayed in her wagon as she headed back home with the bad news. In Olonets province, a relative of the sought-after maiden who had foreseen the refusal might have prepared a cup of *krasnoi gushchi* (reddened sediment) and smeared the matchmaker's cart with the dirt. Consequently, it was said that unsuccessful matchmakers "returned with gushchi" rather than a towel or belt as a pledge of betrothal.[14] In the Ukrainian provinces a rejected suitor was presented with a pumpkin rather than the coveted wedding towel of a betrothal pledge. The spurned matchmaker or suitor could not easily escape public detection and humiliation since the bells on her or his horses, which announced to the entire village the intent of the visit, had already aroused village interest in the outcome of the proposal.

If, on the other hand, the bride's side agreed to the marriage proposal, several steps were taken to formalize the agreement and proceed further with the negotiations. First the contractors hit hands and clasped arms at the elbows. After the handfast the bride's family was under moral, rather than legal, obligation to pursue the matter further. Her parents were expected to inquire about the suitor and inspect, together with relatives and neighbors, his parents' living quarters. This visitation amounted to a verification of the suitor's professed wealth, especially if he came from another village. If the property examination proved favorable to the suitor's proposal, the respective kin groups drank to the bargain.[15] The formal sealing

[13] Kuznetsov, "Semeinoe i nasledstvennoe pravo," p. 221.

[14] P. Pevin, "Narodnaia svad'ba v Tolvuiskom prikhode Petrozavodskago u., Olonetskoi gub.," *Zhivaia starina* 3, no. 2 (1893): 223.

[15] Efimenko, "Narodnyia iuridicheskiia vozzreniia," in her *Izsledovaniia narodnoi zhizni*, 1:11–12.

of the bargain was not complete, however, until the viewing of the betrothed. Dressed in their best attire, the groom and his bride-to-be were
formally introduced to one another before family, godparents, and closest
neighbors. This was a holdover from the pre-emancipation days of arranged marriages when the affianced often had not met each other. Then
the future in-laws shook hands before the witnesses, everyone prayed to
God for his blessing, the parents blessed the betrothed, and the suitor's
side provided drink to seal the marriage contract.[16] In Poshekhon'e district,
Iaroslavl' province, the matchmaker joined the hands of the fathers of the
betrothed and passed over them small loaves of bread, which had been
baked by both the suitor's and bride-to-be's kin. Then she broke each loaf
of bread in half and distributed the halves to the fathers. The ceremony
symbolized the future marriage and subsequent family tranquillity.[17]

Once the marriage contract had been sealed, it took on full juridical significance. Thereafter the breaking of an engagement was dishonorable and
subject to legal action. Cantonal courts required a suitor who broke an
engagement to compensate a bride's father for his daughter's loss of honor
and any expenses incurred in the marital bargaining process. When the
girl's family broke the betrothal contract, custom required that her father
recompense the suitor for his monetary losses. In the more likely event of
a successful engagement, the remaining ceremonies and rituals were "simply supplementary actions that gave public and sacred recognition to the
contract."[18] Nonetheless, peasants insisted that "a bride-to-be is not a wife;
you can get rid of a bride-to-be."[19] In other words, a betrothal did not have
the absolute sanctity and general indissolubility of marriage.

Until the conclusion of an engagement contract the suitor's side covered
all entertaining expenses. The groom's family was obliged to provide the
bride's kin with drink during the examination of the suitor's household and
possessions, and both food and wine at the time of the formal agreement
in the home of the bride-to-be's parents.[20] Social norms demanded that
food and drink flow freely; otherwise the community branded the groom's
father a miser.[21] Thereafter, either the suitor's side paid the wedding expenses by giving the bride-to-be's father a fixed sum of money known as
the kladka or *poklazha* (bride-price), or the expenses were divided equally
between the two kin groups.

---

[16] Ibid., pp. 12–13; and Shein, *Velikoruss*, 1:472.

[17] Aleksandr N. Afanas'ev, "Iuridicheskiia obychai: Po povodu vyzova Etnograficheskago
otdeleniia Russkago geograficheskago obshchestva," *Biblioteka dlia chteniia* (April 1865), nos.
7–8, p. 58.

[18] Efimenko, "Narodnyia iuridicheskiia vozzreniia," in her *Izsledovaniia narodnoi zhizni*,
1:13, 17.

[19] Illiustrov, *Sbornik rossiiskikh poslovits*, p. 135.

[20] Efimenko, "Narodnyia iuridicheskiia vozzreniia," in her *Izsledovaniia narodnoi zhizni*,
1:14.

[21] Shein, *Velikoruss*, 1:469.

In areas of Vladimir, Moscow, Tambov, Nizhnii Novgorod, Samara, Penza, Saratov, Vologda, and Olonets provinces, where the kladka predominated, the bride-price was fixed in the marriage contract. Among poor and middle peasants that sum varied between ten and fifty rubles. In a central industrial province such as Nizhnii Novgorod where rural trades were an important part of household income, a peasant was willing to pay more for a bride skilled in bastmatting, glove making, or some other craft. Extremely wealthy peasants paid as much as one hundred and two hundred rubles. Sometimes food—meat, malt, vodka, flour, and dill—for the wedding repasts was added to the monetary sum.[22] If a bride-price was paid, the bride's family usually was not responsible for providing their daughter with a dowry. Either the bride-price covered the costs of a bride's trousseau or the suitor's family supplied the trousseau as a supplement to the monetary bride-price. The bride's family, nevertheless, provided their daughter with the bed linens she needed in her new family.[23]

Through the simple transfer of property between two kin groups, the bride-price compensated a bride's family for the loss of a laborer and provided the conjugal family with rights to the bride's reproductive powers. The suitor's family, by supplying a bride with clothing and meeting the wedding expenses, in essence acquired absolute authority over its newest member, the daughter-in-law. All links between a daughter and her consanguineal family were now broken.

Olga Semenova-Tian-Shanskaia recorded a black earth province practice whereby both a dowry and bride-price were exchanged, suggesting a blurring of the two types of property. She described the dowry of one Akulina. It included numerous pieces of cloth, clothing, bed linens, a spinning wheel, and other female needs. The groom, meanwhile, presented Akulina's family with a poklazha of ten to fifteen rubles, a sheepskin coat, clothing, flour, groats, and several pints of vodka.[24] The exchange represented a more equitable distribution of the wedding costs. More important, the dowry mitigated the purchase element of the bride-price.[25]

The dowry's contents and its inalienability as the private property of the

[22] N. Astrov, "Krest'ianskaia svad'ba v s. Zagoskine, Penzenskago u. (Bytovoi ocherk)," *Zhivaia starina* 14, nos. 3–4 (1905): 418; M. E. Mikheev, "Opisanie svadebnykh obychaev i obriadov v Buzulukskom uezde, Samarskoi gubernii," *Etnograficheskoe obozrenie* 11, bk. 42, no. 3 (1899): 146; A. N. Minkh, *Narodnye obychai, obriady, sueveriia i predrazsudki krest'ian Saratovskoi gubernii, sobrany v 1861–1888 godakh* (St. Petersburg, 1890), pp. 18n., 115; Zelenin, *Opisanie*, 2:752; and Ol'ga Khristoforovna Agreneva-Slavianskaia, comp., *Opisanie russkoi krest'ianskoi svad'by s tekstom i pesniami: obriadovymi, golosil'nymi, prichital'nymi i zavyval'nymi*, 3 vols. (Moscow, 1887–1889), 2:83–84n.

[23] Efimenko, "Narodnyia iuridicheskiia vozzreniia," in her *Izsledovaniia narodnoi zhizni*, 1:14–15.

[24] Semenova-Tian-Shanskaia, *Zhizn' 'Ivana,'* p. 3.

[25] The same occurred in parts of China. See Johnson, *Women, the Family and Peasant Revolution*, p. 10.

bride and her kin groups were discussed in chapter II. Suffice it to reiterate that the dowry, unlike the kladka, was not a direct property transaction between two kin groups, because its contents remained the bride's uncontested property. Rather it symbolized the intrusion of another kin group into a patrilineal household. Although the dowry was not large enough to threaten the collective capital of the patrilocal household, its nonincorporation into that capital was a constant reminder of the intrusion. At the same time, by providing a bride with essentials, the dowry eased her transition from one household to another.

A major change in dowry contents appeared in the second half of the nineteenth century as the national market and money economy pervaded marital arrangements. Cash became more prevalent, and urban fabrics and luxury items usurped the former domination of homecrafted goods.[26] While the dowry may have changed in content, its form and significance remained the same.

Upon the betrothal, relations between the bride-to-be and her fiancé became more formal. They no longer addressed one another by diminutives of their Christian names but used their full Christian names and patronymics and sometimes the polite form of "you"—*vy*.[27] Such formality was observed at all times, particularly when the groom and his retinue of friends visited his fiancée for the so-called *poezdki na potselui* ("kissing visits").[28] From the point of betrothal onward the maiden was restricted to her parents' home as she "frequented neither street gatherings nor church."[29]

Now all attention focused upon the bride-to-be as she prepared for the last stage of the rite of passage into marriage with the aid of her female peer group and relations. She was freed of all normal household chores as the important preparation of the trousseau began in earnest. Often girlfriends remained at the bride-to-be's home day and night to help sew the trousseau and to act as a support system in the bride's dramatic transition from maidenhood to wifehood.

Until the wedding day Russian peasants expected a bride-to-be to show no joy at the prospects of her new life as wife and mother. Rather, she was to lament her situation through the declamation of ritual songs. Traditionally, she lamented through entire days, standing from morning to evening with a shawl or veil over her head.[30] She decried the impending loss of her

[26] Semenova-Tian-Shanskaia, *Zhizn' 'Ivana,'* p. 3.
[27] Astrov, "Krest'ianskaia svad'ba," p. 457.
[28] Balov, "Ocherki Poshekhon'ia," p. 61.
[29] Kuznetsov, "Semeinoe i nasledstvennoe pravo," p. 223.
[30] F. Giliarovskii, "O tak nazyvaemoi v narode porche brakov, vsledstvie surovosti brachnykh obychaev," *Zapiski Imperatorskago russkago geograficheskago obshchestva po otdeleniiu statistiki* 5 (St. Petersburg, 1878): 146–47.

cherished maidenhood, as well as the conclusion of the more joyous and carefree part of her life. The future offered a bride-to-be an unknown stage of life within a strange hostile family, where she would face new responsibilities and the prospect of little comfort from her blood kin. The following lament demonstrates that a newly married woman's life was not to be envied:

> They are making me marry a lout
> With no small family.
> Oh! Oh! Oh! Oh dear me!
> With a father, and a mother,
> And four brothers
> And sisters three.
> Oh! Oh! Oh! Oh dear me!
> Says my father-in-law,
> "Here comes a bear!"
> Says my mother-in-law,
> "Here comes a slut!"
> My sisters-in-law cry,
> "Here comes a do-nothing!"
> My brothers-in-law exclaim,
> "Here comes a mischief-maker!"
> Oh! Oh! Oh! Oh dear me![31]

While the rigorous observation of the mourning period diminished with the relaxation in parental control over choice in marriage partner, the songs' content and importance did not change. Akin to funeral laments, they were part of the collective normative values of Russian peasant culture that taught a woman subordination in marriage to husband and in-laws. They were usually sung in the presence of other peasant women, who commiserated with the bride on the lot soon to befall her yet urged her to accept without struggle her new position of subordination.[32] The lamentations also gave a bride-to-be an opportunity to honor her parents and thank them for their love and care by extolling them and voicing her reluctance to depart from their household.[33]

The most ritualistic event of the prewedding period involved the bride-to-be's final farewell to her maidenhood. The devishnik (literally, "an evening for maidens") was held at the bride's parents' home on the eve of the wedding. Songs and lamentations pervaded all aspects of the devishnik as

[31] Translated in William Ralston Shedden-Ralston, *The Songs of the Russian People, as Illustrative of Slavonic Mythology and Russian Social Life* (London, 1872), p. 289.

[32] The same collective sympathy and advice of women during wedding lamentations may be seen in present-day Romania. See Kligman, "The Rites of Women," p. 328.

[33] Alexander, *Russian Folklore*, p. 50.

the bride-to-be asked her female peers for advice to prepare her for her
"voyage" to a new family:

> Oh, Mar'ina's gatherings, gatherings, gatherings!
> She gathered all the young girls at her home,
> She sat all of the young girls down at the table,
> And seated herself higher than all of them,
> She bowed her head lower than all of them,
> [And] thought a thought harder than all of them:
> "Well now, young girls, my friends!
> Think [and] advise me:
> How will it be for me to be with strangers?
> How will I become accustomed [to things]?
> What will I call my strange father and mother?
> I do not wish to call him father.
> But he would get angry if I called him by his name.
> I will lessen my haughtiness and pride and increase my reasoning:
> I will call my father-in-law—father,
> And my mother-in-law—mother,
> My brother-in-law—by his patronymic,
> And my sister-in-law—by name [her Christian name]."[34]

In reply the girlfriends counseled the bride on her new responsibilities as
wife and mother:

> Ivan is walking about the yard,
> In a marten fur coat [that reaches] the ground,
> In a sable hat on top,
> In God's graces forever.
> When people say: "Whose is he?"
> Dar'iushka says: "My lord!
> My lord and I will be together forever,
> My lord and I will make a home,
> My lord and I will raise children."[35]

The most important rituals of the devishnik involved the unplaiting of
the bride's maidenly braid and her ritual bath in the presence of female
peers and close relations. On that evening the bride-to-be was first stripped
of the customary belt that protected her maidenly purity. Consequently,
no men were allowed at the ceremony. Amulets and geometric designs in
the embroidered clothing of the bride-to-be were retained to ward away

---

[34] Recorded in Zaraisk district, Riazan province, by Shein, *Velikoruss*, 1:558, #1850.
[35] Recorded in Dankov district, Riazan province, in ibid., p. 563, #1869.

evil spirits and the ever-present threat of the evil eye.[36] Then, in anticipation of her wedding day, the bride-to-be uttered short lamentations beseeching her mother, sister, aunt, and godmother in turn to remove her maidenly beauty or purity, symbolized by her single braid plaited with red ribbons. She subsequently reproached them for having unplaited the braid and having destroyed her maidenly powers.[37]

The female guests led the bride, with her hair loose, to the bathhouse for her ritual bath, where they performed other rituals upon her. The ceremony at the bathhouse invoked an ancient custom whereby a girl married the spirit of the bathhouse—the *baennik*—offering her purity as a sacrifice.[38] Her girlfriends undressed the bride-to-be, washed, and dried her, careful not to make noise or disturb the smoldering brands in the bathhouse fire. A tranquil fire portended a peaceful married life, free of beatings by her husband.[39] The girlfriends carefully wrung out the towel used to wash the maiden and preserved the water in a container. That water was later added to leavened dough so that dumplings (pirogi) could be baked from the dough and presented to the groom prior to the wedding ceremony. The eating of the dumplings symbolized the sacred union of two individuals and ensured that the groom would love his bride. Girlfriends in the Olonets region even washed their faces in the water that a bride-to-be had bathed in to ensure that they too would one day marry.[40]

At the conclusion of the ritual bath, the young girls ceremonially plaited the bride-to-be's hair in the maidenly braid for the last time. In Ermakov canton in Poshekhon'e district, Iaroslavl' province, the bride's closest friend braided the bride's hair together with the same number of colored ribbons as there were girlfriends present. Those ribbons were subsequently distributed among the girlfriends on the wedding day.[41] In Petrozavodsk district of Olonets province girls plaited the bride's hair in as complicated a fashion as possible to make its unplaiting and her deliverance to the state

---

[36] D. B. Chopyk, "The Magic of a Circle: Ceremonial Attire, Food and Dance Symbolism in Slavic Weddings" (Paper presented at the 1983 Annual Meeting of the Canadian Association of Slavists, University of British Columbia, 5 June 1983).

[37] I. M. Kolesnitskaia and L. M. Telegina, "Kosa i krasota v svadebnom fol'klore vostochnykh slav'ian," in *Fol'klor i etnografiia: Sviazi fol'klora s drevnimi predstavleniiami i obriadami*, ed. B. N. Putilov (Leningrad, 1977), pp. 115–16.

[38] E. Kagarov, "O znachenii nekotorykh russkikh svadebnykh obriadov," *Izvestiia Akademii nauk* (15 May 1917), no. 9, p. 645.

[39] An undisturbed fire brought recollection of the hearth fire, which was believed to possess the key to domestic tranquillity and family happiness. See Aleksandr N. Afanas'ev, *Poeticheskie vozzreniia slavian na prirodu: Opyt sravnitel'nago izucheniia slavianskikh predanii i verovanii, v sviazi s mificheskimi skazaniiami drugikh rodstvennykh narodov*, 3 vols. (1865–1869; reprint, The Hague, 1970), 1:35–36.

[40] In some areas the bride was covered with milk and dried with the dough for the sacred dumplings. Balov, "Ocherki Poshekhon'ia," p. 70; and Pevin, "Narodnaia svad'ba," p. 232.

[41] Kolesnitskaia and Telegina, "Kosa i krasota," p. 113.

of matrimony and impurity more difficult. They sectioned off the hair and plaited it very finely, knotting the entwined ribbon several times.[42] The final unplaiting of the bride's hair prior to the wedding ceremony was usually performed by her brother, the keeper of his sister's purity, whose action symbolized the sexual prowess of men who deprived women of their purity.

The wedding day represented the climax of the marriage festivities. It incorporated the ceremonial departures of the groom and bride from their respective patrimonial households, the final break of the bride with her unmarried peers and her transition to the status of married woman, the wedding ceremony, feasting at the groom's parents' home, and, finally, consummation of the marriage. Before a discussion of the most important features of the wedding day, it should be noted that Russian peasants distinguished between the religious wedding ceremony (*venchanie*) and the secular wedding celebrations (*svad'ba*), considering the latter far more important. The svad'ba involved the entire community's active participation in the marriage through the social mechanisms of feasts and other festivities that introduced newlyweds to their new social responsibilities.

As the nineteenth-century juridical historian E. I. Iakushkin pointed out, it is difficult to ascertain the juridical significance of the svad'ba in most Great Russian provinces because the wedding festivities merged with the church ceremony by following upon its heels. Iakushkin noted, however, that in the southern half of Makar'ev district of Kostroma province the religious ceremony and secular festivities were separated in time. Once the sacrament of marriage had been celebrated, the newlyweds proceeded to the groom's father's home, to partake of a wedding repast. Immediately upon its conclusion, the groom returned his bride to her father's home, where she remained alone for at least a week. Despite the religious authorization, the marriage could not be consummated until the conclusion of the svad'ba or communal feasting.[43] In other words, to attain legitimacy a wedding had to be countenanced by community participation and recognition as well as religious ceremony.[44] Community sanctification carried so much weight that the religious ritual could have been dispensed with without censure. Thus, in isolated areas where a priest could not be procured to perform the wedding ceremony, the svad'ba alone, according to customary law, legitimized a marriage. Understandably, sectarians and Old Believers resorted to that practice more frequently than did Orthodox peasants.[45]

[42] Pevin, "Narodnaia svad'ba," p. 235.

[43] Iakushkin, *Obychnoe pravo*, 1:vii–viii; and A. Smirnov, "Narodnye sposoby zakliucheniia braka," *Iuridicheskii vestnik* 10, no. 5 (May 1878): 685.

[44] Efimenko, "Narodnyia iuridicheskiia vozzreniia," in her *Izsledovaniia narodnoi zhizni*, 1:35.

[45] Iakushkin, *Obychnoe pravo*, 1:viii; I. G. Orshanskii, "Narodnyi sud i narodnoe pravo. (Po

At the groom's home on the wedding day the groom's parents and god-parents took various precautions to ensure that their son's married life would be blessed. A feather in the left boot warded off excessively heavy labors, while money in the right boot portended a well-run household economy. The godmother fastened a needle in the groom's shirt to dispel evil spirits and the malevolent intent of village sorcerers.[46] Subsequently participants in the wedding procession assembled at the home for a prewedding repast. In order of importance they included the *tysiatskii*, i.e., the groom's godfather or eldest and closest male relative; the great, middle, and lesser *boiars*, who were also selected from among the groom's relatives and ranked according to degree of relation; the best man, often a nonrelated member of the community capable of directing the complex wedding rituals and constantly interceding on behalf of the groom, who remained a spectator for much of the svad'ba; the groom's male friends; and, finally, the matchmaker and carriage driver.[47] Once the food had been consumed, the wedding party prepared for the departure to the bride's home. The groom's parents remained behind, allowing the ranked retinue to escort their son.

The groom's temporary departure from his paternal home symbolized his initiation as a full adult male with his own responsibilities. It also permitted his mother to come to terms with the change that her son's marriage brought to the family. She lamented the potential diminution of her son's affections for her as he turned his love toward another woman. The mother also ritually decried the potential threat that her new daughter-in-law posed to her position as bol'shukha, or head of the domestic household:

My "natural child" [a euphemism for bastard], . . .
As you are about to marry,
[And] bring back a new wife for yourself,
Do not forsake poor miserable me.
When I am old and sick,
Do not exchange wretched me
For your young wife.[48]

The processional horses were decked out in bells, rattles, drums, and colored ribbons to announce the passage of the wedding procession

---

povodu voprosa o preobrazovanii volostnykh sudov)," *Zhurnal grazhdanskago i ugolovnago prava* 5, no. 3 (May 1875): 104.

[46] Zvonkov, "Sovremennye brak i svad'ba," in Kharuzin, *Sbornik svedenii dlia izucheniia byta*, 1:107–8.

[47] S. M. Osokin, "Sel'skaia svad'ba v Malmyzhskom uezde," *Sovremennik* (1857) no. 1, p. 73.

[48] Cited in Prof. Strakhov, "O svad'bakh i svadebnykh obriadakh i obychaiakh russkikh krest'ian," *Uchenyia zapiski Imperatorskago moskovskago universiteta* 12, no. 11 (1836): 353.

through the village and to protect the groom and later his bride from evil spirits. The entire community lined the street, singing festive songs, obstructing the wagons as they attempted to reach the bride's home, and attesting to community control of as well as active participation in the rite of passage into marriage. It was the duty of the best man to negotiate with the obstructors, buying them off with beer and money.[49] He also asked the neighbors to bless the groom on his new journey "on the road to God's church under the golden crown." He announced that those who refused to give a blessing would find that their sons and daughters would never marry.[50]

As the wedding carriage approached its destination, the bride, dressed in her wedding finery, made a final plea to her father, in the presence of her female peers and extended kin, to save her from the fate that was in his hands:

> Take a look around our heavenly home, my benefactor-father,
> A storm cloud is developing,
> [It is] a thunderous storm cloud
> Strange people
> From foreign faraway parts
> Are driving up to our heavenly home.
> Listen, my lord—benefactor-father,
> My dear falcon brother went
> To buy a lock and tin,
> Keys and copper,
> And to shut the wooden gate
> [So as] not to allow [them] into our heavenly home.[51]

In fact the gates to the bride's home were locked in symbolic representation of the ancient custom of bride abduction. The unlocking of the gates and the groom's access to his bride (past her relatives who were armed with whips and sticks) had to be gained piecemeal through a complex bargaining process and the exchange of gifts from the groom's side. The best man rather than the groom was in charge of the bargaining and gift giving, underscoring the groom's passivity on his wedding day.[52]

---

[49] Ibid., p. 355.

[50] Cited in Pakhman, "Ocherk narodnykh iuridicheskikh obychaev Smolenskoi gubernii," in his *Sbornik narodnykh iuridicheskikh obychaev*, 2:56.

[51] I. Il'inskii, "Svadebnye prichety, detskiia peṣni i pr., zapisannyia v Shchetinskoi, Khmelevskoi i Melenkovskoi volostiakh Poshekhonskago uezda," *Zhivaia starina* 6, no. 2 (1896): 231, #XVII.

[52] For a discussion of medieval Rus' wedding customs see Maxim Kovalevskii, "The Matrimonial Customs and Usages of the Russian People, and the Light They Throw on the Evolution of Marriage," in his *Modern Customs and Ancient Laws of Russia: Being the Ilchester Lectures for 1889–90* (1891; reprint, New York, 1970), pp. 1–31; B. P. Gaideburov, "Brachnye

Knowing that her fate was sealed, the bride turned from her father to her married sisters, asking them that ever-troubling question which pervaded many of the courtship and wedding songs: how was she to live among her alien affinal kin? A sister gave the bride the following answer:

> Live my dear,
> By holding your head down,
> Your heart ardently pumping;
> Call them by their Christian names,
> Honor them by their patronymics;
> Be sweet, affable
> To the alien strangers.
> Also my dear,
> [When you] live with strangers,
> Do not keep bosom girlfriends;
> When you are melancholy [and] sad,
> Go to a virgin field,
> Fall down and pour your soul out to a hot stone.
> The hot stone will not gossip,
> The damp mother earth will not tell.[53]

In other words, a bride was not only about to enter a foreign, potentially hostile family, but she was also leaving the comfortable, insular circle of girlfriends, who were conspicuously absent from the wedding procession and svad'ba festivities, for a life of isolation within a new family. No longer would she be able to count on her blood kin and friends for comfort and advice. Community norms forbade a bride to lament her fate as wife and daughter-in-law to outsiders. Such gossip shamed a family's honor. It was a wife's duty to protect and enhance, not sully, that honor.

The bride's departure from her paternal household for the wedding ceremony further accentuated her loss of maidenly freedom. She left her parents and female peer group with their blessing, but also with their laments:

> As the blue sea overflowed [and] rushed
> In front of our wide gates,
> It carried away, carried away three ships from our yard:
> As the first ship [carried] the soul of a beautiful maiden,
> The second ship [carried] quilts and pillows,
> While the third ship [carried] forged trunks.

podarki," *Iuridicheskii vestnik* nos. 3–4 (July–August 1891): 287–315; Smirnov, "Narodnye sposoby," pp. 661–93; and K. Kavelin, Review of *Byt russkago naroda* by A. Tereshchenko, in *Sochineniia K. Kavelina*, ed. K. Soldatenkov and N. Shchepkin, 4 vols. (Moscow, 1859), 4:121–67.

[53] Il'inskii, "Svadebnye prichety," p. 235, #XXXIII.

When her natural mother came out,
. . . she cried out in a loud voice:
"My child, my child, my dear child!
You forgot, my child,
You forgot three keys, three golden [keys];
You forgot three freedoms:
The first freedom—your maidenhood,
And the second freedom—your natural father,
And the third freedom—your natural mother."[54]

The reference to the second ship laden with quilts and pillows attests to a practice occurring either on the eve of the wedding or immediately upon the departure of the wedding procession for the church. At that time the bride's parents or svakha (the bride's sponsor) loaded a wagon with the bride's dowry chest and delivered it to the groom's parents' home in full view of the neighbors. The spectators commented on the quality of the dowry items and bed linens, bestowing praise and honor upon the bride and her parents, as well as lending another element of public participation to the wedding festivities.[55]

Russian peasants firmly believed in the possibility of local sorcerers' casting spells on newlyweds. They held such spells responsible for a couple's inability to consummate their marriage or, worse, the death of one spouse. Precautions to protect the groom and wedding carriage from evil have already been mentioned. Several other measures were taken when the bride joined the wedding procession. Covering the bride's and, in some instances, the groom's face and shooting firearms were designed to ward off malevolent spirits or spells.[56] At a wedding it was forbidden to address or refer to the bride by name. She was called simply *nevesta* or bride (literally "the unknown one") to thwart the evil eye and evil spirits.[57]

The peasants' obsession with evil spirits was rooted in the reality of some brides' dying shortly after their weddings. Such deaths were frequent enough to prompt a doctor's investigation into the problem. Dr. F. Giliarovskii dismissed the peasants' explanation of malevolent forces at work as superstition. Rather he pointed to the common practice of brides' dousing themselves in ice-cold water if they happened to be menstruating on their wedding day. He noted that the action sometimes deprived women of the opportunity to conceive and caused serious illness, at times resulting

---

[54] Recorded in Epifan' district, Tula province, by Shein, *Velikoruss*, 1:590, #1949.
[55] Strakhov, "O svad'bakh," p. 361.
[56] Kagarov, "O znachenii," p. 648.
[57] E. A. Tudorovskaia, "O vnepesennykh sviazakh narodnoi obriadovoi pesni," in *Fol'klor i etnografiia*, p. 84.

in paralysis and even death.[58] Regardless of the medical explanations for a childless marriage or a bride's death, peasants firmly clung to their superstitious beliefs that the family of a deceased bride was jinxed. As a result, the chances of the deceased's unmarried sisters and brothers' marrying were severely lessened. Wild rumors also might hold the husband responsible for his wife's death. Embroidered tales circulated about the malicious treatment he accorded her. Such stories deterred any sensible woman from considering him as a prospective husband. If he tortured his first wife to death, peasants reasoned, there was no reason why he would not do the same to the second.[59]

With proper precautions against malevolent forces having been rigorously observed, the wedding party carefully scrutinized the conduct of the bride and groom upon arrival at the church, as well as during and immediately following the marriage ceremony. Their actions in relation to one another foretold who would dominate their marriage.[60] For example, whether the groom or bride took the first step into the church or onto the wedding towel therein decided the question of authority between the two. The regulation of such proceedings by friends and relations stymied individual rebellion against the norm. The spectators ensured that the bride acquiesced to the groom's taking the first step.[61] Otherwise a noncomplaisant and shrewish wife threatened to disrupt the patriarchal social order.[62] A bride's willingness to accept subordination to her husband was tested once again at the end of the matrimonial service when the tysiatskii asked the newlyweds which one of them wielded authority over the other. The bride was required to respond by falling to her husband's feet to demonstrate her submissiveness and obedience.[63]

Upon conclusion of the wedding ceremony, the bride's svakha or married female sponsor usually dressed the bride's hair, which had hung loose during the ceremony, in two plaits in the fashion of a married woman. The braids were wound about the head and covered with a *povoinik* or *kichka*— a ceremonial headdress.[64] The ritual was performed in the refectory, out of

[58] Giliarovskii, "O tak nazyvaemoi v narode porche brakov," pp. 129–55.

[59] Zvonkov, "Sovremennye brak i svad'ba," in Kharuzin, *Sbornik svedenii dlia izucheniia byta*, 1:85–86.

[60] French peasants also had various divinatory rites to determine whether a groom or bride would dominate the marriage. See Martine Segalen, *Love and Power in the Peasant Family: Rural France in the Nineteenth Century*, trans. Sarah Matthews (Chicago, 1983), pp. 29–36.

[61] Smirnov, "Ocherki semeinykh otnoshenii," nos. 3–4 (March–April 1877): 103–4.

[62] Segalen, *Love and Power*, p. 37.

[63] Titov, *Iuridicheskie obychai*, p. 36n.

[64] In some areas of Perm and Kostroma provinces the dressing of the bride's hair in the fashion worn by married women did not occur immediately after the wedding ceremony, but when the bridal couple had arrived at the groom's parents' home. See A. Smirnov, "Obychai i obriady russkoi narodnoi svad'by," *Iuridicheskii vestnik* 10, no. 7 (July 1878): 1003.

sight of men, because a woman without a head covering was believed to be unprotected, susceptible to evil spirits and plausibly to the attractions of other men. This practice confirmed the popular belief that women were the perpetrators of sexual corruption. The two plaits symbolized a woman's old allegiance to her blood kin and new loyalty to her husband and affinal kin. The dual loyalties were particularly evident in Samara district, Samara province, where the groom's svakha plaited the bride's right braid and the bride's svakha the left. A married woman's head covering represented her submissiveness to her husband and entrance into his patriarchal household.[65]

Once the ceremonial braiding of the bride's hair had been completed, the bridal party proceeded to the groom's parents' home. There they feasted with the extended kin of both sides and neighbors. The celebration was climaxed by the consummation of the marriage or, more specifically, the deflowering of the bride, as evidenced in the Russian saying, "A maiden in the evening, a young woman at midnight."[66] As in other preindustrial societies, this event was more public than private. Anthropologist Gail Kligman explains this same lack of privacy for a newly married couple in contemporary Romania: "Because a wedding effects the transference of a woman from one household to another, the liminality experienced during the rite of passage temporarily breaches the boundaries between discreet household units."[67]

Right up to the moment when the bridal couple was conducted to the nuptial bed, wedding guests made references, either by word or by symbolic action, to the woman's fecundity and her submissiveness to her husband. The bride's father ceremonially transferred his authority over his daughter to her husband by handing the latter the ceremonial lash, which the husband then tucked into his belt. In several areas of Saratov province the bride was handed a baby, which she dressed in a hat and belt. She was expected to hold the child for some time as a prophetic sign of her ability to produce offspring.[68]

While the guests feasted and toasted the newlyweds (who were forbidden to partake of the wedding repast) the custodians of the nuptial bed (normally the svakha or bride's sponsor and married sister) made the final preparations. Sometimes the bride's maid of honor watched these prepa-

---

[65] Chopyk, "The Magic of a Circle"; and Vsevolozhskii, "Ocherki krest'ianskago byta Samarskago uezda," p. 20. For other interpretations of the double braid and head covering worn by married women, see N. I. Gagen-Torn, "Magicheskoe znachenie volos i golovnogo ubora v svadebnykh obriadakh Vostochnoi Evropy," *Sovetskaia etnografiia* (1933), nos. 5–6, pp. 76–88.

[66] Smirnov, "Narodnye sposoby," p. 668.

[67] Kligman, "The Rites of Women," p. 338.

[68] Afanas'ev, "Iuridicheskiia obychai," p. 54; and Minkh, *Narodnye obychai*, p. 118.

rations to ensure that the room did not contain any sharp objects which the bride might use to cut herself and produce blood if she needed to hide her prior loss of virginity.[69] The bed was located in an unheated hut (*klet'*) or cold-storage room attached to the main residence. The customary use of a cold room was firmly upheld to ensure consummation of the marriage: "Well, let them sleep in the cold—the young bride will love her husband [that much] better," reasoned peasants. Furthermore, privacy, which was at a premium in crowded peasant huts, was a luxury accorded only to young couples. To protect the newlyweds against ever-present malevolent spirits and the evil eye, and to ensure fecundity, the bed custodians placed flaxseed on the bed or put rye sheaves or a fishing net underneath. Sometimes they placed a container of harvested rye or wheat in a corner of the room, adding to it the candles that the newlyweds had held during the wedding ceremony.[70]

Once all preparations of the chamber were completed, the best man and the two svakhas accompanied the newlyweds to the unheated hut, often with the wedding guests following behind. A series of ceremonies then followed, once again stressing the responsibilities of married life. By far the most important obligation of marriage was to produce children. Consequently, it was common for the couple to find a happily married pair, who might be either the bride's or groom's godparent and her or his spouse, upon the nuptial bed. That couple warmed the bed and guaranteed the newlyweds a fecund marriage. The best man either bought off the older couple with vodka or ritually chased them out of the hut or room with a stick.[71] In Zaraisk district, Riazan province, the departing couple blessed the forthcoming marital consummation with the following words: "May God allow you to lie down as two, but arise as three; either a son or daughter on the first night!"[72]

Other rituals emphasized a wife's total subordination to her husband. After the best man and svakhas fed the newlyweds, the bride began the ancient ritual of removing her husband's boots, in one of which he had placed a few silver coins. She was thus reminded of her husband's authority and of the source of her conjugal family's material wealth. Subsequently

[69] Zvonkov, "Sovremennye brak i svad'ba," in Kharuzin, *Sbornik svedenii dlia izucheniia byta*, 1:124.

[70] I. V. Kostolovskii, "Iz svadebnykh obriadov i poverii Iaroslavskoi gubernii," *Etnograficheskoe obozrenie* 19, bk. 75, no. 4 (1907): 106–7; 23, bks. 88–89, nos. 1–2 (1911): 249; and Smirnov, "Obychai i obriady," p. 1004.

[71] P. A. Dilaktorskii, "Svadebnye obychai i pesni v Totemskom uezde, Vologodskoi gubernii," *Etnograficheskoe obozrenie* 11, bk. 42, no. 3 (1899): 165; Mashkin, "Byt krest'ian Kurskoi gubernii Oboianskago uezda," *Etnograficheskii sbornik* 5 (1862), pt. 6, p. 71; Smirnov, "Obychai i obriady," p. 1005; and A. D. Neustupov, "Krest'ianskaia svad'ba Vas'ianovskoi volosti," *Etnograficheskoe obozrenie* 15, bk. 56, no. 1 (1903): 68.

[72] Recorded in Shein, *Velikoruss*, 1:559–60.

the svakhas changed the bride's shirt in the presence of the best man and sometimes other guests, whereupon the bride asked her husband for permission to join him on the nuptial bed. In Kadnikov district, Vologda province, the bride was forced to request permission three times before her husband acquiesced.[73] In the village of Kopalinskaia, Perm district, the groom answered the bride's request by advising her to jump across him, to which she humbly replied, "No, (his name), as a maid I lived without jumping across the garden [i.e., engaging in sexual intercourse] and kept myself pure and noble, and I don't want to jump across you," thus stressing her maidenly purity. Nevertheless, the bride eventually joined her husband.[74]

Before the marriage could be consummated the best man reminded the bride and groom of their obligations to one another. He asked the groom the reasons for his having married. The groom was expected to answer, "To provide my wife with food and drink and to set up house with her." In reply to the same question, asked this time by the bride's svakha, the bride answered, "To sew shirts for my husband, dress him, and bear him sons."[75] Only when the couple was in the procreative position, sometimes with their legs tied together with an embroidered towel or woven belt, did the guests leave the couple alone, locking the door to the room when they departed.[76]

The public importance of the consummation to validate the marital union did not end with the departure of the guests. The act of deflowering the bride was a public celebration. Guests honored the bride's parents, on the one hand, for maintaining their daughter's chastity, and her affinal kin, on the other hand, for their daughter-in-law's fecundity. In the pre-emancipation period verifying the bride's virginity was deemed so important that wedding guests continually badgered the newlyweds from outside the locked door until the act of procreation had been completed. The best man and svakha subsequently entered the bridal room, emerging with the bride's bloodstained nightshirt, presumably from her ruptured hymen, to attest to her chastity. Significantly the nightshirt was called a *kalina*, which is a type of viburnum, a tree or bush with berrylike red fruit.[77] Guests

[73] Dilaktorskii, "Svadebnye obychai," p. 165.

[74] Quoted in Zelenin, *Opisanie*, 3:1054.

[75] Recorded in Semenova-Tian-Shanskaia, *Zhizn' 'Ivana,'* p. 68.

[76] L. N. Chizhikova, "Svadebnye obriady russkogo naseleniia Ukrainy," in *Russkii narodnyi svadebnyi obriad: Issledovaniia i materialy*, ed. K. V. Chistov and T. A. Bernshtam (Leningrad, 1978), pp. 174. In some areas, such as Elat'ma district, Tambov province, consummation of the marriage was postponed until at least three days after the nuptials. Zvonkov, "Sovremennye brak i svad'ba," in Kharuzin, *Sbornik svedenii dlia izucheniia byta*, 1:124.

[77] Evgenii Vasil'evich Anichkov, "Pesnia," *Istoriia russkoi literatury* (Moscow) 1 (1908): 200. The Russian practice of displaying material evidence of the bride's virginity dates back to pre-Christian times. Levin, *Sex and Society*, p. 39.

smashed clay pots and other earthenware dishes to symbolize the breaking
of the hymen, whereupon the svakha sang a song such as the following:

Matchmaker, brother! Why have you come?
Are you drinking, eating, and dancing with us?
I will drink, eat, and dance with you!
Vyshinka-iagatka is red from the sun.
Our light Akhim'iushka is pure from her father's house.
Our light Ulas'ivna is pure from birth.[78]

Proof of a woman's retention of her chastity until her wedding night
continued to be of central importance after emancipation. Generally, in the
second half of the nineteenth century, the newlyweds were allowed to
spend the entire night together before being awakened by the best man
and svakhas. In some villages of Elat'ma district, Tambov province, wedding guests still banged pots at the door of the newlyweds' chamber anx-
iously awaiting the results of the night's intimacy.[79] Everywhere the act of
publicly displaying the bride's nightshirt or at least making public reference
to the bride's chastity or lack thereof was retained.

The bride's parents' honor hung in balance until the question of their
daughter's virginity was settled. If the bride was chaste the wedding guests
praised the parents and blessed them with drink. The groom personally
thanked the bride's mother by presenting her with a gift. This token of his
esteem was normally a pancake (*blin*), in which he had poked a hole to
represent the deflowering of the bride. In Voznesensk suburb and its
neighboring villages (Vladimir province) female guests decorated their
clothing with colored ribbons and walked through the village streets banging screens and pans. They announced the bride's chastity to all residents
and summoned them to pay tribute to the consummation of the marriage.[80] If, however, the bride was not chaste, the groom's mother presented the bride's mother with vodka served in a broken cup. A horse's
harness was sometimes hung around the mother's or father's neck. The
bride herself may have been subjected to a beating from her husband and
his relatives.[81]

[78] Mashkin, "Byt krest'ian Kurskoi gubernii," p. 72.
[79] Zvonkov, "Sovremennye brak i svad'ba," in Kharuzin, *Sbornik svedenii dlia izucheniia
byta*, 1:126.
[80] Zelenin, *Opisanie*, 3:1055, 1:174.
[81] Vsevolozhskii, "Ocherki krest'ianskago byta Samarskago uezda," p. 21; Astrov,
"Krest'ianskaia svad'ba," p. 453; A. O. Kistiakovskii, "K voprosu o tsenzure nravov u na-
rodu," in Matveev, *Sbornik narodnykh iuridicheskikh obychaev*, vol. 1, pt. 1, p. 169; and Chizhikova, "Svadebnye obriady," pp. 174–75. For a comparative analysis of the rituals attesting to
a bride's virginity among all Slavs, see Ján Komorovský, "The Evidence of the Bride's Innocence in the Wedding Customs of the Slavs," *Ethnologia Slavica* (Bratislava) 6 (1976): 137–
46.

The public celebration of a bride's virginity and the consummation of the marriage was an important mechanism of social control over sexual behavior that had its hold even after greater freedom of choice in marriage partner had entered the marriage market in the post-emancipation period. As mentioned earlier, a certain degree of intimacy between a betrothed couple was permitted, but the threat of public censure limited that intimacy. A bride's fear of public shaming drove her to various devices if she was not a virgin on her wedding night or if there was no bleeding upon first intercourse. Blood with which to stain the nightshirt might be procured from animals or other parts of the human body. Sometimes the bride ensured that she would be married while menstruating.[82] Gail Kligman has noted similar practices among present-day Romanian peasants who believe that "all brides are virgins, even if it takes a chicken's blood to prove it."[83] If a bride had to use an animal's blood, she needed to secure her husband's complicity. A groom would in all likelihood go along with the ruse so as to avoid shaming his family. In Novgorod province peasants considered a husband who revealed his bride's secret to be a mischievous child. Better that he hide his wife's shame than publicly disgrace her.[84] Sometimes, however, a husband's protection of his wife's honor was insufficient. In one instance in a black earth province, a bride offered her husband twenty rubles to protect her from public shame. He cut his head in order to soil her nightshirt. Unfortunately for the bride and her kin, however, the svakha overheard the conversation, and the bride and her family were publicly shamed.[85]

The postwedding festivities and feasts continued to focus on the bride. Many of them, including the ceremonial attestation to the bride's prenuptial chastity and the consummation of the marriage, were held at the bride's parents' home. These continued for a few days during which the bride exchanged gifts with her consanguineal and affinal kin. From the perspective of public participation in marriage, the most important ritual took place on the third or fourth day of the wedding celebrations when, at her in-laws' home, the bride was initiated into her new role as housewife, joining the ranks of all the married women in the community. Upon arriving at her in-laws' home, the bride changed her clothing and proceeded to the well, accompanied by a sister-in-law and all the neighboring married

[82] Titov, *Iuridicheskie obychai*, p. 39. Half or more of present-day women experience no bleeding upon first intercourse, because their hymen is very elastic or forms an incomplete ring. The same was probably true in earlier times. I am indebted to Maureen Tighe-Brown, a registered nurse, for this information.

[83] Kligman, "The Rites of Women," p. 334.

[84] D. I., "Zametki o krest'ianskoi sem'e v Novgorodskoi gubernii," in Pakhman, *Sbornik narodnykh iuridicheskikh obychaev*, 2:264.

[85] Semenova-Tian-Shanskaia, *Zhizn' 'Ivana*,' p. 71.

women. Her first task was to fill the buckets at the well and carry them home. However, village women made that task difficult by shouting at and jostling her. Once inside the hut, the bride had to sweep the floor while the female guests threw money at her. The mother-in-law joined in the festivities by instructing her new daughter-in-law in additional household duties, thus firmly establishing the hierarchical relationship between them. In the first years of marriage a young bride, an unknown quantity, could not participate in food preparation. Instead, she was responsible for sweeping the hut and fetching water and firewood. Thus initiated into the community of married women and her position of daughter-in-law, the bride entertained her new peers and affinal kin with food and drink.[86]

Generally, the first year of marriage was celebrated with feasts and ritualized festivities, the most important of which involved Maslenitsa. On the Thursday of Maslenitsa all the newlyweds departed in their best attire for regional celebrations. Crowds of young girls, bachelors, and the elderly waited for them at the crossroads to query them about their married life. The newlyweds were asked questions—"Do you love your wife?" "Is your husband good to you?" "Do you love one another?"—to which they had to respond by kissing one another. If they did not kiss, the crowds took action by dragging them out of their sleds and pelting them with snow. This public control of behavior within married life supplemented controls placed on premarried life.[87] During the Maslenitsa tobogganing festivities in the north the young married couple again had to kiss each other upon request—as many as twenty-five times. If they did not comply right away they were fined another twenty-five kisses.[88]

A Russian peasant woman's subservience to her husband took on a ritualized form on the Sunday of Maslenitsa when a wife asked her husband to tell her his pleasure. To his answer, "*Rybki*" ("My sweetheart"), she replied by bowing to him and kissing him three times or more, depending upon public pressures. Thus once again the couple demonstrated their love for one another, the harmony of that love, and the wife's obedience to her husband. The link between the kissing and the marriage's potential fecundity was also stressed at the festivities.[89]

---

[86] A. Nikolaev, "Krest'ianskaia svad'ba v Zvenigorodskom uezda Moskovskoi gubernii," *Severnaia pchela*, 8 August 1863, p. 926; Smirnov, "Obychai i obriady," p. 1009; and G. V. Zhirnova, "The Russian Urban Wedding Ritual in the Late Nineteenth and Early Twentieth Centuries," *Soviet Anthropology and Archeology* 14, no. 3 (Winter 1975–1976): 31–32.

[87] S. Ponomarev, "Ocherki narodnago byta: Obychnoe pravo," *Severnyi vestnik* (February 1887), no. 2, pt. 2, pp. 51–52.

[88] V. K. Sokolova, *Vesenne-letnie kalendarnye obriady russkikh, ukraintsev i belorusov XIX–nachalo XX v.* (Moscow, 1979), p. 38.

[89] Ibid., p. 40.

The joining of a couple in marriage was both a family and a community affair. As in courtship, family and community maintained strict controls over the rite of passage into marriage. With the engagement, the active courtship of a suitor and his bride-to-be ended. The betrothed became passive spectators to contracts and customs enacted on their behalf. Attention focused on the bride, whose pattern of life was about to be dramatically changed. She would soon depart her parents' home for her in-laws' and sacrifice her maidenhood for the perpetuation of another family line. Her female peers acted as her support group, helping her finish her trousseau and sympathizing with her natural trepidation over the loss of maidenly purity and freedoms. Already in the premarital stage, the collective of married women intruded upon the bride-to-be and her peers. As the betrothed maiden expressed in lamentations her fears about her new life, these elders voiced their collective wisdom. They advised her to accept her subordination to husband and in-laws but also impressed upon her the rewards of her new life. Once the wedding day arrived, a bride's support group of female peers receded to the background, relinquishing its responsibilities to married women in the community. Henceforth the bride was a member of their collective.

Beginning with wedding day festivities, the community jealously guarded its primary function of legitimizing a marriage. Community sanctification was a necessary corollary to the religious sanctification of a marital union. Consequently village members were not mere spectators but important actors in the union of two kin groups. They actively participated in the rituals attending the wedding ceremony and subsequent feasts and wedding celebrations. Through that participation they maintained Russian peasant society's values and norms. Regulation of the interaction between bride and groom and the consummation of the marriage ensured the subordination of women to men and strove to guarantee a bride's virginity. Even if the bride had to resort to chicken's blood to prove her virginity, that proof was vital to the perpetuation of family and community. Upon the arrival of the bride at her in-laws' home the collective of community women introduced her to her household responsibilities and subordination to her mother-in-law. This patriarchal system with its hierarchy of relations within the family now deserves attention.

VI

The Culture of Patriarchy

THE PATRIARCHAL Russian peasant family was but a microcosm of a hierarchical social order that extended from God to his representative on earth, the *batiushka* (little father) tsar to all other fathers. Thus the sanctity of the family could not be questioned. Family quarrels belonged to the private domain, which lay outside the commune's jurisdiction, except in unusual circumstances when a household's economic security was jeopardized or excesses had been committed in disciplining family members. Containing endemic family tensions within the household was the responsibility of the bol'shak (household head), who had various means at his disposal—threats of disinheritance and recruitment, beatings, and refusal to grant passports—to buttress his authority over family members. Although the community at large refrained from interfering in the bol'shak's sphere of influence, its well-defined behavioral code supported his patriarchal position. Domination of men over women, parents over children, and in-laws over affines had become part of the natural order and regularized economic management of households. Having maintained and buttressed the patriarchy for centuries, male Russian peasants firmly believed that tampering with the system would court disaster.[1]

Commune and patriarch together upheld the traditional hierarchy and delineated physical space as well as everyday responsibilities according to gender and age. Male domination over women and children was expressed in men's appropriating the public domain and economic power for themselves. Community matters were a male prerogative. Only household heads—normally male—represented their households at village assemblies. Women might, in exceptional cases, be recognized as household heads; but they were generally barred from filling public office.[2] Ownership of land

---

[1] The origins of Russian patriarchalism are much debated and too complex to be tackled here. For a controversial exploration of this question which suggests that the ancient Slavs had a matriarchal system, see Joanna Hubbs, *Mother Russia*.

[2] Engel claims that in northeastern Kostroma women filled the positions of representative and elder. The frequency with which women did so is unknown. Zhbankov in his study of male out-migration in Kostroma asserted that male village authorities remained at home, suggesting that instances in which women occupied positions of authority were exceptional. See Engel, "The Woman's Side," p. 268; and Zhbankov, *Bab'ia storona*, pp. 2, 33. For a depiction of the popular negative attitude toward women in public office, see the folktale,

7. A woman plowing in Voronovo village along the Volga River, 1900. Photograph from NOVOSTI from SOVFOTO.

8. Making fishnets. Reproduced from Ministerstvo zemledeliia i gosudarstvennykh imushchestv, *Obzor kustarnykh promyslov Rossi*, ed. D. A. Timiriazev (St. Petersburg: Skoropechatnaia M. M. Gutzats', 1902), between pp. 62 and 63.

was also a male preserve. Russian peasants, like other peasant societies, divided everyday tasks along gender lines, relegating heavy agricultural work to men and domestic responsibilities to women. The patriarch or bol'shak supervised the labors of male kin, while his wife, the bol'shukha, had authority over females. Ultimately, the bol'shukha was expected to defer to her husband.

This male-dominated world depended upon an elaborate misogynist ideology that could successfully subjugate just over 50 percent of the peasant population. Like the patriarchy itself, the ideology developed over centuries, beginning in pre-Christian times. Buttressed by the Orthodox Church, it argued that women were inferior because of their polluted bodies and natural propensity toward sexual promiscuity.[3] That message was constantly proclaimed to Russian peasant women in various customs and rituals, extending far beyond the courtship and marriage practices already discussed. Segregation of men and women in the church, the common meeting ground of all village inhabitants, buttressed the functional separation of the sexes and subordination of women at home and in the community. In their religious observances women stood apart from men and did not dare enter the holy sanctuary, another male preserve, for fear of defiling it. In the home husbands subjected wives to beatings and constantly tested their supposedly weak moral nature.

Despite their position as second-class citizens, Russian peasant women supported or, at least, accommodated themselves to the patriarchy. The isolated individual might resist her subjugation, but peasant women did not stand up as a group to protest their oppression. This accommodation may be explained by the nature of the patriarchy itself, which was careful to give women some rewards, power, and safeguards. Russian peasants honored women as mothers and diligent workers. Because men were dependent on their wives' labors in the household and its environs, they gave women a good deal of latitude in managing their affairs. The patriarchy also placed great store in women's honor, so intricately tied to family and male honor. It protected women's reputations, rigorously punishing those who falsely slandered a woman. Evidence of this has already been seen in the case of a slur on a young girl's chastity. Furthermore, the patriarchal system demanded that a husband fulfill his responsibilities to his spouse

---

"The Mayoress," in Aleksandr N. Afanas'ev, comp., *Russian Fairy Tales*, trans. Norbert Guterman (New York, 1973), p. 41.

[3] The view of woman as temptress originated in ancient times and was adopted by Christian societies. See Bonnie S. Anderson and Judith P. Zinsser, *A History of Their Own: Women in Europe from Prehistory to the Present* (New York, 1988), 1:78–79; Juliet du Boulay, "Women—Images of Their Nature and Destiny in Rural Greece," in *Gender and Power in Rural Greece*, ed. Jill Dubisch (Princeton, 1986), p. 139; and Ernestine Friedl, "The Position of Women: Appearance and Reality," *Anthropological Quarterly* 40 (1967): 99.

and set limitations on the extent to which a husband could physically abuse his wife. Even the maintenance of sexual taboos, while stressing women's pollution, at times protected married women from unwanted sexual intercourse.

As a result of the comparatively positive aspects of the patriarchal system, it is impossible to speak of the complete subordination of Russian peasant women or to view them purely as victims. Peasant women not only accommodated themselves to the patriarchy but actively utilized the power channels open to them. They carved out their own subsystems of oppression within and without the household, tyrannizing daughters-in-law and keeping a watchful eye on the behavior of other village women. Control over the domestic hearth, the ability to affect social relationships, the responsibilities of matchmaker, mother, and mother-in-law provided the power bases for women that extended beyond the household. Through these channels women were very much actors in, as well as victims of, the patriarchal system.

Relations between a husband and wife were defined by the marriage contract. According to the civil law code a husband was expected to love and respect his wife, defend her, and support her according to his means. The wife, in turn, was obliged to love and honor her husband. This meant, above all, that she must fulfill her domestic duties and render her spouse unquestioning obedience as family head.[4] Customary practice among Russian peasants did not significantly depart from this legal definition of spouses' mutual responsibilities and female subordination, except with regard to the difficulties in realizing romantic love and the husband's obligation to support his wife. Ideally, peasant marriages were endowed with romantic love. And peasants had a wealth of incantations that were intoned innumerable times at dawn and dusk to ensure a loving relationship between spouses.[5] The utilitarian concerns in selecting a spouse, however, displaced romantic love as an absolute requirement of a successful marriage. Furthermore, emotions of romantic love, familiar in modern societies with leisure time, were largely impossible in post-emancipation Russia with its harsh demographic conditions. The unrelenting fact of high mortality rates among children, spouses, and parents hardened peasant sensibilities.[6] Russian peasants expected wives to obey their husbands and carry out their numerous duties and husbands to fulfill their labor obligations in the name of household survival. And out of economic necessity both hus-

---

[4] *Svod zakonov*, vol. 10, pt. 1, arts. 106–7.

[5] For examples of incantations, see Minkh, *Narodnye obychai*, pp. 80–81.

[6] The mortality rate in imperial Russia declined steadily from 36.9 per 1,000 in 1861–1870 to 34.2 per 1,000 in 1892–1900 and to 31.0 per 1,000 in 1901–1905. Nevertheless, these rates were extremely high and reflective of a premodern society. Rashin, *Naselenie Rossii*, p. 5.

band and wife shared responsibilities in the household economy; the husband was not the sole breadwinner.

In order to maintain their largely self-sufficient family households, spouses divided their tasks along gender lines. Women worked in the home and surrounding garden and tended small animals and fowl, while men concentrated their energies on farming the household's land allotments. Numerous Russian proverbs emphasized the respective roles and expectations of men and women: "Men marry for soup, women marry for meat." "The husband threshes wheat, the wife bakes bread." "The yard is crying for a master, the house for a mistress." "The man and the dog should be always in the yard, the woman and the cat in the house." "The master of the house should smell of wind, the mistress of the house of smoke."[7]

The line separating the domestic and agricultural spheres was not, however, rigid. Economic necessity demanded that at peak periods of the agricultural calendar women join their fathers, fiancés, or husbands in heavy field labors. At such times agricultural tasks were once again divided among men and women. Women harvested rye, winter wheat, and oats with the sickle, tied grain into sheafs, loaded hay, and gleaned harvested fields for precious leftover grain. The heavier tasks of plowing, harrowing, cutting hay, and harvesting with the scythe were left to men.[8] During the winter months when peasants engaged in nonagricultural work, the demarcation between home and fields largely disappeared as men were forced to spend a good deal of time indoors. Men shunned domestic chores as typically women's work and pursued instead such male tasks as mending agricultural implements and making tools. They left the women to spin and weave cloth for family clothing. Husband and wife might also complement each other's work in domestic industries, the revenues from which supplemented the household's agricultural income. In the poor soil areas of the central industrial provinces proceeds from trades relegated meager agricultural income to secondary importance.[9] Consequently men's and women's nonagricultural activities took on the added importance of meeting subsistence needs.

The industries that Russian peasants engaged in varied according to location and availability of raw materials. In central industrial Nizhnii Novgorod province, for example, women worked side by side with men making spoons in Semenov and Balakhna districts, gloves in Gorbatov district, fishing nets in Nizhnii Novgorod district, and bast mats in several districts.

---

[7] Elnett, *Historic Origin*, pp. 117–18.

[8] Hoch, *Serfdom and Social Control*, p. 92.

[9] See, for example, "Zhurnaly nizhegorodskago gubernskago statisticheskago komiteta," *Nizhegorodskii sbornik* 8 (1889): 602–3; V. Borisov, "Kustarnye promysly Sergievskoi volosti, Tul'skago uezda," in *Trudy Kommisii po izsledovaniiu kustarnoi promyshlennosti Rossii* (St. Petersburg, 1881) 7:894–95, 938.

Sometimes the tasks were distributed according to gender and age. In the spoon trade of Semenov and Balakhna districts, for example, a complicated division of tasks ensured that all family members, from the youngest to the eldest, were employed. The patriarch left the village in search of birch, which he purchased at a reduced rate by felling the trees himself. Upon his return to the village he split the wood into pieces. Then nine- and ten-year-old boys squared the ends of the wood pieces and turned them over to their adolescent brothers to hollow out with adzes. An experienced male adult cutter finished tooling the spoon. Then women cleaned and polished each spoon, passing it, in turn, to their adolescent daughters who added the painted decorations. In the bastmatting trade women did the same jobs as men, separating fibers, working the shuttle, or doing the actual basting.[10] Other domestic industries, such as cooperage, blacksmithing, and metalworking, were strictly male occupations, while lace making, knitting, rolling cigarette tubes, and, naturally, wet-nursing were women's work.

In areas of heavy male out-migration, such as Soligalich, Chukhloma, and Kologriv districts of Kostroma province, Poshekhon'e district, Iaroslavl' province, and Arzamas district, Nizhnii Novgorod province, where the soils did not sustain full-time farming, the delineation between male agricultural tasks and female domestic activities did not exist. Gender division of labor applied instead to the agricultural and wage domains. In these localities the burdens of maintaining the domestic household and farming the land both fell heavily upon women. According to D. N. Zhbankov, a nineteenth-century physician, women greatly outnumbered men in the fields of Soligalich and Chukhloma districts during the harvest season. Only at plowing time were significant numbers of men employed.[11] The menfolk were absent from the village for lengthy periods, pursuing trades in towns and cities as far afield as St. Petersburg. In this division of labor women were responsible for feeding their families, and their husbands for meeting the tax and redemption payments on the land. The activities of both spouses were accordingly indispensable for their families' survival. Thus, whether in purely agricultural areas or the mixed economies of central Russia, peasant women performed a crucial function in the agricultural process.

Women's maintenance of a household, a considerable task in itself, was also vital to peasant survival. Through their many domestic duties of cooking, cleaning, looking after farm animals and the garden plot, making clothes, and selling products of their own labors (mushrooms, eggs, milk, flax, hemp, and handicrafts), they met their families' physical needs. By

[10] Mukhin, *Obychnyi poriadok*, pp. 18–19; Plotnikov, *Kustarnye promysly*, pp. 138–47; and Marakin, "Kustarnye promysly Nizhegorodskoi gubernii," pp. 69–70.

[11] Zhbankov, *Bab'ia storona*, pp. 2, 19–20. For a negative appraisal of migrant trades on agriculture, see Plotnikov, *Kustarnye promysly*, p. 33.

bearing children they perpetuated their families and by socializing their offspring they passed on community traditions and mores. As in other peasant societies, "women made it possible for the young to mature and the mature to be regenerated daily, for social relations to be learned and re-created, and for spirits to be shaped and renewed."[12] The response of Russian peasants to the question of whether young girls should be educated attests to their understanding that a woman's labors were an essential component of household economies.

> Why should we teach our girls, ask the peasants. They won't be taken as soldiers, nor as clerks in the stores. They're too busy to read books. On weekdays they work at heavy labor side by side with their men, either in the fields, the woods or in the garden. They have an equal amount of work waiting for them at home, preparing meals for the family, tending the cattle, taking care of the family, and sewing the clothing. On holidays they are busier than ever![13]

Within the larger community proper home management reflected well on the household. Russian peasants often said that "a good housekeeper's home is like a brimming cup." They advised that while "a good housekeeper will save the house, a poor housekeeper will ruin it."[14] A family's hospitality during such public events as name days, weddings, baptisms, and memorial services was measured in terms of a woman's careful food preparation.[15] Food symbolized community sharing of important family occasions, and women took great pride in being the intermediaries in that sharing.

Thus in Russian peasant marriages husbands' support of their wives was not the whole picture. Rather, spouses depended upon each other for maintaining their household economies. The nomenclature for male and female householders, *khoziain* and *khoziaika*, underlines the complementary and interdependent nature of their functions.[16]

Support became an issue only when a spouse defaulted on his or her side of the bargain. According to customary law, throwing a wife out of the

---

[12] Muriel Dimen, "Servants and Sentries: Women, Power, and Social Reproduction in Kriovrisi," in Dubisch, *Gender and Power in Rural Greece*, p. 53.

[13] Quoted in Ben Eklof, "Peasant Sloth Reconsidered: Strategies of Education and Learning in Rural Russia before the Revolution," *Journal of Social History* 14, no. 3 (Spring 1981): 373.

[14] Elnett, *Historic Origin*, p. 118.

[15] In this respect Russian peasant women were not unique. See Jill Dubisch, "Culture Enters through the Kitchen: Women, Food, and Social Boundaries in Rural Greece," in her *Gender and Power in Rural Greece*, p. 197.

[16] Pakhman made this important point in his *Obychnoe grazhdanskoe pravo*, 2:30. Greek peasants also have complementary terms for male and female householders—*nikokyris* and *nikokyra*. See S. D. Salamone and J. B. Stanton, "Introducing the *Nikokyra*: Ideality and Reality in Social Process," in Dubisch, *Gender and Power in Rural Greece*, p. 98.

house, refusing to support a wife with a portion of one's nonagricultural income, or leaving a husband without permission and reneging on one's domestic duties constituted breaches of the marriage contract. Cantonal courts in the central industrial provinces dealt most frequently with cases of spouses' defaulting on their responsibilities. There the attraction of wage labor away from the village disrupted the family household, rendering opportunities for dereliction more frequent.

Migrant laborers' wives were particularly vulnerable to economic hardship if their husbands neglected to send part of their wages home, a fact recognized by the commune and cantonal courts, which sought to ensure that households paid their taxes. Wives were fairly successful in receiving restitution from the legal system when migrant husbands defaulted on their obligations. For example, in 1869 in industrial Ivanovo canton, Shuia district, Vladimir province, a wife charged her husband with willfully neglecting the household economy and throwing her and their daughter out of the house without support. The cantonal judges were sympathetic to the woman's plight. In their indictment of the derelict husband they invoked the sanctity of the marriage agreement and cited the civil law code articles which demanded that a husband maintain his wife, in return for which she owed him unconditional obedience. Far more than marital irresponsibility was at issue in this case, however. The judges also had to address the defendant's long history of incompetence in household management and alleviate the burden he, as an unstable member, placed on the commune. To safeguard the family property and maintain the plaintiff and her offspring, in that order, they took the extreme step of instructing village officials to inventory the property in question and to place it under guardianship. The guardians were to ensure that the indicted man's dependents received a portion of the rent money for their sustenance. The judges further placed limitations on the irresponsible husband's property rights. He had to obtain permission from both the village and the cantonal administration to sell any of his possessions.[17]

In a similar case, this time before the Dievo-Gorodishche cantonal court in industrial Iaroslavl' province, on 16 March 1871, judges were also solicitous of a wife who had been abandoned by her migrant husband. The husband complained to the court that in his absence his wife had left their home for her father's and now, upon his return, refused to live with him. The wife justified her actions, pointing out that her spouse had sent her a mere 9 rubles 50 kopecks of his wages, a sum barely sufficient for the upkeep of her household and two children. Without funds to cover communal taxes, she was forced to move into her father's home. The communal elder, as key witness, testified to the husband's penchant for drunkenness

---

[17] *Trudy Kommisii*, 2:21, #6.

and delinquency, noting that the plaintiff had twice been returned to the commune under police escort. Convinced of the husband's failure to support his wife and children, the judges sentenced the plaintiff to twenty lashes and ordered him to provide for his immediate family. They also insisted that the wife return to her husband. In the end they clearly felt that a woman's place was at her husband's side.[18]

For a wife to default on her obligations to her husband was a no less serious crime, given the complementary and interdependent labor relationship of spouses. In a number of cantonal court cases involving this issue, judges ordered independent-minded wives to compensate their husbands for the loss of their labors. On 26 September 1871, for example, in the Marinsk cantonal court of Mologa district, Iaroslavl' province, a peasant charged his wife with abandoning the household to work for another peasant. As a result, he complained, he had no choice but to hire a laborer out of his own pocket to replace her. The wife, in her defense, accused her husband of forcing her to seek employment against her will. In the face of her obstinate refusal to turn her wages over to her husband voluntarily, the court ruled that until the woman's labor contract expired on 1 November, the husband was entitled to his wife's earnings. Those wages were to cover the auxiliary laborer's salary and other household expenses incurred during the wife's absence. In a slightly different case before the Dovydkov cantonal court in Klin district, Moscow province, on 10 January 1871, a wife asserted her right to be independent of her husband on the grounds of his cruelty and obstinacy in refusing her a passport. Migrant work, she went on to explain, was the only way that she could escape his constant beatings. The husband dismissed his wife's accusations of cruelty, noting that he had committed no offense in following conventional norms regarding the treatment of wives. Nonetheless, he asserted, he was willing out of magnanimity to grant his spouse an annual passport on condition that she give him twenty rubles per annum to hire a laborer in her place. The wife readily agreed to this. The judges then drew up a settlement that obliged her to pay the agreed-upon sum in quarterly installments. Clearly neither judges nor plaintiff took into account the low wages that a woman earned. Twenty rubles a year was a considerable burden for a working woman.[19]

If both husband and wife were guilty of reneging on their marital duties, cantonal judges did not hesitate to punish both parties. For example, in an 1873 case before a cantonal court in Viazniki district, Vladimir province, a wife charged with refusing to sew her husband a shirt and acquiesce in his other requests was sentenced to three days' imprisonment in the cantonal jail. Male judges viewed such a display of female insubordination—a

[18] Ibid., 3:94–95, #26.
[19] Ibid., p. 139, #62; 2:555, #5.

woman's disguised effort to gain some control over her life—as intolerable. Nonetheless, the husband in the case was not entirely blameless. The judges found him guilty of drunkenness, carelessness in managing the household economy, and tax evasion, for which they sentenced him to the maximum sentence of twenty lashes. In this case the spouses' characters determined their respective penalties. Since witnesses had testified to the wife's conscientiousness as a diligent worker, only her lack of respect for her husband was punishable. The husband, on the other hand, was punished because of his derelict character and its debilitating consequences for the household economy.[20]

The interdependent labor relationship between spouses, buttressed by cantonal court decisions, was further strengthened by the harshness of life. The question of survival constantly gnawed at peasant consciousness. By dividing life's responsibilities among men and women, aligned in different spheres of influence, peasants attempted to overcome the powerlessness they felt when faced with nature's imperious demands. Men united behind the commune, which, in turn, ensured that all households tackled agricultural tasks at the same time and in the same manner in order to secure good harvests. Women who were bol'shukhi, or household heads' wives, were given control over the domestic unit where the functions of production, consumption, and socialization so vital for survival were played out.[21] Neither the male nor the female sphere of influence, however, could successfully combat nature, which held at its mercy the success of a harvest or the life of a child, partner, spouse, or indispensable draft animal. This helps explain the Russian peasantry's fatalistic attitudes toward life.

Even with such odds against them, Russian peasant women were able to create at least some beauty and order through their household management.[22] They spent precious time and care weaving and embroidering the colorful linens that adorned the table, oven, and icons in the spiritual corner of the hut. Each linen piece related a different story as women imprinted their individuality and dreams of a well-ordered universe within the confines of colors and designs unique to each village.

As overlords of the domestic sphere, women also played an important role in family decision making. In this respect the bol'shukha exercised al-

[20] Cited in Dobrotvorskii, "Krest'ianskie iuridicheskie obychai" (May 1889): 264. For a discussion of the ways in which women in a patriarchal system try to disrupt normal social relationships for their own and families' ends, see Dubisch, "Introduction," in her *Gender and Power in Rural Greece*, pp. 16–25.

[21] These were typical responsibilities of peasant women elsewhere. See Susan Carol Rogers, "Female Forms of Power and the Myth of Male Dominance: Model of Female/Male Interaction in Peasant Society," *American Ethnologist* 2, no. 4 (November 1975): 745.

[22] For a discussion of how contemporary Greek peasant women beautify their surroundings, see du Boulay, "Women," in Dubisch, *Gender and Power in Rural Greece*, p. 154.

most as much power as her husband, the bol'shak. Without negating the husband's patriarchal authority, she significantly influenced household decisions. She disciplined younger family members, particularly of the female sex, and arranged marriages for her offspring.[23] Russian oral culture recognized the indispensable role of a woman in the saying "Without a husband is the same as without a head; without a wife the same as without a brain."[24] The community, furthermore, buttressed the bol'shukha's position in several ways. However begrudgingly, it accepted women as household heads when their husbands died, leaving small children, and when husbands and adult sons departed the village for work elsewhere. In many areas communes transferred responsibilities of household management to women whose husbands were incompetent. Women also assumed the important task of svakha (matchmaker) in matrimonial arrangements and as caretakers of oral culture, collectively acculturating maidens in the values and norms of the patriarchal system.

Despite the importance of women in economic affairs, decision making, and social control, patriarchal community norms demanded that Russian peasant women be subordinate to their husbands. That subordination must be understood in the context of both the general hierarchical structure of Russian society—in which everyone, male or female, was subject to a higher authority—and that of environmental challenges. Peasants were subordinate to village, cantonal, and state authorities. All of the links in that chain of command, however, were men whose power and obligations were defined in terms of family overlordship, beginning with God, "our Father," and extending to the batiushka (father) tsar and finally the father of every family. The state had a vested interest in supporting the patriarchal system as a means of social control. Peasants were also subordinate to "the powers of the natural world and the pressures of economic reality." Having carved out the public world as their domain, peasant males constantly competed with each other in their struggle against nature.[25] They believed that their success hinged, in part, on total control over both the household and its members, even if that control did not always make rational economic sense. Men's unwillingness to lend a hand in domestic chores during slow agricultural periods, their refusal to allow women significant ownership of property, and their eagerness to beat women were all illogical responses to environmental pressures. Through domination of women, men appear to have been compensating for their inability to master nature.

Male Russian peasants justified their subordination of women on the

[23] The position of the Russian peasant woman was not unique in these matters. See Rogers, "Female Forms," p. 746; and Friedl, "The Position of Women," p. 108.

[24] Elnett, *Historic Origin*, p. 119.

[25] The same was true of Greek peasant society. See du Boulay, "Women," in Dubisch, *Gender and Power in Rural Greece*, p. 154.

basis of a misogynist ideology that stressed women's weaknesses and sub-servient role. The story of Creation and God's fashioning of Eve out of Adam's rib provided a convenient vindication of women's enforced sub-servience. According to one Russian tale of Creation, God would have chosen another part of Adam's body if he had wanted woman to be similar to or better than man. Made from Adam's rib, woman was to be a caretaker and obedient servant:

> Why did not God create Eve out of Adam's foot? In order that the woman should not run from saloon to saloon. Why not out of his hand? So that she should not pull her husband by the hair. Why not out of his head? That she should not be more clever than her husband. She was made out of his rib to take care of him and to serve him faithfully.[26]

Further, Eve's disobedience and introduction of sin into the world attested to woman's restiveness under authority and uncontrolled sexual desires, which needed to be contained by men. If not, disaster on the magnitude of the Fall would once again strike mankind as evidenced by the Russian sayings "Adam listened to Eve and ate the apple" and "A woman was the cause of Adam's banishment from paradise."[27] A priori, man must never listen to woman again.

The Russian Orthodox Church reinforced popular beliefs concerning women's inferiority. The need for male domination over women was a constant refrain of the Russian Orthodox clergy, inspired by the writings of Orthodox Church Fathers. Sermons of Saint John Chrysostom, Saint Basil the Great, Ephrem of Syria, and Herodias all warn against the wick-edness of women, "evil tools of the Devil."[28] Russians had inherited from ancient Middle Eastern religions and Judeo-Christian beliefs a fear of woman's body. Influenced by the Old Testament, the Orthodox Church reinforced taboos concerning menstruating women, suggesting they were polluted and in danger of fornicating with the devil. Consequently it barred all women from entering the church sanctuary and approaching the high altar. Women had to refrain from taking communion while menstru-ating, and only postmenopausal women could bake communion bread.[29]

[26] Quoted in Elnett, *Historic Origin*, p. 111.

[27] Burtsev, *Narodnyi byt velikago severa*, 2:262; and Elnett, *Historic Origin*, p. 111.

[28] Quoted in and discussed by Levin, *Sex and Society*, pp. 52–57. See also Dianne Eckland Farrell, "Popular Prints in the Cultural History of Eighteenth-Century Russia" (Ph.D. diss., University of Wisconsin-Madison, 1980), pp. 151–53.

[29] See V. Iu. Leshchenko, "The Position of Women in the Light of Religious-Domestic Taboos among the East Slavic Peoples in the Nineteenth and Early Twentieth Centuries," *Soviet Anthropology and Archeology* 17, no. 3 (Winter 1978–1979): 31; Dorothy Atkinson, "Society and the Sexes in the Russian Past," in *Women in Russia*, ed. Dorothy Atkinson, Alexander Dallin, and Gail Warshofsky (Stanford, 1977), p. 14; Levin, *Sex and Society*, p. 169; and Worobec, "Temptress or Virgin?" p. 230.

Orthodox peasants also believed that upon delivering a child women were dangerous and vulnerable. In fact, the actual delivery occurred in an isolated place, preferably the bathhouse. Ritual purification of mothers forty days after giving birth was a prerequisite for their reentry into the House of God and larger community.[30]

If women were morally fragile, easily deceived, and physically inferior to men, it stood to reason that they needed male protection and control. In Russian peasant society that control began in childhood when girls were subordinate to their fathers. On their daughters' wedding day fathers relinquished their authority to sons-in-law. According to a popular saying, "Parents take care of their daughter until the wedding, while the husband [takes care] of his wife to the end of her days."[31]

A Russian peasant husband's superiority to his spouse was symbolically expressed in numerous ways. His wife deferred to him in addressing him by his name and patronymic. Sometimes she referred to him as "father." He, on the other hand, called her by her first name or more often by a generic noun such as baba or *starukha* (old woman) that had pejorative undertones. Diminutives of these names, however, were considered more endearing.[32] Communal members referred to a wife by her husband's family name. Denisova or Denis'ikha, for example, literally meant "the wife of Denisov."[33] In other words, women existed "through others' beings" and received honor and social prestige based on their husbands' and conjugal families' standing in the village.[34] Even within the woman's household domain, the place of honor at the dinner table, located directly under the icons of the so-called holy corner, was reserved for the household head.[35] When guests were entertained in the home, the wife was expected to serve them, awaiting her husband's invitation to join them at the table.[36] Through proper management of her own domain she complemented her husband's public profile in the larger community.

[30] For similar beliefs among non-Russian Orthodox peasants, see Dubisch, "Culture Enters Through the Kitchen," in her *Gender and Power in Rural Greece*, p. 196; and Gail Kligman, *Căluş: Symbolic Transformation in Romanian Ritual* (Chicago, 1981), p. 124.

[31] Illiustrov, *Sbornik rossiiskikh poslovits*, p. 149.

[32] Astrov, "Krest'ianskaia svad'ba," p. 457; Sv. P-ii, "Koe chto o krest'ianskoi sem'e," *Penzenskie gubernskie vedomosti* (1887), cited in Iakushkin, *Obychnoe pravo*, 2:206, #1277; Titov, *Iuridicheskie obychai*, p. 44; and Zvonkov, "Sovremennye brak i svad'ba," in Kharuzin, *Sbornik svedenii dlia izucheniia byta*, 1:71n.

[33] Titov, *Iuridicheskie obychai*, pp. 44–45.

[34] Dimen makes this point with regard to Greek peasants; see "Servants and Sentries," in Dubisch, *Gender and Power in Rural Greece*, p. 64.

[35] Minkh, *Narodnye obychai*, p. 7.

[36] S. Ia. Derunov, "Selo Koz'modem'ianskoe, Shchetinskoi volosti, Poshekhonskago uezda: Ekonomichesko-iuridicheskii ocherk," *Iaroslavskie gubernskie vedomosti* (1889), cited in Iakushkin, *Obychnoe pravo*, 2:433, #67.

A woman's subordination to her husband was, however, enforced by more than symbolic gestures and ritualized patterns of behavior. Russian peasants believed that women were prone to excessive behavior. As a result force was necessary to contain it. A husband had the right to beat his wife because, according to popular sayings with a decidedly male voice: "A husband is the law for his wife." "Beat your wife like a fur coat, then there will be less noise." "The more you beat the old woman, the tastier the soup will be." "There is no court for women and cattle." "If the man sins, his sin is outside the house; if the woman sins, she brings her sin home."[37] Beatings reinforced men's political, economic, and psychological authority.[38]

According to the populist ethnographer Aleksandra Efimenko, peasant women regarded beatings as part of the natural order.[39] In other words, the patriarchal ideology was successful in indoctrinating women in the "male-supremacist understanding of what relations between the sexes should be like."[40] They had come to believe that the survival of their families and community rested upon the maintenance of patriarchalism.[41] Russian peasant women had their own sayings regarding men's prowess: "Behind my husband's head it is like being behind a mountain: with him as my shelter I am not afraid of anyone." "A husband may be like a crow, but he is protection for his wife all the same."[42] These suggested that women accepted their inferiority, arguing that physical display of strength enhanced a husband's worth and esteem within the community at large. By curbing his wife's excesses a husband demonstrated his capability of defending her.[43]

Acceptance of male prerogatives and toleration of physical abuse did not mean that Russian peasant women welcomed a husband's beatings. Certainly they did not actively seek out beatings and, in fact, chanted incantations to safeguard against them.[44] During a bride's ritual bath on the eve of her wedding, her girlfriends took precautions to ensure that her hus-

---

[37] Illiustrov, *Sbornik rossiiskikh poslovits*, pp. 144–46; Maxim Gorky, "On the Russian Peasantry," *The Journal of Peasant Studies* 4, no. 1 (October 1976): 17; A. A. Sukhov, "Bytovyia iuridicheskiia poslovitsy russkago naroda," *Iuridicheskii vestnik* 6 (September–October 1874): 65; and G. L. Permyakov, *From Proverb to Folk-Tale: Notes on the General Theory of Cliché* (Moscow, 1979), p. 41.

[38] This a point that Linda Gordon makes in reference to wife beating in general. See her *Heroes of Their Own Lives: The Politics and History of Family Violence: Boston 1880–1960* (New York, 1988), p. 251.

[39] Efimenko, "Zhenshchina," in her *Izsledovaniia narodnoi zhizni*, 1:81–82.

[40] Gordon, *Heroes*, pp. 260–61.

[41] This is a persuasive argument that du Boulay makes regarding Greek peasant women. It also applies to Russian peasant women. See du Boulay, "Women," in Dubisch, *Gender and Power in Rural Greece*, pp. 148–53.

[42] Elnett, *Historic Origin*, p. 119.

[43] Efimenko, "Zhenshchina," in her *Izsledovaniia narodnoi zhizni*, 1:81–82.

[44] See Minkh, *Narodnye obychai*, p. 82.

band would not beat her. Women also acted more forthrightly by running away from a violent husband and even taking a husband to court if his actions exceeded community norms. These norms, defined not only by patriarchs but also by senior village women, did not condone excessive violence, which was counterproductive to the economic functioning of households.[45]

Russian peasant society did not countenance a woman's flight to her parents as a justifiable response to wife beating. In directly challenging her husband's authority, she threatened the entire power structure of the village. The display of a man's strength vis-à-vis his wife was important both inside and outside the household. It maintained his propriety as an upright community member and brought honor upon his household. Respect was readily generated by a husband's ability to contain family quarrels within the household. Washing the home's dirty linen in public was taboo. When a daughter married, her natural parents lost all jurisdiction over her. The husband was her one and only guardian; he looked after her best interests and controlled her behavior. If he was a migrant laborer, the father-in-law and not the natural father assumed full authority in his absence. According to the law of outside noninterference, "A husband and wife quarrel, but a [third] party does not interfere."[46] A runaway wife and meddling parents who sanctioned their daughter's actions had to be properly chastised.

Cantonal courts in both the industrial and agricultural regions of central Russia heard many cases in which wives had run away to their parents' homes to escape abusive husbands either of their own volition or with their parents' encouragement. In either case, male judges were unsympathetic. For example, in an 1869 case heard in the Vysotsk cantonal court in Serpukhov district, industrial Moscow province, a peasant couple and their married daughter charged the daughter's in-laws and husband with beating her and making her life miserable. The defendants justified their behavior by claiming that the daughter-in-law/wife refused to give them their due respect. They accused her of leaving their home without permission and her natural mother with interfering in their household's private affairs. During the trial both mother and father stubbornly upheld their daughter's innocence. In response, the court not only sentenced the daughter to five days in jail for being disrespectful to her husband and in-laws, but gave the mother a like sentence. The judges found the mother's guilt greater than her husband's because she had actively encouraged her daughter's disobe-

---

[45] This was true of other preindustrial societies, such as the Italian, Irish, and Canadian. See Gordon, *Heroes*, pp. 255–56.

[46] Permyakov, *From Proverb to Folk-Tale*, p. 41; and Sukhov, "Bytovyia iuridicheskiia poslovitsy," p. 55.

dience. The father, on the other hand, was ordered to refrain from inviting his daughter home without first seeking her husband's permission.[47]

In other cases cantonal judges treated meddling parents more severely than their offspring. In November 1871 in Pleshcheev canton, industrial Iaroslavl' province, judges sentenced a wife to a full day in jail for disobeying her husband and leaving his household for her father's with her dowry in hand. Eyewitness accounts of the husband's exemplary character gave the judges sufficient reason to doubt the validity of the wife's complaints. The same judges gave the defendant's father a harsher sentence of a full week in jail for instigating his daughter's departure and disrupting her marriage. In a similar case heard on 26 May 1871 in the Staro-Iur'ev cantonal court in Kozlov district, agricultural Tambov province, a wife escaped punishment for leaving her in-laws' home without permission. The judges sentenced her mother to six days in jail, however, for interfering in another family's concerns and disrupting her daughter's marriage by encouraging her willfulness. In both cases the penalties levied against parents were extreme since they took laboring hands away from their household economies for a significant number of days.[48]

While Russian peasants accepted wife beating as a proper way for a man to curb willful character and to ensure obedience, they did not condone criminal action on the part of the husband. Excessive violence threatened anarchy within the village community since such criminal activity could very well extend to other family and community members. Furthermore, an incapacitated battered wife was unable to fulfill her domestic responsibilities, with resultant disruption in a household's productive function. After all, controlled wife beating, according to Russian peasant rationale, was meant to secure the viability of a household economy by deterring a woman from reneging on her commitments, not to destroy that viability.

Obviously there was a fine line between acceptable and unacceptable behavior. Community members reacted to each other with a good deal of cultural baggage that demanded a wife's complete subordination to her husband and the community's nonintervention in marital and household quarrels. They had to decide when it was appropriate to ignore those customary strictures and defend a woman against her husband's excessive beatings. Their responses were invariably conditioned by the husband's social and economic status within the village, the power his kin wielded in the community, the wife's character and relationship to other village women, and so on. Community action regarding an abused woman was accordingly inconsistent.

In the 1880s the inhabitants of a small village in Simbirsk province be-

[47] *Trudy Kommisii*, 2:214–15, #3.
[48] Ibid., 3:15–16, #14; 1:342, #43.

came split along gender lines in the public shaming of a woman who had disobeyed her father-in-law. Here, as in other areas of heavy male out-migration, daughters-in-law in an extended family were subject to their in-laws' authority. At times fathers-in-law abused their power by making sexual demands on daughters-in-law. The title of the newspaper article that reported the incident suggests that *snokhachestvo*, or illicit sexual relations between father-in-law and daughter-in-law, was at issue in this quarrel. The daughter-in-law must have repelled her father-in-law's sexual advances, causing the in-law to charge her publicly with disobedience. Male villagers, in accordance with the father-in-law's wish, armed the unruly daughter-in-law with a broom and led her through the village, forcing her to sweep the windows of every home and the village school. Meanwhile, several women intervened in the public punishment, demanding that they and their children be spared this distasteful spectacle. The male leaders of the procession ignored the women and completed the circuitous route through the entire village. The women's action in this case suggests that they did not believe in the public shaming's legitimacy because snokhachestvo was a sinful act and not to be condoned. The women's collective action against the men of the village thus reasserted, rather than challenged, behavioral norms. It is unclear why male villagers readily came to the father-in-law's aid. Perhaps they felt that maintaining the patriarchal power structure was far more important than protecting a daughter-in-law from rumored snokhachestvo.[49]

In the early 1870s, villagers in agricultural Tambov province interfered more directly in an unjust shaming incident. After withstanding two years of daily beatings from her husband, Maria Miniushina had on several occasions run away from her in-laws' home. This last time when her husband and father-in-law had discovered her whereabouts, they tied her to a cart and forced her to run alongside as they proceeded from village to village whipping both her and the horse. Inhabitants of one village halted the cart and freed the unfortunate woman. Clearly they viewed this punishment as exceeding acceptable wife beating and as shamefully advertising the household's disgrace. But they were unable to do more because tradition dictated that a woman belonged with her husband. Furthermore, the law of non-interference extended to occurrences in other villages: while peasants monitored behavior within their own community, they turned a blind eye to practices outside the village. Indeed, once the cart had proceeded a safe

[49] "Publichnoe posramlenie zhenshchiny za nepochtenie k svekru: Snokhachestvo," *Russkiia vedomosti* (1883): 330, cited in Iakushkin, *Obychnoe pravo*, 2:175, #1164. For a discussion of the higher incidence of snokhachestvo in villages of heavy male out-migration, see L. P. Vesin, "Znachenie otkhozhikh promyslov v zhizni krest'ianstva," *Delo* 20, no. 5 (May 1887): 187–88.

distance from the village the sadistic husband and father-in-law again tied the woman to the cart and resumed the beatings.[50]

Near the end of the century villagers in Baskakov canton, Sychevka district, Smolensk province, were more forthright in opposing an alcoholic husband's repeated unwarranted beatings of his wife. They rushed to the wife's aid each time they heard her loud shrieks. At least temporarily they saved her from her husband's clutches by tying him up. Unfortunately, the source does not evidence any subsequent community actions against the husband. Presumably he would have been required to answer for his behavior before a village assembly.[51]

When all else failed to stop an abusive husband, his wife could appeal directly to the village assembly or cantonal court. Cantonal court records are replete with cases of women taking legal action against their husbands. While the community obliged a wife to refrain from airing domestic squabbles, it countenanced her right to complain to the authorities when her husband threatened her life, beat her without cause, abandoned her and her children, or threatened the household's economic viability.[52] A woman's complaints against her husband gained even more strength if an in-law or village elder represented her in court.[53]

Unfortunately, we know less about what happened when abused wives turned to village assemblies, rather than cantonal courts, for help. The village assembly's role in protecting women against violent husbands can be discerned only indirectly when women appealed village assembly decisions to the cantonal court. In 1871, for example, a peasant woman of the village Goliada in Klin district, industrial Moscow province, complained that the village assembly had unjustly given her a jail sentence in response to her request that her drunken husband be removed from his position as bol'shak. The assembly apparently found her action a clear case of insubordination to her husband.[54] In other instances women appealed to cantonal courts when their husbands, having already been admonished or punished by local authorities, repeated their offenses. Judges usually treated a repeat offender with severity. In still other cases wives used the cantonal court as the first court of appeal, preferring the less prejudicial

---

[50] Iakushkin, *Obychnoe pravo*, 1:xxvii.

[51] Cited in Pakhman, "Ocherk narodnykh iuridicheskikh obychaev," in his *Sbornik narodnykh iuridicheskikh obychaev*, 2:66–67.

[52] A contemporary observer of peasants in Vladimir province noted that community members considered it improper for a woman to take her husband to court and belittled women who did so. It is unclear from the account whether exceptions were made for women who were excessively abused. Dobrotvorskii, "Krest'ianskie iuridicheskie obychai," p. 265.

[53] See, for example, *Trudy Kommisii*, 3:141, #10; 53, #11; 237, #15; "Pis'mo mirovago posrednika iz Riazanskoi gubernii," *Den'*, 25 November 1861, p. 14; and Pakhman, "Ocherk narodnykh iuridicheskikh obychaev," in his *Sbornik narodnykh iuridicheskikh obychaev*, 2:67.

[54] *Trudy Kommisii*, 2:609–10, #23.

opinions of cantonal judges to village assembly meetings packed with their husbands' kinfolk and friends.

In all cases involving wives' complaints against abusive husbands, cantonal judges examined the spouses' characters to determine the guilty party. Here village witnesses played an important role in providing character references. Community members did not hesitate to attest to a woman's upright character when they believed that her husband had treated her unjustly. Thus, for example, on 14 December 1871, in Kukarin cantonal court in Mozhaisk district, industrial Moscow province, a village elder supported a peasant woman's claim that her husband repeatedly mistreated her, and the elder validated a mir document (dated 25 February 1866) that attested to her exemplary character and mistreatment at her husband's hands. On the basis of this evidence the judges sentenced the defendant to the maximum penalty of twenty lashes for his repeated offenses against his wife, and his father to three days in jail for perjury and participation in his son's cruel behavior toward his wife. In a similar case in 1869, heard before the Bol'shesel'sk cantonal court in industrial Iaroslavl' province, a repeat offender was given twenty lashes for his drunkenness and cruelty toward his wife and was threatened as well with expulsion from his commune if he did not mend his ways. The Ivanovo cantonal judges of Rybinsk district, industrial Iaroslavl' province, also gave the maximum sentence of twenty lashes to a migrant laborer who had repeatedly abused his first wife and was currently abusing his second.[55]

Wife-beating cases at the cantonal court level were not confined to the central industrial provinces where women played important roles in local crafts as well as agriculture and might have been expected to take more forthright action against abusive husbands. In an 1872 case, heard before the Gorel cantonal court in agricultural Tambov province, four male villagers testified that on 4 June they had witnessed an unjust beating. On that day they heard female screams outside the home of the defendant, Sergei Antonov Betin. When they investigated they saw Betin and his brother parading the plaintiff, Betin's wife, through the village toward the village elder's quarters. They added that the husband and his family were evil people who frequently indulged in fights. On the basis of this incriminating evidence, the judges sentenced Betin to a week in jail and his brother to three days.[56]

Women who complained about their husbands at the village assembly or cantonal court received the most sympathetic hearing when their spouses were drunkards and squandered their household assets. For example, on 15 October 1871, the Shulets cantonal judges of Rostov district,

[55] Ibid., pp. 274–75, #24; 3:183, #12; 208, #87.
[56] Ibid., 1:37, #1.

industrial Iaroslavl' province, responded to a wife's complaints about her husband's alcoholism and wild behavior by charging the village elder with keeping an eye on the husband's activities. They were concerned not only with the defendant's treatment of his wife, but also with his ability to pay taxes since he already had accumulated arrears. A month earlier, in the same canton, a wife made a legitimate complaint against her husband for beating her and squandering the family property: he had exchanged twenty-five pounds of peas, ten pounds of field peas, six pounds of rye flour, and a pair of scissors for vodka at the local tavern. The judges sentenced the defendant to twenty lashes and ordered the elder to recover the household items from the tavern proprietor.[57] In some areas the village community even sanctioned the transfer of a household headship from husband to wife if the drunken husband was incapable of properly managing the household economy and there were no adult males to assume that position. The new female head could represent her household at village assembly meetings, an honor generally reserved for men.

By tranferring a headship from a man to a woman cantonal judges were not asserting female superiority. Indeed community norms, which cantonal courts upheld, did not generally countenance domineering wives. By undermining their husbands' authority, these women reversed the normative hierarchy of peasant society and threatened social stability. Common wisdom had it that "a goat is no domestic animal among domestic animals; a hedgehog is no animal among animals; a crab is no fish among fish; a bat is no bird among birds; [a husband] who is ruled by his wife is no husband among husbands." "Unfortunate is that house which is run by a wife; unfortunate is that kingdom which is ruled by many." "Hens should not try to sound like roosters."[58] A cuckolded husband was the butt of ridicule and the subject of songs such as the following:

The peasant plowed his small field,
[And] looked at the sun.
". . . all the people have already eaten,
Everyone has had his breakfast;
But my . . . wife
Hasn't brought me something to eat for a long time.
Now I hitch up my horse,
And ride home."
The husband approaches the yard,
[His] wife is wandering about the yard,
The wife is whitened and rouged.

[57] Ibid., 3:261, #102, #118.
[58] Illiustrov, *Sbornik rossiiskikh poslovits*, p. 143; Sukhov, "Bytovyia iuridicheskiia poslovitsy," p. 53; and Alexander, *Russian Folklore*, p. 125.

—"Well, where have you been, wife?
Where, madam, have you been?"
—"I, sir, was
Visiting at a neighbor's."
—"What did you drink, my dear wife?
What, madam, did you drink?"
—"I drank, sir,
Sweet vodka and wine.
I drank a glass of vodka
To your health, sir."
—"Well, thank you, wife
But you forgot about me!"
—"How could I forget about you?
When I don't know how to get rid of you."[59]

Despite the insistence on male domination, Russian peasants, unlike Western European peasants, did not subject a cuckolded husband to a public shaming or charivari. The absence of this type of charivari from the Russian countryside may be explained by the overriding community needs that demanded economically viable and reliable taxpaying households. In exceptional circumstances having an upright woman assume headship of the household was preferable to retaining an alcoholic male head who failed to fulfill his obligations as a sober and respectable community member. Although village men felt threatened by the role reversal, female accession to the headship did occur. It was normally a temporary expedient until a son reached majority age and could take over management of the household economy.[60] In such cases a woman enjoyed the privilege of headship not by virtue of her gender, but by default. It was the woman's husband who was incapable of meeting the community's expectations of a responsible, hardworking man.

The above-mentioned cantonal court decisions against delinquent husbands present, however, only one facet of the court's rulings regarding domestic improprieties. Wronged wives often did not win their legal battles. Furthermore, cantonal court decisions in the post-emancipation period do not suggest any fundamental change in women's positions within the Rus-

---

[59] Quoted in Titov, *Iuridicheskie obychai*, p. 44.

[60] For an account of how peasant males felt threatened by a village woman's assuming her drunken husband's responsibility for working the land, see G. I. Uspenskii, "Krest'ianskie zhenshchiny," in his *Sobranie sochinenii* (Moscow, 1957), 8:515–16. Communities in Karachev, Orel, and Bolkhov districts in Orel province, and Poshekhon'e and Iaroslavl' districts of Iaroslavl' province, did not condone the transfer of household management from husband to wife. See Tsypkin, "Opeka v krest'ianskom bytu," in Tenishev, *Administrativnoe polozhenie*, pp. 162–63.

sian peasant family.[61] Male peasant judges supported the patriarchal system. They sided with a woman only when her husband violated community norms and plunged a household into economic chaos. Even so, they expected the abused wife to continue living with her husband, a circumstance fraught with further dangers for her. Even if judges had a guilty husband swear on paper that he would refrain from beating his wife or appointed the village elder to keep the husband under surveillance, the wife had no guarantee that her humiliated husband would not seek vengeance against her.[62] When judges, on the other hand, felt that women deserved the beatings they received at their husbands' hands, they upheld the behavioral norm whereby women were to be subservient and obedient to their husbands.

Cantonal judges harshly punished "guilty" wives, those whose charges against their husbands could not be substantiated, for perjury and disobedience. In a case of 25 June 1869, which came before the Bun'kov cantonal court in Bogorodsk district, Moscow province, judges refused to comply with a wife's demand that her husband be chastised for beating her. Their decision was based on the stubbornness, rudeness, coarseness of language, and disobedience she displayed toward him in the courtroom: the woman's unacceptable behavior convinced them that she deserved the beating. In another case, in the same province, a wife's insubordination to her husband did not dissuade judges from punishing the husband for his cruelty to her; however, they also brought a jail sentence down upon the wife for her improper conduct. In March 1871 judges in Bukholov canton, Volokolamsk district, also in Moscow province, punished both husband and wife. They sentenced the husband to the maximum sentence of twenty lashes for his alcoholism and his wife to a week in jail for disobeying her husband and leaving home without his permission. In still another case, heard in 1864 in Iaroslavl' province, the court satisfied a woman's request that her husband be punished because of his drunken behavior and because he threw her and her children out of the house. At the same time the judges sentenced the plaintiff to two days' imprisonment for exceeding her subservient role and punishing her husband personally. She reportedly had tied him up and whipped him with a nettle prior to the trial. These penal-

---

[61] Beatrice Farnsworth takes the opposite view in "The Litigious Daughter-in-Law: Family Relations in Rural Russia in the Second Half of the Nineteenth Century," *Slavic Review* 45, no. 1 (Spring 1986): 49–64. Her argument rests on a counting of random cantonal court cases in which daughters-in-law were plaintiffs. Since the records are not complete and were collected by several commissioners, who had their own reasons for deciding to record a case, the cases cannot be subjected to statistical analysis. The percentage of women who came before the courts is also unknown.

[62] See, for example, *Trudy Kommisii*, 2:68, #7; 531, #13; 3:260, #87.

ties served as stern warnings to any woman who dared challenge the normative pattern of female subordination to males.[63]

After appealing to the village assembly or cantonal courts for help, repeatedly abused women had one recourse left: to seek separation from their husbands. That option was, however, severely limited by ecclesiastical prohibitions against divorce and popular attitudes toward the inseparability of spouses, summed up in the folk sayings: "There is marriage but no divorce." "Fate was tied by the hands—it can never be untied." "A husband and wife are like flour and water." "God unites—no one separates." "A wife is not a glove; you cannot remove her from your hands."[64] Divorce, a strictly ecclesiastical matter, was beyond the jurisdiction of cantonal courts and was granted only in cases of adultery, inability to consummate the marriage, entrance of an elderly spouse into a monastery or nunnery, or a heinous criminal act that deprived a spouse of all legal rights.[65]

To circumvent rigid ecclesiastical strictures and the expenses involved in appealing to an ecclesiastical court, village communities sometimes sanctioned separation agreements. These civil agreements, which the church vigorously opposed, were drawn up either in informal tribunals of village elders or, in cases of unresolved disputes, in cantonal courts.[66] Sometimes the settlements did not excuse legally bound spouses from their marital obligations. For example, in Dovydkov canton, Klin district, industrial Moscow province, judges demanded that a spouse compensate her husband for the loss of her labor. The separation agreement reads as follows:

We, the undersigned, peasant S. I. of the village Opalevo and his wife M. N., came to the following agreement in the Pokrov cantonal court: (1) I, S. I., am voluntarily allowing my wife to receive a passport from the Pokrov cantonal administrative [office] and live where she wishes on condition that she pay me twelve rubles in the course of the year in four installments (as I loathe our family situation). (2) I, M. N., promise to pay my husband twelve rubles in the installments he specifies on condition that he cannot demand anything else of me.

30 May 1871[67]

In another case before the Staro-Iur'ev cantonal court in Kozlov district, agricultural Tambov province, on 2 August 1870, an abusive husband

[63] Ibid., 2:151–52; #24; 108, #2; 348, #8; 3:88, #6.

[64] Quoted in Efimenko, "Narodnyia iuridicheskiia vozzreniia," in her *Izsledovaniia narodnoi zhizni*, p. 39; and Illiustrov, *Sbornik rossiiskikh poslovits*, pp. 161–62.

[65] S. V. Kalashnikov, comp., *Sbornik dukhovnykh i grazhdanskikh zakonov po delam brachnym i o zakonnosti rozhdeniia* (Khar'kov, 1891), pp. 97–98, art. 72; and Stefan Pascu and V. Pascu, "Le remariage chez les orthodoxes," in *Marriage and Remarriage in Populations of the Past*, ed. J. Dupâquier et al. (London, 1981), p. 62.

[66] Kalashnikov, *Sbornik*, p. 99, art. 73.

[67] *Trudy Kommisii*, 2:563, #24.

agreed to provide his separated wife and daughter with three measures of rye per month until the daughter reached maturity. In still other cases spouses agreed to forfeit all claims upon one another.[68]

At times spouses separated from each other without first seeking legal permission. Cantonal court records of 1870 reveal a poignant case in which an elderly peasant woman in Bol'shesel'sk canton, Uglich district, industrial Iaroslavl' province, took the initiative to leave her husband after almost forty years of marriage. She had managed the entire household economy throughout their marriage, because her husband was an irresponsible alcoholic. The wife finally abandoned her husband only because blindness had incapacitated her. Rather than become a burden on her spouse, she departed for her cousin's home. She left her husband the cow she had purchased with her own money. A year later the husband sold both the cow and half the home without giving his wife a single kopeck. The blind wife sought compensation by bringing her spouse before the cantonal court. As she lacked support of any kind, the judges awarded her half the proceeds (thirty rubles) from the sale of the house.[69]

Mutual separations were not a license for common-law marriages, although such marriages existed, particularly in areas of seasonal male outmigration. Communities generally frowned upon such relationships, which threatened the sanctity of marriage. According to an observer of peasant life in Sarapul' district, Viatka province, men who entered common-law arrangements were prohibited from participating in communal assemblies. Community members generally treated common-law wives with scorn and called them *poliubovnitsy* (literally "lovers," with a pejorative insinuation of "loose women"). In some areas children of these illegal unions were referred to as *podkrapivniki* (literally "from under a nettle") or *prigul'nye* (from the verb *guliat'*—"to fool around") to stress their illegitimacy. In other areas villagers were more compassionate in their treatment of an illegitimate child, whom they identified as mother's daughter or mother's son (*materin syn* or *materin doch'*). In Perm, Riazan, and parts of Kostroma province illegitimate children did not have a right to communal land allotments. In other parts of Kostroma, Nizhnii Novgorod, areas of Penza, and Iaroslavl', Tambov, and Voronezh provinces, they enjoyed a right to communal land, but in many cases their inheritance rights were limited.[70] A common-law wife also suffered discrimination in property

---

[68] Ibid., 1:343, #16; 3:62, #41.

[69] Ibid., 3:181, #10.

[70] Tikhonov, "Materialy dlia izucheniia obychnago prava," in Kharuzin, *Sbornik svedenii dlia izucheniia byta*, 3:137–38; and Dal', *Tolkovyi slovar'*, 2:475, 3:1070. Other names for illegitimate children are *vygonok*, *vyporotok*, *polivinkin-syn* ("half a son"), *skolotnyi*, *semibat'kovich* ("of seven fathers"), *ubliuden'* ("cur"), *zhuravyi*, and *zazornyi* ("shameful"). See S. Borodaevskii,

matters. Even if her common-law spouse had bequeathed property to her, she could claim it only if all of the following conditions were met: the man had to have recognized the woman legally as his coresident, a fact that had to be confirmed by several witnesses; he or witnesses had to have acknowledged that her children were his; and finally neither the man nor the woman could have a living legal spouse.[71]

Under unusual circumstances common-law marriages were given communal sanction. In 1884, for example, the newspaper *Kievlianin* reported a case in which a village assembly gave formal permission to a couple to live together out of wedlock because their union conformed to community standards. It is worth quoting the decision in full to illuminate the rationale behind it.

> Since the peasant Fedor N., having not lived with his legal wife for several years through the fault of the latter [presumably Fedor's wife had abandoned him], presently desperately needs the female sex, the marriage with the previous wife is considered dissolved. On that basis and the village elder's thrice-repeated request to the commune that we agree to allow N. to take the peasant woman N. into his house with the rights of a wife, we agree to that proposal. If Fedor N. has a grown male child by that adopted second wife we will acknowledge him to be the legal heir to all the real and movable property, not excepting the farmstead and field lands.[72]

Thus Fedor needed both a female laborer to fulfill the household tasks on the farmstead and a sexual partner. A man's hiring a female laborer to support the household economy was certainly not uncommon.[73] The more unusual community recognition of the common-law marriage stemmed from Fedor's childless state, which effectively annulled his first marriage. Even the highly critical peasants of Sarapul' district, Viatka province, distinguished between an unmarried woman who simply labored in a man's home and one who had sexual relations with the man for whom she served as housekeeper. While they scorned the latter, they believed her to have all the responsibilities, obligations, and rights of a wife.[74] Separation and common-law marriages were, nonetheless, rare exceptions to the rule that a woman was subordinate to her husband for life.

"Nezakonnorozhdennye v krest'ianskoi srede," *Russkoe bogatstvo* (October 1898), no. 10, pp. 238–47.

[71] Tikhonov, "Materialy dlia izucheniia obychnago prava," in Kharuzin, *Sbornik svedenii dlia izucheniia byta*, 3:138.

[72] "Original'nyi prigovor," *Moskovskiia vedomosti* (1884): 348, cited in Iakushkin, *Obychnoe pravo*, 2:181–82.

[73] Bondarenko, "Ocherki Kirsanovskago uezda," bk. 7, p. 14.

[74] Cited in "Resheniia volostnykh sudov Sarapul'skago uezda, Viatskoi gub.," in Kharuzin, *Sbornik svedenii dlia izucheniia byta*, 1:45, #24.

The cases involving women's subservience to men presented thus far have concentrated on relationships between spouses. A husband was, however, responsible for more than containing his wife's supposedly willful character within the household. He was also obliged to ensure that she behaved properly within the community. When a wife falsely questioned a communal member's character or committed theft or adultery, she brought shame upon herself, her spouse, and the entire household. Her husband had to answer for her crimes or to participate in her public shaming, both of which reinforced a wife's subordination. For example, in 1881 a husband in Aksenov canton, Pskov province, was found guilty for permitting his wife's disorderly acts. The woman had slurred a neighbor's character by mutilating the neighbor's cock, an important fertility symbol, and throwing the blood-stained animal in her window. For casting aspersions on her neighbor's marital fidelity, the delinquent woman was sentenced to fifteen lashes.[75]

Theft was a particularly odious crime among Russian peasants, given the precariousness of subsistence agriculture. Every item used in farming or in the home was an integral part of a household economy. Peasants considered the theft even of a piece of linen, which could have provided clothing for a family member, to be a heinous crime. Anna Akulicheva of the village Meshkovo in Bolkhov district, Orel province, mentioned in the Introduction, stole a piece of linen from a neighbor.[76] Her co-villagers publicly shamed her. They tied her to a horse, tarred and feathered her, attached an unraveled linen piece to her clothing, and paraded her thus disgraced around the village. Russian peasants generally displayed the stolen object or its facsimile on the thief's body as demonstrative proof of the crime. A stolen beehive or squawking chicken round the neck was extremely unpleasant for the delinquent, adding to the humiliation.[77]

In Akulicheva's case the matter did not end with the public shaming.

[75] Giliarii Sondoevskii, "Po voprosu o narodnykh iuridicheskikh obychaiakh," *Vestnik Pskovskago gubernskago zemstva* (1881): 12, cited in Iakushkin, *Obychnoe pravo*, 2:56, #542.

[76] Tenishev, *Pravosudie*, pp. 41–43.

[77] For examples of such cases in Ukrainian villages of the Russian Empire, see E. I. Iakushkin, *Obychnoe pravo*, vol. 2 (Moscow, 1896), pp. 63–64, #596; p. 71, #641. Evpl. Solov'ev noted that in Chistopol'sk district, Kazan province, if the stolen animal was a calf, piglet, sheep, or goat, then not only was the animal tied round the thief's neck, but as the thief was led through the village, every village member had the right to strike him/her anywhere on his/her body. The more valuable the animal to the household economy, the more severe the public punishment of the thief. Peasants of the Russian Empire saved the deadliest tortures for horse thieves. See E. T. Solov'ev, "Samosudy u krest'ian Chistopol'skago uezda, Kazanskoi gubernii," in Matveev, *Sbornik narodnykh iuridicheskikh obychaev*, vol. 1, pt. 3, p. 15; Christine D. Worobec, "Horse Thieves and Peasant Justice in Post-Emancipation Imperial Russia," *Journal of Social History* 21, no. 2 (Winter 1987): 281–93; Frank, "Popular Justice," pp. 246–47, 257–60.

The spirited woman later sought revenge for her degrading punishment. Completely ignoring community protocol, she reported the illegal shaming to the district land captain. The government official arrested the village elder and at a village assembly admonished the household heads for allowing the shaming. This again provoked the villagers' wrath against Akulicheva. They decided to teach her a lesson once and for all. Instead of subjecting her to another ritual shaming, village assembly representatives ordered her husband to assert his domination over his shrewish wife by whipping her in public. The public humiliation was intended both to punish Akulicheva for having slandered the community and to deter her from such action in future. Far from deterring Akulicheva, however, the sentence provoked her to even greater recalcitrance. Anticipating the village assembly's demand to be compensated in cash or kind for her actions, she craftily removed her dowry items from her husband's home.[78] Normally Russian peasant communities required compensation, usually in the form of vodka, from delinquent community members as an acknowledgment of their guilt. Once the culprits had formally apologized before the village assembly for their actions, they were welcomed back into the fold.[79] Akulicheva's refusal to acknowledge and apologize for her crimes of theft and insubordination was beyond forgiveness. Having challenged community standards, Akulicheva found herself expelled from the village. One can only surmise that villagers subsequently ridiculed the husband for having failed to curb his wife's willful character.[80]

In cases of adultery, the community sympathized with a wronged husband, allowing him to punish his wife in any way he wished, short of murder, for sullying her entire family's reputation. "Illicit sexual penetration" constituted "a violation of the family" and by extension a violation of the community.[81] The following folk song from the Kolomna region of Moscow province is about a woman who had been wrongly accused of adultery. The truth of the matter came to light only after the husband had murdered her for her supposed infidelity.

> A good young man went to a free city,
> To a free city to trade at the fair,
> And two friends ran after him, the good young man.
> They laughed in his, the good young man's face:
> "Our friend, you know nothing, know nothing!
> Your wife went to a feast,

---

[78] Tenishev, *Pravosudie*, pp. 41–43.
[79] Frank, "Popular Justice," p. 249.
[80] Tenishev, *Pravosudie*, pp. 41–43.
[81] Dubisch, "Culture Enters through the Kitchen," in her *Gender and Power in Rural Greece*, p. 210.

She drank all of your sweet brandies,
She rode your jet-black stallion,
And is chasing your favorite stableman out of the yard."
The young man's heart flared up,
The young man turned back at the halfway point.
The good young man rode up to his yard:
He pounded [and] thundered at the gates.
His young wife ran out to meet him,
In only a shirt,
And took him, the good young man, by the right hand.
When the good young man came to the wide yard,
He, the good young man, drew his sharp sword—
And the good young man cut off his wife's raving head,
And went first to the stable—
And his beloved stableman was lying on a cot,
His jet-black stallion was in its stall.
When the good young man entered his palace—
All of his sweet brandies
Were whole and untouched.[82]

Although there are known cases of Russian peasant men's murdering their adulterous wives, such extreme action, for which a husband was criminally and spiritually responsible, was exceptional.[83] Public and private beatings were, however, quite common. In one such case a peasant woman charged that her husband had cut off her hair and threatened to kill her for her adulterous behavior. Even at the end of the nineteenth century some husbands chose to humiliate unfaithful wives publicly. They tied them to wagons and led them, tarred and feathered, through the village streets. Their personal indictment of their wives' behavior assumed a distinctively public character. All villagers could voice their disapproval of adultery by jeering and throwing garbage at the unfortunate women.[84]

If community members discovered a wife with another man in a husband's absence, they sometimes took the law into their own hands and punished the wife publicly by tarring and parading her about the village. Traditionally a man who engaged in illicit sexual relationships was paraded through the village dressed in women's clothing, and the woman in men's. Sexual inversion underlined the unacceptability of adultery as a reversal of

---

[82] Recorded in Shein, *Velikoruss*, 1:243, #986.

[83] See, for example, Iakushkin, *Obychnoe pravo*, 1:xxxxii–xxxxiii; and Il'ia Shrag, "Krest'ianskie sudy Vladimirskoi i Moskovskoi gubernii," *Iuridicheskii vestnik*, nos. 7–8 (1877): 75.

[84] "Nakazanie muzhem zhenu," *Russkiia vedomosti* (1884): 268, cited in Iakushkin, *Obychnoe pravo*, 2:180, #1189; *Trudy Kommisii*, 2:368, #15; and Mironov, "Traditsionnoe demograficheskoe povedenie," p. 84.

the sacred marital union. One such case was reported in the 1880s. A married woman was discovered with a monk from a neighboring monastery. The village inhabitants forced the monk to don a woman's sarafan (jumper) over his cassock and then escorted him back to his monastery amid a pandemonium of yelling, mockery, and banging of pans and oven dampers.[85]

In the post-emancipation period it was more usual for a community to punish an adulterous wife than an adulterous husband. In Viatka province there was a saying, "Secret amours do not adhere to a man, but [stick] more to a wife since she still [*vse-taki*] lives at home."[86] The growth in seasonal male out-migration appears to have affected community norms regarding men's extramarital behavior. Russian male peasants did not expect a husband absent from home for lengthy periods to maintain marital fidelity rigorously. As far as they were concerned, the lures of brothels in towns or the hiring market were perfectly understandable.

Soldiers' wives were notorious for engaging in illicit sexual relations while their husbands were away in the military. This may be explained by the marginality of such women in the village community, especially if they were childless.[87] Fathers-in-law often resented having to support childless women in their households and sometimes turned them out. In nuclear households childless widows without male laborers risked losing their husbands' land allotments. Taking in male laborers solved such a problem. Otherwise, economic needs forced soldiers' wives to leave the village to earn a living elsewhere. Arriving in the cities with only the clothes on their backs, these defenseless women were at the mercy of male employers and were sometimes forced into prostitution. Richard Stites has estimated that approximately one-third of the Russian Empire's prostitutes were soldiers' wives.[88]

The historical record regarding Russian peasant attitudes toward adultery is, however, somewhat biased because only the most sensational stories were reported in the press. It must be noted that Russian peasant communities often failed to act against adulterers. This was especially true in

---

[85] "Nakazanie posramleniem," *Russkiia vedomosti* (1882): 210, cited in Iakushkin, *Obychnoe pravo*, 2:84–85, #723.

[86] Titov, *Iuridicheskie obychai*, p. 102; Semenova-Tian-Shanskaia, *Zhizn' 'Ivana,'* p. 47; and P. M. Bogaevskii, "Zametki o iuridicheskom byte krest'ian Sarapul'skago uezda, Viatskoi gubernii," in Kharuzin, *Sbornik svedenii dlia izucheniia byta*, 1:17.

[87] The soldier's wife has received attention in Farnsworth, "The Soldatka: Folklore and Court Record," *Slavic Review* 49, no. 1 (Spring 1990): 58–73.

[88] Richard Stites, "Prostitute and Society in Pre-Revolutionary Russia," *Jahrbücher für Geschichte Osteuropas* 31, no. 3 (1983): 351. In the 1890s in St. Petersburg soldiers' wives figured among that city's prostitutes, constituting 13 percent of one sample of 2,552 registered women and 7 percent of another sample of 4,220 registered prostitutes. See Engel, "St. Petersburg Prostitutes," pp. 25–26.

such areas of heavy male out-migration as northwestern Kostroma province, Arzamas district, Nizhnii Novgorod province, and Poshekhon'e district, Iaroslavl' province, where married women were left behind to farm
the land. These women saw their husbands for little more than a month or
two a year. Some of them naturally sought emotional support from the
male agricultural laborers they sometimes hired to help them manage the
household economy. Female community members, who outnumbered the
male population, tended to close their eyes to amorous relationships that
developed between a married woman and her agricultural laborer. The
nineteenth-century physician Zhbankov reported witnessing twenty-two
cases of adulterous cohabitation in one district of Kostroma province.[89] At
times young married women in multiple family households came under the
pressure of fathers-in-law who took sexual advantage of their defenseless
wards.[90] Nevertheless, even in regions of out-migration violations of absolute fidelity and obedience to a husband were exceptions. The vast majority of women who remained behind in the village while their husbands
earned a wage elsewhere maintained their temporary celibacy.[91]

The position of Russian peasant women in the family and community
was unenviable. After toiling from before dawn to sunset they found themselves subjected to their husbands' authority, aggression, and capriciousness. Harmony between husbands and wives was rare in a society that condoned wife beating on the basis of a misogynist ideology stressing a
woman's weakness and propensity toward immorality. Women found
themselves discriminated against both inside and outside the home.

Yet, beyond protesting against their oppression by running away from
home, seeking solace from their parents, or taking the bold step of soliciting community and legal aid when conditions became intolerable, Russian
peasant women did not rise up as a group and attempt to overturn the
system. That reality reflects the patriarchy's ability to subdue women,
women's belief in male supremacy, and, finally, their role as actors within
their communities. Russian peasant women were not simply passive victims of the patriarchal system. They were also players in their families and
communities, wielding direct and indirect power, particularly as they aged.
Russian peasant society accorded household heads' wives a great deal of
respect and authority.

In the hierarchy of relations within a multiple family household, a wife
reached ultimate power as a household head's wife and a mother-in-law.
Only in such a position did she possess substantial authority over the
household and subordinate females. By producing and nurturing sons to

[89] See Zhbankov, *Bab'ia storona*, p. 92. Also cited in Engel, "The Woman's Side," p. 268.
[90] See Vesin, "Znachenie otkhozhikh promyslov," pp. 187–88.
[91] Engel, "The Woman's Side," p. 268.

maturity she gained the community's respect. And through her sons she could manipulate the household power structure in her favor vis-à-vis her husband and daughters-in-law. A son could present his mother's opinions to his father without acknowledging their source. A mother could also complain to her son about his wife's attitudes toward her superiors and the fulfillment of her household chores. Such complaints could easily result in a son's striking his wife a punitive blow.

Relations between mothers-in-law and daughters-in-law in the extended family household were inharmonious at best. Russian peasant oral culture and the proceedings of cantonal courts paint a particularly bleak picture. A bride-to-be dreaded leaving the security of her parents' home and living with domineering in-laws who were not averse to using physical force against her. The new burdens of wife, mother, and daughter-in-law contrasted sharply with the relative freedoms of a maiden. A daughter-in-law faced the long and arduous task of ingratiating herself with new in-laws, in particular the mother-in-law. She had to overcome her mother-in-law's hostility toward her as an intruder into her household. That hostility was not totally unfounded. A daughter-in-law was an unknown factor who retained loyalties to her paternal home and who divided a son's loyalty to his own mother. Besides, "by her very youth and strength she was in an ultimately victorious position, waiting only for the older woman to die before she would in turn become the mistress of the house."[92] Furthermore, she might decide not to wait for the old woman's death, instead convincing her husband to leave his parents' home and set up an independent one where she would become a bol'shukha in her own right. Russian oral culture justified a mother-in-law's distrust of her son's wife by noting that "the mother-in-law remembers her own youth and does not trust the daughter-in-law."[93]

For the first year of marriage the daughter-in-law was called nevestka ("the unknown one") and was closely supervised. Her mother-in-law assigned her the heavier tasks of carting wood, sweeping, and looking after the livestock. The higher-status task of preparing food was reserved for more senior sisters-in-law and the bol'shukha herself.[94] Only the birth of children, especially males who would carry on the family tradition, assert the family's position within the community, and support aging parents, confirmed a daughter-in-law's loyalty to her affinal household. Even then,

---

[92] Du Boulay, "Women," in Dubisch, *Gender and Power in Rural Greece*, p. 147.

[93] Elnett, *Historic Origin*, p. 132.

[94] J. Cuisenier and C. Raguin, "De quelques transformations dans le système familial russe," *Revue français de sociologie* 8, no. 4 (October–December 1967): 529; and Paul Friedrich, "Semantic Structure and Social Structure: An Instance from Russia," in *Explorations in Cultural Anthropology: Essays in Honor of George Peter Murdock*, ed. Ward H. Goodenough (New York, 1964), p. 155.

however, the daughter-in-law remained subordinate to her mother-in-law, who supervised domestic tasks and delegated responsibilities to all females under her authority. According to customary law the mother-in-law did not herself have the authority to punish a disobedient daughter-in-law; that honor was reserved for the daughter-in-law's husband or father-in-law. But she could order her son or husband to enforce his wife's obedience to her demands. Daughters-in-law sometimes found conditions in the affinal household to be unbearable.

However, the stereotypic view of the slave-driving mother-in-law has its counterpart in the abusive daughter-in-law. These stereotypes underline the tensions endemic in the multiple family household. Such tensions among women were the product of a power struggle within the domestic sphere. Every woman vied for the position of bol'shukha. While being a mother gave a woman status in her family and community, power came only with the position of mother-in-law. Once a daughter-in-law became a bol'shukha and mother-in-law, she would use her authority exactly as had her mother-in-law to keep her own daughters-in-law in line.

Motherhood was not the crowning pinnacle of a woman's life. In fact, the household's primary economic function relegated a woman's reproductive activity to secondary importance.[95] A pregnant woman continued heavy tasks, including labor in the fields, right up to the time she gave birth (if she had not miscarried in the meantime). Pressing agricultural needs of the summer months demanded that she resume those tasks two or three days after giving birth.[96] Economic concerns overrode the belief that because a new mother was considered impure, she needed to be secluded for forty days. Russian peasants continued to observe the ritual purification ceremony of churching but required women to resume their household and field responsibilities before that time. If after a particularly difficult birth a mother was not strong enough to go back to work, the village midwife's labors were indispensable in caring for the baby and meeting the household's needs during her convalescence.

Pregnancies were fraught with dangers for women. Primitive birthing techniques were sometimes fatal for women with difficult births. A zemstvo doctor noted that in Novgorod province about fifty-nine per thousand women over the age of twenty died in childbirth.[97] With eigh-

---

[95] The secondary importance of reproductive activity was also characteristic of other peasant societies. See Rogers, "Female Forms," p. 754n.; and Beneria Lourdes and Gita Sen, "Accumulation, Reproduction, and Women's Role in Economic Development: Boserup Revisited," *Signs* 7, no. 2 (Winter 1981): 292.

[96] M. K. Gerasimov, "Materialy po narodnoi meditsine i akusherstvu v Cherepovetskom uezda Novgorodskoi gubernii," *Zhivaia starina* 8, no. 2 (1898): 178; and D. A. Sokolov and V. I. Grebenshchikov, *Smertnost' v Rossii i bor'ba s neiu* (St. Petersburg, 1901), p. 35.

[97] Giliarovskii, *Izsledovaniia o rozhdenii i smertnosti detei*, p. xv.

teen to twenty-two years of childbirthing ahead of those who survived their first pregnancy and a lack of knowledge of contraception techniques (outside of herbal abortifacients), Russian peasant women might have as many as seven or eight pregnancies.[98] In regions of heavy male out-migration, peasant women had a lower average of between 5.1 and 5.74 children each. With every pregnancy women risked extreme exhaustion, prolapsed uteri, and various other complications that rendered their heavy labor responsibilities even more burdensome.[99]

The need to maintain domestic rhythms demanded that auxiliary persons look after newborn babies. Elderly mothers-in-law who could no longer perform heavier household tasks and female children who often had not reached even adolescence cared for babes-in-arms. Zemstvo physicians were shocked by infant neglect, particularly during the summer months when mothers worked in the fields.[100] Those babies whose mothers took them to the fields and breastfed them were lucky, although even in such cases a mother's milk supply often ran short because of the hard work, the heat, and the lack of fluids.[101] More often infants were left at home with only the comfort of insanitary *soskas* to satisfy their hunger. These were rags containing bread and other solid foods, such as bacon rind, chewed by an adult or older child. Feeding by this method often caused severe intestinal

[98] In the 1880s Dr. N. I. Grigor'ev studied 1,155 peasant women who were all permanent residents of Myshkin district, Iaroslavl' province. On average these women married at eighteen, had their first babies two years and eleven months later, and their last babies at age thirty-eight, with menopause beginning at approximately age forty-two. The women in this sample averaged seven to eight pregnancies each. A. Muratov, synopsis of Grigor'ev, "O polovoi deiatel'nosti zhenshchin," p. 107. V. K. Neshel' found that the 250 Russian Orthodox and Old Believer peasant women he studied at two hospitals belonging to Count Stroganov in Porkhov district, Pskov province, had on average 6.39 pregnancies each. See his "K voprosu o plodovitnosti zhenshchin krest'ianok," *Vrach* 10, no. 33 (17 August 1889): 725. Hoch estimates a maximum number of seven pregnancies for a pre-emancipation peasant woman. See his *Serfdom and Social Control*, p. 73. See also Mironov, "Traditsionnoe demograficheskoe povedenie," p. 94.

[99] Zhbankov recorded an average of 5.2 pregnancies in areas of heavy male out-migration in Kostroma province. See his *Bab'ia storona*, p. 88. Afinogenov reported the following averages for other industrial regions in the last decade of the nineteenth century: 5.74 in Cherepovets district, Novgorod province; 5.65 in Ruza district, Moscow province; 5.59 in Moscow district, Moscow province; 5.2 in Novgorod province as a whole; and 5.1 in Riazan district, Riazan province. See his *Zhizn' zhenskago naseleniia Riazanskago uezda*, p. 36. For a discussion of diseases affecting pregnant women and the sometimes fatal ailments these women suffered after giving birth, see ibid., pp. 55–66.

[100] The number of births peaked in July and August. Ransel, *Mothers of Misery*, p. 271. For the most detailed account of childrearing practices among Russian peasant women, see A. E. Pokrovskii, *Fizicheskoe vospitanie detei i raznykh narodov, preimushchestvenno v Rossii: Materialy dlia mediko-antropologicheskago izsledovaniia* (Moscow, 1884).

[101] Nancy M. Frieden, "Child Care: Medical Reform in a Traditionalist Culture," in Ransel, *The Family in Imperial Russia*, p. 252.

disorders for infants.[102] Mothers attended to their babies when they returned home in the evening exhausted from backbreaking fieldwork. If the
fields were more than ten versts from the village core, mothers were away
from their newborn children three to four days a week. In some areas
breastfeeding was not introduced until either after the mother had been
churched or after the infant had been baptized.[103] Women's burdensome
labor responsibilities and concomitant physical exhaustion explain such indifference to their children's welfare.[104]

Infant deaths continually robbed a mother of satisfaction from her constant birthing. More that 25 percent of infants died within the first year of
life. An additional 20 percent did not reach adulthood.[105] Such a high infant mortality rate resulted in women's taking various precautionary measures of white magic to safeguard children against the evil eye or illness.
They often swaddled a baby in its father's shirt so that the latter's strength
might be transferred to the child. According to peasant rationale, swaddling also kept infants from harming themselves and helped to shape their
limbs and heads properly. To ward off the *zhikhar'*, an evil household spirit
who was believed to steal babies from cradles in the mothers' absence,
women left scissors and a spindle in a bag (*zybka*) on top of an old twig
broom on the floor. An ancient custom intended to deceive evil spirits involved burying a swaddled inanimate object with all the lamentations of a
regular funeral. In this way a mother hoped to divert the attention of evil
spirits from her living child.[106]

---

[102] Pokrovskii, *Fizicheskoe vospitanie detei*, p. 269; Semenova-Tian-Shanskaia, *Zhizn' 'Ivana,'*
p. 10; Antonina Martynova, "Life of the Pre-Revolutionary Village as Reflected in Popular
Lullabies," in Ransel, *The Family in Imperial Russia*, p. 173; Patrick P. Dunn, " 'That Enemy
Is the Baby': Childhood in Imperial Russia," in *The History of Childhood*, ed. Lloyd deMause
(New York, 1974), p. 388; and Ransel, *Mothers of Misery*, p. 270.

[103] Sokolov and Grebenshchikov, *Smertnost' v Rossii*, pp. 35–38. Presumably this delay in
breastfeeding occurred only if the mother was breastfeeding another child; otherwise, her
breast milk would have dried up.

[104] Eugene D. Genovese found that physical exhaustion of black female slaves in America
also resulted in their seeming indifference to their children. See his *Roll, Jordan, Roll: The
World the Slaves Made* (New York, 1976), p. 496.

[105] Gatrell, *The Tsarist Economy*, pp. 31–37. Pokrovskii cites an infant mortality rate of 32.6
per hundred. See his *Fizicheskoe vospitanie detei*, p. 272. A zemstvo doctor reported that in
Borovichi district, Novgorod province, almost 53 percent of children did not reach adulthood. See V. O. Demich, "Pediatriia u russkago naroda," *Vestnik obshchestvennoi gigieny, sudebnoi i prakticheskoi meditsiny* 11, no. 2 (August 1891), pt. 2, p. 128. According to a later
study, 47 percent of children born in the countryside died before reaching adulthood. See
N. Pismennyi, "O vliianii fabrichnykh uslovii raboty i zhizni materei na smertnost' detei,"
Zhurnal Pirogovskago obshchestva (1904), nos. 1–2, p. 40, cited in Bobroff, "Working
Women," 1:124.

[106] Zelenin, *Opisanie*, 2:584; A. V. Balov, "Rozhdenie i vospitanie detei v Poshekhonskom
uezda, Iarosl. gub.," *Etnograficheskoe obozrenie* 2, bk. 6, no. 3 (1890): 97–98; G. S. Maslova,
"Changes in the Traditional Folk Costume of Riazan during the Soviet Period (Based on

Numerous superstitions reflected the universality of fatalistic attitudes toward life and the grim reality of infant deaths. It was believed that a baby born face down or who did not scream during the christening would not live long. Children born in the month of May, because they had been conceived at the beginning of the harvest season and possibly during the Uspenskii fast period when sexual abstinence should have been observed, were fated to be sickly. Russian peasants believed that death would follow swiftly if a child was born on a day on which a household object had been misplaced or lost. A church funeral on the day of an infant's christening was a herald of doom for the newborn child. To rock an empty cradle was to sign a baby's death warrant.[107]

Even if a baby lived beyond the first year, mothers did not immediately rejoice. Small children were a drain on the household. While, on the one hand, they were a source of future labor, on the other, they demanded attention, food, and clothing. A peasant saying noted that "it is not a misfortune when all the children are under one sheepskin coat, but it is a misfortune when each needs [his/her] own sheepskin coat." Girls were generally poor investments for their parents. They departed from the household when they reached adolescence, just at a point when their labors became a significant element in the household economy. At best girls could bring honor upon their families through good marital matches. Sons, on the other hand, were more coveted as future providers and perpetuators of the family through the male line. Yet even a surviving son was not a guarantee of future aid for his aging parents. Peasants fatalistically reasoned that a family needed at least three surviving sons: "One son is not a son, two sons equal half a son, three sons equal one son." In other words, one son was bound to be unsuccessful and one would be recruited into the army, leaving only the third son as his parents' helper and supporter in their old age.[108] With the military reform of 1874 parents at least no longer had to worry about sons' being drafted for twenty-five years.

The Russian peasant household was as much a social as a productive and consumption unit. Mothers had to prepare children for the duties and functions that lay ahead of them and the proper attitudes of respect and obedience owed parents. They began acculturating children in the cradle.

Data of the Interdisciplinary Expedition, Institute of Ethnography, Academy of Sciences, USSR)," *Soviet Anthropology and Archeology* 7, no. 1 (Summer 1968): 45–46; Kharuzin, "Iz materialov, sobrannykh sredi krest'ian Pudozhskago uezda, Olonetskoi gub." in his *Sbornik svedenii dlia izucheniia byta*, 1:374; and Sheryl Allison Spitz, "The Russian Folk Lullaby in the Nineteenth Century" (Ph.D. diss., Stanford University, 1977), p. 122.

[107] Balov, "Ocherki Poshekhon'ia," *Etnograficheskoe obozrenie* 13, bk. 51, no. 4 (1901): 100, 109; D. I. Uspenskii, "Rodiny i krestiny, ukhod za rodil'nitsei i novorozhdennym. (Po materialam, sobrannym v Tul'skom, Venevskom i Kashirskom uezdakh, Tul'skoi gub.)," *Etnograficheskoe obozrenie* 7, bk. 27, no. 4 (1895): 78; and Balov, "Rozhdenie," p. 95.

[108] Illiustrov, *Sbornik rossiiskikh poslovits*, pp. 175–78.

Through lullabies women defined the gender and age differentiation of labors within the household economy, the social hierarchy of the patriarchal household (with the bol'shak at the top and the daughter-in-law near the bottom of the pyramid), the powers of the bol'shak, and the obligations that children owed their parents. Lullabies steeped a child in the lore of marriage and death, the two pivotal experiences of peasant life, and evoked a world in which fantasy and reality were mingled. Escapism was a necessary corollary to the drudgery and uncertainties of life. Thus peasant mothers at times speculated about the possibilities awaiting male children fortunate enough to travel to the big city:

> You'll go to Petersburg,
> You'll wear silver and gold.
> He'll buy his mother a jacket,
> His father—red bunting,
> His sisters—some ribbons,
> Grandfather gets shoes,
> Grandmother—tomcats.[109]

As children grew older, mothers exchanged folktales and proverbs for lullabies as a way of further educating their children. According to popular sayings, children owed parents an enormous debt that was to be partially recompensed through obedience and respect: "You can buy everything: only you cannot buy a mother and father." "Annushka is a good daughter when she praises her mother and father."[110] Parents expected children to pay off these debts by supporting them in their old age. Numerous folktales inculcated this understanding. The tale "Magic" opens with these typical lines:

> Once there lived an old man and old woman who had a son. The old man was poor; he wanted to place the boy as an apprentice, that he might rejoice his parents in his youth, help them in their old age, and pray for their souls after their death.[111]

The folktale "Riddles" describes even more graphically the ongoing cycle of lending household surpluses to male children so that they might one day repay that debt:

> Near a highway a peasant was sowing a field. Just then the tsar rode by, stopped near the peasant, and said: "Godspeed, little peasant!" "Thank you, my good man!" (He did not know that he was speaking to the tsar.) "Do you earn much

---

[109] Quoted and translated in Spitz, "The Russian Folk Lullaby," p. 33.

[110] Burtsev, *Narodnyi byt velikago severa*, 2:264; and A. Arkhangel'skii, "Selo Davshino, Iaroslavskoi gubernii Poshekhonskago uezda," *Etnograficheskii sbornik* 2 (1854): 73.

[111] Afanas'ev, *Russian Fairy Tales*, p. 399.

profit from this field?" "If the harvest is good, I may make eighty rubles." "What do you do with this money?" "Twenty rubles go for taxes, twenty go for debts, twenty I give in loans, and twenty I throw out of the window." "Explain to me, brother, what debts you must pay, to whom you loan money, and why you throw money out the window." "Supporting my father is paying a debt; feeding my son is lending money; feeding my daughter is throwing it out of the window." "You speak the truth," said the tsar. He gave the peasant a handful of silver coins, disclosed that he was tsar, and forbade the man to tell these things to anyone outside of his presence: "No matter who asks you, do not answer!"[112]

While children had equal responsibilities to both parents, Russian peasants considered a mother's love gentler and purer than a father's. "There is no other friend like your mother," asserted a Russian proverb.[113] A mother's love, like that of the Mother of God, was exalted. A peasant did not denigrate a mother's love for fear of invoking God's wrath. A mother's curse was an unbearable punishment, while "a mother's prayers will save you from the bottom of the sea."[114] In peasant oral culture ambivalence and hostility toward the mother figure were focused on the stepmother, who as a usurper of a natural mother's role could be criticized and mistreated. Folktales always presented the stepdaughter in idealized terms as hardworking, obedient, and abused by an evil stepmother.[115] Apart from its religious underpinnings, a mother's love was rooted in the contrasting role of the father as an authoritative and punitive figure. A father's disciplinary actions, which took the place of the restrictions of tightly bound swaddling clothes, taught children differences between right and wrong. Popular peasant sayings were clear: "An unpunished son has no respect for his father." "Parental blows give health." "If you did not teach your son when you fed him, you will not teach him when it is time for him to feed you."[116] They echoed the words of the medieval *Domostroi* (a manual for household relations), which instructed fathers:

Punish your son in his early years and he will comfort you in your old age and be the ornament of your soul. Do not spare your child any beating, for the stick will not kill him, but will make him healthier; when you strike the body, you save the soul from death. . . . If you love your son, punish him often so that he may later gladden your spirit. Punish your son in his youth, and when he is a

[112] Ibid., pp. 29–30.
[113] Antipov, "Poslovitsy i pogovorki," p. 69.
[114] Illiustrov, *Sbornik rossiiskikh poslovits*, p. 185.
[115] Alan Dundes, *Interpreting Folklore* (Bloomington, Ind., 1980), p. 41. For examples of folktales that deal with the relations between stepmothers and stepchildren, see "Baba Yaga," "Daughter and Stepdaughter," "The Grumbling Old Woman," and "Jack Frost," in Afanas'ev, *Russian Fairy Tales*, pp. 194–95, 363–65, 278–79, 340–41, 366–69.
[116] Illiustrov, *Sbornik rossiiskikh poslovits*, pp. 167–69.

man he will be your comfort and you will be praised among the wicked, and
your enemies will envy you. Raise your child in fear and you will find peace and
blessing in him.[117]

Peasants placed great emphasis upon disciplining sons as a means of instill-
ing filial respect and the obligation to care for elderly parents.

Disciplinary action became more important as sons grew older. Elder
sons, who were either married or about to be married, were resentful of
their father's position as household head, a position that normally became
theirs only in their late thirties or forties. They might manifest their resentment by disobeying their fathers, attacking them verbally and physically, or ultimately abandoning the paternal household. The bol'shak had
several means at his disposal to contain family tensions. He could turn to
the cantonal court for aid in punishing adult sons who no longer feared
their father's strength. With patriarchalism as the basis of a smoothly functioning peasant society, judges invariably sided with fathers who accused
their sons of improper behavior. Sentiments in the cantonal court records—"The authority of a parent needs no justification"; "The father is
old and therefore cannot lie [about his son's behavior]"—reflect this attitude.[118]

Cantonal judges dealt with delinquent sons in various ways. Often without trial they sentenced them to the maximum penalty of twenty lashes.
This humiliating punishment involved whipping the prostrated delinquent
on his naked buttocks with willow switches before peasant witnesses.[119]
Solicitous of a father's authority, cantonal judges also allowed fathers to
set the terms of their sons' punishment. For example, the judges of Prigorod cantonal court, Borisoglebsk district, Tambov province, on 8 May
1871, ruled that three disrespectful sons, ranging in ages from twenty to
twenty-six, should be punished with the number of lashes their father indicated. However, the father was not to exceed the legal limit of twenty
lashes per offender. In similar cases the judges did not restrict the number
of lashes desired by a wronged father. In an extreme 1863 case of a son
beating his mother, the Shalov cantonal court judges of Bogorodsk district, Moscow province, dispensed with the legal limit altogether and sentenced the delinquent son to fifty lashes. They further warned him that if
he did not mend his ways he would be sent to a criminal court.[120]

Cantonal judges considered the permanent departure of a son from his

[117] I. Glazunov, ed., *Domostroi Sil'vestrovskago izvoda*, 3d rev. ed. (St. Petersburg, 1911), pp.
17–18. Based on a translation by Marthe Blinoff, *Life and Thought in Old Russia* (University
Park, Pa., 1961), p. 35. Also cited in Dunn, " 'That Enemy Is the Baby,' " p. 393.
[118] *Trudy Kommisii*, 2:353, #2; 3:3, #8.
[119] Described in Semenova-Tian-Shanskaia, *Zhizn' 'Ivana,'* p. 94.
[120] *Trudy Kommisii*, 1:403, #15; 342, #41; 3:203, #15; 72, #45; 2:138, #26.

father's home without permission to be a particularly odious crime. For example, on 12 September 1871, in Ivanovo canton, Shuia district, Vladimir province, a father charged his son with leaving home and not being respectful of parental authority. When the son defended his action by accusing his father of severely beating him, the father replied that it was a parent's right to punish a disobedient son. The father reasoned that such beatings were merely instructive; they could not lead to maiming. The cantonal court sided with the father, sentenced the son to twenty lashes, and ordered that he return to his parents' home. In a 4 March 1871 case, Fashchev cantonal judges in Lipetsk district, Tambov province, sentenced a delinquent son to eighteen lashes for having left his father's home without permission and actively reversing the norm of patrilocal residence by moving into his in-laws' household.[121]

A father could also threaten a delinquent son with fission and disinheritance (the mechanisms and consequences of which have been discussed in chapter II), refuse a disobedient son's request for a passport to work outside the village, force a son out to work for wages, and, until 1874, threaten him with military recruitment. In March 1871, for example, a father in Dievo-Gorodishche canton, Iaroslavl' province, denied his son's request for a passport renewal. The son had worked in St. Petersburg for twelve years without sending a kopeck back to the village to help his father pay taxes and communal dues. Since the father was having difficulty meeting current payments, he demanded that his son remain in the village and help him on the land. In the same year in Mologa district, Iaroslavl' province, the Kriukov cantonal court judges heartily supported a father's decision to force his delinquent son and daughter-in-law to work outside the family household. The son was perpetually drunk and refused to do his share of agricultural labor. By requiring the son to fend for himself both father and judges hoped that he would abandon his dissolute ways.[122]

One important factor nevertheless limited the choices of disinheritance, passport refusal, and recruitment (until 1874) that a patriarch had for dealing with a problematic son—the effects of those choices upon the household economy. The proper economic functioning of households was, after all, at the root of patriarchalism. The bol'shak's chief tasks were to distribute responsibilities among family members and ensure their fulfillment of duties for the household's subsistence needs and tax payments. If he were delinquent in those obligations, the village community or cantonal judges sometimes chose to overrule his authority. Thus, on 30 November 1871 a cantonal court in Bronnitsy district, industrial Moscow province, sided with a son who charged his father with being repeatedly drunk, creating

---

[121] Ibid., 2:15, #140; 1:666, #2.
[122] Ibid., 2:316–17, #146; 3:93, #17; 148, #12.

disturbances in the home, and generally behaving disgracefully. The judges, presumably on evidence supplied by character witnesses, did not hesitate to sentence the father to twenty lashes. In a 15 May 1871 case before the Borodinsk cantonal court in Mozhaisk district, also in Moscow province, a father falsely charged his son with neglecting to feed him and to pay the household taxes. The defendant's testimony and that of his mother indicated that the son had not been negligent in his duties to his father. Instead, the household's landless state and the father's refusal to grant his son a passport for migrant work had forced the unfortunate son to depend upon community charity to feed the family. On the basis of irrefutable evidence of the father's mismanagement, the judges ordered the father to grant his son permission for a passport. At other times judges transferred a delinquent bol'shak's authority to his eldest son, brother, or wife. A few years before the previous case, Kukarin cantonal judges, also of Mozhaisk district, stripped a drunken, ill-mannered father of his headship in favor of his eldest son. However, because the father was only fifty-one and thus well below the age of retirement, they ordered that he carry a full laboring load in the household economy, now under his son's management. In another case, in Shulets canton, Rostov district, industrial Iaroslavl' province, judges threatened to transfer a headship to a son if the household head did not mend his ways, stop drinking, and cease abusing his family.[123]

The commune's role in ensuring the smooth functioning of a peasant household economy cannot be overemphasized. Russian peasants perceived the patriarchal system as the best way to regulate relations within a family, ensure the full working capacity of all family members, and provide for parents in their old age. Commune and patriarch combined their mutual interests to uphold the sanctity of traditional cultural norms. When, however, the patriarch defaulted in his responsibilities, the communal elders or cantonal court either chastised him or, in extreme cases, transferred his authority to a responsible adult within his household.

The relationship between spouses and the authority wielded by household heads and their wives stood at the center of the Russian peasant patriarchal system. For this reason they have been the focus of attention. The

---

[123] Ibid., 2:426, #120; p. 294, #7; p. 276, #14; 3:256, #28. Village communities and cantonal courts did not countenance a father's excessively cruel treatment or neglect of his children. In 1867, for example, villagers in Novosel'sk canton, Uglich district, Iaroslavl' province, brought a peasant before the cantonal court on those very charges. The judges put the delinquent under community arrest for six days, during which time he was to do some type of community work, perhaps clean the streets and administrative offices. In Morshansk district, Tambov province, the Rybinsk cantonal judges treated an abusive father more leniently by simply warning him that if he continued to treat his children so cruelly, he would have to answer for his actions before the law. Ibid., 3:175, #13; 1:119, #3.

subordination of women to men was based on misogynist beliefs in women's inferiority and moral weaknesses. Men had appropriated for themselves the right to demand complete obedience from their wives as well as the right to beat them for insubordination and infidelity. While Russian peasant women had to suffer abuse daily, they had recourse to village institutions and cantonal courts that did not condone criminal action on the part of husbands. Customary limitations on violence may not have protected women in every instance. However, the more often women used legal channels available to them to protest the cruel treatment they received at the hands of their husbands, the more they helped define the limits of acceptable behavior.

In spite of the oppressive fashion in which they were treated, Russian peasant women did not develop an ethos diametrically opposed to patriarchalism. They were an integral part of the patriarchy, which was at the foundation of their agricultural and protoindustrial economies. They were both actors in and victims of a system that provided them with rewards as well as punishments. As vital laborers in the household economy, they managed all domestic affairs and aided males in their agricultural and artisanal pursuits. For this they were accorded authority and respect both in the household and in the community at large. As indicated by the nomenclatures of khoziain and khoziaika, bol'shak and bol'shukha, a husband and wife's labors were indeed complementary and interdependent. Economic necessity permitted women to assume traditional male roles as tillers of the soil or household heads when men either left the village for migrant work or defaulted in their obligations as household heads. The bol'shukhi's direction of female household activities, as well as women's general responsibilities for educating and socializing their children, and influencing their children's choice in spouses, gave them considerable power in the community at large. The bol'shukha's authority over children and daughters-in-law was no less oppressive than her husband's general authority.

Tensions were endemic in multiple family households in which the distribution of authority subordinated wives to husbands, sons to fathers, and daughters-in-law to mothers-in-law for lengthy periods. Individual resentments were continuously voiced but had to be contained within limits acceptable to family and community. As in courting practices and marriage preparations, the community and its newer extension—the cantonal court—stepped in to define and help maintain the patriarchy. The household head was supported indirectly by the community's noninterference in relations between family members and directly through regulatory repression of offenders who exceeded behavioral norms. Traditional public shaming of delinquents, outlawed by the juridical reforms of emancipation, was still exercised to some extent well into the late nineteenth century. Even so, peasants did not hesitate to turn to peasant-run cantonal courts for punishment of family offenders. These courts complemented village assemblies and informal community courts in maintaining traditional community values. These values did not countenance a spouse's reneging on his or her responsibilities, criminal action by a husband toward his wife, a woman's cuckolding her husband, theft, or a son's disobedience and disrespect for a parent. The cantonal court lash conveniently replaced the bailiff's whip as the time-honored punitive weapon for male peasants. Public shaming and jail sentences were considered the proper punishment for delinquent women. Oppression of peasant by peasant remained strong in the post-emancipation period.[124]

---

[124] Hoch, in *Serfdom and Social Control*, makes a persuasive argument about peasant oppression of peasant in the pre-emancipation period.

Conclusion

THE POST-EMANCIPATION PERIOD provides a panoramic view of peasant Russia. The traditions of the past together with adaptations to changing circumstances are revealed in all of their richness. Over centuries Russian peasants had developed ways to manage and reap benefits from the land, meeting their own needs and those of the ever-demanding state and nobility as best they could. The collective efforts of households were deemed preferable to individual autonomy. Not only economic but social cooperation intertwined family and community in a complex culture of values, behavioral norms, ritual, and drama that guided individuals in their daily lives and through the important rites of passage. By the end of the nineteenth century wasteful extensive agriculture techniques had become outmoded because of rapidly growing population and government-sponsored

9. Women threshing. Photograph from the Library of Congress.

industrialization. Yet, as long as the frontiers and nonagricultural occupations provided outlets for surplus population, peasants continued to farm with the same methods that had served them in the past. Areas on the periphery of cities, particularly in the central industrial provinces, were the exception to the rule, responding to the market demands of increasing urban populations. Nonagricultural opportunities were also affecting the multiple family household. Some sons and their wives chose to leave the parental household and set up on their own, despite the risks involved. Freedom of choice was also entering the marriage market. At the same time, traditional practices were very much alive.

Burdened by subsistence, welfare, social, and tax concerns, heads of households in the repartitional communes of central Russia had devised ways to equalize resources and burdens. They divided the land among themselves to ensure that each household received some of the worst and some of the best. General and partial repartitions at fairly regular intervals readjusted the landholdings of individual households to accommodate changes in laboring power. Property devolution patterns, favoring partible inheritance in the male line, exhibited similar leveling tendencies. All sons inherited equal portions of real and movable property, which they could either maintain together in joint households or use to establish new households.

Equalization of resources was one way of trying to maintain economically viable households. By providing each household with the number of land allotments it could farm effectively, communes hoped to avoid debt-ridden units whose arrears became the responsibility of the remaining households. The commune immediately rewarded newly married couples with land allotments and encouraged them to stay within already established households rather than risk it out on their own. Devolution of property through the male line served as an additional economic safeguard. It was designed to help households fulfill their communal and tax obligations, meet the sustenance needs of retired parents, and look after dependent family members upon a household head's death.

Economic concerns also moved communes to maintain the partriarchal system in which household heads enjoyed absolute authority over household affairs and family members. The commune and cantonal courts buttressed that authority by punishing delinquent sons. Communal officials interfered occasionally in internal household squabbles to prevent sons from leaving their fathers' households and setting up new households with insufficient property. Communes and cantonal courts acted against patriarchs only when the latter threatened the economic well-being of the community and their own households. Thus they might prevent fathers from disinheriting their sons or transfer the headship of households from alcoholic and irresponsible fathers to their eldest sons or, if the sons were underage, to their wives.

The communal and family systems of apportioning property were, however, neither foolproof nor in every instance based on economic reasoning. Households had varying economic success. Biological factors—too many children, too few adult laborers, or no children at all—as well as environmental crises took their toll. Disruptions in the family life cycle, with the premature splintering of households, could also lead to poverty. Furthermore, for one reason or another households did not always meet their tax payments. When a family became temporarily debilitated because of fire, death, or serious illness, the commune and neighbors stepped in to provide aid until the family could stand on its feet again. Woe to that patriarch, however, who brought disaster upon his household through negligence and alcoholism. Community sympathy for delinquent household management was nonexistent.

Subordination of women to men in this misogynist society had little to commend it from the point of view of economic rationality. Male prerogative of land use may have been justified on the basis of men's superior physical ability to do heavy farm work. Taking land allotments away from widows who had maintained productive household economies, however, only satisfied men's greed. Successful women who had appropriated men's roles threatened men's domination and thus, in the opinion of Russian peasant males, could not be countenanced. The same irrationality dominated activities within and outside the households. In spite of the division of domestic and farming obligations along gender lines, women were constantly called upon to help men in their labors, while men refused to sully their hands with female tasks. To this day Soviet women have the double responsibility of laboring a full day for their families' upkeep as well as caring for children, husbands, and the home when not on the job. An ideology that stresses women's inferiority and their need to be beaten is counterproductive to a society's well-being.

Russian women, however, like their counterparts in other peasant societies, accommodated themselves to the patriarchy. First, they shared the belief in their bodies' uncleanliness that had been drummed into them by their immediate male superiors and clergy. Second, women believed that the fate of their families was tied to the maintenance of the patriarchal system. Although certainly not infallible, the patriarchy and its economic institutions helped perpetuate the family. The family household was the primary welfare, productive, reproductive, and social unit. It supported minors, the elderly, the terminally ill, and orphans. Through its community standing and networks, the family provided some stability for its offspring. Mothers played vital roles in acculturating their children in society's values and arranging their marriages. Setting up economically lucrative matches for daughters and presiding over sons' choices of marriage partner gave women power and prestige. Women were ever present at courtship festivities, comparing notes on the talents of prospective brides, teaching them their place in society, and commiserating with their lot as subordinates in multiple family households. Greater power in the household and respect within the community came with age and the position of bol'shukha. As a household head's wife in a multiple family household, a woman managed all domestic tasks, delegating responsibilities to the females under her. Domination of daughters-in-law and influence over sons allowed bol'shukhi to carve out an authoritative position within the patriarchy.

Tensions were endemic in the Russian peasant extended family household. Limited economic resources, land shortages, and increasing wage labor caused disagreements among family members. Brothers resented contributing work to support their siblings' families. Adult sons felt acutely oppressed by their fathers' patriarchal powers and at times waited reluctantly until their midthirties or forties before becoming household heads. Daughters-in-law reacted negatively to domination by in-laws—in particular, demanding mothers-in-law. Tensions and resentments smoldered under the surface during normal times and periodically exploded, on occasion resulting in the premature division of a household into one or more units. Household divisions were normally postponed until after a father's death. The premortem variety, however, was more frequent after 1861, particularly in the central industrial provinces, as nonagricultural opportunities became more plentiful. Even so, usually one married son remained in the father's household to look after his aging parents. Should parents be left on their own, contractual support agreements were drawn up to ensure that sons met their social responsibilities. A father without direct male heirs chose to adopt a son-in-law to look after him and his wife and to carry on the family tradition and household economy.

Tensions were also endemic in the community as a whole. Conditions of life were harsh and life's demands unrelenting. The economic balance was readily tipped from the subsistence level to utter destitution. Privacy was an indulgence for people who had to be constantly aware of the actions of those around them. Disruption of the common value system to which all Russian peasants subscribed threatened the viability of the entire society, or so they believed. It is little wonder that peasants continually quarreled with one another, disputing land boundaries, casting aspersions on the characters of others, and interfering in others' business. Yet, as in the case of family tensions, resolution was possible. Public shaming of unchaste girls, adulteresses, deviant sons, and petty thieves was designed not only to punish transgressors but also to deter others from similar crimes. Delinquents who repented and mended their ways were welcomed back into the fold. Village solidarity was of the utmost importance in terms of survival.

Traditional community values and norms were inculcated not only through punishment of deviants, but also through the extremely rich customs and oral culture that pervaded all aspects of life. Courtship and marriage rituals guided the behavior of young couples and drummed into them their many responsibilities to family and community. While freedom of choice began to enter the post-1861 marriage market, traditional pragmatic criteria for selecting spouses were retained. Numerous festivities welcomed couples to full membership in the community. In such fashion were community and family renewed.

The relative insularity of the Russian village in the second half of the nineteenth century and the viability of peasant social, economic, political, and legal institutions afforded Russian peasants the luxury of making decisions that served their perception of their best interests. While they continually quarreled with each other, they joined forces to fight threats from the external world. Survival against nature, government interference, class oppression, and modernization was after all the fundamental concern of Russian peasant society. An intricate system of relations and institutions evolved to achieve that goal. The post-emancipation repartitional commune, extended family, and informal community proved to be durable institutions that defied or cushioned changes. The twentieth century's intensified market relations, greater urbanization, demographic revolution, universal medical and educational systems, imposed state ideology, separation of work and family, advent of a welfare state, and forced collectivization finally destroyed many rural institutions and traditions. Peasant men and women did everything in their power to lessen the impact of such changes, at every step of the way, angrily shaking their fists. Stalinist collectivization at gunpoint may have rid the countryside of the commune, but it did not destroy the peasant household and valuable garden, nor indeed the mind-set of the Russian peasant. That history continues to unfold.

Glossary _____

bol'shak — household head
bol'shukha (pl. *bol'shukhi*) — household head's wife; female household head
chastushka (pl. *chastushki*) — spontaneously composed rhyming couplets
chetvert' — unit equivalent to 2.375 bushels
desiatina — unit equivalent to 2.7 acres
escheat — real property, normally in the form of a farmstead, which reverts
    back to the commune in the absence of an heir
frérèche — a household made up of two or more conjugal units of married
    brothers
khorovod (pl. *khorovody*) — round dance
kladka — bride-price
mir — commune as an administrative unit
miroed — pejorative term for a wealthy peasant
obrok — quitrent
obshchina — commune as an economic unit
pereverstka (pl. *pereverstki*) — partial repartitional practice in which the to-
    tal number of land allotments at a household's disposal was altered to
    accommodate changes in household composition
podvornoe — type of commune in which land is held on hereditary tenure
posidelka (pl. *posidelki*) — working bee; evening social
prialka (pl. *prialki*) — spinning distaff
pud — unit equivalent to 36.11 pounds (weight)
razdel — household division
sazhen — unit equivalent to 2.3 yards
sel'skii skhod — village assembly
sel'skoe obshchestvo (pl. *sel'skie obshchestva*) — village community on an ad-
    ministrative level
starshina — cantonal official
svad'ba — wedding celebrations
svakha — matchmaker; officiating senior member of a wedding party, ei-
    ther on the bride's or groom's side
svalki i navalki — partial repartitional practice in which the commune re-
    moved a land allotment and taxes on that allotment from one household
    and apportioned them to another
tiaglo (pl. *tiagla*) — labor unit of a married couple
usad'ba — farmstead; land upon which peasants erected their residential
    and farm buildings and cultivated their gardens and orchards

verst — unit equivalent to 0.66 miles

zemliachestvo — living and working with co-villagers in a town or factory

zemstvo (pl. *zemstva*) — elected rural assemblies at the district and provincial levels

zhereb'evki — partial repartitional practice involving the casting of lots

Bibliography

THIS STUDY builds upon and is greatly indebted to the past twenty-five years' path-breaking work on the Western European family by the Cambridge Group for the History of Population and Social Structure and the French Annalistes. Historical inquiry into the family, which until recently had largely been the domain of anthropologists and sociologists, stems to a great degree from the perceived contemporary crisis of the family. The apparent fragility of the family unit in modern times, judged primarily by increasing divorce rates and by alternative relationships' supplanting institutionalized marriage, has sent historians scurrying to uncover a past that was nostalgically assumed to be teeming with sturdy extended families. With the application of historical demography to the study of the family, Peter Laslett and his colleagues in *Household and Family in Past Time* (Cambridge, 1972) have reconstituted family and household structures for such diverse preindustrial societies as Great Britain, Western and Eastern Europe, North America, and the Far East. Their reconstitutions suggest that, contrary to popular belief, the conjugal or nuclear family and not the large extended family predominated in the preindustrial period. In this light, industrialization and individualism did not tear the traditional family apart but rather solidified the conjugal unit.

More recently, however, these same historians in *Family Forms in Historic Europe* (Cambridge, 1983) have modified this conclusion by acknowledging "four sets of tendencies in traditional Europe" in relation to household composition. They argue that the farther south or east a society was positioned in Europe, the greater the tendency for that society to depart—as a result of cultural stimuli and economic factors—from the classical Western model of simple household structures. They also recognize the possibility of household structural diversity within a geographical region. Deeply rooted norms of behavior in each society, in turn, impeded modernization.

The Annalistes, themselves pioneers in historical demography, have also stressed the importance of examining a society's mentalités, which can be defined as "ethical norms, religious beliefs, social representations, economic views, esthetic perceptions, and labor habits" (Confino, "Russian Customary Law," p. 36). Using the interdisciplinary tools of historians, ethnologists, sociologists, anthropologists, and psychologists, they have begun to uncover the belief and value systems of individual cultures over long periods of time. The study of mentalités is meant to provide a new dimension to economic and social history. Economic, particularly Marxist, analysis, the Annalistes argue, is limited by abstract theories that eliminate real people from the stage of everyday life.

The study of mentalités, nevertheless, cannot properly be separated from the empirical evidence of historical demography, which serves as a basis for evaluating the dynamics of any society. Therefore the methodologies of reconstructing families and mentalités have been used together in this effort to uncover the nineteenth-century Russian peasant's inner world of family, community, and land. Examination of the family life cycle and household structure is essential to an understanding of the post-emancipation Russian peasantry and its place within the European spectrum. Russian peasant family life in the central industrial and central agricultural provinces corroborates Laslett's hypothesis that the farther east a society, the more complex its family structures tended to be as a result of different cultural and economic influences. The Russian peasant household was more complex than its preindustrial English counterpart. Unlike the latter, it did not include servants in its composition. Rather it consisted entirely of natal and conjugal relations who provided the labor necessary to perform the household's economic, social, and welfare functions.

Family reconstitution, however, has the tendency to reduce the peasantry to a faceless mass without individual concerns and tastes. Responding to the Annalistes' entreaty that history reveal the personalities, mores, and values of real people, this narrative is punctuated with the rich content of Russian peasant folk songs, proverbs, and other expressions of peasant oral culture that characterized every aspect of daily life. Russian peasants were emotional and expressive in both word and gesture. They understood the limitations of their world but strove to make the most of it. The contradictions that these cultural expressions sometimes contain demonstrate the peasants' flexibility in reacting to ever-changing circumstances and the options they had for gaining some control over their lives. At times women and men spoke with the same voice, and at other times with two distinct voices. Through exploration of all nuances in meaning, the complexities of the peasant worldview are revealed.

The collections of oral culture are not without their problems, however. All of them suffer from the static nature of the written word. Peasant oral culture is so rich because its raconteurs continually improvised songs and stories. The best collections are those that provide several variations of the same song or tale. Recording oral poetry among peasants, who were suspicious of amateur and professional ethnographers from the big cities or nearby estates, was a formidable task. Mistrustful peasants would have freely sung songs and told stories that ethnographers expected to hear, leaving bawdy versions for occasions when the village was free of outsiders. Any off-color songs and tales would in any case not have reached the printed page because of censorship laws. The collectors themselves had their own biases, and they sometimes unfavorably compared village mores with those of the privileged, educated society they represented. Most of them were men who at times were insensitive to the repressive nature of the patriarchal system. The works by Ol'ga Khristoforovna Agreneva-Sla-vianskaia, Aleksandra Ia. Efimenko, and O. P. Semenova-Tian-Shanskaia, are refreshing for their analyses from women's perspectives.

In addition to the general problems of collecting materials in the nine-teenth century, the first attempts to preserve the Russian national epos were unsophisticated. I. P. Sakharov, a pioneer in Russian ethnography, compiled five volumes of songs, *Pesni russkago naroda* (St. Petersburg, 1838–1839). The songs are not regionally differentiated and are marred by textual errors. His successors, A. V. Tereshchenko, V. I. Dal', and Petr Kireevskii, paid some attention to authenticity of textual material, regional differentiation, and variations in dialect. However, it was not until the foundation of the Imperial Russian Geographical Society in 1845 that eth-nographic studies could be systematized and coordinated throughout Eu-ropean Russia. The society set project goals, defined methodologies, and established scholarly standards.

Despite the shortcomings of Russian oral cultural records, comparative and critical analysis of the voluminous folktales, songs, and courtship and wedding rituals illuminates popular mentalités. Several folkore and ethno-graphic collections stand out for their completeness and sophisticated methods of selection. This book has benefited greatly from the works of Aleksandr N. Afanas'ev, V. I. Dal', and D. K. Zelenin; I. I. Illiustrov's *Sbornik rossiiskikh poslovits i pogovorok* (Kiev, 1904); P. V. Shein's *Velikoruss v svoikh pesniakh* 2 vols. (St. Petersburg, 1900); the journal *Etnograficheskoe Obozrenie* (1889–1916) published by the Imperatorskoe obshchestvo liu-bitelei estestvoznaniia, antropologii i etnografii; as well as the numerous publications of the Imperial Russian Geographical Society, including its journals and serials *Etnograficheskii sbornik* (1853–1864), *Zapiski po otdele-niiu etnografii* (1867–1917), and *Zhivaia starina* (1890–1916).

Russian peasants also revealed their attitudes and beliefs through their legal activity. Fortunately for the modern historian, they were a litigious lot. They made use of the *volost'* (cantonal) courts, which the emancipation legislation of 1861 established exclusively for their estate. There peasants brought disputes involving inheritance, property claims, personal relations with family and community members, broken engagements, and the guardianship of orphans. Records of these court proceedings, at least for the late 1860s and early 1870s, have survived in published form.

The seven-volume reports of the Liuboshchinskii Commission for Re-forming the Cantonal Courts (*Trudy Kommisii po preobrazovaniiu volostnykh sudov . . .* , [St. Petersburg, 1873–1874]) is a unique compilation of cus-tomary law provisions and cantonal court decisions. Set up by Alexander

II, the commission investigated courts in fifteen provinces selected as representative of all regional, economic, and ethnic variations of European Russia. Rather than depend exclusively upon provincial and local official reports, commissioners traveled to the fifteen provinces with a specific program. Twenty-eight questions were devised to elicit responses from peasant officials, cantonal court judges, and ordinary peasants on such matters as the functioning of a guardianship system, the extent and content of last wills and testaments, the frequency and mechanisms of household fissions, property devolution, and women's property rights. Commission members also polled governors, representatives of the nobility, presidents of local zemstvos, justices of the peace, peace arbitrators, and circuit court procurators about the functioning of the cantonal courts. In addition to exercising these broad mandates, the commissioners copied out cases that had been heard by the courts in 1871. A few cases from previous years and from 1872 were also included in the final listings.

Unfortunately, the Liuboshchinskii commissioners did not pursue their tasks uniformly in all provinces. Thus, for example, they investigated eighty-two cantonal courts in twelve districts of Tambov province and only eleven in four districts of Vladimir province and three in one district of Nizhnii Novgorod province. Of the cases relating to provinces of central Russia, only those for Tambov, Iaroslavl', and Moscow provinces can be claimed representative.

The published compilation of the findings and cantonal court records demonstrates that the Liuboshchinskii Commission fell short of its original mandate. Stock peasant explanations about various customary practices suggest that the questions officials put to peasants were phrased in such a way as to elicit those responses. Also, given the peasantry's suspicions of government officials and their intentions, the lack of variation in the peasants' explanations for their practices is understandable. Then too, the commissioners may have standardized their answers. Thus the published accounts of responses to the commission's questionnaire must be treated with extreme caution and, in most cases, simply ignored. The commissioners also did not achieve their goal of providing statistical data concerning the frequency of cases before the cantonal courts in a given year and the proportion of criminal to civil cases.

On the other hand, the listings of cantonal court cases in the commission reports are a fairly reliable source of customary law practices and the influence of the written law upon those practices. Except for a few instances in which cases dealing with peasant arrears and drunkenness appear to have been recorded at the expense of other types of cases, the listings reflect local practices. Nevertheless certain reservations are proper in the use of these court records. They are incomplete because cantonal court scribes normally did not record those frequent cases which were settled amicably among the contesting parties. The extant records, on the other hand, present regional and interdistrict variation in customary law and inconsistencies in the judgments of mainly peasant judges. Furthermore, in order to justify their (sometimes false) claims, peasants often lied and were not averse to bribing district court judges and their scribes with vodka. At the same time, however, nineteenth-century observers of the countryside, whose works have constituted a major source for students of the Russian peasantry, applied their urban bourgeois prejudices to the peasants. For instance, they exaggerated the extent of corruption in cantonal courts, pointing to the common use of vodka in deciding a case. Little did they realize that drink was a common symbol of agreement among peasants. All marriage and labor contracts, for example, were sealed with drink. Why should agreements made at court have been any different? It thus becomes the task of the historian to examine nuance when sorting out custom and self-interest on the part of peasant plaintiffs and defendants.

Court cases, by their very nature, reveal only one side of the coin. Cases that came before a tribunal were disputes which could not be settled amicably among family or community members. For example, the premature death of a household head or spouse, remarriages, and the lack of direct heirs created problems in inheritance matters that needed external arbitration. Nor were cantonal courts necessarily courts of first resort. The village assembly and informal peasant courts continued in the post-emancipation period to provide forums for airing grievances and settling disputes. Entire communities sometimes took the law into their own hands and sometimes publicly shamed moral delinquents. The community expected such deviants to apologize and mend their ways in order to be welcomed back into the community fold. At other times anger against outlaws, such as horse and cattle thieves who threatened the economic viability of the communities, resulted in horrendous illegal tortures and lynching. Unfortunately, these vital local institutions left a scant written record. The role and influences of the village assembly and community behavioral norms can only be gleaned indirectly from the cantonal court records. Fortunately, ethnographic materials, field studies conducted by scholars of customary law, and newspaper reports are invaluable in supplementing such impressions.

Empirical information, such as the numerous reports published by the statistical bureaus of local zemstva and statistical data released by the Central Statistical Committee of the Ministry of Internal Affairs, provide the modern social historian with an understanding of the Russian repartitional commune, ages at marriage, household sizes and structure, and the productive functioning of the Russian peasant household. Many multivolume zemstvo compilations, especially those for the provinces of Moscow, Tver, and Orel, are particularly rich in purely descriptive listings of individual communes and their land tenure practices. The Imperial Russian Free Economic Society also made a valuable contribution to the study of the commune with its sponsorship of the *Sbornik materialov dlia izucheniia sel'skoi pozemel'noi obshchiny* (1880), edited by F. L. Barikov et al. The society sent researchers out into the field to investigate land tenure in individual communes in various provinces of European Russia. Data concerning the method, types, and frequency of repartition, soil quality, the influence of interest groups on communal practices, and the commune's policy with regard to land use by widows, returning soldiers, and illegitimate children illustrate the mechanisms of land tenure. At the same time, they evince the complexities of peasant life, which continually had to adapt to changing circumstances, sometimes temporarily departing from established patterns.

Zemstvo household censuses, because of their aggregate nature, offer limited help for the study of the composition of post-emancipation Russian peasant households. They provide the family historian with only mean household sizes for thousands of peasant villages, which can then be used comparatively with the data provided by the 1897 first national census. Zemstvo statisticians were most interested in the economic rhythms of Russian peasant society and the reasons behind increasing peasant indebtedness, pauperization, and landlessness. Although they cited household fissions as a major cause of worsening economic conditions in the countryside, they did not focus their attention upon changes in household structures. Rather they emphasized the labor strength of households as a measure of their economic performance.

One zemstvo study, however, stands apart. F. A. Shcherbina's *Krest'ianskie biudzhety* (Voronezh, 1900) is a unique sample of raw data concerning 230 families in the province of Voronezh between 1887 and 1896. Intent upon reconstructing a typical Voronezh village, Shcherbina selected representative data from the thousands of household budget studies that his colleagues at the Voronezh zemstvo statistical bureau had collected since the mid-1880s. Shcherbina provided a detailed case history for each of the 230 families, identifying them by name, age, relation, occupation, and nationality. His analysis of each family's economic situation ranged from the amount of land at its disposal to the value of its property, to its participation in market relations, and finally to its profits and outstanding debts. Although he failed to provide detailed information about changes in household structure over time, the raw data are rich enough to enable the researcher to reconstruct families, to measure the frequency and effects of fissions, and to gain a sense of the family's life cycle.

The broad range of published sources makes possible a concentrated examination of the postreform Russian peasant family, community, inheritance patterns, and communal land tenure in the central industrial and central agricultural regions. At times, data from other provinces, particularly in regard to courtship practices and marriage preparations, can be used to illustrate broader cultural patterns in European Russia.

Primary Sources

Afanas'ev, Aleksandr N., comp. *Russian Fairy Tales*. Translated by Norbert Guterman. New York: Pantheon Books, 1973.

Alexander, Alex E. *Russian Folklore: An Anthology in English Translation*. Belmont, Mass.: Nordland, 1975.

Antipov, V. "Poslovitsy i pogovorki (Novg. g. Cherepov. u.)." *Zhivaia starina* 15, no. 1 (1906), pt. 2, pp. 69–74.

Blagoveshchenskii, N. A. *Svodnyi statisticheskii sbornik khoziaistvennykh svedenii po zemskim podvornym perepisiam*. Vol. 1: *Krest'ianskoe khoziaistvo*. Moscow: Tipolit. T-va I. N. Kushnerev, 1893.

Burtsev, Aleksandr Evgen'evich. *Narodnyi byt velikago severa: Ego nravy, obychai, predaniia, predskazaniia, predrazsudki, pritchi, poslovitsy, prisloviia, pribautki, peregudki, pripevy, skazki, priskazki, pesni, skorogovorki, zagadki, schety, zadachi, zagovory i zaklinaniia*. 3 vols. St. Petersburg: Tip. I. Efrona, 1898.

Dal', V. I. *Poslovitsy russkago naroda: Sbornik poslovits, pogovorok, rechenii, prislovii, shistogovorok, pribautok, zagadok, poverii, i proch.* Moscow: Izd. Imp. ob-va istorii i drevnostei rossiiskikh, 1862.

Dobrovol'skii, V. N., comp. *Smolenskii etnograficheskii sbornik*. Vols. 3–4. Zapiski Imperatorskago russkago geograficheskago obshchestva po otdeleniiu etnografii, vols. 23, 27. St. Petersburg: Tip. S. N. Khudekova, A. V. Vasil'eva, 1894–1903.

Glazunov, I., ed. *Domostroi Sil'vestrovskago izvoda*. 3d rev. ed. St. Petersburg: Tip. Glazunova, 1911.

Iakushkin, E. I. *Obychnoe pravo: Materialy dlia bibliografii obychnago prava*. 3 vols. Vol. 1, 2d rev. ed. Moscow: Tovarishchestvo tip. A. I. Mamantova, 1896–1910. Vol. 2. Iaroslavl', 1896.

Il'inskii, I. "Svadebnye prichety, detskiia pesni i pr., zapisannyia v Shchetinskoi, Khmelevskoi i Melenkovskoi volostiakh Poshekhonskago uezda." *Zhivaia starina* 6, no. 2 (1896): 226–41.

Illiustrov, I. I. *Sbornik rossiiskikh poslovits i pogovorok*. Kiev: Tip. S. V. Kul'zhenko, 1904.

Ivanov, V. V., ed. *Obychnoe pravo krest'ian Khar'kovskoi gubernii*. 2 vols. in 1. Khar'kov: Izdanie Khar'kovskago gubernskago statisticheskago komiteta, 1896–1898.

Kratkoe sel'sko-khoziaistvennoe opisanie po Urzhumskomu uezdu, Viatskoi gubernii: Po dannym zemskoi statistiki. Viatka: Tip. Maisheeva, 1892.

Kuznetsov, Ia. "Semeinoe i nasledstvennoe pravo v narodnykh poslovitsakh i pogovorkakh." *Zhurnal Ministerstva iustitsii* 16, no. 6 (June 1910), pt. 2, pp. 201–43.

Mal'kovskii, V. N. "Svadebnye obychai, pesni i prigovory: Zapisany v Rybinskoi volosti, Bezhetskago uezda, Tverskoi gub. v 1903 godu." *Zhivaia starina* 13, no. 4 (1903): 426–40.

Materialy po statistike narodnago khoziaistva v S.-Peterburgskoi gubernii. 17 vols. St. Petersburg: Izd. S.-Peterburgskago gubernskago zemstva, 1882–1895.

Minkh, A. N. *Narodnye obychai, obriady, sueveriia i predrazsudki krest'ian Saratovskoi gubernii, sobrany v 1861–1888 godakh.* Zapiski Imperatorskago russkago geograficheskago obshchestva po otdeleniiu etnografii, vol. 19, no. 2. St. Petersburg: V tip. V. Bezobrazova, 1890.

Moskovskaia guberniia po mestnomu obsledovaniiu 1898–1900 g.g. Vols. 1–4. Moscow: Statisticheskoe otdelenie Moskovskoi gubernskoi zemskoi upravy, 1903–1908.

Nizhegorodskii sbornik. Nizhnii Novgorod, 1868–1877.

"Pis'mo mirovago posrednika iz Riazanskoi gubernii." *Den'* 25 November 1861, pp. 13–14.

Rittikh, A. A., ed. *Krest'ianskii pravoporiadok.* St. Petersburg, 1904. *Svod trudov mestnykh komitetov po 49 guberniiam Evropeiskoi Rossii.*

Russia. Kommisiia po preobrazovaniiu volostnykh sudov. *Trudy Kommisii po preobrazovaniiu volostnykh sudov: Slovesnye oprosy krest'ian, pis'menny otzyvy razlichnykh mest i lits i resheniia: volostnykh sudov, s''ezdov mirovykh posrednikov i gubernskikh po krest'ianskim delam prisutstvii.* 7 vols. St. Petersburg, 1873–1874.

———. Laws, Statutes, etc. *Polnoe sobranie zakonov Rossiiskoi Imperii.* Ser. 2. 55 vols. St. Petersburg, 1830–1884.

———. Laws, Statutes, etc. *Polnoe sobranie zakonov Rossiiskoi Imperii.* Ser. 3. 33 vols. St. Petersburg, 1885–1916.

———. Laws, Statutes, etc. *Sbornik dukhovnykh i grazhdanskikh zakonov po delam brachnym i o zakonnosti rozhdeniia.* Compiled by S. V. Kalashnikov. Khar'kov: Tip. I. M. Varshavchika, 1891.

———. Laws, Statutes, etc. *Svod zakonov Rossiiskoi Imperii.* 16 vols. St. Petersburg, 1876.

———. Ministerstvo finansov. *Trudy mestnykh komitetov o nuzhdakh sel'skokhoziaistvennoi promyshlennosti.* 58 vols. St. Petersburg, 1903.

———. Ministerstvo vnutrennikh del. Tsentral'nyi statisticheskii komitet. *Pervaia vseobshchaia perepis' naseleniia Rossiiskoi Imperii, 1897 goda.* Edited by N. A. Troinitskii. 89 vols. St. Petersburg, 1899–1905.

———. Ministerstvo vnutrennikh del. Tsentral'nyi statisticheskii komitet. *Statisticheskii vremennik Rossiiskoi Imperii.* Ser. 2, vols. 17–22. Ser. 3, vol. 7. St. Petersburg, 1881–1887.

———. Ministerstvo vnutrennikh del. Tsentral'nyi statisticheskii komitet. *Statistika Rossiiskoi Imperii.* 90 vols. St. Petersburg, 1887–1914.

———. Ministerstvo vnutrennikh del. Zemskii otdel. *Svod zakliuchenii gubernskikh soveshchanii po voprosam, otnosiashchimsia k peresmotru zakonodatel'stva o krest'ianakh.* 3 vols. St. Petersburg, 1897.

———. *Trudy kommisii po izsledovaniiu kustarnoi promyshlennosti Rossii.* 15 vols. St. Petersburg: Tip. V. Kirshbauma, 1879–1885.

Sbornik statisticheskikh svedenii po Orlovskoi gubernii. 3 vols. Moscow and Orel: Izd. Orlovskago zemstva, 1886–1887.

Sbornik statisticheskikh svedenii po Saratovskoi gubernii. 3 vols. Saratov: Izd. Saratovskago gubernskago zemstva, 1883–1884.

Sbornik statisticheskikh svedenii po Tverskoi gubernii. Vols 2–12. Tver: Izd. Tverskago gubernskago zemstva, 1889–1895.

Sbornik statisticheskikh svedenii po Voronezhskoi gubernii. Vol. 3, pt 1: *Zemlianskii uezd.* Voronezh: Izd. Voronezhskago gubernskago zemstva, 1886.

Shcherbina, F. A. *Krest'ianskie biudzhety.* Voronezh: Izd. Imperatorskago vol'nago ekonomicheskago obshchestva, 1900.

Shedden-Ralston, William Ralston. *Russian Folk-Tales.* London: Smith, Elder, 1873.

———. *The Songs of the Russian People, as Illustrative of Slavonic Mythology and Russian Social Life.* London: Ellis & Green, 1872.

Shein, P. V. *Velikoruss v svoikh pesniakh, obriadakh, obychaiakh, verovaniiakh, skazkakh, legendakh i t.p.* 2 vols. St. Petersburg: Imp. Akademiia nauk, 1900.

Statisticheskii ezhegodnik Moskovskoi gubernii za 1893 g. Moscow: Statisticheskoe otdelenie Moskovskoi gubernskoi zemskoi upravy, 1893.

Statisticheskii sbornik po S.-Peterburgskoi gubernii 1897 god. St. Petersburg, 1898.

Sukhov, A. A. "Bytovyia iuridicheskiia poslovitsy russkago naroda." *Iuridicheskii vestnik* 6 (September–October 1874): 45–67.

Tverdova-Svavitskaia, Z. M., and N. A. Svavitskii. *Zemskie podvornye perepisi 1880–1913: Pouezdnye itogi.* Moscow: Izd. Tsentral'nogo Statisticheskogo Upravlenii SSSR, 1926.

Zelenin, D. K. "Iz byta i poezii krest'ian Novgorodskoi gubernii." *Zhivaia starina* 14, nos. 1–2 (1905): 1–56.

———. *Opisanie rukopisei uchenago arkhiva Imperatorskago russkago geograficheskago obshchestva.* 3 vols. Petrograd: Izd. Imperatorskago russkago geograficheskago obshchestva, 1914–1916.

———. "Sbornik chastushek Novgorodskoi gub. (Po materialam iz bumag V. A. Voskresenskago)." *Etnograficheskoe obozrenie* 17, bks. 65–66, nos. 2–3 (1905): 164–230.

Secondary Sources

Pre-1917 Monographs and Articles concerning Russia

Afanas'ev, Aleksandr N. "Iuridicheskiia obychai: Po povodu vyzova Etnograficheskago otdeleniia Russkago geograficheskago obshchestva." *Biblioteka dlia chteniia* (April 1865), nos. 7–8, pp. 45–61.

———. *Poeticheskie vozzreniia slavian na prirodu: Opyt sravnitel'nago izucheniia slavianskikh predanii i verovanii, v sviazi s mificheskimi skazaniiami drugikh rodstvennykh narodov.* 3 vols. 1865–1869. Reprint. The Hague: Mouton, 1970.

Afinogenov, A. O. *Zhizn' zhenskago naseleniia Riazanskago uezda v period detorodnoi deiatel'nosti zhenshchiny i polozhenie dela akusherskoi pomoshchi etomu naseleniiu: Mediko-statisticheskoe izsledovanie.* St. Petersburg: Tip. Shtaba otdel'nago korpusa zhandarmov, 1903.

Agreneva-Slavianskaia, Ol'ga Khristoforovna, comp. *Opisanie russkoi krest'ianskoi svad'by s tekstom i pesniami: obriadovymi, golosil'nymi, prichital'nymi i zavyval'nymi.* 3 vols. [Moscow: Tip. A. A. Levenson, 1887–1889].

Anichkov, Evgenii Vasil'evich. "Chto takoe narodnaia slovesnost'?" *Istoriia russkoi literatury* (Moscow) 1 (1908): 1–15.

———. "Pesnia." *Istoriia russkoi literatury* (Moscow) 1 (1908): 173–220.

Arkhangel'skii, A. "Selo Davshino, Iaroslavskoi gubernii Poshekhonskago uezda." *Etnograficheskii sbornik* 2 (1854): 1–79.

Astrov, N. "Krest'ianskaia svad'ba v s. Zagoskine, Penzenskago u. (Bytovoi ocherk)." *Zhivaia starina* 14, nos. 3–4 (1905): 415–58.

Azarevich, D. "Russkii brak." *Zhurnal grazhdanskago i ugolovnago prava* 10, nos. 5–6 (September–December 1880): 82–132, 97–139.

Babarykin, V. "Sel'tso Vasil'evskoe, Nizhegorodskoi gubernii, Nizhegorodskago uezda." *Etnograficheskii sbornik* 1 (1853): 1–24.

Balov, A. V. "Ocherki Poshekhon'ia." *Etnograficheskoe obozrenie* 9, bk. 35, no. 4 (1897): 57–76; 11, bks. 40–41, nos. 1–2 (1899): 193–224; 13, bk. 51, no. 4 (1901): 81–134.

———. "Rozhdenie i vospitanie detei v Poshekhonskom uezda, Iarosl. gub." *Etnograficheskoe obozrenie* 2, bk. 6, no. 3 (1890): 90–114.

Balov, A. V., S. Ia. Derunov, and Ia. Il'inskii. "Ocherki Poshekhon'ia." *Etnograficheskoe obozrenie* 10, bk. 39, no. 4 (1898): 69–92.

Barikov, F. L., et al., eds. *Sbornik materialov dlia izucheniia sel'skoi pozemel'noi obshchiny.* Vol. 1. St. Petersburg: Izd. Imperatorskikh vol'nago ekonomicheskago i russkago geograficheskago obshchestva, 1880.

Bondarenko, V. N. "Ocherki Kirsanovskago uezda, Tambovsk. gub." *Etnograficheskoe obozrenie* 2, bks. 6–7, nos. 3–4 (1890): 62–89, 1–24.

Borodaevskii, S. "Nezakonnorozhdennye v krest'ianskoi srede." *Russkoe bogatstvo* (October 1898), no. 10, pp. 233–51.

Borzhovskii, Valerian. " 'Parubotstvo,' kak osobaia gruppa v malorusskom sel'skom obshchestve." *Kievskaia starina* (August 1887): 765–76.

Brzheskii, N. K. "Krest'ianskie semeinye razdely i zakon 18 marta 1886 goda." *Russkoe ekonomicheskoe obozrenie* 4, nos. 4–6 (April–June 1900): 39–79, 68–110, 48–82.

———. *Nedoimochnost' i krugovaia poruka sel'skikh obshchestv: Istoriko-kriticheskii obzor deistvuiushchago zakonodatel'stva.* St. Petersburg: Tip. V. Kirshbauma, 1897.

———. *Ocherki iuridicheskogo byta krest'ian.* St. Petersburg, 1902.

Chernenkov, N. *K kharakteristike krest'ianskago khoziaistva.* Vol. 1. Moscow: Tip.-lit. Russkago tovarishchestva, 1905.

Demich, V. O. "Pediatriia u russkago naroda." *Vestnik obshchestvennoi gigieny, sudebnoi i prakticheskoi meditsiny* 11, nos. 2–3 (August–September 1891), pt. 2, pp. 125–45, 187–212; 12, nos. 1–3 (October–December 1891), pt. 2, pp. 66–76, 111–23, 169–86.

Dilaktorskii, P. A. "Svadebnye obychai i pesni v Totemskom uezde, Vologodskoi gubernii." *Etnograficheskoe obozrenie* 11, bk. 42, no. 3 (1899): 160–65.

Dobrotvorskii, N. "Krest'ianskie iuridicheskie obychai: Po materialam, sobrannym v vostochnoi chasti Vladimirskoi gubernii (uezdy Viaznikovskii, Gorokhovetskii, Shuiskii i Kovrovskii)." *Iuridicheskii vestnik* (May 1889): 261–93; (October–November 1891): 197–208, 326–63.

————. "Pozemel'naia obshchina v Orlovskom uezde, Viatskoi gubernii." *Russkaia mysl'* 5, no. 9 (September 1884), pt. 2, pp. 26–60.

Druzhinin, Nikolai Petrovich. *Iuridicheskoe polozhenie krest'ian: Izsledovanie, -s prilozheniem statei: I. Polnopravnyia sel'skiia obshchestva i bezpravnyia seleniia. II. Krest'ianskaia zhenshchina. III. "Vy" i "ty." IV. Nakazanie bez suda. V. Preobrazovannyi volostnoi sud. VI. Iuridicheskaia bezpomoshchnost' krest'ian.* St. Petersburg: Izd. Iuridicheskago knizhnago magazina N. K. Martynova, 1897.

Efimenko, Aleksandra Ia. *Izsledovaniia narodnoi zhizni.* Vol. 1: *Obychnoe pravo.* Moscow: Izd. V. I. Kasperova, 1884.

Efimenko, P. S., comp. *Materialy po etnografii russkago naseleniia Arkhangel'skoi gubernii.* Izvestiia Imperatorskago obshchestva liubitelei estestvoznaniia, antropologii i etnografii 30, nos. 1–3 (1878). Trudy etnograficheskago otdela, 5, nos. 1–2.

Fon–Nos, St. "Pokrytka." *Kievskaia starina* 1, no. 2 (February 1882): 427–29.

Gaideburov, B. P. "Brachnye podarki." *Iuridicheskii vestnik* nos. 3–4 (July–August 1891): 287–315.

Gerasimov, M. K. "Materialy po narodnoi meditsine i akusherstvu v Cherepovetskom uezda Novgorodskoi gubernii." *Zhivaia starina* 8, no. 2 (1898): 158–83.

Giliarovskii, F. "O tak nazyvaemoi v narode porche brakov, vsledstvie surovosti brachnykh obychaev." *Zapiski Imperatorskago russkago geograficheskago obshchestva po otdeleniiu statistiki* (St. Petersburg) 5 (1878): 129–55.

Giliarovskii, O. V. *Izsledovaniia o rozhdenii i smertnosti detei v Novgorodskoi gubernii.* Zapiski Imperatorskago russkago geograficheskago obshchestva po otdeleniiu statistiki, vol. 1. St. Petersburg: V tip. K. Vul'fa, 1866.

Gol'msten, A. Kh. *Iuridicheskiia izsledovaniia i stat'i.* 2 vols. St. Petersburg: Tip. M. M. Stasiulevicha, 1894–1913.

Golovin, K. *Sel'skaia obshchina v literature i deistvitel'nosti.* St. Petersburg: Tip. M. M. Stasiulevicha, 1887.

Iakushkin, E. I. "Zametki o vliianii religioznykh verovanii i predrazsudkov na narodnye iuridicheskie obychai i poniatiia." *Etnograficheskoe obozrenie* 3, bk. 9, no. 2 (1891): 1–19.

Isaev, Andrei. "Znachenie semeinykh razdelov krest'ian: Po lichnym nabliudeniiam." *Vestnik Evropy* (July 1883): 333–49.

Kagarov, E. "O znachenii nekotorykh russkikh svadebnykh obriadov." *Izvestiia Akademii nauk* (15 May 1917), no. 9, pp. 645–52.

Kavelin, K. *Sochineniia K. Kavelina.* Edited by K. Soldatenkov and N. Shchepkin. 4 vols. Moscow, 1859.

Kharuzin, Nikolai, ed. *Sbornik svedenii dlia izucheniia byta krest'ianskago naseleniia Rossii: Obychnoe pravo, obriady, verovaniia i pr.* 3 vols. Moscow, 1889–1891. Vols. 2–3 in Izvestiia Imperatorskago obshchestva liubitelei estestvoznaniia, antropologii i etnografii, vol. 69. Trudy etnograficheskago otdela, vol. 11.

Kostolovskii, I. V. "Iz svadebnykh obriadov i poverii Iaroslavskoi gubernii." *Etnograficheskoe obozrenie* 19, bk. 75, no. 4 (1907): 104–7; 23, bks. 88–89, nos. 1–2 (1911): 248–51.

Kostomarov, N. I. "Velikorusskaia narodnaia pesennaia poeziia: Po vnov' izdannym materialam." In *Sobranie sochinenii N. I. Kostomarova: Istoricheskiia monogra-*

fii i izsledovaniia, bk. 5, vol. 13, pp. 517–62. 21 vols. 1903–1905. Reprint. The Hague: Europe Printing, 1967.

Kovalevskii, Maxim. *Modern Customs and Ancient Laws of Russia: Being the Ilchester Lectures for 1889–90*. 1891. Reprint. New York: Burt Franklin, 1970.

"Krest'ianskii sud: 'Trudy Komissii po preobrazovaniiu volostnykh sudov.' Spb. 1873." *Otechestvennyia zapiski* 36, no. 1 (January 1874): 182–237.

Leont'ev, A. A. *Krest'ianskoe pravo: Sistematicheskoe izlozhenie osobennosti zakonodatel'stva o krest'ianakh*. 2d ed. St. Petersburg, 1914.

Levitskii, Pavel. "Cherti nravov krest'ian Totemskago uezda." *Etnograficheskii sbornik* 5 (1892): 54–57.

Lichkov, L. S. "Krest'ianskie semeinye razdely." *Severnyi vestnik* (January 1886), no. 1, pt. 2, pp. 84–108.

Maksimov, S. V. *Nechistaia, nevedomaia i krestnaia sila*. St. Petersburg: Tov. R. Golike i A. Vil'borg, 1903.

Manotskov, V. I. "Chto takoe krest'ianskii vopros?" *Vestnik Novgorodskago zemstva* 7, no. 20 (15 October 1905): 63–76.

Marakin, F. I., et al. "Kustarnye promysly Nizhegorodskoi gubernii: Nizhegorodskii uezd." *Nizhegorodskii sbornik* (Nizhnii Novgorod) 7 (1887): 1–373.

Mashkin. "Byt krest'ian Kurskoi gubernii Oboianskago uezda." *Etnograficheskii sbornik* 5 (1862), pt. 6, pp. 1–119.

Matveev, P. A., ed. *Sbornik narodnykh iuridicheskikh obychaev*. Vol. 1. Zapiski Imperatorskago russkago geograficheskago obshchestva po otdeleniiu etnografii, vol. 8. St. Petersburg: Tip. v Kirshbauma, 1878.

———. "Svod zakonov i krest'iane: Po povodu sostavleniia novago Grazhdanskago Ulozheniia." *Rus'* 3, no. 9 (1 May 1883): 20–32.

Mikheev, M. E. "Opisanie svadebnykh obychaev i obriadov v Buzulukskom uezde, Samarskoi gubernii." *Etnograficheskoe obozrenie* 11, bk. 42, no. 3 (1899): 144–59.

Miller, O. F. "Zametki o russkikh svadebnykh pesniakh. (Po povodu stat'i N. I. Kostomarova: 'Velikorusskaia narodnaia pesennaia poeziia po vnov' izdannym materialam' v VI kn. *Vestnika Evropy* za 1872 g.)." *Filologicheskiia zapiski* 11, no. 4 (1872): 1–24.

Mukhin, V. F. *Obychnyi poriadok nasledovaniia u krest'ian: K voprosu ob otnoshenii narodnykh iuridicheskikh obychaev k budushchemu grazhdanskomu ulozheniiu*. St. Petersburg: Tip. Pravitel'stvuiushchago Senata, 1888.

Muratov, A. Synopsis of N. I. Grigor'ev, "O polovoi deiatel'nosti zhenshchin Myshkinskago uezda, Iaroslavskoi gubernii (*Vracheb. Ved.* (1883) nos. 21–33)." *Meditsinskoe obozrenie* 20 (July 1883): 107.

Neshel', V. K. "K voprosu o plodovitosti zhenshchin krest'ianok." *Vrach* 10, no. 33 (17 August 1889): 725.

Neustupov, A. D. "Krest'ianskaia svad'ba Vas'ianovskoi volosti." *Etnograficheskoe obozrenie* 15, bk. 56, no. 1 (1903): 52–69.

Nikolaev, A. "Krest'ianskaia svad'ba v Zvenigorodskom uezda Moskovskoi gubernii." *Severnaia pchela*, 8 August 1863, p. 926.

Orlov, V. *Formy krest'ianskago zemlevladeniia*. Sbornik statisticheskikh svedenii po Moskovskoi gubernii: Otdel khoziaistvennoi statistiki, vol. 4, pt. 1. Moscow: Izd. Moskovskago gubernskago zemstva, 1879.

Orshanskii, I. G. *Izsledovaniia po russkomu pravu obychnomu i brachnomu*. St. Petersburg: Tip. A. E. Landau, 1879.

———. "Narodnyi sud i narodnoe pravo. (Po povodu voprosa o preobrazovanii volostnykh sudov)." *Zhurnal grazhdanskago i ugolovnago prava* 5, nos. 3–5 (May–October 1875): 60–142, 140–223, 1–71.

———. "O pridanom." *Zhurnal grazhdanskago i torgovago prava* (December 1872): 986–1045, 175–206.

Osokin, S. M. "Sel'skaia svad'ba v Malmyzhskom uezde." *Sovremennik* (1857), no. 1, pp. 54–87.

Pakhman, S. V. *Obychnoe grazhdanskoe pravo v Rossii: Iuridicheskiia ocherki*. 2 vols. St. Petersburg, 1877–1879.

———, ed. *Sbornik narodnykh iuridicheskikh obychaev*. vol. 2. Zapiski Imperatorskago russkago geograficheskago obshchestva po otdeleniiu etnografii, vol. 18. St. Petersburg: Tip. A. S. Suvorina, 1900.

Pevin, P. "Narodnaia svad'ba v Tolvuiskom prikhode Petrozavodskago u., Olonetskoi gub." *Zhivaia starina* 3, no. 2 (1893): 219–48.

Plotnikov, M. A. *Kustarnye promysly Nizhegorodskoi gubernii*. Nizhnii Novgorod: Izd. Nizhegorodskago gubernskago zemstva, 1894.

Pokrovskii, A. E. *Fizicheskoe vospitanie detei i raznykh narodov, preimushchestvenno v Rossii: Materialy dlia mediko-antropologicheskago izsledovaniia*. Izvestiia Imperatorskago obshchestva liubitelei estestvoznaniia, antropologii i etnografii, vol. 45, nos. 1–3. Moscow: Tip. A. A. Kartseva, 1884. Trudy antropologicheskago otdela, 7, nos. 1–3.

Ponomarev, S. "Ocherki narodnago byta: Obychnoe pravo." *Severnyi vestnik* (February 1887), no. 2, pt. 2, pp. 45–63.

Semenova-Tian-Shanskaia, O. P. *Zhizn' 'Ivana': Ocherki iz byta krest'ian odnoi iz chernozemnykh gubernii*. Zapiski Imperatorskago russkago geograficheskago obshchestva po otdeleniiu etnografii, vol. 39. St. Petersburg: Tip. M. M. Stasiulevicha, 1914.

Semevskii, V. I. "Domashnii byt i nravy krest'ian vo vtoroi polovine XVIII v." *Ustoi* 1, nos. 1–2 (January–February 1882): 90–132, 63–107.

———. *Krest'iane v tsarstvovanie Imperatritsy Ekateriny II*. 2d rev. ed. 2 vols. in 3. St. Petersburg: Tip. M. M. Stasiulevicha, 1903.

Shcherbina, F. A. "Dogovornyia sem'i." *Severnyi vestnik* (September 1888), no. 9, pt. 2, pp. 85–96.

Shmakov, I. N. "Svadebnye obychai i prichitaniia v seleniiakh Terskogo berega Belogo moria." *Etnograficheskoe obozrenie* 15, bk. 59, no. 4 (1903): 55–68.

Shrag, Il'ia. *Krest'ianskie sudy Vladimirskoi i Moskovskoi gubernii*. Moscow: V Universitetskoi tip. (M. Katkov), 1877. Reprinted from *Iuridicheskii vestnik* nos. 7–8 (1877).

Smirnov, A. "Narodnye sposoby zakliucheniia braka." *Iuridicheskii vestnik* 10, no. 5 (May 1878): 661–93.

———. "Obychai i obriady russkoi narodnoi svad'by." *Iuridicheskii vestnik* 10, no. 7 (July 1878): 981–1015.

———. "Ocherki semeinykh otnoshenii po obychnomu pravu russkago naroda." *Iuridicheskii vestnik* 9, nos. 1–12 (January–December 1877): 49–74, 98–128,

92–131, 177–224, 118–76, 92–142. Reprinted as a monograph. Moscow: V Universitetskoi tipografii (M. Katkov), 1877.

Sokolov, D. A., and V. I. Grebenshchikov. *Smertnost' v Rossii i bor'ba s neiu.* St. Petersburg: Tip. M. M. Stasiulevicha, 1901.

Stepanov, V. I. "Derevenskiia posidelki i sovremennyia narodnyia pesni-chastushki." *Etnograficheskoe obozrenie* 15, bk. 59, no. 4 (1903): 69–98.

Strakhov, Prof. "O svad'bakh i svadebnykh obriadakh i obychaiakh russkikh krest'ian." *Uchenyia zapiski Imperatorskago moskovskago universtiteta* 12, nos. 10–11 (1836): 187–204, 351–72.

Strakhovskii, I. M. *Krest'ianskiia prava i uchrezhdeniia.* St. Petersburg: Izd. T-va obshchestvennaia pol'za, 1903.

Sumtsov, N. F. *O svadebnykh obriadakh preimushchestvenno russkikh.* Khar'kov: Tip. I. V. Popova, 1881.

Tenishev, V. V. *Administrativnoe polozhenie russkago krest'ianstva.* St. Petersburg: A. S. Suvorin, 1908.

———. *Pravosudie v russkom krest'ianskom bytu.* Briansk: Tip. L. I. Itina, 1907.

Titov, A. A. *Iuridicheskie obychai sela Nikola-Perevoz Sulostskoi volosti, Rostovskago uezda.* Iaroslavl': Tip. Gubernskoi zemskoi upravy, 1888.

Tiutriumov, I. "Krest'ianskaia sem'ia: Ocherk obychnago prava." *Russkaia rech'* (April, July, October 1879), nos. 4, 7, 10, pp. 270–94, 123–56, 289–318.

Tsypkin, P. "Obshchinnoe vladenie: Svod dannykh, dobytykh etnograficheskimi materialami pokoinago kniazia V. N. Tenisheva." *Zhurnal Ministerstva iustitsii* 15, no. 1 (January 1909), pt. 2, pp. 123–74.

Uspenskii, D. I. "Rodiny i krestiny, ukhod za rodil'nitsei i novorozhdennym. (Po materialam, sobrannym v Tul'skom, Venevskom i Kashirskom uezdakh, Tul'skoi gub.)." *Etnograficheskoe obozrenie* 7, bk. 27, no. 4 (1895): 71–95.

Uspenskii, M. "Maripchel'skaia krest'ianskaia svad'ba. (Bytovoi ocherk)." *Zhivaia starina* 8, no. 1 (1898): 80–104.

Vesin, L. P. "Znachenie otkhozhikh promyslov v zhizni krest'ianstva." *Delo* 19, no. 7 (November 1866): 127–55; 20, no. 2 (February 1887): 102–24; no. 5 (May 1887): 161–204.

Vorob'ev, N. "Il'inskaia volost' Iur'evskago uezda po perepisiam 1881 i 1899 g." *Vestnik Vladimirskago gubernskago zemstva* 19, nos. 15–16 (1904): 35–64.

Vorontsov, V. P. *Krest'ianskaia obshchina: Obshchii obzor zemskoi statistiki krest'ianskago khoziaistva.* Itogi ekonomicheskago issledovaniia Rossii po dannym zemskoi statistiki, vol. 1, edited by A. F. Fortunatov. Moscow: Tip. A. I. Mamontova, 1892.

Vsevolozhskii, E. "Ocherki krest'ianskago byta Samarskago uezda." *Etnograficheskoe obozrenie* 7, bk. 24, no. 1 (1895): 1–34.

Zhbankov, D. N. *Bab'ia storona: Statistiko–etnograficheskii ocherk.* Kostroma: V Gub. tip., 1891.

Post-1917 Monographs, Articles, and Papers concerning Russia

Aleksandrov, V. A. "Semeino-imushchestvennye otnosheniia po obychnomu pravu v russkoi krepostnoi derevne XVIII–nachala XIX veka." *Istoriia SSSR* (November–December 1979), no. 6, pp. 37–54.

Alekseichenko, G. A. "Prigovory sel'skikh skhodov kak istochnik po istorii krest'ianskoi obshchiny v Rossii vtoroi poloviny XIX veka. (Po materialam Tver-skoi gubernii)." *Istoriia SSSR* (November–December 1981), no. 6, pp. 116–25.

Anfimov, A. M., and P. N. Zyrianov. "Elements of the Evolution of the Russian Peasant Commune in the Post-Reform Period (1861–1914)." *Soviet Studies in History* 21, no. 3 (Winter 1982–1983): 68–96.

Atkinson, Dorothy. "Society and the Sexes in the Russian Past." In *Women in Russia*, edited by Dorothy Atkinson, Alexander Dallin, and Gail Warshofsky, pp. 3–38. Stanford: Stanford University Press, 1977.

Baker, Anita B. "Deterioration or Development? The Peasant Economy of Moscow Province prior to 1914." *Russian History* 5 (1978): 1–23.

Baklanova, E. N. *Krest'ianskii dvor i obshchina na russkom severe: Konets XVII–nachalo XVIII v.* Moscow: Izd. Nauka, 1976.

Benet, Sula, ed. and trans. *The Village of Viriatino*. New York: Anchor Books, 1970.

Bernshtam, T. A. "Devushka-nevesta i predbrachnaia obriadnost' v Pomor'e v XIX–nachale XX v." In *Russkyi narodnyi svadebnyi obriad: Issledovaniia i materialy*, edited by K. V. Chistov and T. A. Bernshtam, pp. 48–71. Leningrad: Izd. Nauka, 1978.

Blinoff, Marthe. *Life and Thought in Old Russia*. University Park: The Pennsylvania State University Press, 1961.

Blum, Jerome. *Lord and Peasant in Russia: From the Ninth to the Nineteenth Century*. Princeton: Princeton University Press, 1972.

Bobroff, Anne Louise. "Working Women, Bonding Patterns, and the Politics of Daily Life: Russia at the End of the Old Regime." 2 vols. Ph.D. diss., University of Michigan, 1982.

Bohac, Rodney Dean. "Family, Property, and Socioeconomic Mobility: Russian Peasants on Manuilovskoe Estate, 1810–1861." Ph.D. diss., University of Illinois at Urbana-Champaign, 1982.

Bolotenko, George. "Administration of the State Peasants in Russia before the Reforms of 1838." 2 vols. Ph.D. diss., University of Toronto, 1979.

Brown, Julie. "Peasant Survival Strategies in Late Imperial Russia: The Social Uses of the Mental Hospital." *Social Problems* 34, no. 4 (October 1987): 311–29.

Bushnell, John. "Peasants in Uniform: The Tsarist Army as a Peasant Society." *Journal of Social History* 13, no. 4 (Summer 1980): 565–76.

Calina, Josephine. *Scenes of Russian Life*. London: Constable, 1918.

Chaianov, A. V. *A. V. Chayanov on the Theory of Peasant Economy*. Edited by Daniel Thorner et al. Homewood, Ill.: Richard D. Irwin, 1966.

Chizhikova, L. N. "Dwellings of the Russians." *Soviet Anthropology and Archeology* 5, no. 1 (Summer 1966): 32–55.

———. "Svadebnye obriady russkogo naseleniia Ukrainy." In *Russkyi narodnyi svadebnyi obriad: Issledovaniia i materialy*, edited by K. V. Chistov and T. A. Bernshtam, pp. 159–79. Leningrad: Izd. Nauka, 1978.

Chopyk, D. B. "The Magic of a Circle: Ceremonial Attire, Food and Dance Symbolism in Slavic Weddings." Paper presented at the 1983 Annual Meeting of the Canadian Association of Slavists, University of British Columbia, 5 June 1983.

Coale, Ansley J., Barbara A. Anderson, and Erna Härm. *Human Fertility in Russia since the Nineteenth Century*. Princeton: Princeton University Press, 1979.

Confino, Michael. "Russian Customary Law and the Study of Peasant Mentalités." *The Russian Review* 44, no. 1 (January 1985): 35–44.

Cuisenier, J., and C. Raguin. "De quelques transformations dans le système familial russe." *Revue français de sociologie* 8, no. 4 (October–December 1967): 521–57.

Czap, Jr., Peter. " 'A Large Family: The Peasant's Greatest Wealth': Serf Households in Mishino, Russia, 1814–1858." In *Family Forms in Historic Europe*, edited by Richard Wall, Jean Robin, and Peter Laslett, pp.105–51. Cambridge: Cambridge University Press, 1983.

———. "Marriage and the Peasant Joint Family in the Era of Serfdom." In *The Family in Imperial Russia: New Lines of Historical Research*, edited by David L. Ransel, pp. 103–23. Urbana: University of Illinois Press, 1978.

———. "The Perennial Multiple Family Household, Mishino, Russia 1782–1858." *Journal of Family History* 7, no. 1 (Spring 1982): 5–26.

Donnorummo, Robert Pepe. "The Peasants of Central Russia and Vladimir: Reactions to Emancipation and the Market, 1850–1900." Ph.D. diss., University of Pittsburg, 1983.

Druzhinin, N. M. *Russkaia derevnia na perelome 1861–1880 g.g.* Moscow: Izd. Nauka, 1978.

Dunn, Patrick P. " 'That Enemy Is the Baby': Childhood in Imperial Russia." In *The History of Childhood*, edited by Lloyd deMause, pp. 383–406. New York: Harper & Row, 1974.

Eklof, Ben. "The Myth of the Zemstvo School: The Sources of the Expansion of Rural Education in Imperial Russia, 1864–1914." *History of Education Quarterly* 24, no. 4 (Winter 1984): 561–84.

———. "Peasant Sloth Reconsidered: Strategies of Education and Learning in Rural Russia before the Revolution." *Journal of Social History* 14, no. 3 (Spring 1981): 355–86.

———. *Russian Peasant Schools: Officialdom, Village Culture, and Popular Pedagogy, 1861–1914*. Berkeley: University of California Press, 1986.

Elnett, Elaine. *Historic Origin and Social Development of Family Life in Russia*. 1926. Reprint. New York: AMS Press, 1973.

Engel, Barbara Alpern. "Peasant Morality and Pre-Marital Relations in Late 19th Century Russia." *Journal of Social History* 23, no. 4 (Summer 1990): 695–714.

———. "St. Petersburg Prostitutes in the Late Nineteenth Century: A Personal and Social Profile." *The Russian Review* 48 (1989): 21–44.

———. "The Woman's Side: Male Out-Migration and the Family Economy in Kostroma Province." *Slavic Review* 45, no. 2 (Summer 1986): 257–71.

Engel, Barbara Alpern, and Clifford N. Rosenthal, eds. and trans. *Five Sisters: Women against the Tsar*. New York: Alfred A. Knopf, 1975.

Engelstein, Laura. "Morality and the Wooden Spoon: Russian Doctors View Syphilis, Social Class, and Sexual Behavior, 1890–1905." *Representations* 14 (Spring 1986): 169–208.

Farnsworth, Beatrice. "The Litigious Daughter-in-Law: Family Relations in Rural

Russia in the Second Half of the Nineteenth Century." *Slavic Review* 45, no. 1 (Spring 1986): 49–64.

———. "The Soldatka: Folklore and Court Record." *Slavic Review* 49, no. 1 (Spring 1990): 58–73.

Farrell, Dianne Eckland. "Popular Prints in the Cultural History of Eighteenth-Century Russia." Ph.D. diss., University of Wisconsin-Madison, 1980.

Figes, Orlando. "Collective Farming and the 19th-Century Russian Land Commune: A Research Note." *Soviet Studies* 38, no. 1 (1986): 89–97.

Frank, Stephen P. "Popular Justice, Community and Culture among the Russian Peasantry, 1870–1900." *The Russian Review* 46, no. 3 (July 1987): 239–65.

Frieden, Nancy M. "Child Care: Medical Reform in a Traditionalist Culture." In *The Family in Imperial Russia: New Lines of Historical Research*, edited by David L. Ransel, pp. 236–59. Urbana: University of Illinois Press, 1978.

Friedrich, Paul. "Semantic Structure and Social Structure: An Instance from Russia." In *Explorations in Cultural Anthropology: Essays in Honor of George Peter Murdock*, edited by Ward H. Goodenough, pp. 131–66. New York: McGraw-Hill, 1964.

Frierson, Cathy. "Razdel: The Peasant Family Divided." *The Russian Review* 46, no. 1 (January 1987): 35–51.

Gagen-Torn, N. I. "Magicheskoe znachenie volos i golovnogo ubora v svadebnykh obriadakh Vostochnoi Evropy." *Sovetskaia etnografiia* (1933), nos. 5–6, pp. 76–88.

Gatrell, Peter. *The Tsarist Economy 1850–1917*. London: B. T. Batsford, 1986.

Goldman, Wendy. "Alimony in the Peasant *Dvor*: Family Law and Soviet Life." Paper presented at the Eighteenth National Convention of the American Association for the Advancement of Slavic Studies, New Orleans, November 1986.

Gorky, Maxim. "On the Russian Peasantry." *The Journal of Peasant Studies* 4, no. 1 (October 1976): 11–27.

Gromyko, M. M. "Obychai pomochei u russkikh krest'ian v XIX v. (K probleme kompleksnogo issledovaniia trudovykh traditsii)." *Sovetskaia etnografiia* (1981), nos. 4–5, pp. 26–38, 32–46.

———. *Traditsionnye normy povedeniia i formy obshcheniia russkikh krest'ian XIX v.* Moscow: Nauka, 1986.

Hoch, Steven L. *Serfdom and Social Control in Nineteenth Century Russia: Petrovskoe, A Village in Tambov.* Chicago: University of Chicago Press, 1986.

———. "Serfs in Imperial Russia: Demographic Insights." *Journal of Interdisciplinary History* 13, no. 2 (Autumn 1982): 221–46.

———. "Sharecropping and Peasant Tenancy Relations in Post-Emancipation Russia." Paper presented at the Annual Convention of the American Association for the Advancement of Slavic Studies, November 1986.

Hubbs, Joanna. *Mother Russia: The Feminine Myth in Russian Culture.* Bloomington: Indiana University Press, 1988.

Ivanits, Linda J. *Russian Folk Belief.* Armonk, N. Y.: M. E. Scharpe, 1989.

Johnson, Robert Eugene. *Peasant and Proletarian: The Working Class of Moscow in the Late Nineteenth Century.* New Brunswick, N. J.: Rutgers University Press, 1979.

Kaiser, Daniel H. "Death and Dying in Early Modern Russia." Paper presented at the Kennan Institute for Advanced Russian Studies, Washington, D.C., 22 May 1986.

Kerblay, Basile H. *L'isba d'hier et d'aujourd'hui: L'évolution de l'habitation rurale en U.R.S.S.* Lausanne: Editions L'Age d'Homme, 1973.

Klimova, Nina T. *Folk Embroidery of the USSR.* New York: Van Nostrand Reinhold, 1981.

Kolesnitskaia, I. M., and L. M. Telegina. "Kosa i krasota v svadebnom fol'klore vostochnykh slav'ian." In *Fol'klor i etnografiia: Sviazi fol'klora s drevnimi predstav-leniiami i obriadami,* edited by B. N. Putilov, pp. 112–22. Leningrad: Izd. Nauka, 1977.

Komorovský, Ján. "The Evidence of the Bride's Innocence in the Wedding Customs of the Slavs." *Ethnologia Slavica* (Bratislava) 6, (1976): 137–46.

Lenin, Vladimir I. *The Development of Capitalism in Russia: The Process of the Formation of a Home Market for Large-Scale Industry.* Moscow: Foreign Languages Publishing House, 1956.

Leshchenko, V. Iu. "The Position of Women in the Light of Religious-Domestic Taboos among the East Slavic Peoples in the Nineteenth and Early Twentieth Centuries." *Soviet Anthropology and Archeology* 17, no. 3 (Winter 1978–1979): 22–40.

Levin, Eve. *Sex and Society in the World of the Orthodox Slavs, 900–1700.* Ithaca: Cornell University Press, 1989.

Lewin, Moshe. "Customary Law and Russian Rural Society in the Post-Reform Era." *The Russian Review* 44, no. 1 (January 1985): 1–20.

———. "The Obshchina and the Village." Paper presented at a Conference on the Peasant Commune and Communal Forms in Russia, School of Slavonic and East European Studies, University of London, July 1986.

Mandel, James Ian. "Paternalistic Authority in the Russian Countryside, 1856–1906." Ph.D. diss., Columbia University, 1978.

Martynova, Antonina. "Life of the Pre-Revolutionary Village as Reflected in Popular Lullabies." In *The Family in Imperial Russia: New Lines of Historical Research,* edited by David L. Ransel, pp. 171–85. Urbana: University of Illinois Press, 1978.

Maslova, G. S. "Changes in the Traditional Folk Costume of Riazan during the Soviet Period (Based on Data of the Interdisciplinary Expedition, Institute of Ethnography, Academy of Sciences, USSR)." *Soviet Anthropology and Archeology* 7, no. 1 (Summer 1968): 36–48.

Melton, Edgar. "Proto-Industrialization, Serf Agriculture and Agrarian Social Structure: Two Estates in Nineteenth-Century Russia." *Past and Present* 115 (May 1987): 69–106.

Miller, Forrestt A. *Dmitrii Miliutin and the Reform Era in Russia.* [Nashville, Tenn.]: Vanderbilt University Press, 1968.

Min'ko, L. I. "Magical Curing (Its Sources and Character, and the Causes of Its Prevalence)." *Soviet Anthropology and Archeology* 12, nos. 1–3 (Summer 1973–Winter 1974): 3–33; 34–60; 3–27.

Mironov, Boris N. "The Russian Peasant Commune after the Reforms of the 1860s." *Slavic Review* 44, no. 3 (Fall 1985): 438–67.

———. "Russkaia sel'skaia obshchina posle reform 1860-kh gg. (Reformi sverkhu i sotsial'nie izmeneniia vnizu)." Unpublished extended version of above paper, 1983.

———. "Traditsionnoe demograficheskoe povedenie krest'ian v XIX–nachale XX v." In *Brachnost', rozhdaemost', smertnost' v Rossii i v SSSR: Sbornik statei*, edited by A. G. Vishnevskii, pp. 83–104. Moscow: Statistika, 1977.

Mixter, Timothy. "Of Grandfather-Beaters and Fat-Heeled Pacifists: Perceptions of Agricultural Labor and Hiring Market Disturbances in Saratov, 1872–1905." *Russian History* 7, pts. 1–2 (1980): 139–68.

———. "Women Migrant Agricultural Laborers in Russia, 1860–1913." Unpublished paper.

Munting, R. "Outside Earnings in the Russian Peasant Farm: Tula Province 1900–1917." *The Journal of Peasant Studies* 3, no. 4 (July 1976): 428–46.

Netting, Anthony. "Images and Ideas in Russian Peasant Art." *Slavic Review* 35, no. 1 (March 1976): 48–68.

Oinas, Felix J., and Stephen Soudakoff, eds. *The Study of Russian Folklore*. Bloomington: Indiana University, Dept. of Slavic Languages, 1971.

Pallot, Judith. "Agrarian Modernization on Peasant Farms in the Era of Capitalism." In *Studies in Russian Historical Geography*, edited by James H. Bater and R. A. French, 2: 423-49. 2 vols. London: Academic Press, 1983.

———. "The Development of Peasant Land Holding from Emancipation to the Revolution." In *Studies in Russian Historical Geography*, edited by James H. Bater and R. A. French, 1: 83–108. 2 vols. London: Academic Press, 1983.

———. "Khutora and Otruba in Stolypin's Program of Farm Individualization." *Slavic Review* 43, no. 2 (1984): 242–56.

Pascu, Stefan, and V. Pascu. "Le remariage chez les orthodoxes." In *Marriage and Remarriage in Populations of the Past*, edited by J. Dupâquier, E. Helin, P. Laslett, M. Livi-Bacci, and S. Sogner, pp. 61–66. London: Academic Press, 1981.

Pearson, Thomas S. "Authority and Self-Government in Russian Peasant Village Administration (1881–1917): Problems and Perceptions." Paper presented at the Conference on the Peasantry of European Russia, 1800–1917, University of Massachusetts-Boston, 19–22 August 1986.

Permyakov, G. L. *From Proverb to Folk-Tale: Notes on the General Theory of Cliché*. Moscow: Nauka, 1979.

Pershin, P. N. *Zemel'noe ustroistvo dorevoliutsionnoi derevni*. Vol. 1: *Raiony: Tsentral'no-promyshlennyi, tsentral'no-chernozemnyi i severo-zapadnyi*. Moscow, 1928.

Ransel, David L. *Mothers of Misery: Child Abandonment in Russia*. Princeton: Princeton University Press, 1988.

Rashin, A. G. *Naselenie Rossii za 100 let (1811–1913 g.g.): Statisticheskie ocherki*. Moscow: Gosudarstvennoe statisticheskoe izdatel'stvo, 1956.

Ripets'kyi, Oleksa. "Parubochi i divochi zvychai v seli Andriiashivtsi, Lokhits'koho povitu na Poltavshchyni." *Materialy do ukrains'koi etnol'ohii* 18 (1918): 155–69.

Robinson, Geroid Tanquary. *Rural Russia under the Old Regime: A History of the*

Landlord-Peasant World and a Prologue to the Peasant Revolution of 1917. Berkeley: University of California Press, 1972.

Shanin, Teodor. *The Awkward Class: Political Sociology of Peasantry in a Developing Society, Russia 1910–1925.* Oxford: Oxford University Press, 1972.

————. *The Roots of Otherness: Russia's Turn of Century.* Vol. 1: *Russia as a 'Developing Society.'* London: Macmillan, 1985. Vol. 2: *Russia, 1905–07: Revolution as a Moment of Truth.* New Haven: Yale University Press, 1986.

Sokolova, V. K. *Vesenne-letnie kalendarnye obriady russkikh, ukraintsev i belorusov XIX-nachalo XX v.* Moscow: Izd. Nauka, 1979.

Spitz, Sheryl Allison. "The Russian Folk Lullaby in the Nineteenth Century." Ph.D. diss., Stanford University, 1977.

Stites, Richard. "Prostitute and Society in Pre-Revolutionary Russia." *Jahrbücher für Geschichte Osteuropas* 31, no. 3 (1983): 348–64.

Svavitskii, N. A. *Zemskie podvornye perepisi: Obzor metodologii.* Moscow: Gosstatizdat, 1961.

Tudorovskaia, E. A. "O vnepesennykh sviazakh narodnoi obriadovoi pesni." In *Fol'klor i etnografiia: Obriady i obriadovyi fol'klor*, edited by B. N. Putilov, pp. 82–90. Leningrad: Izd. Nauka, 1974.

Uspenskii, G. I. *Sobranie sochinenii.* 9 vols. Moscow, 1957.

Vovk, Khvedir. *Studii z ukrains'koi etnohrafii ta antropolohii.* Prague: Ukrainskyi hromads'kyi vydavnychyi fond, [1926].

Wheatcroft, S. G. "The Agrarian Crisis and Peasant Living Standards in Late Imperial Russia: A Reconsideration of Trends and Regional Differentiation." Paper presented at the Conference on the Peasantry of European Russia, 1800–1917, University of Massachusetts-Boston, 19–22 August 1986.

Worobec, Christine D. "Customary Law and Property Devolution among Russian Peasants in the 1870s." *Canadian Slavonic Papers* 26, nos. 2 and 3 (June–September 1984): 220–34.

————. "Horse Thieves and Peasant Justice in Post-Emancipation Imperial Russia." *Journal of Social History* 21, no. 2 (Winter 1987): 281–93.

————. "The Post-Emancipation Russian Peasant Commune in Orel Province, 1861–1890." In *Land Commune and Peasant Community in Russia: Communal Forms in Imperial and Early Soviet Society*, edited by Roger Bartlett, pp. 86–105. London: Macmillan, in association with the School of Slavonic and East European Studies; New York: St. Martin's Press, 1990.

————. "Temptress or Virgin? The Precarious Sexual Position of Women in Postemancipation Ukrainian Peasant Society," *Slavic Review* 42, no. 2 (Summer 1990): 227–38.

Yaney, George. *The Urge to Mobilize: Agrarian Reform in Russia, 1861–1930.* Urbana: University of Illinois Press, 1982.

Zaionchkovsky, Peter A. *The Abolition of Serfdom in Russia.* Edited and translated by Susan Wobst. Gulf Breeze, Fl.: Academic International Press, 1978.

Zelenin, D. K. "Zhenskie golovnye ubory vostochnykh (russkikh) slavian." *Slavia* (Prague) 5 (1926–1927): 303–38, 535–56.

Zhirnova, G. V. "The Russian Urban Wedding Ritual in the Late Nineteenth and

Early Twentieth Centuries." *Soviet Anthropology and Archeology* 14, no. 3 (Winter 1975–1976): 18–38.

Modern Literature on Peasant Societies and the Family outside Russia

Anderson, Bonnie S., and Judith P. Zinsser. *A History of Their Own: Women in Europe from Prehistory to the Present.* 2 vols. New York: Harper & Row, 1988.

Beauroy, Jacques, et al., eds. *The Wolf and the Lamb: Popular Culture in France from the Old Regime to the Twentieth Century.* Saratoga, Calif., 1976.

Berkner, Lutz K. "Inheritance, Land Tenure and Peasant Family Structure: A German Regional Comparison." In *Family and Inheritance: Rural Society in Western Europe, 1200–1800*, edited by Jack Goody, Joan Thirsk, and E. P. Thompson, pp. 71–95. Cambridge: Cambridge University Press, 1978.

Burguière, André. "The Charivari and Religious Repression in France during the Ancien Régime." In *Family and Sexuality in French History*, edited by Robert Wheaton and Tamara K. Hareven, pp. 84–110. Philadelphia: University of Pennsylvania Press, 1980.

Davis, Natalie Zemon. *Society and Culture in Early Modern France.* Stanford: Stanford University Press, 1975.

D'Emilio, John, and Estelle B. Freedman. *Intimate Matters: A History of Sexuality in America.* New York: Harper and Row, 1988.

Dubisch, Jill, ed. *Gender and Power in Rural Greece.* Princeton: Princeton University Press, 1986.

du Boulay, Juliet. *Portrait of a Greek Mountain Village.* Oxford: Clarendon Press, 1974.

Dundes, Alan. *Interpreting Folklore.* Bloomington: Indiana University Press, 1980.

Friedl, Ernestine. "The Position of Women: Appearance and Reality." *Anthropological Quarterly* 40 (1967): 97–108.

Genovese, Eugene D. *Roll, Jordan, Roll: The World the Slaves Made.* New York: Vintage Books. 1976.

Goldschmidt, Walter, and Evalyn Jacobson Kunkel. "The Structure of the Peasant Family." *American Anthropologist* 73 (1971): 1058–76.

Goody, Jack. *The Development of the Family and Marriage in Europe.* Cambridge: Cambridge University Press, 1983.

———. "Inheritance, Property and Women: Some Comparative Considerations." In *Family and Inheritance: Rural Society in Western Europe, 1200–1800*, edited by Jack Goody, Joan Thirsk, and E. P. Thompson, pp. 10–36. Cambridge: Cambridge University Press, 1978.

———. "Introduction." In *Family and Inheritance: Rural Society in Western Europe, 1200–1800*, edited by Jack Goody, Joan Thirsk, and E. P. Thompson, pp. 1–9. Cambridge: Cambridge University Press, 1978.

———. "Strategies of Heirship." *Comparative Studies in Society and History* 15, no. 1 (January 1973): 3–16.

Gordon, Linda. *Heroes of Their Own Lives: The Politics and History of Family Violence: Boston 1880–1960.* New York: Viking, 1988.

Hajnal, J. "European Marriage Patterns in Perspective." In *Population in History: Essays in Historical Demography*, edited by D. V. Glass and D.E.C. Eversley, pp. 101–43. London: Edward Arnold, 1965.

Hammel, Eugene A., Kenneth W. Wachter, and Peter Laslett. "Household Hypotheses." In *Statistical Studies of Historical Social Structure*, edited by Kenneth W. Wachter, Eugene A. Hammel, and Peter Laslett, pp. 29–42. New York: Academic Press, 1978.

Hareven, Tamara K. "Family Time and Historical Time." *Daedalus* 106, no. 2 (Spring 1977): 57–70.

Johnson, Kay Ann. *Women, the Family and Peasant Revolution in China*. Chicago: University of Chicago Press, 1983.

Kligman, Gail. *Căluş: Symbolic Transformation in Romanian Ritual*. Chicago: University of Chicago Press, 1981.

———. "The Rites of Women: Oral Poetry, Ideology, and the Socialization of Peasant Women in Contemporary Romania." In *Women, State, and Party in Eastern Europe*, edited by Sharon L. Wolchik and Alfred G. Meyer, pp. 323–43, 419–25. Durham: Duke University Press, 1985.

Laslett, Peter. "Family and Household as Work Group and Kin Group: Areas of Traditional Europe Compared." In *Family Forms in Historic Europe*, edited by Richard Wall, Jean Robin, and Peter Laslett, pp. 513–63. Cambridge: Cambridge University Press, 1983.

Laslett, Peter, and Richard Wall, eds. *Household and Family in Past Time: Comparative Studies in the Size and Structure of the Domestic Group over the Last Three Centuries in England, France, Serbia, Japan and Colonial North America, with Further Materials from Western Europe*. Cambridge: Cambridge University Press, 1972.

Lee, Robert. "Family and 'Modernisation': The Peasant Family and Social Change in Nineteenth-Century Bavaria." In *The German Family: Essays on the Social History of the Family in Nineteenth- and Twentieth-Century Germany*, edited by Richard J. Evans and W. R. Lee, pp. 84–119. London: Croom Helm, 1981.

Le Goff, Jacques, and Jean-Claude Schmitt, eds. *Le Charivari*. Paris, l'Ecole des hautes études en sciences sociales, 1981.

Le Goff, Jacques, and Pierre Nora, eds. *Constructing the Past: Essays in Historical Methodology*. Cambridge: Cambridge University Press, 1974.

Leonard, Diana. *Sex and Generation: A Study of Courtship and Weddings*. London: Tavistock, 1980.

Löfgren, Orvar. "Family and Household among Scandinavian Peasants." *Ethnologia Scandinavica* 4 (1974): 1–52.

Lourdes, Beneria, and Gita Sen. "Accumulation, Reproduction, and Women's Role in Economic Development: Boserup Revisited." *Signs* 7, no. 2 (Winter 1981): 279–98.

Mosely, Philip E. "The Distribution of the Zadruga within Southeastern Europe." In *The Zadruga: Essays by Philip E. Mosely and Essays in His Honor*, edited by Robert F. Byrnes, pp. 58–69. Notre Dame, Ind.: University of Notre Dame Press, 1976.

Rheubottom, D. B. "Dowry and Wedding Celebrations in Yugoslav Macedonia." In *The Meaning of Marriage Payments*, edited by J. L. Comaroff, pp. 221–49. London: Academic Press, 1980.

Rogers, Susan Carol. "Female Forms of Power and the Myth of Male Dominance:

A Model of Female/Male Interaction in Peasant Society." *American Ethnologist* 2, no. 4 (November 1975): 727–56.

Ross, Ellen, and Rayna Rapp. "Sex and Society: A Research Note from Social History and Anthropology." In *Powers of Desire: The Politics of Sexuality*, edited by Ann Snitow, Christine Stansell, and Sharon Thompson, pp. 51–73. New York: Monthly Review Press, 1983.

Rotberg, Robert I., and Theodore K. Rabb, eds. *Marriage and Fertility: Studies in Interdisciplinary History*. Princeton: Princeton University Press, 1980.

St. Erlich, Vera. *Family in Transition: A Study of 300 Yugoslav Villages*. Princeton: Princeton University Press, 1966.

Sarmela, Matti. *Reciprocity Systems of the Rural Society in the Finnish-Karelian Culture Area with Special Reference to Social Intercourse of the Youth*. Helsinki: Suomalainen Tiedeakatemia, 1969.

Scott, James C. "Peasant Moral Economy as a Subsistence Ethic." In *Peasants and Peasant Societies: Selected Readings*, edited by Teodor Shanin, pp. 304–10. 2d ed. Oxford: Basil Blackwell, 1987.

Segalen, Martine. *Historical Anthropology of the Family*. Translated by J. C. Whitehouse and Sarah Matthews. Cambridge: Cambridge University Press, 1986.

———. "Life-Course Patterns and Peasant Culture in France: A Critical Assessment." *Journal of Family History* 12, nos. 1–3 (1987): 213–24.

———. *Love and Power in the Peasant Family: Rural France in the Nineteenth Century*. Translated by Sarah Matthews. Chicago: University of Chicago Press, 1983.

Shorter, Edward. *The Making of the Modern Family*. New York: Basic Books, 1975.

Thompson, Edward P. "Rough Music: le charivari anglais." *Annales: Economies, Sociétés, Civilisations* (March-April 1972): 285–312.

Weber, Eugen. *Peasants into Frenchmen: The Modernization of Rural France, 1870–1914*. Stanford: Stanford University Press, 1976.

Wrigley, E. A. *Population and History*. New York: McGraw-Hill, 1976.

Index